D0934396

The Collected Writings of Walt Whitman

# WALT WHITMAN

# Daybooks and Notebooks

## VOLUME I: DAYBOOKS
### 1876–November 1881

*Edited by* William White

 NEW YORK UNIVERSITY PRESS 1978

© 1977 BY NEW YORK UNIVERSITY PRESS

LIBRARY OF CONGRESS CATALOG CARD NUMBER: 75–27382

MANUFACTURED IN THE UNITED STATES OF AMERICA

ISBN: 0–8147–9167–0–Vol. I

# The Collected Writings of Walt Whitman

GENERAL EDITORS

*Gay Wilson Allen and Sculley Bradley*

ADVISORY EDITORIAL BOARD

*Roger Asselineau*     *Harold W. Blodgett*

*Charles E. Feinberg*     *Clarence Gohdes*

*Emory Holloway*     *Rollo G. Silver*     *Floyd Stovall*

GRATEFUL ACKNOWLEDGMENT IS MADE TO

Mr. Charles E. Feinberg,

WHOSE ASSISTANCE MADE POSSIBLE THE ILLUSTRATIONS
IN THIS VOLUME AND WHO ALSO MADE
AVAILABLE TO THE PUBLISHER THE RESOURCES OF
THE FEINBERG COLLECTION.

THE PREPARATION OF THIS VOLUME,
AND COSTS ASSOCIATED WITH ITS PUBLICATION,
WERE SUPPORTED THROUGH GRANTS FROM THE

Editing and Publication Programs
of the National Endowment for the Humanities,

AN INDEPENDENT FEDERAL AGENCY.

# Preface

This book should have been called *Daybooks, 1876–1891, Diary in Canada, Miscellaneous Journals, Autobiographical Notes, Words, The Primer of Words, Other Notebooks, &c. on Words*, if we believe that titles should describe contents. But given the size and current fashion of title-pages, the spine of a book, and the running titles at the top of each page, such a title was obviously impossible. So we have compromised by using *Daybooks*—which text does, after all, take up two-thirds of this work—and giving the term *Notebooks* to all the rest of the material.

Most of this material here is published for the first time, except for very brief excerpts from the *Daybooks* (often called the *Commonplace Book* but reverting to Walt Whitman's own title); *The Diary in Canada* and *The Primer of Words* were both published in limited editions in 1904, the latter under the title of *An American Primer* (again I restore Whitman's title and follow the MS. text, not the printed version). With the exception of some of the material from *The Diary in Canada*, a few excerpts from *Faint Clews & Indirections*, edited by Clarence Gohdes and Rollo G. Silver for Duke University Press, and the Livezey-Whitman MSS. in the University of California, the texts published in the present addition to *The Collected Writings of Walt Whitman* are in the Feinberg Collection, now housed in the Library of Congress. The sources for all of this, the MSS. and printed matter not in the Feinberg Collection, are documented in footnotes in their proper place.

The publication of the *Daybooks* has been delayed, first, because there was some doubt as to whether they belonged in Whitman's *Collected Writings*, though there is no question that they should be made easily available to scholars somewhere. For the *Daybooks* are not meant to be read in the same way as *Leaves of Grass*, *Specimen Days*, and the poet's *Correspondence*: the writings in the present volumes are, strictly speaking, reference works and meant to be consulted for names, dates, activities, ideas both half-formed and fully developed, jots and doodles that help us to understand how a great man's mind works, where some of what he has written came from, where he was at all times, and also what he was like. What is in the text of the *Daybooks and Notebooks*, except for the clippings and few names and addresses written by others, is all by Walt Whitman. Though it is in his *Collected Writings*, it is certainly not Literatue (even with a small *l*), nor often very literary. Yet it has its values and uses, and the heavy annotations—the second reason for the delay in publication—are designed to increase the value and make the volumes more useful. One could have spent another lifetime tracking down every name in the *Daybooks* (but to what end, for Whitman never saw many of them but once, and they had little bearing on his life or work); yet sooner or later one must stop searching and researching, and go to print.

Without the help of the previous volumes in Whitman's *Collected Writings*, edited by Edwin Haviland Miller, Harold W. Blodgett, Sculley Bradley, Floyd Stovall, and Thomas L. Brasher, especially the *Correspondence* volumes, identifications and other such discoveries would have been very difficult if not impossible. The General Editor of the collections of Whitman (with Sculley Bradley), Gay Wilson Allen, has been, both in his writings on Whitman and personally, of enormous help. And also patient.

In proof-reading, I am indebted to Artem Lozynsky, Elizabeth Wells, and Maurice Brown; for going over the entire manuscript for the Center for Editions of American Authors, I am indebted to Ronald Gottesman; for the index I am indebted to John Beesing; to Wayne State University, I must acknowledge with thanks several summertime grants; and to the National Endowment for the Humanities, the Modern Language Association of America, and the CEAA, under the direction of Matthew J. Bruccoli, I am not only grateful for more than one large grant but for its seal to Walt Whitman's *Daybooks and Notebooks* as An Approved Text.

Yet, as has been said before so often, without Charles E. Feinberg this work and much else on Whitman would not exist at all.

*WILLIAM WHITE*

*Franklin Village, Michigan*
31 May 1976

CONTENTS

# Introduction

"Another damned thick book! Always scribble, scribble, scribble! Eh, Mr. Gibbon," was the Duke of Gloucester's affable remark to the author of the *Decline and Fall of the Roman Empire*. But it might well have been applied a hundred years later to Walt Whitman, who seemed always to be writing something, from the time when he was a young boy in his teens to the last days before he died in Camden. Newspaper copy, short stories, a novel, poetry (and he could never leave his poems alone, not even after they were in print), editorials, letters, reminiscences, interviews with himself for newspapers, magazine pieces, journals, diaries notebooks. So with Whitman as it was with Edward Gibbon, always scribble, scribble, scribble. These *Daybooks and Notebooks* are testimony to that: he was a writer.

But just what the *Daybooks* are is a question. There were two of them, the first with entries from March 1876 to 30 May 1889, the second from his seventieth birthday on May 31, 1889 to December 2, 1891, just a very few months before his death in March 1892. A young friend, Clayton Wesley Peirson, rebound the first one—which Whitman had just about worn out—at the same time he presented the poet with a new one. Because of the nature of the entries in the two volumes, those who have used the books long after Whitman's death referred to them as the *Commonplace Books*. But Whitman used the word *Daybooks* for them. So in the publication of them for the first time I have used the word Whitman used, *Daybooks*.

Well, just what are they? Generally, as anyone will observe by turning over the leaves, the right-hand pages contain day-to-day entries, the names and addresses of those to whom he sold and shipped copies of the Centennial *Leaves of Grass* and *Two Rivulets*, a collection of his poetry and prose which he put together in 1876. As with all of his editions, with two brief exceptions, he was not only the author but the publisher of his works: he was likewise his own business manager, shipper, and promoter. Whatever records he kept, of his sales and distribution, of printing and binding figures, of poetry and prose he sent to newspapers and magazines (their acceptance or rejection, payment for them, and their appearance), tax bills, water bills, subscription to daily papers, of payments for the keep of his brother Edward, his own board and room when he lived with his brother George, of letters received and letters sent, where he went and when he came home: these and a whole variety of other things he entered on the right-hand pages.

This would indicate that Whitman meant, in the beginning, to keep an account book for book sales, with information on the purchasers. He entered these names and addresses meticulously, closing the entries with a note "paid," and often the date. These entries he made in ink or in black, red, blue and indelible pencil; later he seemed to use red for special events, but that changed. We can say that Whitman simply used whatever writing instrument or ink was nearest at hand. Some notes were jotted down on paper fragments and pasted or pinned to the pages. The first 25 pages were numbered in blue pencil. Then the nature of the entries on these right-hand pages seemed to change, but Whitman always retained their chronological order, more or less daily—but he certainly did not make an entry every day in what became a diary.

The account-book phase of the *Daybooks* continued almost to the very end, even the final entries on the right being names of book-buyers of *Leaves of Grass*. But after about six months, early in September 1876, he began making other kinds of entries: thus begins the diary phase. These are of enormous variety, and there is no consistency about them, except that they are about Walt Whitman: his activities, literary and social, his friendships, his habits, his health and the weather (toward the end there was more on these two facets than anything else), his trips, his finances, whom he visited and who visited him, whom he wrote to, and who wrote to him.

While there is a wealth of information about Whitman's daily comings and goings and doings on the right-hand pages—which here in their printed version mean the odd-numbered pages (not Whitman's numbers, which do not exist beyond the first 25, but the numbers in brackets which I have supplied as editor)—there is a lack of completeness in the entries. We know from extant letters written by Whitman, from letters to him, and from other available information, that he wrote to people and did not record this in his *Daybook*, and others wrote to him; and we know that he did other things and kept no note of them. However, much that Whitman did do is chronicled here in the holograph pages on the right side of the two volumes of memoranda.

These entries, it must be remarked very early, cite all this variety of activity, but there is little, if any, commentary by the poet. We have in the *Daybook* the *what* of this activity, but almost no *why*. We see almost nothing here of how Whitman *feels* about anything he does or sees or anywhere he goes. Toward the end of the diary entries, in the last year or two, there occurs a longish passage—though most of the time, nothing which comes remotely close to baring his soul. Far from it. The greatest man of his age dies, and all Whitman can say is, "Emerson died, aged 79," and on the next line, "Death of Emerson." (On the other hand, he did underline the entry heavily in red.) Again, the President is assassinated, and what does Whitman say? "President Garfield shot." And that's all.

In fairness to Whitman, one must add that these *Daybooks* were by no means meant for publication, and there is not the slightest doubt whatever that he meant them for his own private use, his own personal record, largely of a business nature. His commentary on what took place during those 16 years of the *Daybooks*, his reaction to events in his private life, in Camden and places he visited, and in the nation: these he recorded in letters to numerous friends, and in his writings for newspapers and magazines in both poetry, and in conversations with Horace Traubel, among others. There was really no need to say much more than "Death of Emerson" or "President Garfield shot," for on both events he wrote something within a short time for publication.

So much for the matter on the right. What do we have on the left-hand pages, the ones that have, in this printed version of the *Daybooks*, even page numbers? These pages have still more varied entries than the opposite pages, for it is here that we get the "commonplace book" flavor that has given that title to this work (used by scholars, not by Whitman himself). Thus on the left we find names and addresses, both in Whitman's handwriting and quite often in the hand (supposedly) of Whitman's guest, or a friend, or simply someone Whitman met somewhere—at a ferryboat in the harbor, on a horse-drawn streetcar (could Whitman have had the book with him?), or written on slips of paper, or on calling cards; then there are calling cards themselves, with the dates the person named came to see Whitman, addresses clipped from the left-hand upper corner of envelopes; also advertisements for a wide variety of goods and services, clipped from newspapers; other newspaper clippings, occasionally very long ones, about Whitman and his activities; and sometimes a card, pasted on the left, with an entry on the right noting that person's visit. At other times the left-hand page entries bear no relationship whatever to diary notations (always dated in contrast to the undated material on the left).

Opposite Whitman's *Daybook* entries for August 1876, for example, is the following complete entry on the left-hand page: "John Hay/506 Euclid av/Cleveland Ohio/Call'd on me in/NY. in May/'79". And some of the lists of names can be very long, indeed, such as the 45 people to whom Whitman sent "complimentaries" in 1876—could they have been complimentary copies of the Centennial Edition of *Leaves of Grass?* And the 41 to whom he sent copies of the Philadelphia *Sunday Times* of 26 January 1879, containing his prose piece, "Winter Sunshine: A Trip from Camden to the Coast." Another list was of 21 people he saw, or meant to see, when he visited West Hills, New York, his birthplace, between July 29 and August 1, 1881. But the longest list of all (on the left-hand pages) was written in London, Ontario, in June 1880, when he was visiting Dr. Richard Maurice Bucke, and sent papers, postals, and letters to 81 relatives, friends, and acquaintances.

If most of the notations in the *Daybooks* ("postal to Pete Doyle," "Harry here," "paid Bradbent & Taylor $5," "X Lou 20," "Wm M F. Round, call'd," and "Lewis More/RR man I met on the ferry/friend of Pete's") are about as exciting as reading the telephone book, but once in a while such an entry as this turns up (under April 1878:)

> 9<sup>th</sup> (evening) Mr Belisle call'd this evening.  Said
>         that G   W   Childs desired him to call & say to me
>         he would assist me in bringing out a new
>         edition of my poems, <u>leaving out the objec-</u>
>         <u>tionable passages</u> — said it could be arranged
>         on that condition —    I told him to thank
>         Mr C from me very deeply for his kindness
>         & liberality — (decided at once to decline on any such
>                     condition)

This really doesn't tell us much, but it's far better than Whitman's one-liners.

Somewhat out of place, chronologically, is this left-hand-page entry opposite diary notations for August 1880:

<u>Tennyson</u>    Farringford, Freshwater, Isle
            <u>of Wight,</u>  "about seven months
                    in the year – the winter especially ["]
                    address 1882   [in blue pencil]
                    Aldworth, Haslemere, Surrey [encircled in blue pencil]
                    four months of the summer
                    (& then a month or five weeks in London)

but probably as good as any address

care of Frederick Locker
        25 Chesham Street
        London   S W
(Tennyson started for Venice ab't
  middle of May, '80, on a visit
  of a month)
(Lionel Tennyson     4 Sussex Place
        Regents' Park – London  N W)
(Mrs Gilchrist has been at Locker's house
        to copy old letters of Blake for the
        new ed'n)

Below this, on the same page, are a calling card of Chas. S. Gleed, and addresses of Stephen F. Smart, E. C. Stedman, R. Worthington, T. W. H. Rolleston, and Pete Doyle. Again, the Tennyson item is far from a great deal, though it does show that Whitman had been in touch with the British Poet Laureate.

Among the entries for 1880, we find this on the left:

June 17 & 18 – Sent "Summer Days" to following:
- Tribune, Denver                                10
- Boston Herald                                  10
- New York Tribune                               12
- Phil Press                                     10
- Cin Commercial                                 10
- Chic Tribune                                   10
- Louisville Courier Journal                     10
    New Era   Lancaster Pa
— 3 Washington Post ————————
    Eve Star, Washington [cancelled in
                        blue pencil]             10
- Free Press   Detroit                           10
/ Globe, St Johns   New Brunswick                10
- Chronicle, Halifax  N S ————                   10
- John C Dent, Globe newspaper, Toronto          10
- Witness, Montreal.                             10
- Register, Woodstown N J                         7
- Post   Camden, free                          free

We learn from this that Whitman sent his prose piece, "Summer Days in Canada" (which he later used in *Specimen Days*) to at least 15 newspapers, asked $10 from most of them, $12 from the New York *Tribune*, $7 from the Woodston, New Jersey, *Register*, and no fee from the Camden *Daily Post*. It was published in the Philadelphia *Press* and the Camden *Daily Post*; some of the others may also have printed it.

When Walt Whitman's favorite brother Jeff, who was a successful engineer in St. Louis, died on November 25, 1890, the poet noted the fact in the second volume of his *Daybook*. Between a mundane entry on November 24 ("Sunny, dry, cold—belly ache—bad head—bad digestion") and an equally dull one for 26, 27, 28, 29, 30 November ("cold, cold"), Whitman wrote on November 25, 1890:

> 25    My brother Jeff died at St Louis, Mo:
>
> typhoid pneumonia    heart attack
> at last[3193]
>
> in his 58<sup>th</sup> year – born July 18 1833
> Geo: went on to St: L – Jessie who was in N J:
> got there the 2<sup>d</sup> day after the death

He also wrote about Jeff in "An Engineer's Obituary," published in the *Engineering Record* (New York), December 13, 1890 (reprinted in *Good-Bye My Fancy*, 1891, and *Prose Works* 1892). A few lines later, he made a very brief entry under December 4, 1890 which was an uncharacteristic comment for the *Daybook*: "gloomy days—death of Jeff—."

Another uncharacteristic entry, to go along with the names, addresses, the comings, goings, and the mere listing of letters to and letters from Whitman, appears this rather long one for 13 April 1887:

> April
> 13th    Went on to New York – R P Smith was
> my convoyer & host – went to Westminster
> Hotel, Irving Place. – Stedman, Johnston, Gilder
> & John Burroughs Evn'g – next afternoon, Ap. 14th
> my "Death of Lincoln" piece at Madison Sq: Theatre[2307]
> – good audience – next day, 15th – sat to C C
> Cox, photographer, 12th and Broadway – also to
> Miss Wheeler, portrait painter – good time – [2308]
> felt pretty well – rather overwhelm'd with friends,
> & pulling, & talk – R P Smith very kind, faith-
> ful, & liberal – Wm Duckett with me – A

> Thursday Evn'g
> grand ovation $_\wedge$ – reception, two or more hundred –
> at Westminster Hotel Parlors, to me, Thursday
> returned to Camden April 16th
> Evn'g, April 14 $_\wedge$ – (If I had staid longer, I sh'd
> have been kill'd with kindness & compliments)[2309]
> rec'd $~~~~$ $600   Andrew Carnegie $350 [2310]

And beginning about this time Whitman made some equally lengthy comments on his health every few weeks or so, which a reader can observe as the first *Daybook* closes and the second volume begins. Slightly larger in format, 28 by 22 cm. to 20 by 16 cm. (for the first volume), this second volume has only about 60 pages containing entries by Whitman: he did not live to fill it up. Except for the longish entries every now and then, the material does not vary much from the earlier *Daybook*.

One of the most curious and interesting kind of entries, and there are several similar ones, has to do with lists of names of young men whom Whitman encountered in Camden or Philadelphia. The first one appears on a left-hand page opposite the page dated September and October 1876, although this list of young men appears to have been made at two or more times in March and April 1880:

> Drivers, Conductors, Ferrymen[107]
> Gideon Jackson, driver 2$^d$ st. North Cam
> John Williamson, tall, young, (old driver) 5th st
> John McLaughlin black eyed, (old driver) 5th st
> Jerry Robbins, driver Stevens St cars [in pencil]
> Danl Garwood driver Scull's wagon [in pencil]
> Jo Cline, Stevens St. (and all round)
> John Emery, 46 car Haddington, March '80
> Harry Miller Market st Phil
> Wm Wilson " " "
> Robert Norris [last name in pencil] 144 Car
>                      105 Car       Clark Hilton
> April '80 – Johnston Love McFetridge, $_\wedge$ young conductor    $\wedge$   extra
>    Edward Wilson conductor car (open) No 8 Market St
>    Frank St John coal agent, Maine man, I saw at
>                              the ferry

One may make guesses, psychological or otherwise, as to why Whitman seemed compelled to make this and the several other lists of young men, sometimes with comments on their personal appearances. The names almost never appear later in the *Daybooks* or in Whitman's *Correspondence*, so most likely he never saw any of them again.

Whitman makes a brief and touching observation in the *Daybook* in February 1883: "14$^{th}$—the group I saw this afternoon and to-night in the Phila. ferry house—the two women—the three or four fine little children—that 12 or 13 year old boy that reminded me of myself, 50 years ago."

These last 16 years of Whitman's twilight, the period covered by the *Daybooks*, were not without noteworthy incidents in the life of the poet, though his production of memorable poetry was just about over. It was the time of editions of *Leaves of Grass*: the Centennial, the Author's, the Osgood, the Death-bed. It was the time of Mrs. Anne Gilchrist's visit to America, where she had romantically come from England to marry Whitman, not realizing how impossible such a dream was; yet they did become the best of friends, and we see in the *Daybooks* how often they visited each other. It is really a great pity that Whitman made no comments in the *Daybook* about this: even when she died on November 29, 1889, all that he wrote under the date of December 15, 1889 was: "death of Mrs: Gilchrist—news rec'd to-day/she must have been buried Dec. 1."

These were the years of his acquaintanceship with George and Susan Stafford, and he duly records in the *Daybooks* the numerous visits to their farm near Timber Creek, observing nature, taking notes, writing essays, and recovering his health. And he seemed to be traveling more than he ever did before, on both long and short trips: to New York, to Boston, to St. Louis and the West as far as Denver and Colorado Springs, to London, Ontario, Montreal, and Quebec. All these are quietly recorded either in the *Daybooks* themselves, on slips of paper later pasted in the *Daybooks*, or on separate pieces of paper meant (perhaps) to be pasted or pinned into the books. His lectures on President Lincoln's death and on Thomas Paine are noted here, and several celebrations of the poet's own birthdays. Despite his 1873 stroke, from which he never fully recovered, and his calling himself a half-paralytic, he appears to have led a fairly active life until near the end of his 73 years. Always, in addition, most assuredly, he was writing, writing, writing.

The 16 years of the *Daybooks* supplement the biographical information in the six volumes of Whitman's *Correspondence*, Traubel's *With Walt Whitman in Camden* (beginning March 28, 1888), and *Specimen Days*. The *Daybooks* give us the bare bones of the poet's outward life, which he fleshed out in his letters, talks to Traubel, and his literary reminiscences.

The other matter published in the volumes of *The Collected Writings of Walt Whitman*, both in their respective places in footnotes and as an appendix, fill out the record. They are concerned with a few parts of Whitman's life, such as his visit to Dr. Richard Maurice Bucke in Canada in the summer of 1880, and with his great interest in the English language. Other than what is said about these documents in the footnotes in their proper places below, little needs to be added. They belong in an edition of Whitman's collected works if such productions are to achieve anything approaching completeness.

As with the *Daybooks*, I should note that the Canadian diary, the other journals and notes, and the two works on language called *Words* and *The Primer of Words* were not published during their author's lifetime because they were never finished. Again, as with the *Daybooks*, they are by and large, reference works. As readable and interesting as some parts of them are, they are not meant in any sense to be considered or read as pieces of literary endeavor. They are what many of us call scholarship, and for the use of scholars concerned with both Whitman and the English language in America. They are included here for the convenience of scholars. But I like to think that Walt Whitman would have appreciated my including these. Of one thing there is no question: he would have relished the preservation, the study, the concern, the attention, and most certainly the acceptance he and his writings now enjoy.

# Editorial Statement

The text of Walt Whitman's two *Daybooks* (1876–1891) published here is a diplomatic transcription of the poet's holograph manuscript. That is, the complete text is reproduced not only word for word but mark for mark and in the full context of spacing, alignments and as many other idyosyncratic features of physical appearance as is possible to occomplish with type and short-hand editorial commentary.

The first *Daybook* measures 20 by 16 cms. and consists of 404 unnumbered pages, with barely visible lines; it is bound in dark cloth, with a leather spine. For the convenience of readers I have written a number, placed in square brackets, for each page of the *Daybook*; but obviously such a number does not appear in the book itself. The earliest date in this *Daybook* is March 2, 1876, the latest date May 30, 1889. The second *Daybook* is slightly larger, 28 by 22 cms.; and though it consists of 278 pages, also unnumbered, only the first 61 contain writing, and the last three. Its dates are May 31, 1889 to December 2, 1891. This book is bound in half leather, lettered on the front cover, *Walt Whitman*; it was given to him by Clayton Wesley Peirson, who had rebound the first *Daybook*, as the poet says in the *Daybook* itself. The pages of this book I have also numbered (and put the numbers in square brackets) and put a number 2 before each page-number—"2:3," "2:4," and so on.

Most of Whitman's writing has been written in black ink, with some material in black, blue, red, and purple pencil, and some in red ink. He frequently used red ink to indicate special events, such as one that took place during August 1879, when the poet headed a page, "St Louis and Colorado Trip," and in 1881 he wrote "Boston" in red ink at the top of some pages, to indicate his trip there concerning the Osgood *Leaves of Grass*. Whitman often used a blue pencil to write "rec'd" sideways across the name of a person to whom he had sent a copy of *Leaves of Grass*; he also numbered the first 25 right-hand pages—the only pages he numbered at all—in blue pencil. But there is no consistency to the use of colored pencils and ink, as these are sometimes used for entries of little or no importance. In all cases where Whitman's autograph matter is written in some other manner than in black ink, I have so indicated by a comment in square brackets, such as: "[in red ink]," "[in pencil]," "[in purple pencil]," and so on.

What characterizes the *Daybook* is that Whitman never really made up his mind what he wanted it to be, though it does follow a roughly chronological order. In general, the pages on the right contain day-by-day entries; and the left-hand pages have general memoranda, accounts, names and addresses (often written by the person whose name and address is there), advertisements and clippings, either pasted to the page or pinned. Judging from the first entries (after the material on the fly leaf), Whitman intended the *Daybook* to be something of an account book for sales of *Leaves of Grass* and (then) of *Two Rivulets*, published that year (1876) as companion volumes similarly bound as a Centennial Edition in celebration of the hundredth anniversary of the nation. (Later it became a diary— just that.) As may be seen, Whitman listed the names, addresses, numbers and titles of books sent and paid for, with dates and amounts of money. When the poet-publisher-bookseller wrote checkmarks to indicate the sale and transaction were complete I have naturally retained Whitman's checkmark. I have also retained his cancellation of words, lines, and whole passages (there are not many of these); all of Whitman's lines, horizontal —especially those he often wrote between entries—vertical, at angles, in circles, and all over the page, are faithfully reproduced just as Whitman drew them.

However, because of typesetting difficulty, when Whitman wrote a word vertically across or beside another word—such as "rec'd" when a buyer got his copy of *Leaves of Grass*—I have inserted the word horizontally on the page and noted in square brackets "[sideways]." On all other occasions—and there are not very many of them on the right-hand pages—where I, as editor, have added anything, I have put my words in square brackets. All material not in square brackets or not otherwise described may be assumed to be by Walt Whitman, written by him in black ink.

In transcribing and recording the material on most of the left-hand pages, such as letter heads clipped from sheets of stationery, return addresses from the upper corners of envelopes, newspaper and magazine ads, calling cards, and other printed material, I have put in square brackets my comments, "Not in WW's hand," "From a letter-head," or simply "Printed" after every line that is not in Whitman's autograph. Again, without my comment, the reader may assume all the other material is written by the poet.

Corrections, strike-overs, inserted words (usually with a caret) I have transcribed exactly the way Whitman has left them. Where a letter has been cancelled, I have cancelled it; if the letter is obliterated, I have simply written an "x." If several words or a line are wholly illegible, I have put the line in square brackets with a question mark: "[——?——]." There are no silent corrections or changes. All of Whitman's errors that he did not correct—and there are very few of them, mainly in the spelling of a person's name—I have left just as he left them. When he misspelled names, or got places or dates wrong, or titles of his poems or prose are wrong or not clear to the reader today, I have not changed them in the text, but have used footnotes to make these corrections. Indeed, I have made the fullest possible use of footnotes, which I shall explain below.

I have employed no symbols of my own, other than square brackets, x's, and question marks. Symbols, lines, and other nonverbal markings here in the printed *Daybook* are all by Whitman: he was especially fond of the pointed finger. Similarly, without editorial comment, except for noting printed material, I have transcribed Whitman's partial words, false starts, cancellations, careted-in words, corrections. It will be seen, in the transcription of the *Daybook*, that much of the editorial comment deals with colored inks and pencil, and with the printed matter pasted or pinned on the left-hand pages. There are so few emendations (which I have put in square brackets), that I have no emendation "policy." When I correct, I do so in footnotes.

My heavy use of footnotes needs explanation. Every name of a person, place, book, poem, prose work, or a "situation" in Whitman's life and times that seemed to me to call for annotation, I have annotated in order that the reader, or more aptly the user, of these *Daybooks* might get the fullest possible value and benefit from this wealth of Whitman material. All of Whitman's poems and prose writings, to which he refers often by short names, I have fully identified and located, both in their original publication and in *The Collected Writings of Walt Whitman*. I have done the same with letters to which he refers in the *Daybook*: when Whitman refers to a letter he has sent or received, I have recorded in footnotes where the letter has been published, often where the MS. is located, and if the letter is lost, I have noted that too. Letters to Whitman, when he makes note of this correspondence, are similarly annotated as to MS. location and present publication (if it has been published). In a word, I have keyed in the *Daybook* with the *Prose Works 1892*, Volumes I and II, with the Comprehensive Reader's Edition of *Leaves of Grass*, and especially with the first five volumes of *The Correspondence*. Furthermore, in the diary entries in the first volume of the *Daybooks*, between May 28, 1888 and

September 14, 1889, the dates of the five published volumes of Horace Traubel's *With Walt Whitman in Camden*, have also been "cross-referenced" or keyed in with the Traubel's work.

As I explain in the Introduction above, Whitman often made reference in the *Daybook* to an event, either in his life or in the political or social activities of his time, and then said little or nothing whatever about it: Emerson's death, the shooting of President Garfield, some catastrophe or tragedy. On these occasions, I have either given more details of the event or, if Whitman wrote a poem or an article about it, I have recorded in a footnote where Whitman's piece may be found. I have attempted to identify as many of the people as possible whom Whitman mentions, which includes those he met, wrote to, sold books to, received as visitors, heard from, or otherwise was "associated" with through the *Daybook*. In a number of instances, I have fully described their relationship with Whitman. When the names of persons occur again and again, I refer the reader to the first footnote that details the individual's connection with Whitman. In brief, the footnotes serve a necessary function. Without them, the *Daybooks* would be far less useful to the researcher from 1876 to 1892.

In order that the reader of the Whitman *Daybooks* may get something of the "feeling" or atmosphere or spirit of the holograph manuscript which the poet wrote and kept during the last 16 years of his life, a number of facsimile pages of the original have been reproduced. Unfortunately, though print makes the material more easily readable and has many other advantages, nothing can replace seeing and using the very pages Whitman himself saw and used for recording his daily coming and goings. In this edition we have attempted to come as close as possible to the original, and we have considerably increased the bulk, and we hope the value, by the annotation.

# CHRONOLOGY
## OF WALT WHITMAN'S LIFE AND WORK

| | |
|---|---|
| 1819 | Born May 31 at West Hills, near Huntington, Long Island. |
| 1828 | May 27, Whitman family moves to Brooklyn. |
| 1825–30 | Attends public school in Brooklyn. |
| 1830 | Office boy for doctor, lawyer. |
| 1830–34 | Learns printing trade. |
| 1835 | Printer in New York City until great fire August 12. |
| 1836–38 | Summer of 1836, begins teaching at East Norwich, Long Island; by winter 1837–38 has taught at Hempstead, Babylon, Long Swamp, and Smithtown. |
| 1838–39 | Edits weekly newspaper, the *Long-Islander*, at Huntington. |
| 1840–41 | Autumn, 1840, campaigns for Van Buren; then teaches school at Trimming Square, Woodbury, Dix Hills, and Whitestone. |
| 1841 | May, goes to New York City to work as printer in *New World* office; begins writing for the *Democratic Review*. |
| 1842 | Spring, edits a daily newspaper in New York City, the *Aurora*; edits *Evening Tattler* for short time. |
| 1845–46 | August, returns to Brooklyn, writes for *Long Island Star* from September until March. |
| 1846–48 | From March, 1846, until January, 1848, edits Brooklyn *Daily Eagle;* February, 1848, goes to New Orleans to work on the *Crescent;* leaves May 27 and returns via Mississippi and Great Lakes. |
| 1848–49 | September 9, 1848, to September 11, 1849, edits a "free soil" newspaper, the Brooklyn *Freeman*. |
| 1850–54 | Operates printing office and stationery store; does free-lance journalism; builds and speculates in houses. |
| 1855 | Early July, *Leaves of Grass* is printed by Rome Brothers in Brooklyn; father dies July 11; Emerson writes to poet on July 21. |
| 1856 | Writes for *Life Illustrated*; publishes second edition of *Leaves of Grass* in summer and writes "The Eighteenth Presidency!" |
| 1857–59 | From spring of 1857 until about summer of 1859 edits the Brooklyn *Times*; unemployed winter of 1859–60; frequents Pfaff's bohemian restaurant. |
| 1860 | March, goes to Boston to see third edition of *Leaves of Grass* through the press. |
| 1861 | April 12, Civil War begins; George Whitman enlists. |
| 1862 | December, goes to Fredericksburg, Virginia, scene of recent battle in which George was wounded, stays in camp two weeks. |
| 1863 | Remains in Washington, D.C., working part-time in Army Paymaster's office; visits soldiers in hospitals. |

1864    June 22, returns to Brooklyn because of illness.

1865    January 24, appointed clerk in Department of Interior, returns to Washington; meets Peter Doyle; witnesses Lincoln's second inauguration; Lincoln assassinated, April 14; May, *Drum-Taps* is printed; June 30, is discharged from position by Secretary James Harlan but re-employed next day in Attorney General's office; autumn, prints *Drum-Taps and Sequel*, containing "When Lilacs Last in the Dooryard Bloom'd."

1866    William D. O'Connor publishes *The Good Gray Poet*.

1867    John Burroughs publishes *Notes on Walt Whitman as Poet and Person*; July 6, William Michael Rossetti publishes article on Whitman's poetry in London *Chronicle*; "Democracy" (part of *Democratic Vistas*) published in December *Galaxy*.

1868    Rossetti's *Poems of Walt Whitman* (selected and expurgated) published in England: "Personalism" (second part of *Democratic Vistas*) in May *Galaxy*; second issue of fourth edition of *Leaves of Grass*, with *Drum-Taps and Sequel* added.

1869    Mrs. Anne Gilchrist reads Rossetti edition and falls in love with the poet.

1870    July, is very depressed for unknown reasons; prints fifth edition of *Leaves of Grass*, and *Democratic Vistas* and *Passage to India*, all dated 1871.

1871    September 3, Mrs. Gilchrist's first love letter; September 7, reads "After All Not to Create Only" at opening of American Institute Exhibition in New York.

1872    June 26, reads "As a Strong Bird on Pinions Free" at Dartmouth College commencement.

1873    January 23, suffers paralytic stroke; mother dies May 23; unable to work, stays with brother George in Camden, New Jersey.

1874    "Song of the Redwood-Tree" and "Prayer of Columbus."

1875    Prepares Centennial Edition of *Leaves of Grass* and *Two Rivulets* (dated 1876).

1876    Controversy in British and American press over America's neglect of Whitman; spring, meets Harry Stafford, and begins recuperation at Stafford farm, at Timber Creek; September, Mrs. Gilchrist arrives and rents house in Philadelphia.

1877    January 28, gives lecture on Tom Paine in Philadelphia; goes to New York in March and is painted by George W. Waters; during summer gains strength by sun-bathing at Timber Creek.

1878    Spring, too weak to give projected Lincoln lecture, but in June visits J. H. Johnston and John Burroughs in New York.

1879    April to June, in New York, where he gives first Lincoln lecture, and says farewell to Mrs. Gilchrist, who returns to England; September, goes to the West for the first time and visits Colorado, because of illness remains in St. Louis with his brother Jeff from October to January.

1880    Gives Lincoln lecture in Philadelphia; summer, visits Dr. R. M. Bucke in London, Ontario.

1881    April 15, gives Lincoln lecture in Boston; returns to Boston in August to read proof of *Leaves of Grass*, being published by James R. Osgood; poems receive final arrangement in this edition.

1882    Meets Oscar Wilde; Osgood ceases to distribute *Leaves of Grass* because District Attorney threatens prosecution unless the book is expurgated; publication is resumed in June by Rees Welsh in Philadelphia, who also publishes *Specimen Days and Collect*; both books transferred to David McKay, Philadelphia.

1883    Dr. Bucke publishes *Walt Whitman*, a critical study closely "edited" by the poet.

1884    Buys house on Mickle Street, Camden, New Jersey.

1885    In poor health; friends buy a horse and phaeton so that the poet will not be "house-tied"; November 29, Mrs. Gilchrist dies.

1886    Gives Lincoln lecture four times in Elkton, Maryland, Camden, Philadelphia, and Haddonfield, New Jersey; is painted by John White Alexander.

1887    Gives Lincoln lecture in New York; is painted by Thomas Eakins.

1888    Horace Traubel raises funds for doctors and nurses; *November Boughs* printed; money sent from England.

1889    Last birthday dinner, proceedings published in *Camden's Compliment to Walt Whitman*.

1890    Writes angry letter to J. A. Symonds, dated August 19, denouncing Symond's interpretation of "Calamus" poems, claims six illegitimate children.

1891    *Good-bye My Fancy* is printed, and the "death-bed edition" of *Leaves of Grass* (dated 1891–2).

1892    Dies March 26, buried in Harleigh Cemetery, Camden, New Jersey.

The Collected Writings of Walt Whitman

Walt Whitman: Daybook, 1876–1891

[Inside front cover]

[All material here written on two scraps of paper, pasted inside front cover:]

John Boyle O'Reilly[1]   [In pencil, three lines,

left for me in             Boston –    not in WW's hand]

_Progress_ office         Mass

Phila:

    April 16 '80 [2]

    Walt Whitman

      James W. Christopher      [Three lines, not in WW's hand]

        47 Day St

        New York City[3]

[On both sides of a scrap of paper, now in the Feinberg Collection, Whitman has written some notes, which he may have intended to insert in his _Daybook_; but he did keep them, and as they are dated in three places, February 1876 and May 1877, and are similar to entries in this notebook, they belong with other _Daybook_ matter:]

---

1.  The earliest mention of John Boyle O'Reilly (1844–1890) occurs in _The Correspondence of Walt Whitman,_ III, 224; he was coeditor of the Boston _Pilot_ from 1876 until his death.

2.  The notes and other material inside the front cover must have been put there more than four years after Whitman bought the notebook, for the first entry on p. 1 is dated 2 March 1876, when the _Daybook_ started out simply as an account book, recording his sales of the 1876 _Leaves of Grass_ and _Two Rivulets._ It continues as such for 21 right-hand pages, with names, addresses, and other miscellaneous data on the left-hand pages. Finally, on the page Whitman numbered 22, the _Daybook_ has its first "diary" entry on the arrival of Mrs Anne Gilchrist and her family in Philadelphia, 10 September 1876 at 1929 22nd Street, though he writes "Fred Vaughan called" on the page numbered 12.

3.  James W. Christopher's and O'Reilly's names and addresses are, it may be assumed, in their hand, as is the case with numerous signatures in the _Daybook_; these people either signed the book in Whitman's home, on Stevens Street or on Mickle Street, Camden, or Whitman may have taken the book with him on visits, to New York, to Canada, or elsewhere.

Feb. '76

Sam'l Deal, small, y[oung?]
    red hair'd, new cond.[uctor]
    on 5<sup>th</sup> & 2<sup>d</sup>

Joseph Davis, driver on [the]
    Kins' Express, tall, you[ng]
    blonde, very light thin m[ ? ]
    Friend of Nat. Jones

May '77

Jos C Baldwin
    Elliottstown
    Effingham Co.  Ill.

John Strattor  40 yr's
    4 child – carpenter – 10 mos in 23<sup>d</sup>

Hugh Harrop  boy 17  fresh Irish
                     wool sorter

Press People

W<sup>m</sup> V. McKean, Ledger
[ ? ] Nevin, Press
  . Alf. C. Lambdin
          Managing Ed. } Phil
[W]<sup>m</sup> Drysdale, Rep } Times

[C]has Reddy, Rep.  New Rep  &
               Chic. Tribu[ne]

Ch  H  Spieler
    Photographer
722 Chestnut  [st]
    top floor
  son Jacob

[Some of these names — Hugh Harrop, Joseph C. Baldwin, and Charles H. Spieler — occur in other places in the *Daybook*: Spieler in an entry for 25 October 1876 (when Whitman mentions having his niece's picture taken), Baldwin on 4 May 1877 (when Whitman sent him a paper and letters), and Harrop on 28 April 1878 (when Whitman sent him a Sunday paper). From then on, their names come up from time to time. As for the newspapers referred to, the Philadelphia *Public Ledger,* the Philadelphia *Times,* the Camden *New Republic,* and the Chicago *Tribune,* the *Public Ledger* was published by George W. Childs, a very good friend of the poet; the *Times* published pieces by him and supported him in his difficulties with censors; the *New Republic* was owned by a friend Henry Lummis Bonsall and it was in this paper that Whitman met Harry Stafford; and the *Tribune* was sometimes sent pieces by Whitman though they were not used.]

[1]

[Clippings, from newspapers, of two poems:]

## COME, YE DISCONSOLATE.

Come, ye disconsolate, where'er ye languish,
   Come, at the shrine of God fervently kneel:
Here bring your wounded hearts, here tell your anguish:
   Earth has no sorrow that heaven cannot heal.

Joy of the desolate, light of the straying,
   Hope when all others die, fadeless and pure;
Here speaks the Comforter in God's name, saying,
   Earth has no sorrow that heaven cannot heal.

Go ask the infidel what boon he brings us,
   What balm for aching hearts he can reveal;
Sweet as the cheering lay, hope ever sings us,
   Earth has no sorrow that heaven cannot heal.[4]

---

## CANADIAN BOAT SONG.

Faintly as tolls the evening chime,
Our voices keep tune and our oars keep time;
Soon as the woods on the shore look dim,
We'll sing at St. Ann's our parting hymn;
Row, brothers, row, the stream runs fast,
The rapids are near, and the daylight's past.
Why should we yet our sails unfurl,
There's not a breath the blue wave to curl;
But when the wind blows off the shore,
Oh, sweetly we'll rest our weary oar.
Blow, breezes blow, the stream runs fast,
The rapids are near, and the daylight's past.

---

4. "Come, Ye Disconsolate" is a familiar hymn, found in Methodist hymnals and other Protestant collections.

[2]

[Written in pencil on a scrap of paper pasted into *Daybook*:]
    <u>at Sarnia   Canada June '80</u>

        Dr Archibald McLean
        Robert Gurd
        Willie Gurd [5]
Timothy Blair Pardee, Commissioner
    of Crown Lands,[6] (one of the 6
    Members, forming the Canada Gov't)
        Adams

[Clipped from the bottom of a letter, not in WW's hand:]

      Your Affectionate friend,
        Lillian Edgerton.
  Please destroy this. It is entre nous.
     Care Mrs. A. Adams,
       1501 State Street,
         St. Louis,
          Mo.

[3]

1876 [in blue pencil]      1 [in blue pencil]
   March 2 '76
         sent L of G. & T. R.
<u>Albert B. Otis[7]</u> &
<u>Mrs. L. N. Fairchild</u> [8] } then another T. R.
242 Washington st.     paid in full
  Boston, box 561      $15

    March 2
<u>Edw. Dowden</u>[9]    sent L of G & T. R. by mail
     Winstead  March 14, sent 12 books
Temple road      by express
    Rathmines     all paid
Dublin  Ireland

---

5. Robert and Willie Gurd were related to Dr Richard Maurice Bucke's sister, Matilda Gurd.

6. Timothy Blair Pardee was one of Whitman's hosts on the poet's trip to Canada in the Summer of 1880, when this sheet was most likely pasted in the *Daybook*; see *The Correspondence of Walt Whitman*, III, 183.

7. Albert B. Otis was a Boston lawyer; see *The Correspondence of Walt Whitman*, II, 190.

8. Mrs Fairchild was the wife of a paper company executive whom Whitman probably met in Boston in 1881; see *The Correspondence of Walt Whitman*, III, 354.

March 2 '76                    sent L of G & T. R.
Albert B Otis &            then another  T. R.
Mrs. L. N. Fairchild)      paid in full
242 Washington St,                  #15
Boston, box 561


March 2                    sent L of G & T. R. by mail
Edw. Dowden                March 14. sent 12 books,
Temple road Winstead            by express
        Rathmines               all paid
Dublin Ireland


March 2                    L of G, T R
Rev. J. B. Harrison        & (April 20)
     box 168                  Mem
Vineland N J.              all paid #10


John Newton Johnson        L of G
Guntersville               & T R
    Marshall co Ala         all paid
                              #10

March 2
Rev. J. B. Harrison ⎱ L of G, T R
box 168 ⎰ & (April 20)
Vineland N J. ⎰ Mem.
⎰ all paid $10

John Newton Johnson[9a] ⎱ L of G
Guntersville ⎰ & T R
Marshall co Ala ⎰ all paid
⎰ $10

[4]

F R Buckmen (with Frank [in pencil on letterhead of Hunter & Drennen, Commission Merchants; another card: Buchanan, Smedley & Bromley, Photographic Supplies . . . Philadelphia. Presented by Alfred E. Bennett; another card is of a manufacturers' and printers' supplies company.]

[5]

76 [in blue pencil]                    2 [in blue pencil]
March 12

Kate Hillard [10]          T R, one lost   [written in    both Vols
                            (but one      pencil sideways:]
                            paid $5        sent & recd
                                        recd [in red pencil]

Belisle[11]  [in blue pencil,   T R not paid $5
            sideways:]             May 23
            dead

                                        [in pencil:]
John Burroughs[12]      T R paid      both vols
                        $5            sent

9. Edward Dowden (1843–1913), professor of English literature in the University of Dublin, the first of whose letters from Whitman is dated 22 August 1871. See *The Correspondence of Walt Whitman*, II, 133, III, *passim*.

9a. John Newton Johnson, of Mid, Alabama, a self-styled philosopher, eccentric and colorful, whose thirty letters to Whitman are in the Feinberg Collection, but Whitman's replies, 1874–1890?, are all lost. See *The Correspondence of Walt Whitman*, II, 324–325n; III, 94, 103, 107, 158n.

10. Katharine Hillard (1839?–1915), poet, translator, editor of Mrs Blavatsky, she said Whitman "is the only poet fit to be read in the mountains"; they met in 1876; see *The Correspondence*, II, 224n.

11. D. W. Belisle called on Whitman 9 April 1878, at the behest of George W. Childs about an edition of the *Leaves* "leaving out the objectionable passages"; Whitman declined at once. See *Daybook* entry for that date; also *The Correspondence of Walt Whitman*, III, 146n.

12. John Burroughs (1837–1921), the naturalist, one of Whitman's closest associates; Burroughs said of him, "I loved him as I never loved any man."

| | | |
|---|---|---|
| March 11 | L of G & T R | |
| <u>Alfred Webb</u> | sent by mail | $\sqrt{x^{12a}}$ |
| 74 Middle Abbey st. | paid | |
| Dublin | $10   [in red pencil:] recd | |

| | | | | |
|---|---|---|---|---|
| Thos Dixon[13] | [in blue pencil, | L of G & T R | [in blue pencil, | |
| 15 Sunderland st | sideways:] | sent by mail | sideways:] | |
| Sunderland, | dead | paid $20 – | dead | |
| Eng | | | [in red pencil:] | |
| | | | recd | |

[6]

Hunting case, chased, key winding
gold watch   No 42630
    ~~M~~   White Dial   black figures,
        ~~M Tobias~~
        M T Tobias & Co: Liverpool, makers
Silver [covered by piece of paper   1 line:]
[On slip   ~~Col~~ first class
of paper:]   M. T. Tobias & Co, Liverpool [in red ink]
        English lever ʻ adjusted
                white faced dial, with black figures [in red ink]
        balance,   <u>heavy gold painting</u>
[in red ink:]          on case winder "G. C. Allen   ["] [in red ink]
case   small,   ⎫
    written plain ⎰        <u>No. 42, 630</u>
chased
    shield on one side   case peculiarly chased in
                                chain work
Exchanged with J H Johnston, New York[13a]
            for stem-winder, gold
Silver   watch.


[next 6 lines on sheet of paper pasted down:]
    Full plate, stem-winding

    12a.  These checkmarks and crosses are Whitman's notations that the book has been re-
ceived ($\sqrt{}$) and paid for (X).
    13.  Thomas Dixon, an uneducated English corkcutter and one of Whitman's early
English admirers who bought a copy of *Leaves of Grass* in 1856, which led, through W. M.
Rossetti, to the British reception of Whitman. See *The Correspondence of Walt Whitman*, II,
99–100n.
    13a.  John H. Johnston (1837–1919), New York jeweler, one of Whitman's most "endur-
ing" friends, often to be mentioned in the *Daybook*; their long correspondence began on 19
April 1876 — see *The Correspondence of Walt Whitman*, III, 40. There are 29 Whitman-to-
Johnston letters in Vols. III-V.

March 15
Wm. M Rossetti
5.6 Euston Sq
London n w
Eng:

Two Riv 2 copies
L of G. 1 copy
both by mail
paid

(one copy J R
March 20)

March 15
Mrs Ann Gilchrist
1 Torriano Gardens
Camden road
London

L of G & J R
by mail
paid

March 17
N M Johnson
506 12th st
Washington

L of G & J R
paid 20
(April 20 sent
Mem)

March 21
Keningale Cook
Shorter's Court
Throgmorton st.
London Eng

sent by mail
L of G & J R
paid 20

✓x

March 22
Henry Abbey
Rondout
Ulster co
N. Y.

by mail J R
paid 5

Appleton-Tracy movement,
Silver case with gold joints,
hunting style, 18 size four prs jewels,
expansion balance adjusted —
    plate No. 967030 – case No. 5985
[rest of page in pencil:]
gold watch  1889      Hunting case
back case "Warranted    stem-winding

                    14 K
white dial   U S Assay
black figures
                    41561"
front case plain


                                                                    [7]

'76 [in blue pencil]                    3  [in blue pencil]
    March 15
Wm M Rossetti[14]         Two Riv  2 copies   [in red    (one copy   T R
    56 Euston Sq          L of G, 1 copy       pencil,         March 20)
    London  n w               both by mail    sideways:]
        Eng:        paid.                      recd
                                               both


    March 15
Mrs Ann Gilchrist[15]      L of G & T R
    1 Torriano Gardens        by mail     [in red pencil, sideways:]
    Camden road [in blue pencil      paid            recd
    London            sideways:]
              dead


    March 17
N M Johnson[16]            L of G & T R
    506 12th st           paid  $20       [in red pencil, sideways:]
    Washington           (April 20 sent            recd
                              Mem )

    14.  William Michael Rossetti (1829–1919), critic, brother of Dante Gabriel Rossetti, and
one of those most responsible for introducing Whitman to England.
    15.  Mrs Anne Gilchrist (1828–1885), the English woman who fell passionately in love
with Whitman on reading his poetry and came to America to fulfill her desires. See *The
Correspondence of Walt Whitman,* II, 1–2; III, 1–2, *et passim.*
    16.  Mrs Nancy M. Johnson, a Washington widow and friend of Ellen M. O'Connor, who
ordered books from Whitman; see *The Correspondence of Walt Whitman,* III, 25n, 32–33n.

| | | |
|---|---|---|
| March 21 | sent by mail | |
| Keningale  Cook | L of G & T R | |
| Shorter's Court | paid | [in red pencil:] |
| Throgmorton st. | ? $20 | recd |
| London  Eng | | |

√x

| | |
|---|---|
| March 22 | |
| Henry Abbey[17] | by mail T  R |
| Rondout | paid |
| Ulster co | $5 |
| N. Y. | |

[8]

[In pencil on scrap pasted on page:]

Hiram Grosot      [in blue pencil, sideways:]
   203 Broadway      dead
John W. Earley
Geo. Anderson

[On scrap pasted on page:]

Mrs. Edeson
Robena Edeson

[On letterhead Packard & Jones, District Agents, Office No. 2 Pike Block, Syracuse, N.Y.:] Benton H. Wilson, care of
PACKARD & JONES [printed line]
   No. 2 Pike block
      Syracuse, N. Y.
   [on scrap pasted on page]
   Willard Johnson [in red ink]
   [seven lines in pencil]
      over Winterer's
n. e.      Beer Saloon
   Cor 4th 3d & Noble Sts
   Office Coast Survey
   — Willard Johnson
      R M Bache
         in charge

17. Kenningale Cook and Henry Abbey both ordered books from Whitman; see *The Correspondence of Walt Whitman,* III, 440, 442.

Hiram Grost
203 Broadway
John W. Earley
Geo. Anderson

Mrs. Edeson
Robena Edeson

**William Dens**

Bento H. Wilson care of
PICKARD & JONES,
DISTRICT AGENTS.
No. 2 Pike Block
Syracuse, N.Y.

Office No. 2 Pike Block,

Syracuse, N.Y.

Willard Johnson
Over Winterer's
Beer Saloon
n e.
Cor 13th & Noble St
Office Coast Survey
Willard Johnson
R. M. Bache
in Charge

'76 [in blue pencil]          4 [in blue pencil]                    [9]

March 29     ⎞ send <u>Pub'n Copy</u> of L of G
To <u>W M Rossetti</u>[18] ⎰ & T R – also letter – (must have gone
                          by the Java   29th)

March 28
<u>John McEntee</u>          ⎞
McEntee & Dillon        ⎰ T R by mail
  Iron Works            ⎰ paid
Rondout   Ulster Co     ⎰
        N Y

April 9
<u>Mrs Amelia F. Johnston</u> [sideways in ⎞ L of G & T R      [sideways in red:]
113 east 10th st.          blue:]       ⎰ paid                    recd
      N. Y. City           dead         ⎰ April 20 sent J. H.J.
J H J  150 Bowery                       ⎰    Mem
    car[e?] Broome

April 13
<u>F B Sanborn</u>      ⎞              took L of G & T R     [sideways in red:]
                    ⎰              for the Alcotts (to send        recd
                    ⎰                  paid     the money)
                    ⎰              p.o. order
                    ⎰              $10 recd

April 14
<u>E C Stedman</u>        ⎞            sent by Adams Express [sideways in red:]
      Stock Broker    ⎰            L of G & Two Riv            recd
80 Broadway           ⎰            with MS photo &c
    N Y City          ⎰            paid $30

[Bottom of page covered by a sheet with two names and addresses:]
    John Y Foster
      Editor Fram [?] Leslie
        53, Park Place
            N Y.

---

18. For Whitman's letter to Rossetti, see *The Correspondence of Walt Whitman*, III, 33–34.

W B Crooks
929 Chestnut St
Phila

[10]

[Blank.]

[11]

1876

sent letter to <u>London Times</u> with <u>Song of</u>
    <u>Exposition</u> (price £12)[19] must have gone on
    steamer from N.Y.    April 22 – (2$^d$ letter Ap

April 21

rec'd by money order p.o. $21:97 from Edw. Carpenter[20]
        3 Wesley Terrace   Shaw Lane Headingley Lee
            (wrote ack. April 23)   sent L of G, one copy ⎫
                sent slips         & T R one copy    ⎬
                                         sep. pac   ⎭

[sideways in red ink in left margin:]  sent
                        rec'd
                        4
                        vols

May 5 – sent letter to <u>W M Ros.</u>[21] acknowledging   £28.4
    "     also to R. Bu. with extract of  ¶

sent S of E to <u>Chicago</u> <u>Tribune</u> May 5, ask'd   50
[on slip of paper:]
        Memoranda      750
        Rivulets       700
                (have taken 50 since

19.  "Song of the Exposition" was the title first used in *Two Rivulets* of 1876 for a poem written in 1871 as "After All, Not to Create Only" and published in a dozen newspapers in 1871 with that title, and also published as a booklet and added at the end of the 1871 *Leaves of Grass*. (See the Comprehensive Reader's Edition of *Leaves of Grass*, pp. 194–196n.) This may or may not be the same text (or version) sent to the London *Times* on 22 April 1876 and to the Chicago *Tribune* on 5 May (returned 10 May as too late for publication).

20.  Edward Carpenter (1844–1929), a fervent English enthusiast who first wrote Whitman in 1874 because the poet had given him "a ground for the love of men"; he visited Whitman in 1877 and 1884, and the two corresponded for the rest of Whitman's life. See *The Correspondence of Walt Whitman*, III, 41, *et passim;* the last three volumes of letters include 22 from Carpenter.

21.  For Whitman's letter to Rossetti, see *The Correspondence of Walt Whitman*, III, 43–45; the letter to Dr Bucke of the same date is not extant.

Centennial        700
                    (taken 50
        on hand [in WW's hand]
[This writing (five lines in pencil above) is not in WW's hand. In left margin,
sideways, in pencil, in WW's hand:]
        from Jas Arnold [22]
            May 5   '76

                                                                    [12]
    [Blank.]

                                                                    [13]

'76 [in blue pencil]                5   [in blue pencil]
April 21
Dr F Seeger[23]              ⎞ sent by A Express prepaid
    718 Lexington av         ⎟ L of G & T R
            near 58th st     ⎜ paid
            N Y City         ⎠ $10


    April 21                 ⎞
B G Morrison                 ⎟ sent by A Ex. prepaid     [in red pencil,
    Karns City               ⎨ L of G & T R                  sideways:]
    Butler Co   Penn         ⎟ paid                          recd
                             ⎠    $10


    April 21                 ⎞
Miss Anna Ballard            ⎟ sent by A Ex prepaid      [in red pencil,
office Daily Sun             ⎨ L of G & T R                  sideways:]
        editorial rooms      ⎟ paid                          recd
        N Y City             ⎠    $10


    April 19                 ⎞ paid $10 for L of G & T R   [in blue pencil,
Joaquin Miller[24]           ⎟   both Vols. furnish'd to him  in right margin
through letter from J H      ⎨   to be call'd for by him      sideways:]
    Johnston         N Y     ⎠       Sept. '76               rec'd
                             J. M. call'd May 11    [in blue pencil]
                                "     "     Sept 24

22.  James Arnold was a binder at 531 Chestnut Street, Philadelphia, to whom Whitman
had sent for binding these copies of *Memoranda During the War, Two Rivulets,* and the
Centennial Edition of *Leaves of Grass.*
    23.  Dr Ferdinand Seeger had ordered books from Whitman, as had B. G. Morrison and
Therese C. Simpson; see *The Correspondence of Walt Whitman,* III, 38, 42, 45, 51, 440, 441.

April 23
to
Thérèse C Simpson
1 Alva st
Edinburgh

sent T R by mail
(Rossetti also sent T. R.
to her)
paid

[in blue pencil,
in right margin
sideways:]
rec'd     √x

[14]

[Clipping:] General European Agency — Land & Passenger Departments . . .
R. B. Groat, General Agent, Queen Anne Chambers, 1 & 2, Poultry, London,
E.C.
[Three addresses, in pencil, not in WW's hand:]

Stephen F. Smart
Office Queen Anne's Chambers
First Floor 1 and 2
Poultry
London E. C.
England
#
E. C. Devereux
Agt  Union Pacific Ry
Topeka  Kansas
#
Chas. S. Gleed [25]
Union Pacific Ry
Kansas City
Mo.

[Clipping:]

## JUST THE MAN.

Chas S. Gleed, for some time connected
with the advertising department of the Union
Pacific, has been appointed by Mr. White, general passenger agent of the Santa Fe, to take
charge of the advertising department of that
road. Mr. Gleed has had valuable experience

---

24. Joaquin Miller (1839–1913), an author whose poetry Whitman was fond of and who
called Whitman "The greatest, and truest American I know." They met in 1872; see *The
Correspondence of Walt Whitman,* II, 155, 182n; III, *passim.*
25. Two letters from Whitman to Charles S. Gleed, 25 July and 28 September 1880, are
among Whitman's lost letters.

in this branch of railroading, having been in
charge of that department for the Kansas Pacific for some time prior to the consolidation
with the Union Pacific. He is well known in
[End of clipping.]

[15]

'76 [in blue pencil]                    6 [in blue pencil]
    April 23 – sent <u>Mem</u> <u>War</u> & Sheets T R to O'C

| | | |
|---|---|---|
| April 25<br>Edw'd Carpenter[26]<br>45 Brunswick Sq.<br>Brighton<br>Eng | sent L of G & T R<br>in sep packages &<br>p. card —<br>☞ rec'd p.o.m. order<br>$21.97<br>April<br>from E C    22 | [in blue    both<br>pencil,    sets<br>sideways:]    sent<br>both sets<br>recd |
| April 26<br>Rev. <u>A. P. Putnam</u>[27]<br>263 Hicks st.<br>Brooklyn<br>N. Y. | sent L of G & T R<br>by Ad Ex prepaid<br>paid  $10<br>by p   order | [in red pencil,<br>sideways:]    √x<br>recd |
| May 2<br><u>J T Trowbridge</u>[28]<br>Arlington<br>Mass | by mail  <u>Two</u> <u>Riv.</u><br>also <u>Mem.</u>  with slips | [in red pencil,<br>sideways:]    √x<br>recd |

[16]

[In pencil, on 2 slips of paper covering the page:]
Flinn's Bed Springs
248 So 2ᵈ St
Phila :

26.  See footnote 20.
27.  The Rev. A. P. Putnam ordered books from Whitman; see *The Correspondence of Walt Whitman*, III, 440.
28.  John T. Trowbridge (1827–1916), novelist and poet, who met Whitman in Boston in 1860, said "no book approached the power and greatness of" *Leaves*; Trowbridge was highly thought of by Whitman; see *The Correspondence of Walt Whitman*, I, 190–191n, *et passim*.
28a.  See footnote 567, below.
29.  William Michael Rossetti; see footnote 14.
30.  See footnote 16.

John O'B  Inman[28a]
20 North 9th
St
N Y  City

---

Charles  Cohen
311 Washington
St
(he has a family
there)

---

Lipman's  MS  paper
51 So:  4th St  Phila

[17]

Feb 18  $9 closing up acc't with Sampson Low & Co.

London

by letter from W M R.[29] April 19,        [in red ink, sideways:]
with
from London which see ☞ list        £  s        all
– by draft on Drexel & Co.        28.4        sent
March 15  '76 – Mrs Johnson, Wash. $20[30]  [in red ink,
sideways:]  sent &/rec'd

March $\overset{16}{\wedge}$ from Murat Halstead[31] $50. for pay for articles in
Cin. Com

May 4 recd check $10 from Laura Curtis
Bullard[32] 35 East 39th St  N Y for set   (sent books / books rec'd)
sent p. card May 5
from John Swinton[33] $50 – 5 sets  all sent  [in red ink, all / sent
sideways:]  / & recd

---

31.  Murat Halstead was editor of the Cincinnati *Commercial;* the money was for "extracts" from *Memoranda During the War,* published 16 February 1876. See *The Correspondence of Walt Whitman,* III, 24.

32.  Laura Curtis Bullard's letter to Whitman, 3 May 1876, is in Horace Traubel's *With Walt Whitman in Camden,* III, 555–556; his letter to her, 5 May, is lost.

33.  John Swinton (1829–1901), newspaperman on the New York *Times,* New York *Sun,* his own *John Swinton's Paper,* and mayoralty candidate of New York; wrote Whitman in 1874 what the poet called "almost like a love letter"; see *The Correspondence of Walt Whitman,* I, 74–76, 252–253, 263; II, III, *passim.* See also William White, "Whitman and John Swinton: Some Unpublished Correspondence," *American Literature,* XXXIX (January 1968), 547–553.

Feb 18th /9 closing up acc't with Sampson Low & Co.
London

by letter from W M R. April 19.
from London which see with list all sent   L   s
— by draft on Drexel & Co.                    28. 4
March 15th /76 — Mrs Johnson, Wash.n  $20
March 16 from Marat Halstead 50. for pay for articles in
Cin. Com

May 4 rec'd check $10 from Laura Curtis (sent books rec'd)
Bullard 35 East 39th st N Y for set
sent p. card May 5
all sent from John Swinton $50 — 5 sets all sent

May 10 — draft $50 from J. Burroughs
sent book G. Aug 1 — rec'd Middletown N. Y.

April 2 sent book £25 from Robt Buchanan London
sent book Strahan & Co. 36 Paternoster
Sept 5.
— June 6th J. L. A. Ward $50 sent package
3 Vols — slips sheets & printed rec'd

June 5 rec'd letter dated May 23 Toft, Knuts
ford England, from Rafe Leycester,
— P.O. order £2 — wants both books one sent
both sent           £3 S. R. to be sent yet (rec'd) 12

June 12 rec'd order from M D Conway
London on L B Harrison
First National Bank
for £6.   Cincinnati O

May 10 — draft $50   from J. Burroughs[34]     [in red ink,    sent / & / recd
                                                  sideways:]
    sent L of G. Aug 1 – rec'd   Middletown N Y.


April 28   £25 from Rob't Buchanan[34a] London       [in red ink,   all / sent
                                                       sideways:]
sent books    Strahan & Co.   36 Paternoster road   [sideways:] sent / 17 vols /
    Sept 5                                              & large / photo


— June 6 J. Q. A. Ward [35] $50    sent package   [in red ink,   all / sent / &
                                                    sideways:]              recd
                    3 Vols – slips, sheets
                        & prints –        [sideways:] sent all /
                            rec'd                      10 vols
                                            / altogether / with slips
                                            / & pict


[three lines in pencil:]
June 5   rec'd letter, dated May 23. Toft, Knuts-
    ford, England, from Rafe Leycester,      [in red ink,    sent & / rec'd
    – p.o.order £2 – wants both books         sideways:]
  both sent   [in pencil]                     one
            ☞   T. R. to be sent yet          sent June
                                              (rec'd)      12


June 12   rec'd order from M D Conway[36]    [sideways:]  sent / the Vols /
                                                              3 sets
        London on L B Harrison               [in red ink,   books all / sent
            First National Bank               sideways:]
        for £6.          Cincinnati  0


                                                              [18]
    [Blank.]

34.  See footnote 12.
34a.  Robert Buchanan (1841–1901), English poet and critic, who lauded Whitman in Britain but felt his poor reception was caused by W. M. Rossetti and Swinburne's sponsorship; see *The Correspondence of Walt Whitman*, II, 152n, 321; III, 47–48 *et passim*.
35.  John Quincy Adams Ward (1830–1910), American sculptor; see *The Correspondence of Walt Whitman*, III, 39; and *Walt Whitman Review*, XXI (September 1975), 131.
36.  Moncure D. Conway (1829–1907), American clergyman who spent most of his life in England and became Whitman's foreign representative in 1866, later joined by W. M. Rossetti; see *The Correspondence of Walt Whitman*, I, 14, 332–333, 346–349; II, III, *passim*.

[19]

June 13 – rec'd instalment
   of $48:44 from Trübner
   & Co:  (with statement)

June 20 – rec'd draft from W M R, £45.9.6        [Rossetti]

June 20 – rec'd (& drew) p. o. order $5.47
   for T. R. for
      Chas G. Oates[37]      book sent
      Meanwoodside       rec'd
         Leeds, Eng.

recd pay £3.3 from London Athenæum
   for Man-of-War-Bird [38]

Aug 3, rec'd $20 cash from Jas S Inglis
144 Fifth Av. N Y for two sets –

                  [sideways:]  all
   Aug 4, sent Two Copies L of G.      rec'd
     two copies T R yet to be sent &
            rec'd         4 Vols

     Sept 2 – all sent
       4 Vols

       p o orders
Oct. 11th — rec'd draft   for  £21.18 ($116.01)
   from W M Rossetti

   "   10 from W J Linton[39] for set  [sideways:]  sent
Oct 19 $5 from Wm Avery

[20]

   [Blank.]

37. See Whitman's letter to Charles G. Oates, *The Correspondence of Walt Whitman*, III, 58.

38. "To the Man-of-War-Bird" first appeared in the London *Athenaeum*, 1 April 1876; it was an intercalation in some copies of the Centennial *Leaves*, and was placed among the "Sea-Drift" group in 1881. See the Comprehensive Reader's Edition of *Leaves of Grass*, pp. 257–258; see also footnote 497, below.

39. William J. Linton (1812–1897), a wood engraver, born in England, who lived near New Haven, Conn., edited *Poetry of America, 1776–1876* (London, 1878), including eight Whitman poems. See *The Correspondence of Walt Whitman*, II, 171–172; III, 116–117.

[21]

cts
1878 – Jan 2 – p o order for $9. 99  from
    Edw'd Carpenter – for one set of books
    for E T Wilkinson,⁴⁰ York – books sent
                    Jan 2

[22]

    [Blank.]

[23]

                    7  [in blue pencil]

'76  [in blue pencil]
  May 4
to A J Davis⁴¹        2 L of G  by Adams Ex    [in red pencil,
  24 East 4th st      2 Two R       paid         sideways:]
  N Y City            paid                       recd          √x

  May 4
to Alf E Giles        1 L of G  by Adams Ex    [in red pencil,
  Fairmount av.                     paid        sideways:] recd
  Hyde Park           1 Two R
  Mass                paid

  May 5
J B Harrison⁴²                      for Miss Norris
  Vineland            sent Mem of War.
    N. J              paid

  May 6
Laura Curtis Bullard ⁴³   one set Two Vols     [in blue pencil,
  35 East 39th st         by Ex — pre-paid      sideways:] recd
    N Y.                  paid

---

40. Edward T. Wilkinson was a haberdasher of 13 Micklegate, York, "in a large way of business," according to Edward T. Carpenter, who ordered the 1876 *Leaves* and *Two Rivulets* for him on 18 December 1877; see Horace Traubel, *With Walt Whitman in Camden*, I, 189.
    41. A. J. Davis was a New York lawyer, one of whose copies was for his wife, Mary F. Davis; Whitman's presentation copy to her and A. J. Davis's letter are in the Feinberg Collection.
    42. This is the same Rev. J. B. Harrison to whom Whitman sent *Leaves of Grass* and *Two Rivulets* on 2 March 1876 and *Memoranda During the War* on 20 April; see above.
    43. See footnote 32.

May 6
John Swinton[44]
   134 East 34th st
     N. Y.
        One set – Two Vols
        by Ex – prepaid

            [in blue pencil,
            sideways:] recd   √x

[24]

[Pasted sheet contains all of following:]
    at Mrs Wroth's[45]
      July – 1881

    Lieutenant Commander
      Chas. A Schetky U.S.N.
  U. S. R. S. "St Louis" –
    League Island Navy Yard
        Philada
  Stephen P. Belched
    39 Franklin Str
      Newark N. J.
        [These 8 lines, in pencil, not in WW's
        hand, but by two others, perhaps
        by the two men themselves.]

[25]

'76  [in blue pencil]        8  [in blue pencil]
  May 18
J Leicester Warren[46]
  67 Onslow Sq.
London  S W
      one set – Two Vols – mail
         L of G & T R
      paid

            [in blue pencil,
            sideways:] recd   √x

  May 18
C W Reynell[47]
  Forde House
    Putney
London  S W
      one set – by Mail
        Two Vols – L of G
          & T R
      paid

            [in blue pencil,
            sideways:] recd   √x

  May 18
W B Scott[48]
  Belleview House
    Battersea Bridge
    Chelsea
London  S W
      one set  by mail
        Two Vols – L of G
          & T R
      paid

            [in blue pencil,
            sideways:] recd   √x

44.  See footnote 33.
45.  Mrs Caroline Wroth, wife of a Philadelphia importer, at whose home at 319 Stevens Street, Camden, Whitman took his meals beginning 2 July 1881.

May 19
<u>A G Dew – Smith</u>    ⎱  one set by mail
  7ª  Eaton Sq.       ⎰  Two Vols L of G        [in blue pencil,
  London  S. W.                 & T. R.        sideways:] recd    √x
                   paid

[26]

[On three separate slips of paper: the first in WW's hand, the other two with corrections in his hand.]

    Dr. Ruschenberger
      Pres.
        Acad. Natural Sciences
        cor. 20th & Chestnut
            Phil.

  65 yrs old – been
    Surg in Navy
      40 yr's

    Nov 8ᵗʰ 1875
      Helene d'Apéry
       ~~302 North 38th st.~~        [WW's hand]
      ~~57 Saunders Ave~~
      3825 Haverford St        [WW's hand]
      West Philª

    <u>C A Hale</u>            [in pencil]
    ~~421 N. 3ᵈ Camden~~     [WW's hand]
    708 Market          [in pencil]
      Phila             [in blue pencil, in WW's hand]

[27]

'76 [in blue pencil]        9 [in blue pencil]
May 19
<u>E W Gosse[49]</u>        ⎱  One set   by Mail
  Townshend House    ⎰     L of G. & T R       [in blue pencil,
    North Gate              paid             sideways:] rec'd    √x
    Regents Park
  London

46. John Byrne Leicester Warren (1835–1895), third Baron de Tabley, an English poet; see *The Correspondence of Walt Whitman*, III, 34, 44, 51.

47. Charles W. Reynell was also sent *Memoranda During the War* on 14 or 15 June 1876.

48. William Bell Scott (1811–1890), an English poet and painter who learned about

| May 23 | one Vol | |
| Robt Smeaton | T. R. by mail | [in blue pencil, |
| 249 Harrison st | prepaid | sideways:] recd |
| Brooklyn | paid by | |
| N Y | p. order $6 | |

| May 24 | | |
| T W H Rolleston[50] | one Vol  T R by | [in blue pencil, |
| glass house | mail  prepaid | sideways:] |
| Roscrea | | recd  √x |
| co. Tippy | paid | |
| Ireland | by p. order | |

| May 29 | | |
| N Bangs Williams & Co. | L of G  Ed'n 1867 | |
| booksellers | paper | |
| 52 Westminster st | paid | |
| Providence | | |
| R I | | |

[28]

[On two slips of paper:]

    Cyril Flower[51] Furzedown – Streatham

                Surrey    Eng:   [these 2 lines in WW's hand]

[Four lines in pencil, not in WW's hand:]

           Cyril Flower

           Furzedown

           Streatham

    England            Surrey

---

*Leaves of Grass* from Thomas Dixon, and it was Scott who first sent *Leaves* to W. M. Rossetti. See *The Correspondence of Walt Whitman,* II, 99–100n; III, 44n.

49.  Sir Edmund W. Gosse (1849–1928), writer and English literary critic, who used this copy of *Two Rivulets* for a review in *The Academy,* IX (24 June 1876), 602–603; he visited Whitman in Camden in 1885. See *The Correspondence of Walt Whitman,* III, 48, 384; and also William White, "Sir Edmund Gosse on Walt Whitman," *Victorian Studies,* I (1957), 516–517.

50.  T. W. H. Rolleston (1857–1920), Irish poet, biographer, historian, who corresponded with Whitman from 1879 until his death; several of Whitman's letters to Rolleston are lost. For Whitman's letters, see *The Correspondence of Walt Whitman,* III, 254, V, 320–321, *et passim;* for both men's letters, see Horst Frenz, editor, *Whitman and Rolleston: A Correspondence* (Bloomington, Indiana, 1951).

51.  Cyril Flower, an English barrister and friend of Tennyson, whom Whitman met in Washington in December 1870; see Whitman's letter to him, 2 February 1872, *The Correspondence of Walt Whitman,* II, 162–163.

Budapest                          see

45  Dob utcza              over  [WW's hand]
        [not WW's hand]
                     (visited me
      Paul Liptay[52] [printed]   Aug 26  [WW's hand]
                       '76)
*Correspondent for Hungarian Journals.* [printed]
Philadelphia [not WW's hand]
1736 Warnock Street. [not in WW's hand]

                                              [29]

76  [in blue pencil]            10  [in blue pencil]
  June 7
  Geo: Wallis[53]                sent the Two Vols.
  Art Museum                     by mail      [in blue pencil:]      √x
  South Kensington   s w                      recd
          England                paid

  June 8                         sent 3 Vols.  (2 L of G &
  J Q A Ward[54]      [in blue pencil,              1 Riv
    140 East 38th st.   sideways:        by Ex. paid              [in blue
      New York       all / rec'd]           all sent & rec'd [in blue      pencil,
                                                          pencil] sideways:]
                                         — recd $50 — 6 or 7 Vols      rec'd
                                                  yet to go
                                         (sent Mem: Notes: Strong B.
                                            & Gurney's Photo — with other
                                                pict. & slips

[Three lines in red ink:]
July 26, '79 rec'd letter     both Vols   [in blue pencil:] recd    [sideways:]
from R L dated          sent   Lof G. only                 both Vols
6 Cheyne Walk, London     ☞        Two R due               rec'd  √x
    June 12             paid   June 16 sent Mem             Mem. also

52.  Paul Liptay, the correspondent for Hungarian journals, is mentioned in a letter from Whitman to Charles W. Eldridge; see *The Correspondence of Walt Whitman,* II, 315.
53.  George Wallis (1811–1891), artist and Keeper of the Art Gallery at the South Kensington Museum, 1860–1891; W. M. Rossetti asked that the 1876 *Leaves* be sent to him (see *The Correspondence of Walt Whitman,* III, 51).
54.  See footnote 36.

Rafe Leycaster
   F. Toft
   Knutsford
     England
County of
  Cheshire

☞ T. R. to be sent yet
sent
Aug 31

June 12
Therese C. Simpson[55]
  1 Alva st.
    Edinburgh

sent L of G.
[in blue pencil:]
paid    recd

√x

[30]

Moncure D   Conway[56]
   2 Pembroke Gardens
      Kensington
was here in
Jan. & Feb       London, W.
  '76  also
    1880      England

[Bottom of page covered with announcement from *Trübner's American, European and Oriental Literary Record* for 1880 ( ? ), with a vertical blue line in the margin to indicate interest in Charles John Plumptre's third edition of *King's College Lectures on Elocution*.]

[31]

76  [in blue pencil]
  June 12
N MacColl[57]
  Athenæum office
20 Wellington st
   London

11  [in blue pencil]
sent Mem. (2 copies
  one in sheets
  one bound

[in red pencil,
  sideways:]
  recd
[in blue pencil,
  sideways:]
  recd

√x

[Card from Athenæum Office, 20, Wellington Street, Strand, W. C., dated July 4, 1876.]

June 14 and 15
to W   B   Scott[58]

---

55. See footnote 23.
56. See footnote 36.
57. Norman MacColl (1843–1904), editor of the London *Athenaeum*, 1871–1900.
58. See footnote 48.

C  W  Reynell      ⎫ sent <u>Mem</u>
J Lec Warren[59]    ⎪
& Thos Dixon[60]    ⎪
Rafe Leycester     ⎬
W  M  Rossetti      ⎪
Robt Buchanan[61]   ⎪
J  Newton Johnson[62] ⎪
    for Walt       ⎭

July 11       ⎫ [in blue                          [in blue
to Philip Hale[63] ⎪ pencil,     ☞   all sent       pencil,
  Northampton ⎨ sideways:]   sent L of G. one Vol  sideways:]
    Mass      ⎪ both vols   ☞ T. R. is to be sent ☜  one V
              ⎭ recd        $10 paid p o order      rec'd

July 27       ⎫
to Miss Kate Hillard[64] ⎪   sent L of  G       [in red pencil,
  care of Smith Beede ⎬    paid — one Vol         sideways:]
    Keene Flats   ⎪                                  recd
      New York   ⎭

                                                    [32]

                              [in red ink:]
              John Hay[65]     call'd on me in
              506 Euclid av      N Y. in May
              Cleveland  Ohio       '79

                                                    [33]

'76 [in blue pencil]      12 [in blue pencil]
  Aug 1.           ⎫   L̶ ̶o̶f̶ ̶G̶,̶ ̶o̶n̶e̶ ̶V̶o̶l̶ ̶o̶n̶l̶y̶
sent John Hay      ⎪  ☞    both Vols sent
1 Cushing's block  ⎬  T̶w̶o̶ ̶R̶i̶v̶.̶ ̶i̶s̶ ̶y̶e̶t̶ ̶t̶o̶ ̶b̶e̶ ̶s̶e̶n̶t̶
  Cleveland        ⎪  paid $10  [in red pencil,   recd
    Ohio           ⎭  July 28    sideways:]    one vol

---

59. See footnote 46.
60. See footnote 13.
61. See footnote 34a.
62. See footnote 9a.
63. Philip Hale (1854–1934), music critic and program annotator for the Boston Symphony Orchestra, who wrote on Whitman in *The Yale Literary Magazine* in November 1874; see *The Correspondence of Walt Whitman*, III, 53.
64. See footnote 10.
65. John Hay (1838–1905), Lincoln's private secretary, historian, and Theodore Roosevelt's Secretary of State; see *The Correspondence of Walt Whitman*, III, 53. On 22 March 1892 Hay wrote Whitman for a copy of the Centennial Edition (letter in the Feinberg Collection).

Aug 1   sent
John Burroughs     } one Vol L  of  G  [in blue pencil,
  Esopus on Hudson } paid              sideways:]  recd  one
       N Y                                              vol

Aug 4                                  {4 Vols        [sideways:]
James S  Inglis [in blue pencil,  ☞ all (are sent      all 4 Vols
144 Fifth avenue    sideways:] } sent two copies L  of  G.    rec'd
    N. Y. City          recd       ☞   all sent       [in red pencil,
  at Cottier & Co's             ☞ Two copies T  R are  sideways:]
                                   yet to be sent            recd
                                 paid for all $20

Aug 22
to Mrs Matthews     } one copy L  of  G      [in red pencil, sideways:]
      of Birmingham } paid                          recd
Care  of  Rossetti  }
           London

Some time in August (? or July) Fred Vaughan[66]
                              called

                                                              [34]

    [Blank.]

                                                              [35]

76  [in blue ink]        13   [in blue ink]
   Aug 23                          the
R Hannah            } sent L  of  G  one
   Craven House               Vol
Queen's Elm  Brompton } paid                              √x
   London  s w      } [in red pencil:] recd

Aug 30              }                    [sideways and
R Spence Watson     } sent one set Two Vols    across other   √x
  101 Pilgrim st    } ☞ another set to go   writing:]
Newcastle-on-Tyne   } sent £5   (two sets sent)   two
     England        } [in red pencil, sideways:]   sets
                          all recd                 sent

66. Fred Vaughan, a New York driver who knew Whitman as early as March 1860, whose
eight letters 1860–1862 and one of 11 August 1874 to Whitman are in the Feinberg Collection;
Whitman's replies, at least four, are lost; see *The Correspondence of Walt Whitman,* I, 182n,
364, 365, 371, 372; II, 371.

Aug 30
Geo: Saintsbury[67] } sent one set Two Vols
Savile Club                    [in blue pencil,
15 Savile Row                 sideways:] rec'd                    √x
   London W


Aug 31
Godfrey Lushington } one set – Two Vols        [in blue pencil,
   16 Great Queen street { ☞ another set to go    sideways:] recd
          Westminster              sent £5                              √x
       London   S W
              E


   Aug 31
Vernon Lushington }  one set Two Vols      [in blue pencil,
   Spring Gardens {     another set to go      sideways:] recd
London   S   W  {  ☞       sent  5                              √x
         E        } rec'd 2 Vols Complete   ack their rec.
                        by postal card Nov 8


                                                    [36]

          L  of  G – 19½  oz  [in pencil]
          T       R – 19   oz  [in pencil]
   postage to N  S  Wales –  newspaper 4^cts
        "                "        letters      12


                                                    [37]

76  [in blue pencil]    14  [in blue pencil]
   Aug 31      } sent T  R      [sideways:] Two Vols    [in blue pencil,
Rafe Leycester {  [in red ink:]           & Mem – Recd      sideways:]
☞ see back    ) (see back)                                    all recd
                                                            3 Vols


   Aug 31      }                              [in red pencil,
                                              sideways:]
W  M  Rossetti { sent a set Two Vols
                 wrote R a letter  [in pencil]      recd

---

67. George Saintsbury (1845–1933), British critic, who favorably reviewed *Leaves of Grass* in *The Academy*, VI (10 October 1874), 398–400, subscribed to the Centennial Edition of the *Leaves*, and contributed to a fund collected by W. M. Rossetti in 1885–1886.

| | | |
|---|---|---|
| Aug 31 | | [in blue pencil, |
| G H Lewes[68] | sent a set | sideways:] rec'd |
| The Priory – 21 North Bank | Two Vols | [in blue pencil, |
| Regent's Park | | sideways:] dead |
| London  n  w | | [in red pencil, |
| Eng | | sideways:] <u>recd</u> |

Heath Edge Haslemere
         Surrey

| | | |
|---|---|---|
| Aug 31 | | [in red pencil, |
| G H Boughton | sent a set | sideways:] |
| Grove Lodge | Two Vols | <u>recd</u> |
| Palace Gardens Terrace | | |
| Kensington | | √x |
| London  W | | |

| | | |
|---|---|---|
| Sept 1 | | |
| Geo: Fraser[69] | | √x |
| 3 Middleton road | a set – Two Vols | |
| Camden road | [in blue pencil,    ? | |
| London  W N | sideways:]  rec'd | |

| | | |
|---|---|---|
| Sept 1 | | |
| W T Arnold | | |
| University College | sent L of G. [in blue pencil,   ? | √x |
| Oxford  Eng | sideways:]  recd | |

[38]

[Four lines in pencil:]
Ziegler
Castor, tailor
Young John Wanamaker[70]
J. M Scovel[71]

---

68. George Henry Lewes (1817–1878), associated with George Eliot, whose life of Goethe Whitman admired; he also said to Traubel, "I never seem to have any but the best feeling for Lewes — he is a man I respect: a man of a thousand parts," despite his flippant remarks to George Eliot about Whitman's poetry. See *With Walt Whitman in Camden*, II, 433–434.

69. George Fraser's letter to Whitman, ordering the books, is in the Library of Congress.

70. Wanamaker's store is mentioned in *With Walt Whitman in Camden*, I, 98, as first selling *Leaves of Grass* when McKay brought it out in 1882, then deciding not to handle it. This 1876 reference to "Young John Wanamaker" is not entirely clear: Whitman may simply have seen him, or he may have been at Scovel's — though this is doubtful.

71. James Matlack Scovel, a Camden lawyer, politician, colonel, U. S. Treasury agent, at whose home in the 1870s Whitman breakfasted frequently on Sundays; see *Walt Whitman's Diary in Canada* (below), and *The Correspondence of Walt Whitman*, II, 337; III, 63–64, 389, *et passim;* V, 75, 306.

[39]

'76  [in blue pencil]          15  [in blue pencil]
Sept 2
Whitney & Adams[72]                   a set Two Vols        [in blue pencil,
  "Old Corner Bookstore"         $10 due me           sideways:]
    Springfield                   sent p. card          recd &
      Mass                         Sept 24            paid


Sept 2
Scribner, Armstrong & Co[73]    two copies T  R.
  743 & 745 Broadway          $10 due me            [in blue pencil, recd &
    New York City           [in blue pencil:]          sideways:]    paid
                   paid


Sept 2
J S Inglis    [in blue pencil,
         sideways:]        two copies T  R
  see back        recd


Sept 3
Philip Hale[74]          T  R
  see back         [in blue pencil:]
            recd


  ?  ?
Sept 3 — 10.[th] — Walter & Garry Storms[75] called
~~Send~~


[40]


Send complimentaries[76] to
———

Dr Ridge X                         Capt Frazee \
Col Johnston &XFamily              Dave Moore \

72.  Whitman's letter of 24 September 1876 to Whitney & Adams is among the lost letters.
73.  Whitman sent Burroughs's *Notes on Walt Whitman* on 30 March 1877 to Scribner and Company, in addition to the 2 September copies of *Two Rivulets*; these are the forerunner companies to the present-day Charles Scribner's Sons.
74.  See footnote 63.
75.  Walter Storms is Walt Whitman Storms, the son of a New York horsecar conductor, George I. Storms, whom Whitman knew and who wrote to Whitman 29 June 1856 (letter in the Feinberg Collection) that he was naming his son after Whitman. Whitman's letter, 11 June 1856, to George I. Storms is lost; as are letters to Walt Whitman Storms.
76.  Inasmuch as nothing else is used to identify "complimentaries" they may have been copies of the second printing of the Centennial Edition (called the Author's Edition) of *Leaves of Grass*; and the 45 people to whom he gave them, here listed, between September 1876 (when

Dr Brown,\ the druggist
Dr Rowand ✗
Jo Adams \
John P Foley 2
Al Johnston N Y
J H Johnston /
Gutekunst ✗ ✓
Dr Babbitt ✗
Mr English ✓
    Atlantic City Review ✗
Mr Zimmerman ✗
Mr Freeman ✗
Wᵐ Taylor
    Woodstown Register
the Mingles
the Odenheimers
Gen Sewell
Amos Cooper
Dr Mitchell \
R  Buchanan
Conductor – Market St Phil\

Ed Lindell \
Capt Thomson \
Capt Hand \
Tilghman Hiskey
Olly Wood
John McLaughlin
Dan
Ed Cattell
Isaac Frazee  \
Isaac Pennypacker
Megargee \ \
Morgan  \
Davis    } reporters
Bolger  / \
Harry Bonsall \
Col Ingersoll
Siegfried
[five lines in blue pencil:]
Alice Elverson
Jake Spieler \
Young Moore
    "   Stratton
        Parks

it was printed) and 1879 (when the next list appears here, see below), were mainly acquaintances in Camden or nearby. Those who can be identified are: Colonel John R. and Mrs Rebecca
B. Johnston, and their two children Ida and Jack (John Jr), a Camden artist, who had a studio
in Philadelphia; Al Johnston is Albert B. Johnston, the son of the New York jeweler, John H.
Johnston, one of the poet's best friends; F. Gutekunst was the photographer, 712 Arch Street,
Philadelphia, who made numerous pictures of Whitman; D. M. Zimmerman was secretary-
treasurer of the Camden & Atlantic Railroad, who gave the poet railway passes; William
Taylor was editor of the Woodstown (N. J.) *Constitution* in October 1878 when Whitman
wrote him about a job for Harry Stafford; Ed Lindell is Captain Respegius Edward Lindell,
who worked for the Camden ferries and was also a viola player; other ferry friends (see *Prose
Works 1892*, I, 183) were Captain A. B. Frazee, Dave Moore, Tilghman Hiskey, Captain
Thompson, Captain Hand; Edward Cattell was a farm hand and friend of the Staffords, of
Timber Creek, N. J. (see *The Correspondence of Walt Whitman*, III, 77); General William
J. Sewell's letter to Whitman of 8 January 1884 is owned by Mrs Doris Neale; Whitman's letters
to him of 24 February 1878 and 6 May 1880 are lost; Dr S. Weir Mitchell (1829–1914), Phila-
delphia poet, novelist, and one of Whitman's physicians, who saw the poet first in April 1878
(see *The Correspondence of Walt Whitman*, III, 114n); for Robert Buchanan see footnote 35;
Harry Bonsall, son of Henry L. Bonsall, editor of the Camden *Daily Post* and *New Republic* —
Harry was in and out of the Insane Asylum at Blackwoodtown; Colonel Robert G. Ingersoll
(1833–1899), noted lawyer and agnostic, whom Whitman heard lecture for evidently the first
time on 25 May 1880 (see *The Correspondence of Walt Whitman*, III, 175); Alice Elverson was
the daughter of Joseph Elverson, Jr, assistant editor of the Philadelphia *Saturday Night*; Jake
Spieler may be the Philadelphia photographer who took a picture of Mannahatta (Hattie) Whitman (the poet's niece) on 25 October 1876.

[41]

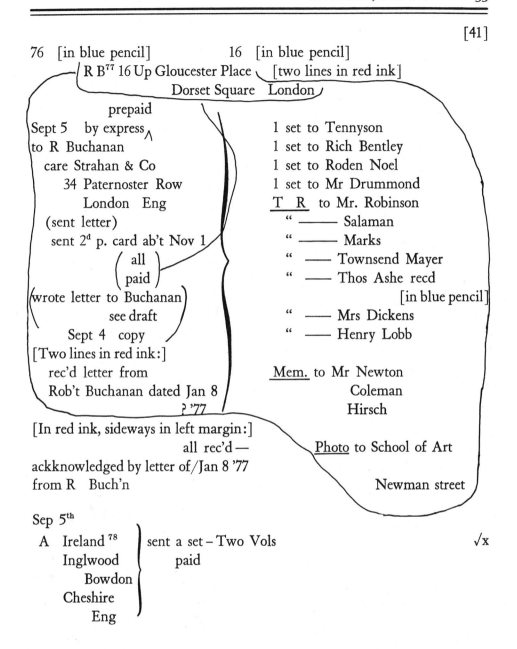

76  [in blue pencil]           16  [in blue pencil]

R B⁷⁷ 16 Up Gloucester Place   [two lines in red ink]
                Dorset Square   London

            prepaid
Sept 5   by express
to R Buchanan
   care Strahan & Co
      34 Paternoster Row
         London   Eng
      (sent letter)
      sent 2ᵈ p. card ab't Nov 1
            all
            paid
wrote letter to Buchanan
         see draft
      Sept 4   copy
[Two lines in red ink:]
   rec'd letter from
   Rob't Buchanan dated Jan 8
                  ? '77

[In red ink, sideways in left margin:]
               all rec'd —
ackknowledged by letter of/Jan 8 '77
from R   Buch'n

1 set to Tennyson
1 set to Rich Bentley
1 set to Roden Noel
1 set to Mr Drummond
T  R  to Mr. Robinson
 "  ——— Salaman
 "  ——— Marks
 "  —— Townsend Mayer
 "  —— Thos Ashe  recd
                  [in blue pencil]
 "  —— Mrs Dickens
 "  —— Henry Lobb

Mem. to Mr Newton
         Coleman
         Hirsch

Photo to School of Art

               Newman street

Sep 5ᵗʰ
   A  Ireland ⁷⁸      sent a set – Two Vols        √x
      Inglwood            paid
         Bowdon
      Cheshire
         Eng

---

77.  See Robert Buchanan's letter from Whitman (*The Correspondence of Walt Whitman*, III, 47–48 and 56), in which the poet writes that he will send to Tennyson and other subscribers listed here a copy of his latest book or books, a portrait and an autograph; Buchanan had started the campaign on Whitman's behalf in April 1876; the books sent on 5 September 1876 were received on 8 January 1877. Richard Bentley & Son were London publishers; Mrs Dickens presumably was the wife of the novelist; Roden Noel was a poet and critic (see *The Correspondence of Walt Whitman*, III, 60).

78.  Alexander Ireland (1810–1894), English author and biographer of Emerson; see *The Correspondence of Walt Whitman*, III, 49, 57.

Sept 5
Mrs Mentia Taylor ⎫ sent a set            [in blue pencil,
  22 Marine Parade ⎬ the Two Vols       sideways:] rec'd
    Brighton  Eng ⎭ paid


Sep 5
M   D   Conway[79]        ⎫ sent a set
  2 Pembroke Gardens ⎬ the Two Vols                           √x
    Kensington        ⎭ paid
  London     Eng

[42]

[Blank.]

[43]

76  [in blue pencil] ⎫  17  [in blue pencil]
    Sept. 6
Benj   Eyre          ⎬ a set
  19 Old Sq.           Two Vols        [in blue pencil,          √x
  Lincoln's Inn                        sideways:] rec'd
  London   W   C ⎭


    Sept 6           ⎫
Edw   ~~Dannra~~     ⎬ a set
    Dannreather       Two Vols       [in blue pencil,          √x
  12 Orme   Sq                        sideways:]  recd
  London   W ⎭


    Sept  6          ⎫
Rev  T  E  Brown ⎬ a set                                            √x
  Clifton College      Two Vols
    Bristol  Eng ⎭


    Sept 6            ⎫
    ~~Puppard~~       ⎬   a set              [in red ink,          √x
C   W   Sheppard          Two Vols          sideways:] rec'd
  13 Albion Terrace
    Horsham       ⎭ sent 2ᵈ card about 1ˢᵗ Nov.
  Sussex          Eng      card rec'd & answered

---

79. As is evident from these details, W. M. Rossetti, Moncure D. Conway, and Robert Buchanan were quite busy in obtaining subscriptions for Whitman's books in England; see also *The Correspondence of Walt Whitman*, III, 59–60.

Sep  6
E  J  A  Balfour
   Trinity College  } a set          [in blue pencil,
   Cambridge      } Two Vols       sideways:]  recd     √x
   Eng

[44]

Sent Phil Sund <u>Times</u>   Jan 26 '79 [80]

| | |
|---|---|
| Ed Carpenter | Hannah |
| Prof Dowden | Mary |
| Rudolf Schmidt[81] | Jeff |
| W  M  Rossetti | Elmer Stafford |
| J  H  Johnston  N Y | Harry |
| John Lucas | Ed Cattell |
| Jo  Browning | Mrs Lippincott |
| Winfield S Fullerton | Mr English (also picture) |
| Will Tinker | Wm Biddle |
| J  A  Symonds | John Burroughs |
| Thos Dixon | Smith Caswell |
| Dr Bucke | John Newton Johnston |

80.  The Philadelphia *Times* for 26 January 1879 contained Walt Whitman's piece, "Winter Sunshine: A Trip from Camden to the Coast," reprinted in *Specimen Days and Collect* (in various places in the text); the 35 paragraphs that Whitman did not reprint are in an appendix to *Prose Works 1892*, I, 330–338.

81.  Of the 41 people to whom Whitman sent copies of the Philadelphia *Times* with his article, many have been identified above; those not previously identified are: Rudolf Schmidt (1836–1899) was a poet and editor who introduced *Leaves of Grass* to Scandinavia and translated *Democratic Vistas* (see *The Correspondence of Walt Whitman*, II, 1, *et passim;* III, *passim*); John Lucas was a Philadelphia paint manufacturer (1028 Race Street); Jo Browning was to be the husband of Debbie Stafford, the daughter of the Staffords whom Whitman visited at Timber Creek, N. J.; John Addington Symonds (1840–1893), was an English author, translator, poet, critic (*Walt Whitman — A Study,* 1893), who first wrote to Whitman in October 1871 (see *The Correspondence of Walt Whitman*, II, 158–159; III, 171, *et passim;* IV, 34, *et passim;* V, 72–73, 182, *et passim*); see also *The Letters of John Addington Symonds,* edited by Herbert M. Schueller and Robert L. Peters (Detroit, 1967–1969 in 3 vols.); Richard Watson Gilder (1844–1909) was assistant editor of *Scribner's Monthly* (1870–1881) and editor of *The Century* (1881–1909), who first met Whitman in 1877, and of whom the poet thought highly (see *The Correspondence of Walt Whitman*, III, 110n, IV and V, *et passim*); in addition to sending the Philadelphia *Times* to friends, members of his family, Hannah, Mary, and Jeff, he also sent it to nearby newspapers, Bridgeton *Pioneer*, Cape May *Wave*, and Tom's River *Courier*); Elmer Stafford was Harry's cousin; Harry can only mean Harry Stafford, one of the most important young men in Whitman's life (see *The Correspondence of Walt Whitman*, III, 2–9, IV and V, *et passim*); Smith Caswell was one of John Burroughs's hired hands; Hattie refers to Mannahatta, Jeff Whitman's daughter; Marvin refers to Joseph B. Marvin, co-editor of *The Radical* (1866–1867), who later worked in the Treasury Department and wrote on Whitman in *The Radical Review* in 1877 (see *The Correspondence of Walt Whitman*, II, 317n, 340–341; III, *passim*); Pete refers to Peter Doyle, the Washington horsecar conductor, who was the poet's closest young friend in his Washington days (see *The Correspondence of Walt Whitman,* II, 3–4, *et passim;* III, *passim*); Francis E. Dowe was the husband of Emma Dowe, Louisa (Mrs George) Whitman's sister; Mrs Louisa Orr was another member of George W. Whitman's family.

R  W  Gilder

Bridgeton Pioneer

Tom's River Courier

Cape May Wave

Woodstown Register

Lord Houghton

John R  Rowand

Mrs Gilchrist

Hattie

Marvin

Pete

Capt Frazee

Mrs Stafford

Mr Zimmerman

Mr Freeman

F  E Dowe

Mrs Louisa Orr

[45]

76  [in blue pencil]

Sept 7

P  B  Marston

20 Ladbrooke Grove r'd

Notting Hill

London w  Eng

18  [in blue pencil]

Two Riv      [in blue pencil, sideways:] recd

[clipping:]

Mr. Philip Bourke Marston, the clever
English poet, of the school of Rossetti, is the
son of Dr Westland Marston, the dramatist.
He is only 26 years old, and has already published two volumes of delicately imaginative
and beautiful verse. He has been blind since
his third year, but he excels in description of
nature. He has a devoted sister, who is his
amanuensis. He is tall and slight, and his large
brown eyes, though sightless, are very expres-
sive.

√x

Sept 7.

Chas G Oates,[82]

Meanwoodside

Leeds      E

Two Riv

[in blue pencil,
sideways:]  recd

√x

Sept 7

A  C  de Burgh

care T W H Rolleston

38 Trinity Coll

Dublin      I

a set

Two Vols

[sideways:]
~~There sh'd~~
~~have been but~~
~~one Vol~~
~~sent him~~
right as it is

82.  Whitman wrote similar letters to Marston and Oates on 7 September 1876; see *The
Correspondence of Walt Whitman*, III, 58.

Sept 7
J  H McCarthy[83]
  48  Gower st
    Bedford Square   WC   }Two   Riv  [in blue pencil,
London  ~~W C~~   Eng                  sideways:]  recd        √x

Sept 7
J  H  Ingram[84]                         [in blue pencil,
   Howard House         Two Riv   sideways:] recd      √x
     Stoke Newington  Green
  London   N   Eng

Sept 7
Rev R  P  Graves
1  Winton R'd  Leeson Park  }A set ?  Two   [in blue pencil,
  Dublin    I           Two Vols  Riv   sideways:] rec'd  √x

[46]

[On letterhead of The Willmer & Rogers News Company, 31 Beekman Street, New York, importers of newspapers, periodicals and books:]
They sent letter to me Jan 1 '79        C  K   Willmer manager
& I sent circ.

[On long slip of paper:]

Jan 79   [rest of this one address & name (in pencil) not in WW's hand]
              John V  Sears
             304 Chestnut St.
                Inquiry  Office

[In pencil:]
       Harry  Garrison
Jan '79        RR man on ferry – blonde
            I meet

Jan '79
     Andrew  Blair  Frazee[85]

83.  Justin H. McCarthy, Jr (1860–1936) thanked Whitman on 23 September 1876 for *Two Rivulets* and said that his father, the novelist, had met Whitman in 1870; see *The Correspondence of Walt Whitman*, III, 64n.

84.  In a letter to Anne Gilchrist, November 1880, Whitman said that John H. Ingram (1848–1916), editor of Poe and author of books on Chatterton and Marlowe, wanted to publish Whitman's prose in London; see *The Correspondence of Walt Whitman*, III, 193.

85.  Andrew Blair Frazee was a Camden ferryboat captain; see footnote 76 and *Prose Works 1892*, I, 183.

[47]

'76 [in blue pencil] &rbrace;    19 [in blue pencil]
  Sept 7
Rev T  E  Brown &rbrace;Two Vols    √x    p 17 — have <u>two</u>
  Clifton College       a set              <u>sets</u> been sent
  Bristol                                      him?
                                            See back

  Sept 7
A  C  deBurgh
care of T  W  Rolleston { Two Riv                                    √x
  F  S  Ellis
    29 New Bond st
London  W     Eng

    Sept 7
W Brockie[86]    &rbrace;    Two Riv    [in blue pencil,
  22 Olive Street                       sideways:] recd            √x
  Sunderland
      Eng

  Sept 8
Edw'd Carpenter[87] &rbrace;        a set
              Sq:                Two Vols    [in blue pencil,
  45 Brunswick ~~st~~    ☞        makes      sideways:] both sets
    Brighton                    2 sets sent         rec'd
      Eng                          him

[48]

    Prof: Edward Dowden
        Temple r'd – Winstead – Rathmines
                Dublin  Ireland

[49]

'76 [in blue pencil]    20  [in blue pencil]
    Sept 8                                  [in blue pencil,
  Prof  Edw: Dowden &rbrace;    1 L  of G    sideways:] rec'd
  Temple r'd Winstead        2    T  R          4    sets
        Rathmines          (acknowledged by     sent         √x
    Dublin    I             letter dated Oct 4)  together

---

86. As in the case of Marston and Oates (footnote 82), Whitman wrote identical letters to Ellis and Brockie; see *The Correspondence of Walt Whitman*, III, 57–58.

87. Whitman said in letters to Carpenter, 23 and 25 April 1876, that he was sending two volumes; see *The Correspondence of Walt Whitman*, III, 41, 43.

Sept 8
Rev  A  B  Grosart[88]          a set          [sideways:]
    care of Prof E. Dowden          Two vols              see alluded to in
        as above          (acknowledged by letter     Ros.'s letter of  √x
                          from ED dated Oct 4)          May 26 '76
                                        [in blue pencil:]
                                            recd


Sept 8
Rev  Prof  Dowden
    North  Brantisfield Pl     a  set
        Edinburgh          Two Vols                    √x
            Scotland


    Sept 9
John Hay[89]      } sent  T  R
☞    see back


    Sept 9
R Spence Watson    } a set — Two Vols          [sideways:]
    see back          (the second set)          see Ros's letter of
                                        May 3ᵈ
                                            [in blue pencil:]
                                            recd


---

Morse here — the <u>sculping</u>[90]
1223 Chestnut st — Sept 7th to 14th

                                                    [50]

[On slips of paper, only the first (in pencil) in WW's hand:]

            S  P  Dyke

[On letterhead of Frank Leslie's Publishing House, 53, 55 and 57 Park Place:]

            John Y. Foster.

---

88.  For the Dowden and Grosart orders, see *The Correspondence of Walt Whitman*, III,
58–59; Grosart (1827–1899) was an editor of Elizabethan texts. Whitman's letter to W. M.
Rossetti, 10 September 1876, partially explains the comment "alluded to in Ros.'s letter of May
26 '76." (Rossetti letter is not extant.)
    89.  See footnote 65.
    90.  On 16 February 1879 (see *Daybook* below) Whitman received the sculptured head
from Sidney H. Morse and commented "head recd / bad — wretchedly bad". (See footnote
421.)

[Plain sheet, seven lines:]  Dec '80 [sideways in WW's hand in blue pencil]

D. Y. Kilgore[91] 605 Walnut
house 517 Preston St
bet 40 & 41st Sts
just above Lancaster
Avenue —
Walnut St Last Car
or Vine St

[51]

'76 [in blue pencil]    21  [in blue pencil]

Sept 10
G F E Pearsall[92]   Two R   [in blue pencil,
298 Fulton st              sideways:] recd
Brooklyn

Sept 11
John Swinton[93]
134 East 34th st  3 copies  L of G    [in blue pencil,
by Express    2 "    T R    sideways:]  all recd
paid    3 "  Memoranda
see back

Sept 11
J Q A Ward[94]  2 copies  L of G    [in blue pencil,
140 East 38th st  2 "    T R    sideways:]  all
by Express    2 "  Memoranda    rec'd
paid
see back

Sept 13 — sent papers <u>with</u> <u>circulars</u> enc. to
    Buchanan, Dowden, Rossetti & J L Warren[95]

---

91. Damon Y. Kilgore (1827–1888), Philadelphia lawyer and member of the Liberal League of Philadelphia; Whitman spent Thanksgiving Day 26 November 1880 with the Kilgore family; see *The Correspondence of Walt Whitman*, III, 61, 75–76, 199.

92. G. F. E. Pearsall, artist and photographer, took Whitman's picture in September 1872 (see *The Correspondence of Walt Whitman*, III, 49–50) and it was used as the frontispiece to *Two Rivulets*; it remains one of the best known likenesses of the poet.

93. See footnote 33.

94. See footnote 35.

95. Buchanan, Dowden, and Rossetti were Whitman's English "representatives"; J. L. Warren refers to John Byrne Leicester Warren, third Baron de Tabley (see footnote 46).

Sept 14 — sent Two Vols, L and R, also John B's <u>Notes</u>    [in blue pencil,
 with slips, papers – & letter – to <u>Jeannette L Gilder</u>[96]    sideways in left
  77 Brunswick st.   Newark N   J    margin:]   rec'd

Sept 14 — letter to Tennyson[97]    [in blue pencil:]
        recd & ans'd

                   [52]

[On long sheet from a notebook, all in pencil, except two *Map* lines:]

Beatrice Carnvardine Gilchrist. [not WW's hand]
 33  Warrenton St    Boston
Herbert Haslakenden Gilchrist.[98]
Lemuel Stephens [not WW's hand]    Gir: Coll.
   Res. 2320 Green St.
<u>Maps</u> – J   L   Smith    27 South 6th
     St.   Phil
perfumery – 26   4th
 Frank Wadsworth Parsons [not WW's hand]

Jeff    Office Water Commissioners
   City  Hall – St Louis[99]

[Three lines, in pencil, not WW's hand:]

Wister  Shoemaker
Asst  Tkt  Agent  P.R.R.
Market St   Wharf

  ratan  work, chairs & baskets
  Becker   712 South   4th
    Camden

                [53]

'76  [in blue pencil]       22   [in blue pencil]
 Mrs G & family arrived Sept 10  '76    1929 North 22d st[100]

 96.  Jeannette L. Gilder (1849–1916), sister of Richard Watson Gilder, whom Whitman met in June 1878, though he wrote her in 1875 when she was on the New York *Herald*; she was co-founder and editor of *The Critic* (1881–1906). See *The Correspondence of Walt Whitman*, III, 141n, IV, 58, 68, 118, 224n; V, 79n, 145, 256, 257. This letter of 14 September 1876 is lost.
 97.  Whitman's letter to Tennyson of 14 September 1876 is also apparently lost; but see the letter of 9 August 1878, *The Correspondence of Walt Whitman*, III, 133.
 98.  Beatrice and Herbert Gilchrist were the daughter and son of Mrs Anne Gilchrist, who went to Boston in the fall of 1878 and winter 1879 after leaving Philadelphia.
 99.  Thomas Jefferson ("Jeff") Whitman (1833–1890), Walt's favorite brother, planned and built the St Louis water works and was its superintendent and chief from 1867 until 1887.
 100.  This may be cited as the first "diary" entry in Whitman's *Daybook*, recording the arrival of Mrs Anne Gilchrist from England in her attempt to become "Mrs Whitman."

My visits to Montgomery House   Phil. $\cancel{12}^{th}$

13$^{th}$ 14$^{th}$ of Sept &c (house 1929 North 22$^d$ st.)

& 15$^{th}$                called Sept 25 – Oct 9 [101]

John Burroughs there   Sept 14 and 15 '76

$\cancel{W}$ Sept 16
W J Linton[102]   L of G   [in blue pencil, sideways:] recd          √x
box 489
New Haven
Conn

<u>Favorita</u>  opera – Brignoli          Saturday
the superb "spirto gentil"          Sept 16 '76
went with Hatty – [103]
Phil – Academy –
the disagreeable night –
⸮ equinoctial storm, Saturday night 16th
Sunday 17$^{th}$

'76

Sept 17$^{th}$ (Sunday) equinoctial storm to-day
& last night, & up to 9 o'clock to night
Sept 18 – This (Monday) a rich, sweet, bracing
beautiful day – fresh sunshiny morning

⌈also Oct 1,
Sept 19$^{th}$ to 23$^d$ – Down at White Horse – [104] (4 days)⌋2, & 3
saw E. C.[105]
composed the Tom Paine bit[106]

101.  Whitman was to visit Mrs Gilchrist often during her stay of about two years at 1929 North 22nd Street, Philadelphia.

102.  See footnote 39.

103.  Hatty was Mannahatta Whitman, Jeff's daughter and Walt's niece from St Louis, 16 years old; the poet and Hattie (as her name was sometimes spelled) heard Pasquale Brignoli (1824–1884), the Italian tenor, sing in the opera *La Favorita* by Donizetti. "Spirto Gentil," a popular romanza for tenor, was a special favorite of Whitman. See "Letter from Paumanok," reprinted in *Uncollected Poetry and Prose*, I, 255–258, from the New York *Evening Post*, 14 August 1851; see also *The Correspondence of Walt Whitman*, III, 69; and Robert D. Faner, *Walt Whitman & Opera* (Philadelphia: University of Pennsylvania Press, 1951), pp. 8, 181, *et passim*.

104.  White Horse is Whitman's name for the Stafford farm, a mile and a half from Kirkwood, Glendale, New Jersey, 12 miles from Camden; he also used the name Timber Creek.

105.  E. C. refers to Edward Cattell, a Stafford farm hand; see *The Correspondence of Walt Whitman*, III, 77.

106.  The Tom Paine bit was a piece read by Whitman in Philadelphia on 28 January 1877

[54]

<u>Drivers</u>, <u>Conductors</u>, <u>Ferrymen</u>[107]
Gideon Jackson,  driver 2ᵈ st.  North Cam
John Williamson, tall, young, (old driver) 5th st
John McLaughlin   black eyed, (old driver) 5th st
Jerry Robbins, driver  Stevens St cars  [in pencil]
Danl  Garwood  driver Scull's wagon  [in pencil]
Jo  Cline, Stevens St. (and all round)
John Emery, 46 car  Haddington, March '80
Harry Miller    Market st  Phil
Wm  Wilson      "    "    "
Robert Norris  [last name in pencil]   144 Car
                         105 Car          Clark Hilton
April '80 – Johnston Love McFetridge,ʌ young conductor    ʌ    extra
     Edward Wilson   conductor car (open) No 8 Market St
     Frank St John   coal agent, Maine man, I saw at
                                             the ferry

[On slip of paper (in pencil) at bottom:]

                    Hudson R Greenleaf
                    Union Depot
                    23ᵈ & Col

[55]

'76  [in blue pencil]    23  [in blue pencil]
Sept 24 —
    W  J ∖ Linton[108]      sent T  R     [in blue pencil,
           box 489      (see back)    sideways:]  all recd
    New Haven                               Two Vols
       Conn                                   recd

Sept 24 – wrote postal card to Whitney & Adams
            paid [in blue pencil]   see back

on the 140th anniversary of Paine's birthday, later included in *Specimen Days* as "In Memory of Thomas Paine" (*Prose Works 1892,* I, 140–142); the MS in the Feinberg Collection is endorsed: "For the inauguration of the Thos. Paine bust. Written out in the woods, Kirkwood (White Horse) Oct. 2 '76 WW". See the letters to Damon Y. Kilgore, *The Correspondence of Walt Whitman,* III, 61, 75.

107.  This is the first of such lists of young men which Whitman made on the left-hand pages of his *Daybook*; these entries were made in March 1880, somewhat later than the 1876 entries of the right-hand pages. One may conjecture the reason why Whitman, then more than 60 years old, jotted down these boys' names with some occasional comments. The names almost never reappear in the *Daybook* or anywhere else, so most likely Whitman never saw them again.

108.  See footnote 39.

Sept·24th & 5th – visited J M [109] at Mr & Mrs Mingle
near
2347 at St Alban's Place &    24th st Phil

---

Sept 25th – answered    A  K  Butts postal card [110]
to 34 Dey st   N   Y

---

talk with H    S [111] & gave him    r Sept 26 '76 –(took r back)

---

Jeff ar    at    431 Stevens – Sept 26

---

At Kirkwood [112] Oct 1, 2, 3[d]    '76

---

Oct 9 – drew $100 from bank

X  Oct 9 – paid Arnold $50 – binding[113]

"   "    paid Lou[114] 50 – up to Oct 1, '76

Oct 10, – rec'd p. o. orders, $116 from Rossetti

At Kirkwood from from Oct 10 to Oct 19
paid Mrs S. $5

Oct 19 – Wm & Margaretta Avery[115] here
Sold Wm    T    R    $5 – gave M a Mem for
Mrs Cornelia Thompson of Va

Oct 19   Chas Eldridge here[116]

109. J. M. cannot be positively identified, although it may be Joseph B. Marvin, a Washington friend; see footnote 81.

110. A. K. Butts, of 36 Dey Street, New York (whose letter from Whitman of 25 September 1876 is lost), a book agent who was labeled, with O'Kane and Somerby, as three who "had embezzled the proceeds" from books he entrusted to them to sell. See *The Correspondence of Walt Whitman*, II, 273–274, 275; III, 42n.

111. H S refers to Harry Stafford. The "r" refers to a ring Whitman gave Harry as a marriage symbol. See *The Correspondence*, III, 6–7; and E. H. Miller's *Walt Whitman's Poetry: A Psychological Journey* (New York, 1968), pp. 53–54.

112. References to Kirkwood indicate that Whitman was visiting the Stafford Farm; Timber Creek, White Horse (or Whitehorse), Glendale, also refer to the Stafford Farm.

113. Arnold was James Arnold; see footnote 22.

114. Lou refers to Mrs Louisa Whitman, George's wife, with whom Whitman boarded on Stevens Street, Camden.

115. William and Margaretta Avery were evidently cousins of Whitman's mother from Brooklyn; Whitman sold Avery a copy of *Two Rivulets* while they were in Camden, and gave Mrs Avery a copy of *Memoranda During the War* for Mrs Cornelia Thompson.

116. Charles W. Eldridge was an old friend, publisher of the third (1860) edition of *Leaves,* and one who helped Whitman get a position in Washington. Numerous references to

July, Aug,
$\Big($ Hattie & Jessie here – $\wedge$ Sept. & Oct [117]
here four months – left Oct 25 '76 for St. L. $\Big)$

[56]

[On a slip of paper:]

Maps –
Breuner & Atwood
402 Locust st

[Three clippings from newspaper classified ads, on sheet of notebook paper:]

One from Philadelphia Agency, 900 Walnut   Street; another —
COPYING AND ENLARGING PICTURES
a specialty.  R.  Newell  &  Son, 626  Arch  st.

Third one:

Rub[b]er Hand Stamps,
For bank and business purposes, the best in the
market, warranted  two  years.   S.  J.  Brown  &
Co., 149 South Fourth street.

[57]

'76 [in blue pencil]          24 [in blue pencil]
Mem – Send O'Grady[118] my Photo, to care
$\Big($ Dowden's letter to me $\Big)$
of Dowden, Dublin.          dated Oct 4

Oct. 9 – Rossetti's p o'orders $116 – rec'd

Oct 21 – Sent circ's & slips to Henry King, P M, Topeka
Kansas

Oct 24, went probably Oct 25

Miss Blind,[119] 52 Torrington Sq. WC London    T R        √x

him throughout the *Correspondence of Walt Whitman* and letters to him.
117.  Hattie and Jessie, of course, were Whitman's nieces, Jeff's daughters from St Louis.
118.  Standish James O'Grady (1846–1928), Irish lawyer and poet, author of "Walt Whitman: the Poet of Joy," *The Gentleman's Magazine*, n.s. XV (December 1875), 704–716; see
*The Correspondence of Walt Whitman*, II, 153n.
119.  Mathilde Blind and the other 13 English recipients of *Two Rivulets*, with or without
its companion *Leaves of Grass*, got their books through Rossetti; four are mentioned in Whitman's letter to Rossetti of 10 September 1876 (see *The Correspondence of Walt Whitman*, III,

Ford Madox Brown[120] 37 Fitzroy Sq. W  "   Two Vols [in red ink, rec'd   √x
                                                                        sideways:]

R   Hannah   Craven House   Queen's Elm   Brompton SW   T R

Lady Hardy[121] 126 Portsdown r'd   W              Two Vols       √x

                                    Regent's
J  T  Nettleship[122] 233 Stanhope St᜕Park NW   Two Vols √x [in red ink,
                                                                        sideways:]
                                                                        rec'd

R  R  Whitehead    Balliol College Oxford    T  R  √x [in blue pencil,
                                                                        sideways:]
                                                                        recd  /  recd

R  L  Nettleship[123]      "       "       "       T R              √x [in blue
                                                                   pencil, sideways:]
                                                        recd  /  recd [in red ink]

H  S  Theobald [124] 50 Talbot road   Bayswater W  T R       √x [in blue
                                                                   pencil sideways:]
                                                                   recd / recd [in
                                                                        red ink]

                        Camden Cottage
H  R  Ricardo[125] ⋀ Christ Church r'd   Hampstead W Two Vols √x [in red
                                                                   ink, sideways:]  recd

H  G  Dakyns  Clifton College  Bristol              Two Vols √x

Hubert Herkomer[126] Bushey, Herts.                 Two Vols √x

Francis Hueffer[127] 37 Fitzroy Sq   W              T  R    √x

59-60); Whitman wrote letters to two of them, at least. Miss Blind (1841–1896), a minor and pedestrian poet, was the author of *The Prophecy of St. Oran* (1882), *The Heath on Fire* (1886), *The Ascent of Man* (1889), on the debate over evolution, and other verse influenced by her travels.
    120. Ford Madox Brown (1821–1893), an English painter in the Romantic tradition, specializing in historical, religious, and literary subjects, who inspired the Pre-Raphaelite Brotherhood.
    121. Lady Hardy was probably the wife of Herbert Hardy, first Baron Cozens-Hardy (1838–1920), an English judge.
    122. John Trivett Nettleship (1841–1902), painter and author who was a friend of Rossetti; see *The Correspondence of Walt Whitman*, II, 153n.
    123. R. R. Whitehead (unidentified) and Richard Lewis Nettleship (1846–1892) — the latter's *Philosophical Lectures and Remains* was published in London in 1897 and 1901, and his *Theory of Education in Plato's Republic* in Oxford in 1935.
    124. H. S. Theobold was a London art collector and dealer.
    125. H. R. Ricardo: unidentified further than by data in the *Daybook*.
    126. Sir Hubert von Herkomer (1849–1914), Bavarian painter and Oxford professor of fine arts, 1885–1894.
    127. Francis Hueffer (1845–1889), one of the three editors of *The New Quarterly Magazine*, n.s. Vols. I–III, 1873–1880.

W  J  Stillman[128] St Helen's Cottage Ventnor          T  R  [in red ink,
                                                         sideways:]  rec'd

Cha's Rowley Jr   Harpushey   Manchester          Two Vols √x [in blue
                                                  pencil, sideways:] recd

            The Centennial Exposition          [in blue pencil]
                    Phila.                      [in blue pencil]

                                                              [58]

   [Blank.]

                                                              [59]

'76  [in blue pencil]          25  [in blue pencil]
Oct 24 — was taken by
    Mrs Fannie L   Taylor,[129]
(1810 Olive street   St Louis   Missouri)
to the Exposition – the 2 1/2 hours there
    wheel'd about in the chair — the Japanese
    summer-house – the figure of Carlyle —
— the visit to the Annex – the statuary —
the crowd — the delightful ride along the
Schuylkill, evening

   Oct 25 — Hattie's picture   photo'd
        (paid Mr. Spieler $5 )     [130]
   Nov 12 "          "      $5 )

Oct 28–31 — down at White Horse[131]

Eve. Oct 31 — visited at Mrs. G.[132]

                rec'd
Oct 31 – $10 p o order  from Henry King   p m
       Topeka, Kansas\books sent Nov  1

128.  William J. Stillman (1828–1901), American painter and art critic, a correspondent
for the London *Times*, 1875–1898; Whitman wrote to him and to Theobold (see above) when
he sent *Two Rivulets*; see *The Correspondence of Walt Whitman*, III, 63.
   129.  Mrs Taylor, with whom Whitman visited the Centennial Exposition in Philadelphia,
probably had come to Camden to escort Mannahatta (Hattie) and Jessie Louisa Whitman,
daughters of Jeff, back to St Louis after their four-month stay with their uncles George and
Walt. See *The Correspondence of Walt Whitman*, III, 69.
   130.  See end of footnote 76.
   131.  See footnote 112.
   132.  Mrs Anne Gilchrist.

Nov. 1  
Henry King p m ⎫ a set  
Topeka ⎬ Two                    √x  
Kansas ⎭ Vols

Nov. 1 — Talk with H S [133] in front room S street – gave him r

again

Nov. 3 — wrote letter to Rossetti – (will get there ab't 13th)

Nov. 5th–8th — down at White Horse — went over  
to Blackwoodtown & around through Chew's  
Landing, "Greenland" &c.  (Election day)   Nov. 8 paid Mrs S [134]

$5

Name of young man at station   Pettit

[60]

[Two slips of paper covered by printed ad (on purple and pale green card-board) of The Sierra Grande Mining Company of New Mexico, Sierra City, Dona Ana Co., New Mexico. One slip reads: Lord Houghton / Traveller's Club / Pall Mall / London. (not WW's hand). The other reads: Should you intend to send / them please direct it to Mr. Otto Behrens / City. 140 Eight Avenue. (not WW's hand).]

[61]

'76  [in blue pencil]  
Nov. 11 – paid Jas Arnold, $100 [135]  
"   "    went down to White Horse – there 12th, 13th, 14th  
"   14th sent 6 Photo Cards to Children's Home  

¶  
"   "    A̶d̶v̶.̶ of Photo. in "Visitor" to different people

Nov 16 – at White Horse one day

Nov 17, commenced furnishing Children's Home Matron  
with the pictures, (& selling some myself) for the  
benefit of the orphans.[136]

133. Harry Stafford. See footnote 111.  
134. As seen above on 10 October, Whitman paid Mrs Stafford $5.00 for his room and board when he visited the family at White Horse.  
135. The binder of Whitman's *Leaves* and other books; see footnote 22.  
136. Whitman aided the Camden Children's Home, Haddon Avenue, by giving them

Nov. 18, 19, 20 – Visit at Mrs G's, 22ᵈ street

        dark & rainy three days

   also Nov. 24 –

Nov. 21

Wᵐ  A Stagg[137]        a set  2 Vols

  68 Broadway                          [in red ink,

     room No 12                      sideways:]  recd

New York City

Nov. 21 – sent letter to R. Buchanan – see draft

Nov  21 – sent full set of slips &c to J  H  McCarthy[138]

"    "      "        "        "        Mrs Ritter, Po'keepsie[139]

Nov 25, 26, 27, 28 – Down at White Horse – Memorable

   talk with H S — settles the matter.[140]

                                   [62]

[On three calling cards:]

      George Jeffeau

   Machinist.      19 yr's

      23 Marseilles

       bet. 19ᵗʰ & Broad

-------

    *Dr.  William  Baker.* [printed on calling card]

(Inscribed  in Col Johnston's room)  [in pencil]

    Hospital Univ. of Penn'a.  [printed on calling card]

3400

3400 Spruce St.        West Philad'a. [printed on calling card]

---

signed copies of the Pearsall photograph of himself to sell for $1.00; full proceeds went to the orphanage. See "The Poet Aids an Orphanage," *Walt Whitman Review,* VI (September 1960), 58–59.

    137.  William A. Stagg had written Whitman on 17 November 1876 requesting an autograph (letter in the Feinberg Collection).

    138.  See footnote 83.

    139.  Mrs Ritter, musician and a friend of William D. O'Connor, was the wife of Professor Frédéric Louis Ritter (1834–1891) of Vassar, who composed a musical setting for "Dirge for Two Veterans." Whitman visited the Ritters on 28 April 1879. See *The Correspondence of Walt Whitman,* III, 153n.

    140.  As Professor Edwin H. Miller points out, in *The Correspondence of Walt Whitman,* III, 2–9, Harry Stafford was a difficult and moody person.

*Richard Ashbridge, Jr.* [printed on card]
Doctor – assistant in
  Penn: Univ: Hospital
(I spent 3 or 4 hours there)


call'd on me in Camden
  *W. L. Shoemaker,* [printed on card]
      Georgetown, D. C. [printed on card]

[63]

'76 [in blue pencil]
Dec 1.

| | | | | |
|---|---|---|---|---|
| Ed T. Potter | sent 2 copies old | [in red pencil, | | √x |
| Newport | <u>Leaves of Grass</u> | sideways:] | | |
| R I | rec'd $5 | recd | | |

Dec 11
Mrs Louise Chandler
     Moulton[141]     1 L of G
  care Phil Bourke Marston          [in blue pencil:]
  20 Ladbroke Grove Road  rec'd $5 — rec'd
     Notting Hill w
       London

Dec 12
Mrs F R Ritter[142]  sent L of G        √x
  63 South Hamilton st     [in blue pencil:]
  Poughkeepsie N Y  rec'd $5  rec'd

Dec 14
Philip Ripley[143]  sent MSS     [in blue pencil:]
American Cyclopædia office  & autograph  rec'd  recd  √x
  551 Broadway
    N Y City

141. Mrs Ellen Louise Chandler Moulton (1835–1908), an American poet, was staying in England with Philip Bourke Marston (1850–1887), a blind English poet whose works she edited; see entry above for 7 September 1876; and *The Correspondence of Walt Whitman,* III, 58 and 65.

142. See footnote 139.

143. Whitman's letter to Ripley, 14 December 1776, is lost.

Dec 13, 14 wrote to

Mr Johnston    150 Bowery

Pete

Mr Childs

Miss Nicholson, Children's Home

Joe Allen, (sent Photo, Mem,

       & letters) [144]

[64]

[Clippings from *Daily Post* for Thursday, March 29, 1877, with title "Walt Whitman," beginning:]

> He visits New York after 5 years ab-
> sence  High tone Society now takes
> him to its bosom — Yet he rides again
> atop of the Broadway Omnibuses
> and Fraternizes with drivers and
> boatmen — He has a New Book under
> way — He is better in health.

[The article of several hundred words is about WW's visit. Attached is a small card with 'Walt Whitman / March 8th 77' on one side (not WW's hand), on the verso are ten signatures, one of which is Whitman's.]

[65]

'76

                                      paid

  Dec 19 – Paid Mr. Twoes[145] $10 – (owe him now $9) in full

                                  conv'n

evening, sitting in room, had serious inward rev'n & ~~con~~

                        –saw clearly

  about ————————  what it really meant –

–very profound meditation on all – ~~more~~ happy & satisfied at

last about it – singularly so. It ——————— like – more

m————————————— (that this may last now

                              without any more perturbation)

---

144. The letters to Peter Doyle and to John H. Johnston are in *The Correspondence of Walt Whitman,* III, 67–68; but those to Joe Allen, George W. Childs, and Miss Nicholson of the Camden Children's Home are among the lost letters.

145. H. B. Twoes, the poet's tailor, 134 Federal Street, Camden.

Dec 29
David Sobieski White
   75 West 54<sup>th</sup> street   } sent L of G
      New York City

1877  [in blue pencil]
  '77 – Jan 6<sup>th</sup> to 10<sup>th</sup>
    Down at White Horse

Jan 10<sup>th</sup> to 16<sup>th</sup>
   at the G's 1929 north 22<sup>d</sup> Phila

        to 23d
Jan 18<sup>th</sup> ∧down at White Horse

Jan 25<sup>th</sup> at 1929   22<sup>d</sup> st   till Feb 2

Feb 7<sup>th</sup> to 13<sup>th</sup> at White Horse

Feb 15 to 17<sup>th</sup> at 1929   22<sup>d</sup> st    (John Burroughs there)
   – to 21<sup>st</sup>   ditto

<u>In New York</u>  from March 2<sup>d</sup> to March
   27, '77 – (at Esopus   March 16<sup>th</sup> – 29<sup>th</sup>) [146]
   [in blue pencil:] visit to New York[147]

X  March 30 – paid L. $50 – pays up to April 1, '77.[148]
     "   "   "   Jas Arnold $50 [148a]

March 26 '77 – Monday night – Death of Mrs A. F. Johnston

---

146. As will be seen from Whitman's visits to the Stafford farm at White Horse, with Mrs Gilchrist and her family at 1929 North 22nd Street, Philadelphia, and with John Burroughs at Esopus-on-Hudson, during January, February, and March 1877, he was increasingly dissatisfied with life in his brother George's home on Stevens Avenue in Camden.

147. Whitman's visit to J. H. Johnston, the New York jeweler, was his first, lasting almost a month, but ending in sadness with Mrs Johnston's death. See Gay Wilson Allen, *The Solitary Singer,* pp. 478–479.

148. Nevertheless, despite his absences, Whitman paid Louisa Whitman $50 for his room and board.

148a. The $50 for James Arnold was for binding *Leaves of Grass,* as usual (see footnote 22).

[66]

[On sheet pasted in notebook:]¹⁴⁹

| | |
|---|---|
| Han | ⎧ Mrs Searing ⎫ |
| Mary | ⎩    Howard Glyndon ⎭ |
| Hattie | Mrs Smith |
| Mrs Gil ¹⁵⁰ | E  C  Stedman |
| G  W  Waters¹⁵¹ | E . T  Potter¹⁵³ |
| J  H  Johnston | Mrs Hewson |
| Cin Com | Ida Johnston¹⁵⁴ |
| Eve Star | Ellen O'Connor |
| John Bur | Mrs Mingle |
| Ed Cattell | Addington Symonds |
| Debbie S | |
| Thos  J  W ¹⁵² | |
| Pete Doyle | |
| John Newton John . . . | |
| Tom Freeman | |
| May  Johnston | |
| Al     " | |
| Mrs  Bowne  Woodside | |
| Mrs  Croly¹⁵⁵   [in blue pencil] | |
| Mrs  Bigelow¹⁵⁶ | |

149. Although there is no notation on this list, we may assume, because of its being in the *Daybook* next to an article headed "Walt Whitman," from the New York *Daily Post,* 29 March 1877, that Whitman sent clippings of this article to the 30 listed (two of them newspapers).

150. Hannah and Mary, Whitman's sisters; Mannahatta (Hattie), his niece; Mrs Gilchrist, his friend; J. H. Johnston, the New York jeweler; the Cincinnati *Commercial*; the Washington *Evening Star*; John Burroughs; Edward Cattell (see footnote 105); Debbie Stafford; Peter Doyle; John Newton Johnson (see footnote 9a); May and Al Johnston, J. H. Johnston's daughter and son; E. C. Stedman, the critic and anthologist; Ellen O'Connor, William D. O'Connor's wife, of Washington; and John Addington Symonds, the Englishman, may all be easily identified; the other 12 in this list are identified below — if identification is possible.

151. George W. Waters (1832–1912), a painter, who did a portrait of Whitman in 1877 (now in the frontispiece of Vol. V of the 1902 edition of the *Complete Writings*), which Whitman thought "grand" and John H. Johnston bought from him for $200 in 1884. See *The Correspondence of Walt Whitman,* III, 68, 80, 83–84, 99, 115–116, 139.

152. "Thos J W" is most likely Thomas Jefferson Whitman, though the poet usually referred to his brother as Jeff; on 5 June 1880 referred to "Thos J Whitman."

153. Edward Tuckerman Potter was a resident of Newport, Rhode Island, to whom Whitman sent two copies of *Leaves of Grass* on 1 December 1776, and several articles from time to time.

154. Ida Johnston was the daughter of Colonel John R. Johnston, a Camden artist friend; see *The Correspondence of Walt Whitman,* II, 322; III, 85.

155. Mrs Croly may refer to Mrs Jenny C. Croly, who asked Whitman for a poem for *Demorest's Illustrated* on 21 May 1882; or the wife of David G. Croly (1829–1889), editor of the New York *Daily Graphic* until 1878.

156. Mrs Bigelow may be the wife of John Bigelow (1817–1911), minister to France (1865–1866) and co-editor, New York *Evening Post* (1848–1861), whom Whitman visited in West Point, New York on 16 June 1878. See *The Correspondence of Walt Whitman,* III, 121.

[67]

'77 / March 30 – paid Jas Arnold $50 – (leaves $108 due)

1877

| | | |
|---|---|---|
| March 30<br>sent Lawrence Hutton<br>229 West 34<sup>th</sup> st<br>New York City | } a set<br>Two Vols<br>~~to be paid for~~ $10<br>paid | [in blue pencil:]<br>recd |

| | | |
|---|---|---|
| March 30<br>Scribner & Co.[157]<br>743 Broadway | } John Burroughs<br>Notes<br>to be paid for $1 | [in blue pencil:]<br>rec'd &<br>paid |

| | | |
|---|---|---|
| April 1<br>G W Waters[158]<br>113 east 10th st<br>N Y | } a set<br>two vols | [in blue pencil:]<br>rec'd |

| | | |
|---|---|---|
| April 1<br>J Addington Symonds<br>Clifton Hill House<br>Bristol Eng | a set<br>Two Vols<br>paid | [in blue pencil:]<br>recd    √x |

Tuesday  Ap. 24  to Ap 30 – down at White Horse
(the scene in the front room Ap. 29, with H)

E. Carpenter here May 1

[68]

X   Edward Tuckerman Potter[159]
          Newport  Rhode Island

X   Mrs F R Ritter[160]
          Poughkeepsie  N Y

X   J  Addington Symonds
          Clifton Hill House
          Clifton
                    Bristol  Eng:

157.  See Whitman's letter, *The Correspondence of Walt Whitman*, III, 81.
158.  See footnote 151.
159.  See footnote 153.
160.  See footnote 139.

[Next two addresses on slips of paper, in pencil, not in WW's hand:]

Paul  Berger
1248  South   13th  St
          Phila

Studio  \        [in  WW's  hand]
  '78 & '9  \

J. B.  Studley
   277 Hudson  St:
   New York

Studio |        [in  WW's  hand]
  '79  |

[69]

1877
May  2 – to                  ⎞
   E   J   Ellis             ⎟      the two Vols
      25 Argyll  road        ⎬            paid                        √x
      Kensington             ⎟
          London    W        ⎠

May   2  –  to               ⎞
   A   Cordery               ⎟      L  of  G
143 Haverstock  Hill         ⎬            paid                        √x
   London   N  W             ⎠

May  2 – to                  ⎞
   J   T  Nettleship[161]     ⎟      a paper
      233 Stanhope st        ⎬      with  circ's  &c                  √x
          London   N   W      ⎠      – postal card –

May  3 – to                  ⎞
   E   A   Veght             ⎬ sent circ in ans to his
      Somerville   N   J     ⎠     x Ap 9
                                letter asking abt books

May  3  to                   ⎞
      J Addington Symonds     ⎟  Two Vols
Clifton  Hill  House         ⎬      The second set    see back
   Clifton   Bristol, Eng    ⎠  [in red ink, sideways:]   rec'd

161.  On 24 October 1876, Nettleship was sent *Leaves of Grass* and *Two Rivulets*; see
entry above for that date and footnote 122.

May 3 to
    F W Cozens
    27 Queen's Gate
    London  S W

Two Vols
(pay not yet rec'd May 1 (2)    √x
[in red ink, sideways:] rec'd
    paid

[70]

[Three calling cards: the first, John D. Hylton, Palmyra, N. J., dealer in Pensauken Creek Clay & Kaolin, for fire brick, chimney tops, garden vases, etc.; the second, N. C. Smith, 129 South Eighth Street, Philadelphia, dealer in stationery and fancy goods; the third, Edward MacHarg, Professor of Memory, &c., 1304 South Seventeenth St., Phila. Only the' last has any marginalia:]
Introduced to me at Ferry reception/room Phil. side Feb '79

[71]

1877
May 4 letters to
    Editor Secularist
      care G  W  Foote[162]
      12 Gower street
      London  W C
& to
    Editor Examiner[163]
      London

June 5 '78 – G  W  Foote
owes me yet, at least £3
money subscribed for me
in London    [in blue pencil:]
never rec'd    lost
  embezzled    to me
          embezzled
            in London

C
paper & letter to Joe  Baldwin,  Elliottstown[164]
[in red ink:]
Effingham Co.  Ill  rec'd ans

May 4 – Wrote to Tom Freeman  Sloan's Station[165]

162.  George William Foote (1850–1915), a freethinker who refused to pay £3 for the books to Whitman, saying the money was stolen by an employee; Whitman called Foote a "fraud" (see entry below for 12 February 1878). See The Correspondence of Walt Whitman, III, 55n.

163.  These letters to the Editor, Secularist and the Editor, London Examiner were apparently not published and are among Whitman's lost letters.

164.  At least four Whitman letters to Joseph C. Baldwin, 4 May and about 20 September 1877, 23 September 1878, and 20 June 1880, are lost; among those from Baldwin, one, 17 June 1875, is in the T. E. Hanley Collection, University of Texas, and four, 13 May, 11 August, 11 and 21 September 1877, are in the Feinberg Collection. The last two deal with a loan of money from the poet.

165.  This is the same Thomas B. Freeman to whom Whitman sent material about 26 January 1879, 9 April 1878, and about 29 March 1877. See footnotes 76 and 81. Freeman's letters to Whitman, 1 February 1877 and 13 May 1878, are in the Feinberg Collection; Whitman's to Freeman, 4 May 1877, is lost.

Jefferson County  Ohio   (short letter)
              [in red ink:]
              rec'd ans
                     invited to visit them

[Next five lines in pencil:]
May 15 — have been down to White Horse
    for a week, – return'd  this evening.
    ⎛ Mr Carpenter call'd on me there  [165a] ⎞
    ⎝ Herbert Gilchrist    "         "       ⎠

16th return'd to White Horse –
    [rest of page, eight lines, in red ink:]
    remained at W  H  till 22[d]

23[d], 24[h] & 25th – at dinner each day at 1929 22[d] st Phil[166]

May 23[d] – recd "Birds & Poets" J  B's book[167]

May 25      ⎞
W  Hale White │
   Admiralty   ⎬ sent  Two  Riv
      Whitehall │ paid              [sideways:] rec'd
   London  Eng  ⎠

                                                    [72]
[On three slips of paper, the first and second names and addresses not in
WW's hand:]

Joaquin Miller[167a]
  2347 StAlbans Place
          Philadelphia

     ⎛ Near the Naval  ⎞
     ⎝ Assylum –       ⎠

Mrs. Fannie L. Taylor –[168]
No 1810 Ohio Street –
    St. Louis  Mo –

165a.  For Edward Carpenter see footnote 20; for this visit see *The Correspondence of
Walt Whitman,* III, 82n.
    166.  These were visits, of course, to Mrs Anne Gilchrist's, and to the Stafford farm.
    167.  John Burroughs's "The Flight of the Eagle" (on Whitman) appears in his *Birds and
Poets* (Boston, 1877), pp. 185–235.
    167a.  For Joaquin Miller see footnote 24.
    168.  See footnote 129.

J  H  Stafford
            Horner[169]
  p o box 1093
       Oberlin
Lorain Co    Ohio

[73]

'77  [in blue pencil]
[First three lines in red ink:]                    [in black ink:]
June – first part at White Horse              ⎛Edwd
                                                              ⎞ Carpenter
    "     last part at north 22ᵈ st            ⎝ there

June 25 – went down to White Horse

July 4 – Lou very sick – (I return'd 6ᵗʰ or 7ᵗʰ)

July 13 to 20ᵗʰ '77 – down at White Horse
  ⎛Came up in the light wagon with Mrs S   July 20   ⎞
  ⎝      July 20ᵗʰ '77, in the room at White Horse "good bye" ⎠
Herbert's paintings at the creek – July '77 [170]

last of June or early in
  ab't July 12 – Two Riv: to Gen Carse for
         Mr Keasbey — (paid)

July 27 – E  J  Loomis[171]  ⎞ sent Two Riv      √x
   Nautical Almanac Office  ⎬ paid $5      [in blue pencil, sideways:] rec'd
   Washington  D  C            ⎠

July 21st⎞
July 29  ⎬ wrote Mrs S — (28th   over at 22ᵈ st)

July 22ᵈ to 30ᵗʰ  '77 — very hot — therm 90–96–
       in Camden — feeling pretty well, for me —

---

169.  Horner was the nickname of Jacob H. Stafford (1850–1890), Harry's cousin, whose mother was Mary Horner. See *The Correspondence of Walt Whitman*, III, 204n.
  170.  Herbert Gilchrist seems to have made some paintings at Timber Creek, or brought some down to show to Whitman; "good bye" most likely refers to another quarrel with Harry Stafford.
  171.  Professor Elias J. Loomis (1811–1889), astronomer and Yale professor, to whom Whitman sent *Leaves of Grass* in 1882, as well as this *Two Rivulets* in 1877.

Aug 4 '77 — For the last 3 or 4 days    Herbert
    home (at 1929 no 22$^{d}$ st)    from White Horse
    – I am over there for a couple of hours every eve-
    ning — Aug 3 – letter from Mrs S rec'd — Aug 4
    sent Mrs S the big photo. by Herbert – [172]
    — still feeling well for me

[74]

[On two slips of paper:]

Manvill Winterstein[173]

6$^{th}$ O Cav.

Hampden

Geanga Co

Ohio

Reuben Farwell[174]

Nankin P  O

dead )    Wayne Co

Mich

Benton H  Wilson

care of Packard & Jones

2 Pike Block

Syracuse    N  Y

Wm  H Millis[175]

Dover

Kent Co

Del

Camden   July 14  '76
[Left margin torn] night – Ed: Ambler Armstrong[176]

172. Herbert Gilchrist seems to have been spending a number of days at Timber Creek; meanwhile Whitman has been visiting Mrs Anne Gilchrist in Philadelphia. This page from the *Daybook* is reproduced as illustration no. 8 in *The Correspondence of Walt Whitman*, III, 202.

173. Manvill Wintersteen's letters to Whitman are in the Berg Collection, New York Public Library; Whitman's letters, February and March 1875, are lost.

174. Reubel Farwell, a Michigan Cavalryman, met Whitman in Armory Square Hospital, Washington; they corresponded after his release and discharge (Farwell's letters are in the Trent Collection). See *The Correspondence of Walt Whitman*, II, 328; Professor Miller says "Bucke wrote to Farwell after WW's death," but this must mean the Farwell family, as Reuben Farwell — according to Whitman's own notation here — died before the poet.

175. Whitman's letters to William H. Millis, Jr, an ex-soldier, about 12 February 1874, and about 27 February 1875, are among those lost; of those from Millis, one, 20 January 1868, is in the Yale University Library, and four, 16 February 1874, 28 February 1875, 4 April 1875, and 27 September 1875, are in the Berg Collection, New York Public Library.

176. Edward Ambler Armstrong, president of one of the earliest mentioned Walt Whitman

age 18 – born & raised in Salem
N.J. large family 7 or 8 – liv
cor 4th & Arch – studying law
Pres. W.W. club – evening, 2 hours
t[?]k.   (buried the baby that afternoon)[177]

[75]

'77 [in blue pencil]
[Clipping from the *Daily Post,* Thursday, August 2, 1877:]

"The Old Gray" under a tree.

Walt Whitman, the poet, is considerably improved in health, and, we understand, (says the Washington *Evening Star,*) contemplates making a visit soon to this city. His familiar form on the Avenue once more, would be a welcome sight to his many friends. Of late the poet has been sojourning quietly at a farm house with his friends Mr. and Mrs. George Stafford, at Timber Creek, a pleasant stream, near Kirkwood, N. J., some twelve miles from Philadelphia. One of his English admirers, Herbert Gilchrist, a young artist, who is visiting this country, having found the poet in his retreat, has been staying some weeks in the same neighborhood, and visiting the poet daily, in order to paint his portrait. The painting, which is now well advanced, and promises to be an excellent likeness, represents Mr. Whitman sitting in an easy chair under a favorite tree. It is hoped that the painting will be retained in this country.[177a]

———o———

clubs, was among those who attended the celebration of Whitman's 70th birthday, 31 May 1889; Traubel (*With Walt Whitman in Camden,* V, 249) says Armstrong's speech was "simply clap-trappy, telling in a style laboring to be pathetic and personal, things of W. of a very dubious authenticity."

177. This refers to Walter Orr Whitman, 8-month-old son of George Whitman, who died on 12 July 1876.

177a. For commentary on Gilchrist's painting and a reproduction of it, see Gay Wilson Allen, "The Iconography of Walt Whitman," in Edwin Haviland Miller, ed. *The Legacy of Walt Whitman* (New York, 1970), pp. 137–140.

Aug 5  Wm Gardner Barton[178]  ⎞  sent J B's <u>Notes</u>
       88 Bridge Street    ⎟  "      Vistas
       Salem  Mass       ⎟        Mem                   √x
                         ⎠  paid  [in blue pencil, sideways:] recd

Aug 4 & 5th  Harry [Stafford] here

Aug 12, 13, 14 – down at White Horse

Aug 13.  Harry went to Woodbury – (two weeks)

Aug 15 – up at Camden for the day – went
       back to White Horse evening
Sept meetings with Ed C by the pond moonlight nights[179]

Aug 15 – sent Dr R  M  Bucke, Asylum
      for the Insane, London, Ontario, Canada,
      Two Rivulets — (paid)
  "  wrote to Harry [Stafford]

Sept 10 – recd p o order $23:30 from Rossetti

[76]

[On three slips, only the last one in WW's hand:]

Thomas B. Freeman
Sloan's Station
Jeff Coty   Ohio

Rev  Geo  L  Chase
Faribault
Min

Philip Ripley[180]
Cyclopædia Office
551 Broadway
N. Y. City

178.  The year before this, on 12 November 1876, Barton wrote to Whitman, asking for an autograph (the letter is in the Feinberg Collection).
179.  Harry Stafford and Whitman were visiting each other in Camden and at Timber Creek, the poet also spending some time with Edward Cattell, the Stafford hired hand. Whitman's letter to Stafford, mentioned below, is lost.
180.  Whitman's letter to Ripley, 14 December 1876, is lost.

[77]

'77 [in blue pencil]

a

<u>Sept 10 '77</u> – return'd from a long (months)
    stay at Kirkwood — (left good bye
    note for Mrs S   and Harry   Monday
                  Sept 10 '77)

Sept 10 – Hattie & Jessie here on a two
    weeks Visit — (five days with Mrs Gilchrist)

Sept 16   Jas Anderson Rose   }   sent both    [in blue pencil:]
    11 Salisbury Street – Strand }   Vols    rec'd        √x
    London   W   C        }   paid

Sept 21 – saw Geo Staf   at the market, (sent the
    little dinner basket to Ruth – Geo: wanted me to go down
                      with him)

Sept 23. Sent circular to Lawrence Kohoe
        9 Barclay street N   Y   Catholic Publication
                    Society

Sept 23 – Wrote long letter to John Newton Johnson[181]

Sept 24   Hattie & Jessie went back to Ellicott
        City
    (wrote to Jeff and Mary)
    Herbert Gilchrist at John Burroughs's
    Mrs. G   ill in bed (the operation)

[78]

[On three slips:]
            D.   W.   Belisle,[182]
                     [name and address not in WW's hand]

dead )      No. 110   Market St
              Camden, N. J.
Lock Box 45 P. O.

181.   Unfortunately this letter to John Newton Johnson is lost.
182.   See footnote 11.

nephew of Capt.
<u>Thompson</u>
John K.   R. Hewitt. [printed in script]
   with Jim Scovel

The Congregationalist,
   Congregational House,
      Boston, Jan. 31  1876    [all but month and day
    Edward Abbott[183]                                    printed]
      Literary Editor. [these two lines and date not in
                       WW's hand]

                                                   [79]

'77

Sept 26 – paid Jas Arnold $50 (leaves
                       $58 due)

Sept 29–30 – Harry here with me

Oct 2: letter from Edw'd Carpenter

  "    postal order from E  C  $50:12

  "    sent p  card to E  C  45 Brunswick[184]
    Sq:  Brighton, Eng: acknowledging rec't

Oct 2, (evening) wrote to Hattie and Jess[185]

  "     "     also to Ed Cattell

Oct 5  Seymer Thompson ⎫
     Christ's College  ⎬
(Ed Carpenter's      ⎪  L  of  G  [in blue pencil:]
   order)  Cambridge ⎬  & T  R    recd        √x
        Eng ⎭  paid

---

183. Edward Abbott asked, about May 1880, for a poem for the Emerson number of
*The Literary World,* and Whitman sent him instead "Emerson's Books (the Shadows of
Them)," *The Literary World,* XI (22 May 1880), 177–178, reprinted in *Specimen Days and
Collect;* see *Prose Works 1892,* II, 514–518, and 767–768; and *The Correspondence of Walt
Whitman,* III, 178.
   184. A transcript of Whitman's letter is in *The Correspondence of Walt Whitman,* III, 100.
   185. Whitman's letter to Mannahatta and Jessie Louisa Whitman is in *The Correspondence
of Walt Whitman,* III, 99; but the letter to Edward Cattell is lost.

Oct 5

Clement Templeton[186]     L   of   G
    Abernethy House     & T   R    [in blue pencil:]   √x
         Mount Vernon     paid      rec'd

(Ed: Carpenter's
   order)    Hampstead


        London

[80]

[On three cards:]

     Edward Carpenter     Bradway
       45 Brunswick Sq      near Sheffield
x          Brighton   Eng:       Eng

---

    Mʳ Edward Tuckerman Potter. [printed caps]
x        Newport, R. I.   [not WW's hand]

    Pres'dt University of Minnesota.    [not WW's hand]
x        William W. Folwell    [printed caps]
     Minneapolis,
       Minnesota.   [these two lines not in WW's hand]

[in red ink:]     E   C   Stedman
   8 Pine St
     N Y            49 East 9ᵗʰ St. [not WW's hand]
   June
     ~~March~~ 81       New York, April 24ᵗʰ 1880   [not WW's hand]
[In blue pencil:]
80
Broadway

[81]

'77 [in blue pencil]
Oct 5

   J   J   Harris Teall[187]
     University Extension Lecturer    T   R   (only)
       Nottingham           paid       [in blue pencil:]   √x
                                        rec'd

186. Clement Templeton was a concert master in London; see *The Correspondence of Walt Whitman,* III, 100.
    187. J. J. Harris Teall taught science in Nottingham, and the Rev. H. R. Haweis is described as "a popular London preacher"; Haweis and his wife visited Whitman in Camden in

(Ed Carpenter's
        order)     England

Oct 5

   Rev. H  R  Haweis       L  of  G
(Ed:        16  Welbeck  street    &  T  R
Carpenter's     Cavendish  Square    paid         √x
order)          London  W
(Broadbent & Taylor's photos)

Oct 5 to E  Carpenter[188]
  45 Brunswick Sq–  }notifying the sending
     Brighton        of the Vols

Oct 5  after nearly f three weeks absence
       visited Mrs G's – Mrs G temporarily sitting
       up — Herbert return'd —

Oct 11 – wrote to Rossetti  spoke  of the Examiner
      claim, told him to take no further trouble —
      — enclosed a letter to Secularist[189] care G   W
      Foote, 12 Gower Street   W   C   (ought it not
                      [in blue pencil:]
      to be 13 Bookseller's row?)    no)
Oct 11 – sent a set Two Vols each to
        Mr Broadbent & } 914 Chestnut st
      W Curtis  Taylor }    Phil

Oct 13 – Harry here

[82]

[On four calling cards:]
       C  H  Bratton
      124 Vine St
      Philadelphia
          Pa     [this name and address not in WW's hand]

December 1885; see *The Correspondence of Walt Whitman*, III, 100–101.
    188.  Whitman's letter to Edward Carpenter is in *The Correspondence of Walt Whitman*, III, 100.
    189.  Both of Whitman's letters, to Rossetti and to the *Secularist*, are lost; the "trouble" may refer to Foote's refusal to pay £3 for the books Whitman sent him; see footnote 162, and *The Correspondence of Walt Whitman*, III, 55n.

Col. Jno. R. Johnston,[190]    [printed]
Artist.                        [printed]
722 Sansom  3ᵈ floor
~~728 Chestnut Street~~ [printed]
434 Penn  Camden

with Ziegler & Swearingen
36 North 4ᵗʰ St  Phila.
John R. Johnston, Jr.[191] [printed]
A  R  McCown & Co:
623 Market St Phil
                    434 Penn St. [printed]
Cam

[Calling card of John P. Miller,[192] manufacturer and dealer in gentlemen's furnishing goods, etc., Philadelphia.]

[83]

'77⟩ Oct 15 – sent Two Vols – to Col Forney[193]
      "    "       "    "      to Thos A Scott

Oct 17 – Carse tells me of Mr Keasbeay's[194]
  X (U  S  Att.  Newark  N  J) vehement adhesion
    to L  of  G & T R.  (I must go on to Newark
    & see K.)

Oct 17 — Dr Bucke call'd  [these seven lines on Dr Bucke's calling card]
      book
   took a set, & is to send the
         paid    [in red ink]
   money      –(money sent) [in red ink]

---

190.  Colonel John R. Johnston, a Camden artist, to whose daughter Ida and son John R., Jr, Whitman wrote (see *The Correspondence of Walt Whitman*, III, 85, and 88–89), and with whom the poet spent Sunday evenings (see ibid., II, 322).

191.  John R. Johnston, Jr (referred to above), was employed by Ziegler & Swearingen, sellers of notion in Philadelphia, after working for A. R. McCown & Co. (whose name and address is here cancelled), a Philadelphia hosiery store.

192.  See footnotes to entries below for 18 April 1879; these notes were meant to be included by Whitman in the *Daybook* upon his return from New York to Camden.

193.  Colonel John W. Forney (1817–1881), Philadelphia and Washington newspaper publisher, who published Whitman's "The First Day of Spring on Chestnut Street," Philadelphia *Progress*, 8 March 1879; reprinted in *Specimen Days and Collect* (see *Prose Works 1892*, I, 188–190). Forney also accompanied Whitman on his 1879 trip to Kansas; see *The Correspondence of Walt Whitman*, III, 150n, 163n–165, 213, 256; see entry below for 12 December 1881. Whitman's letters to him are lost.

194.  A. Q. Keasby is mentioned in William Sloane Kennedy's *The Fight of a Book for*

Dr R. Maurice Bucke [printed in script]
Asylum for the Insane
London   Ontario
Canada


Oct 17 – Rec'd good letter from Harry – Wrote to
H quite a long letter — [195]


Oct 19–20 – Harry here – [195a]


the World (West Yarmouth, Mass., 1926), p. 109, a leading lawyer of the Newark bar who lectured on Whitman during the season of 1887–88.

195.   Harry Stafford's letters to Whitman, of this date and others of 1877, are in the Feinberg Collection; but only two of six to Stafford from the poet are extant for that year, 18–19 June and 7 August 1877; see The Correspondence of Walt Whitman, III, 86–87, and 93–95.

195a.   There is no entry, obviously, for 18 October 1877; but on a scrap of paper in the Feinberg Collection are these notations by Whitman, perhaps made with the intention of using them in the Daybook:

> Columbia st road
> driver Chas Knight   135
> "     Wilson Bray   115
> "     Chas Saunders   110
> "     Harry Cooper   120
> Oct. 18 '77 – calls on Col Forney
> — the passes rec'd – the scene at
>     the "retirement"
>
> Old Washington Clerk
> '77 Oct 18 – met Thos J Hibsman
>     young, blonde, fat, on Chestnut
>     St. to-day – he told me he had
>     left Wash: & was employed
>     in mercantile bus: getting
>     orders I think, selling &c
> 22d St. Sept & Oct. '77
>     Arthur Peterson, neighb[or of]
> the Gilchrists – a paymast[er in]
> the navy
>     Wm Blair
>         yn'y m'n in Richardsons
>         confect'ry store   Phil
>
> Ellie young wm'n at
> fruit stand – Market st.   Phil
>
>     Porter C Bliss
>     Office Library Table
>         47 Lafayette Place
>             New York City
>     (Nov. '77)

Like so many other lists of names in the Daybook, especially those of workmen on the ferries or horse cars, or of young men, most of the people are never mentioned again. Colonel John W. Forney, however, is an exception: he was a very good friend who went to Kansas with Whitman in 1879 (see footnote 193). Arthur Peterson is another exception; a poet (1851–1932) who wrote Songs of New-Sweden (1887), Whitman refers to him in letters to Mrs Anne and Herbert Gilchrist: see The Correspondence of Walt Whitman, III, 139, 171, and 254.

Oct 25  Edwd Carpenter ⎞ 1 copy L  of  G          [in blue pencil,
    Cobden Road ⎟ "   "   Two Riv          sideways:] recd
    Chesterfield ⎬ 4 Dem Vistas
    Derbyshire ⎠

Oct 25 – Letter from Ed Cattell – wrote to him[196]
    (Herbert down at White Horse – (ret'd 26th Oct)

Oct 22–26 – Visited at Mrs G's to supper every evening
                   this week

Oct 27 – good letter from Harry

[84]

[On three calling cards:]
        Operas
     Lucia – by Donnizetti
    Sonnambula –" Bellini
x           John A Johann,[197]  [printed]
Public Ledger.        Philadelphia. [printed]

a good word – "oase"
       Mrs. F. B. Odenheimer [printed in script]
         north
    No. 40  Fourth St.  [not WW's hand]
       Camden  [not WW's hand]

        Dec. '78
      Miss Jeannette L. Gilder[198]
x       No 148 East 18th St
          N Y
  or
New York Herald   [these five lines not in WW's hand]

[85]

'77 [in blue pencil]

196. This letter is missing; the only extant letter from Whitman to Edward Cattell is that of 24 January 1877; see *The Correspondence of Walt Whitman*, III, 77.
197. John A. Johann, of the Philadelphia *Public Ledger*, was suggested by Whitman on 31 January 1879 as one of George W. Childs's "young men [to] come down & meet me at the foot of Market Street . . . at ¼ to 8, and convoy me up to your house." See *The Correspondence of Walt Whitman*, III, 146.
198. See footnote 96.

Elmer[199]

Oct 28th Sunday   sent letter to Harry    called


        Elmwood            6 m

Oct 29   Saml M  Duffell, Yardville,   near
         Trenton, N J. invited me to his farm to
         visit ~~from~~  Dr Street knows him

"    "  – very pleasant day –(Monday)

"    "  sent photos, circ's, &c (quite a batch,
         with adv. of books) to Prof R M Anderson[199a]
         University of Wisconson         Drawer
              Madison   Wisconsin         165


Oct 29 – Mr Shoemaker, of Washington,
         visits me – Speaks of Mr Loomis, &
         of Mr Seaver, Librarian, there[200]


Nov. 1 – paid Spieler a $5 gold piece[201]
         (superb day – walked a-foot in Phil: and C –
         – more than for four years, at any one time)
         – Elmer[202] spending the evening with me —


Nov 3 – sent E  F  Strickland, Milwaukee,[203]
         Wis:  Photo & Circulars – rec'd $1 —


        (Sunday)
Nov. 4th – breakfasted at J  M  Scovel's[204]
         – wrote long good letter to Harry —


---

199.  Elmer refers to Elmer E. Stafford (1861–1957), Harry's cousin who was then (1877) 16 years old. See *The Correspondence of Walt Whitman*, III, 91n.

199a.  Rasmus B. Anderson (not R. M.), Professor of Scandinavian at the University of Wisconsin, first heard of Whitman in 1872 from Bjørnsterne Bjørnson in Norway. See R. B. Anderson, *Life Story* (Madison, Wisconsin: privately printed, 1915). Quoted by Gay Wilson Allen, "Walt Whitman's Reception in Scandinavia," *Papers of the Bibliographical Society of America*, XL (Fourth Quarter 1946), 263–264. See also footnotes 258 and 270 in the *Daybook*, below.

200.  Mr Loomis is Professor Elias J. Loomis (see footnote 171), at this time in the Nautical Almanac Office of the Navy Department in Washington; Mr Seaver is unidentified.

201.  Spieler is Jake Spieler, Philadelphia photographer (see end of footnote 76).

202.  See footnote 199.

203.  E. F. Strickland, Jr's letter of 7 April 1876, asking for an autograph, is in the Feinberg Collection.

204.  This was a frequent occurence; see footnote 71.

Nov 5   Benj: Hosteller Barr – at Mrs G's to tea

"   "   Elmer here – (he returns home to the farm)

"   "   (Herbert walk'd down to White Horse on the
        4th & returned on the 5th   )[205]

[86]

[On a calling card and a slip of paper:]
    Sept. '79 – Lower Shincliffe
        Durham   Eng:

---

    M$^{rs}$ Alexander Gilchrist[206] [printed in script]
1929 North 22
via [in purple pencil]   Columbus Av:

[On scrap of paper, in pencil:]

    Williams's copper plate
        Map of U S, Canada,
        Central Am, West Indies
            pub by
                Brenner & Atwood
                402 Locust st
                    Phil
        Size about
        6 ft x 6

[87]

'77

Nov 6 – Supper at Mrs G's – Miss Selons there – her
        talk about Victor Hugo & his family, doings, con-
        duct &c. at Guernsey – his treatment of his wife,
        daughter, & sister-in-law — (Miss Reichenbach not there)

Nov 9 – Met Wm Taylor, of "Woodstown (N J) Regis-
        ter," on 8th St. Phil.   He invited me to Woodstown[207]

---

205. I cannot identify Benjamin Hosteller Barr, but the others referred to in these lines
are Harry Stafford (Whitman's letter to him is lost), Elmer E. Stafford, and Herbert Gilchrist;
the walk to White Horse was 12 miles.

206. Alexander Gilchrist, the biographer of William Blake, and late husband of Mrs Anne
Gilchrist; she usually, except in formal circumstances, used the name of Mrs Anne Gilchrist.

207. William Taylor, editor of the Woodstown (New Jersey) *Register*; the next year he
must have become editor of the *Constitution,* for Whitman wrote to him about a job for Harry
Stafford: see *The Correspondence of Walt Whitman,* III, 133n. (See above, footnote 76.)

[Clipping:]

– ? go down W J RR to Swedesboro            Swedesboro Stage.
      ? afternoon                                    ———

Nov.  10 – Arthur Henry call'd –                 THE undersigned will run here-
  –he is at Lippincott's —                      after a DAILY STAGE from
  – J Foster Kirke Ed'r L's Mag:[208]      WOODSTOWN to SWEDESBORO. Starts
  – he was with Prescott, & edited         from the Woodstown House at 6:45
  Prescott's works since ——                o'clock  A.M.  Returning,  leaves
  – the "Press" has 15,000 circulation     Swedesboro' on arrival of Phil. af-
                                                   ternoon Train.

Nov. 10 – Harry, up with me – spent              ALL  ERRANDS  in  Philadel-
  the afternoon & went back in the 6        phia, Camden or Swedesboro, will
  train — Geo:  S. quite unwell —           be Promptly Attended to.
  — I wrote him an affectionate             GEO. W. CROTHERS.
  letter[209] by Harry, & sent him a              ———
  little bottle of wh:

Nov. 13 — Horner Stafford [210] visited me — G[eorge] S[tafford] is very
  sick[211]

Nov 13 — to E   D   Bellows   356 Fifth st   Jersey       √x
  City   N   J   sent circ's adv. (he wants John B's Notes)[212]

Nov 14 to 17 — down at White Horse — took provisions
  &c to old Mr and Mrs Morgan —[213]
                      æ
  — Geo: Stafford ill with hæmatemesis – Dr Stout —

                                              [88]

[On three calling cards and a smaller slip:]
  her husband deserted her & she has gone
  back to Russia — her wonderful
  voice & singing (never was I more impress'd)

---

    208.  Whitman went to a dinner party on 26 March 1879, and mentioned the "jolly time"
he had with Kirk (which he spelled Kirke) and others; see *The Correspondence of Walt
Whitman,* III, 150. Kirk (1824–1904) edited *Lippincott's Magazine,* 1870–1886.
    209.  This letter to George Stafford is, unfortunately, lost.
    210.  Harry's cousin; see footnote 169.
    211.  For more details of George Stafford's illness, see *The Correspondence of Walt Whit-
man,* III, 102n.
    212.  See Whitman's letter to Edward D. Bellows, 20 November 1877, *The Correspondence
of Walt Whitman,* III, 102–103; see entry below for 18 November 1877.
    213.  Will and Rachel Morgan, who visited Whitman at White Horse on 15, 16, 17 March
1878; Will Morgan died on 13 June 1878 (see both entries below).

– her Tartar physionomy –
Mme. Sophia G. Logeenova,     [printed in script, five lines]
   (Of St. Petersburg, Russia.)
   2107 Columbia Avenue,
   Philadelphia.

(Over.)

[Also cards of W. Howard Michener, artist, Phila.; Wm. Righter Fisher and
Mary Wager-Fisher;[214] and Wm. Righter Fisher's return address — Attorney
at Law, 33 S. 3rd St., Phila.]

[89]

1877                                   √x

Nov. 18 – Edward D Bellows          sent by express
    356 Fifth Street, bet Monmouth    L of G   [in blue
                  (June 5 '78 sent     T R      pencil,
    & Brunswick Streets    "W W for 1878")  J B's     sideways:]
      Jersey City N J             Notes       rec'd
                                (circ's)

Nov 23 – sent 2ᵈ copy of J B's notes by mail ——
Nov 28 – sent Good Gray Poet

---

Nov. 19 – sent little box to Geo: Staf: letter — flaxseed &c   [after 'box,' in blue
                                          pencil, sideways:]   recd

Nov 19–to–23 – visited in 22ᵈ st every evening

Nov 23 – sent Kit of fish to G[eorge] S[tafford], Kirkwood   [in blue pencil,
                                                  sideways:]  recd

Nov 24 Saturday, & especially Saturday night, <u>severe
   storm,</u> 24ᵗʰ loss of the <u>Huron</u> steam sloop of war
                    100 lives

Nov 26 – sent circ. to John R Aiken   628 East
   9ᵗʰ st N Y City

Nov 26 – Debbie, Jo: B, and Harry – Dr Cullen's
                       funeral [215]

---

214. Mrs Mary E. Wager-Fisher wrote "Poets' Homes: Walt Whitman," *Wide Awake
Pleasure Book,* VI (February 1878), 109–114, on which she drew for another one in *The Long-
Islander,* 5 August 1878.
   215. Debbie and Harry Stafford, with John Burroughs, attended the funeral of Dr
Cullen (?).

Nov 27 – Mrs G   here to dinner

Nov 27 – Sidney H Vines B A[216]          } a set          [in blue pencil,
        Christ's College                  } L  of  G    sideways:]  rec'd  √x
through                                    } &
E  Car       Cambridge  Eng               } T  R
        28th   rec'd postal money order $10 } from E  C  paying

Nov 29 – wrote to Elmer – sent Mr Lucas's letter
              to Horner[217]
        evening at Mrs Odenheimer's

Nov 30 to A   Williams & Co  }  by Adams' Express   [in blue pencil,
              Booksellers    }  sent x 3 copies     sideways:]  recd
        283 Washington St    }  Ed '72 – Leaves        & paid
        Boston    Mass[218]  }  of Grass –
                    $5.25 due

                                                    [90]

[On three slips of paper (all in pencil):]

              July '79
        Wm  H  Nice    in         )        Greeley
                       p o        )           Weld Co:
Will  Tinker   married            )        Colorado
        lives  on  his  farm      )
                                  )
W    S  Fullerton                 )
        works  at  trade          )

        letter from Nice, June 20  '79

                is with florist
              Keeping  bachelor's
                    hall

216.  Whitman wrote Edward Carpenter on 27 November 1877 that he was sending Vines, a lecturer at Christ's College, Cambridge, *Leaves of Grass* and *Two Rivulets*; see *The Correspondence of Walt Whitman*, III, 103.
217.  Whitman apparently sent a letter from John Lucas, a Kirkwood and Philadelphia paint manufacturer, to young Jacob H. (Horner) Stafford in an attempt to get Horner a job; see *The Correspondence of Walt Whitman*, III, 102–103.
218.  See Whitman's letter to A. Williams and Company, owners of the "Old Corner Bookstore," *The Correspondence of Walt Whitman*, III, 103–104.

Louella  Del Co  Pa
Jos  C  Baldwin[219]
Elliottstown
Effingham  County
Ill

[91]

'77/
Dec 1 – John R Aiken[220]  } sent by mail
    628 East Ninth Street  {   the Two Vols
    Station  D         L of  G  &  T  R
    New York City       paid

Dec 2 – Sunday – breakfast at J  M Scovel's –[221]
    – Mrs S – Mrs O – Harry & Annie &c
    — supper in the evening at Col: Johnston's[222]

Dec 4 – sent letter to Debbie S. in answer to hers[223]
    — papers to G  S  —

Dec 5 – sent circ's (in answer to letter) to Mary J
    Perigo, Upper Lake, California

"  "  Letter from Elmer —

"  "  Sent word to W  B  Clarke,[223] Bookseller  340
    Washington st  Boston, that he could have
    3 copies of the 1872 ed'n & 2 copies of the 1867
    edition, for $8 —

Dec 6 – wrote to J  B  Marvin[223] asking him to get the   [in blue pencil,
    wooden & stereotype lines from the Chronicle   sideways:] recd
                            office         them
                                                both

Dec 7 – sent J  H  Ambruster, Phil: Tool Co: office 1716
    Barker St.  circ. (is the gentleman I met on boat)

219.  See footnote 164.
220.  Whitman sent circulars to Aiken on 26 November 1877; see above.
221.  See footnote 71.
222.  See footnote 190.
223.  Neither Whitman's letter to Deborah Stafford, nor hers to him are extant; nor are the poet's to W. B. Clarke and to Joseph B. Marvin, below.

Dec 8 – sent by Adams' Ex to  } 3 copies 1872 Ed. L of G.
    W B Clarke              } 2 "    1867 "      "
        340 Washington st   } 1 J B's Notes
            Boston          } paid

Dec 9 – breakfast at
    J M S[224]

Dec 10 – sent "Blade o' Grass" to Elmer[225]

[92]

[In pencil, on a slip of paper, and two calling cards:]

    Shirt M              George S McWatters
    42 No 4              221 East 18th street
    good                 betw 2d & 3 Avs  [name and address
                                          not in WW's hand]

[Also cards of A. Williams, glove manufacturer of Phila., and William Tait, optician, of Phila.]

[93]

'77

    Dec 11 – sent to
        Claxton, Remsen & Haffelfinger[226]  } 2 L of G      3.50    [in blue
                        626 Market st        } 1 Dem Vist     50     pencil,
                            Phil             } 1 Strong Bird  50     sideways:]
                                             } 1 T Riv    –  3.50    paid
                                                            ─────
                                                             8.00

Dec 10–to–30 – fine spell of weather – out
    every day – evenings at Mrs G's
    — walks at 1 & 2 o'clock along Chestnut
    st — the crowds of promenaders,
    purchasers, visiters from the country &c
                    by
    — the toy-sellers along  the curbstones

224. James Matlack Scovel: see footnote 71.
225. "Blade of Grass" was Whitman's way of referring to a poetical manuscript he had used or was to use in an edition of *Leaves of Grass*; he gave them to close friends, but this one he gave to Elmer Stafford cannot be identified.
226. Claxton, Remsen & Haffelfinger were Philadelphia booksellers; letters from the company to Whitman, 3 October 1877, 5 January 1878 are in the Library of Congress.

—the shows of goods & really rich,
wonderful, ingenious things in the
shop windows[227]

Dec 23 – letter from Mrs Stafford – ans'd —

Dec 24 with Joaquin Miller at "the Danites" [228]
          at Walnut Street Theatre

"   27 – same play with the G's
          Joaquin Miller in Phila:   [in blue pencil]

Dec 24 sent circ (at request of J   M   S)[229] to F   C   Van
     Horn, 155 Worcester st   Boston – Mass

Dec 25 – Christmas – dinner at north   22$^{d}$ st.[230]
     (Herbert's crayon with the hand up)

Dec 22 – "Book of Gold" to Mrs S – picture books
                                        to Mont, Van,
     "     Bible to Elmer[232]        Georgie & Ruth[231]

[94]

[On three slips of paper:]
          James Knowles[233]
          Editor Ninetee[n]th
          Century
          care Henry S King
                    & Co
     _____   _____
          London
          England

227.  Another of Whitman's few instances of commentary on anything in this *Daybook*.
228.  "The Danites" was Joaquin Miller's play, the opening of which Whitman attended, as seen here, with Miller; see also Miller's letter to Whitman in *With Walt Whitman in Camden*, III, 225 (MS. in the Feinberg Collection). Whitman saw the play again on 27 December, at which time he introduced Miller to the Gilchrists, with whom he seems to have spent much time during this month. See *The Correspondence of Walt Whitman*, III, 104–105.
229.  James Matlack Scovel; see footnote 71.
230.  The home of Mrs Anne Gilchrist and her family, 1929 North 22nd Street, Philadelphia.
231.  These are all members of the Stafford family: Montgomery (1862–1926?), Van Doran (1864–1914), and George (1869–1924) were brothers and Ruth (1866–1939) the sister of Harry, who was the favorite of Whitman's and the eldest at 19; at that time Mont was 15, Van 13, Georgie 8, and Ruth 11. The *Book of Gold,* which Whitman gave Mrs Stafford, was a book of poems by John Townsend Trowbridge (New York: Harper & Brothers, 1878).
232.  Elmer was Harry's 16-year-old cousin (1861–1957).
233.  Chronologically, although this slip of paper is on the left-hand page, James Knowles,

[In pencil, eight lines, not in WW's hand:]
Emile Zola
Author of l'Assommoir[234]
& Dramatic Editor of
the Sciecle Paris

[WW's
hand:]————————————————

Jan 16  William Minturn            [WW's hand:]
  '78    of New York City –        a great friend
         60 Fifth Av               of young
                                   J  G  Bennett[235]

————————————————

     John E Coale
     1128 Walnut St. Philad[a]

         [Clipping:]

                 M. Emile Zola, the author of "L'Assomoir," and
              the leader of the French Realistic school, is described
              as a grave, quiet-looking gentleman, still quite young,
              with dark hair, eyes and beard.

                              Tribune April 23   [WW's hand]
                                   '78

                                                        [95]

1878
Jan 2 – Edward T Wilkinson[236] ⎫ sent L  of  G     [in blue pencil,
    13 Micklegate                ⎬ & T  R            sideways:]    √x
from       York   England        ⎭ paid              rec'd
  Edw Carpenter                                      rec'd

editor of the London *Nineteenth Century,* seems out of place, for it was not until August 1885
that this periodical published anything by Whitman: "Fancies at Navesink," *The Nineteenth
Century,* XVIII (August 1885), 234–237, eight short poems; see *Leaves of Grass,* Comprehensive
Reader's Edition, pp. 513–516.
     234. *L'Assommoir* (1877), a study of the effects of drinking on the lives of working class
people, was the novel that brought fame to Zola (1840–1902). Although he had written
*Thérèse Raquin* (1867), Zola was still earning his living as a journalist, listed here as dramatic
editor of *Siècle Paris.*
     235. James Gordon Bennett, Jr (1841–1918), publisher of the New York *Herald* (founded
by his father), who sent Stanley to Africa to find Livingston, financed the transatlantic cable,
started the Paris edition of the *Herald*; Whitman did not appear in the *Herald* until 1887,
when he was made "poet laureate" by the new managing editor, Julius Chambers, with
Bennett's consent, and wrote 32 poems for the paper between 15 December 1887 and 12 August
1888, and two letters (on Cleveland's free trade message, and a tribute to General Sheridan)
on 28 January and 8 August 1888. See *Leaves of Grass,* Comprehensive Reader's Edition, pp.
521–534, 545–546, as well as *Daybook* entries for January–March 1888, below.
     236. See footnote 40.

Jan 3 – Sent circular (on application) to Hen
          Moore, 44 South 5th Street – Ph[237]

Jan 9 – Kind letter from J  B (15)[238]

Jan 7 – letter from Jo Baldwin – he wants me to come out there & live
          with him – Hon John S Dewey owns the farm he works –[239]

Jan 10 sent to Claxton,
          Rennsen & Haffelfinger[240]

    2 half leather L  of
       G @  2.75 &          [in blue pencil,
    1 Two Riv at 2.75          sideways:]
      ~~7.50~~                  paid
  & 3 marble L 8          $12.75
  G at $1.50

Jan 13–14 John Burroughs here)

Jan 16   rec'd Register'd letter from Dr Bucke  $15

Jan 16  Dr A  S  Frazer      sent  L  of  G  &          [in blue pencil,
          Sarnia  Ontario            T  R                        sideways:]
                    Canada           paid                        rec'd

Jan 16 – Dr R  M  Bucke      sent L  of  G          [in blue pencil,
          Asylum for the Insane          paid          sideways:] rec'd
          London  Ontario  Can

[three lines in pencil:]

Jan 16   Mr Minturn of N  Y  call'd
                    talk about Emile Zola of Paris
                    Dante Rossetti, Swinburne & O'Shaughnessy

Jan 15 – Letter from Dr Bucke – invites me strongly to visit
          him & Mrs Bucke at the Asylum – (I must go)[241]

237.  Henry W. Moore, formerly of the Camden Philotechnic Institute, moved to St Louis,
and planned to go to Venezuela, according to a clipping from the Camden *New Republic* of
4 August 1877, which Whitman sent to Harry Stafford, who knew Moore when he was in
Bingham's school and printing office. See *The Correspondence of Walt Whitman*, III, 94.
238.  This is most likely John Burroughs, rather than Joseph Baldwin, who wrote Whitman on 7 January 1878 and would hardly write again so soon.
239.  John S. Dewey: an elected public official, such as governor or senator, not otherwise
identifiable.
240.  See footnote 226.
241.  Whitman did visit Dr and Mrs Richard Maurice Bucke from June to September 1880
in London, Ontario; see *Walt Whitman's Diary in Canada*, appended to this *Daybook*.

[96]

W  J  Press – Jan 16 '78 [242]
Pete Doyle
Mary
Hannah
Jessie
John Swinton
Gen Sewell
Mr Zimmerman
Mont
Mrs Fisher
G  W  Childs
Thos Dixon
Watson Gilder
E  T  Potter, Newport
Cin: Commercial
Wash: Eve Star [244]
Reuben Farwell [247]
    Nankin p o Wayne co Mich
H  Buxton Forman [248]
R  J  Hinton [249]  Eve Post office
    500 Montgomery st
    San Francisco  Cal

Wide Awake Feb [243] '78
Jessie
Mary
Hannah
Warren & Amy Dowe [245]
Ruth & Georgie Stafford
Elmer
Grace & Bertha Johnston [246]

242. *West Jersey Press,* 16 January 1878, contained an unsigned article, "Walt Whitman for 1878." Whitman sent either the newspaper or an off-print (one is in the Feinberg Collection).

243. Mary E. Wager-Fisher, "Poets' Homes: Walt Whitman," *Wide Awake Pleasure Book,* VI (February 1878), 109–114. See footnote 214 above.

244. Of the 15 listed here, several have been identified in footnotes 76 and 81; Mont is Montgomery Stafford (see footnote 231); George W. Childs (1824–1894) was co-owner of the Philadelphia *Public Ledger* (see *The Correspondence of Walt Whitman,* III, 142, 146, 263, 368n); Thomas Dixon was an English admirer (see footnote 13).

245. Amy Haslam Dowe was the niece of Louisa Orr Whitman (George's wife); see her "A Child's Memories of the Whitmans" in Edwin Haviland Miller, "Amy H. Dowe and Walt Whitman," *Walt Whitman Review,* XIII (September 1967), 73–79; Warren was Amy's brother.

246. Grace and Bertha Johnston were members of the family of John H. Johnston, the New York jeweler and staunch Whitman friend.

247. See footnote 174.

248. H. Buxton Forman (1842–1917), British critic and editor of Keats, Shelley, and others, later associated with literary forger Thomas James Wise. Forman made "highly respectful references to Whitman" in *Our Living Poets* (1871), p. 11; Whitman and Forman corresponded for several years (see *With Walt Whitman in Camden,* II, 265–267, 433–434, for Forman's letters of 21 February 1872, 26 January 1876, and 26 September 1888), the Englishman saying he was "a constant reader and great admirer of Whitman's poetry"; he also dedicated his edition of Shelley's *Masque of Anarchy* to Whitman; and the American considered Forman "a man of considerable power without any considerable individuality" (*ibid.,* II, 439; see also V, 87, 408).

249. Colonel Richard J. Hinton (1830–1901), a Londoner who came to America in 1851, was a printer, newspaperman, officer in the Union army, author of several books, and the one who suggested that Thayer & Eldridge publish *Leaves of Grass;* he saw Whitman while wounded in a Washington hospital, wrote pieces about him (Rochester *Evening Express,* 7 March 1866; *The Kansas Magazine,* I [8 December 1872], 499–502; *The New Voice,* XVI [4

W  J  Linton[250]
Edw'd Dowden,[251] with N  Y
    letter of July 4 '78, & "Sun"

[On slip of paper, in pencil:]
begins  N  Y  Sun – Dec. 23
   — at 5 cts a copy

        James F. Baker
   all      114 Federal St
paid up to
   Jan 1 '79    Camden

[97]

1878

Jan 19 – sent Dr R M Bucke, London, On-    [in blue pencil, sideways,
   tario, Canada, photo of large head     across two lines:]
           postage 15[cts]       recd
Herbert commenced large picture, life size,
    in rocking chair ( ?"the old gray poet")
letter from Harry – Jan 20 – wrote to Harry –[252]

Jan 20, 21, Sunday, Monday, rainy, cloudy — in my
    room most of the time

  "  " letter from Elmer –

Jan 22, 23 — Harry up here with me –

Jan 22 – sent papers to Wesley Stafford [253]
       Dixie, Polk Co  Oregon

          ?
  (editress (& owner) "Wide Awake" L  of  G
Jan 24 – Mrs Ch's Stuart  Pratt      also photo [in blue pencil,  √x
  69 Chandler st  Boston Mass[254]   also circ's  sideways:] recd

  "  " to Jessie, Wide Awake[255]

February 1899], 2, among others); see *The Correspondence of Walt Whitman*, II, 30–31n, 157n,
189n, *et passim.*
   250.  See footnote 39.
   251.  See footnote 9.
   252.  Harry Stafford's letters to Whitman are in the Feinberg Collection; Whitman's letters
to his young friend referred to here are lost.

Jan 25 – sent Dr Ridge a set – Two Vols   [in blue pencil, sideways:]  recd

Jan 27 (Sunday)   rode down to Kirkwood, & back

Jan 29 – sent Central News Co   505 Chestnut st
        Phil:   one copy "Leaves of Grass" — 2.80

Jan 31 – snow — heavy storm all day —
        – wrote to Reuben Farwell – sent W J Press ☞ see opp.
                                          page
        – sent to Mont:[256]

[98]

Mrs Chs: Stuart  Pratt   editress Wide Awake
    sent Cor slip
      Dec '78        69 Chandler Street   Boston
    [in pencil]

        [Rest of page has holograph material on three slips:]
        call'd Feb 6 '78
                    Miss Woodward [printed in script]
            1702 Ross St [not WW's hand]

                        [Nine lines in pencil, all in WW's hand:]
                        driver on Union line   No 103
                            Taylor Wilgus  M
                        father 75 – grandmother over 90
                                (mother died) – age 30
                            two children – one girl of 6
                        (drove 103   3 yr's) one baby
                                Taylor Wilgus

253.  Wesley Stafford was another of Harry's cousins; he was married to Lizzie Hider on 9 February 1881 (see *The Correspondence of Walt Whitman*, III, 194, 210, 262).
254.  Whitman's letter to Mrs Charles Stuart Pratt, editor of *Wide Awake Pleasure Book*, dated 27 December 1878, is lost.
255.  Whitman must have sent his niece, Jessie, Jeff's daughter, a copy of *Wide Awake Pleasure Book*, containing Mrs Wager-Fisher's article (see footnote 214 above).
256.  For Reuben Farwell, see footnote 174; for Mont, see footnote 231.

Feb 12 '78 – Coming over the Market st
ferry
Harry Gile and Jesse Wilson[257]
Called Feb 6 '78  [in WW's hand]
R. B. Anderson[258] [not WW's hand]
Madison Wis. [not WW's hand]

[99]

'78

Feb 1 – Sent W J Press of Jan 16, & circ's: to
H Buxton Forman, 38 Marlborough Hill
St John's Wood, London   N W. Eng[259]

"   " sent postal card asking address to John M Rogers,[260]
New Britain, Conn

Jan 31 & Feb 1 '78 — Severe snow storm, wind &
rain — heaviest fall of snow, this winter —
– wreck of the Metropolis,   (bound from Phila
to Para, Brazil, a 900 ton vessel with RR
iron & 250 laborers) on Currituck shoals,
N. C.   6.50 p m Feb 1 '78 – over 100 lost[261]

x

Feb 2 – paid Lou $20 (pays up to Jan 1 '78) [262]

"   " sent circ: to W  L  Tiffany[263]  325  South  Ninth
street  Minneapolis  Minn:

Feb 3 – Sunday – fine bright day —

"      papers to Hattie – Geo. Stafford

257.  Taylor Wilgus, Harry Gile, and Jesse Wilson cannot be otherwise identified.
258.  Professor R. B. Anderson, of the University of Wisconsin, wrote to Whitman on 17 September 1877, asking for an appointment (letter in the Feinberg Collection); see entry below for 6 February 1878.
259.  See footnote 248.
260.  John M. Rogers was a Brooklyn driver, who apparently moved to Connecticut and then to Arredondo, Florida; 11 letters from him to Whitman, from 9 February 1871 to 21 February 1878 are in the Feinberg Collection; 10 letters from Whitman to Rogers, about 8 February 1870 to 14 March 1878, are lost.
261.  Whitman apparently did not, on this occasion, as he did in June 1889 after the Johnstown flood, write a poem about the tragic loss of life; see entry below after 31 May 1889.
262.  This was the payment to Louisa Orr Whitman for the poet's board.
263.  W. L. Tiffany's letter to Whitman, 29 January 1878, is in the Feinberg Collection.

Feb 4 – Monday – bright day – papers to Wesley Stafford [264]
   – over at Phila: called at Col. Johnston's — [265]
   – (items in the papers quite generally
   ab't my going on a lecturing tour to
   California) — [266]

Feb 5 – sent papers to Geo: Stafford, Will Tinker & Jo: Baldwin[267]

"   6   letter to Mr & Mrs Stafford – papers also[268]

"   "   Prof. R B Anderson[269] of Wisconsin University, Madison, call'd, (with Miss   √x
   Woodward) – told me of his visit to Bjornsen
   the     poet, & of B's mention of me — [270]

"   photo to Wesley Stafford, Dixie, Polk Co   Oregon

                    [100]

[Opposite card of Siam O'Coupcio, Professor of Physiognomy, Physiology and
Phrenology[271] (examinations, $1.00, charts, $2.50):]
Phrenologist
the "Professor"
– at Studio
'78 & Jan '79
 his chum
 Edw'd Conners
 "Humpty Dumpty"

[Opposite card of Hillman Rowand & Son, manufacturers of pulverized charcoal for rectifying and chemical purposes, Kirkwood, Camden Co., N. J.:]

---

 264. Hattie was Jeff's daughter Mannahatta, Walt Whitman's niece; George Stafford was
the head of the household at Timber Creek; and Wesley Stafford was Harry's cousin (see
footnote 253).
 265. Colonel John R. Johnston, the Camden artist who maintained a studio in Philadelphia.
 266. Whitman certainly did not make a lecture tour to California at that time; he did
make a trip to Colorado, followed by a three-months' stay in St Louis in the fall of 1879, and
he did read poems at public gatherings, hardly a "lecturing tour."
 267. George Stafford (see above), Will Tinker (see list of those sent the Philadelphia
Sunday *Times* of 26 January 1879), and Joe Baldwin (see footnote 164) often were sent items
by the poet.
 268. This letter to George and Susan Stafford is lost.
 269. See footnote 258.
 270. Bjørnstjerne Bjørnson (1832–1910), Norwegian dramatist, who is known for his
plays dealing with Norway.
 271. See Thomas L. Brasher, "Whitman's Conversion to Phrenology," *Walt Whitman
Newsletter,* IV (June 1958), 95–97.

Met on Ferry
   on charcoal wagon
   Feb '79
   ———————
his brother Walter
   "Schooner"
   ———————
sent him "Winter
         Sunshine" [272]


[Opposite card of W. P. Mockett, 353 Birch St.:]
Met at Col J's
      Feb. '79
   ?

teacher of languages
lived several years in Spain


[Opposite card of Henry Whitall,[273] 502 S. Second St., Camden: "A miniture
(*sic.*) copy of the Movable Planisphere of the whole Heavens at every min-
ute. . . .":]
                  Old man met on
                  Ferry – night –
                  Feb '79


                                                            [101]

'78

Sunday – Feb 10 – sent papers to Hattie, Mont
          & Elmer, – to W  S  Fullerton, Greeley[274]


   "      sent W  J  Press & Circ's to R  J  Hinton,[275] office Evening
          Post, 500 Montgomery st.  San Francisco  Cal


   "      wrote to Ed Cattell [276] –(send carte visite photo)

272. "Winter Sunshine. A Trip from Camden to the Coast," by Walt Whitman, Philadelphia *Times,* 26 January 1879; reprinted in *Specimen Days* in nine different places, with 35
of the 60 short paragraphs in the Appendix (see *Prose Works 1892,* I, 330). See footnote 80
above. The entire piece, as it appeared in the Philadelphia *Times,* is in Herbert Bergman, "Walt
Whitman on New Jersey: An Uncollected Essay," *Proceedings of the New Jersey Historical
Society,* LXVI (October 1948), 139–154.
273. Hillman Rowand, Walter Rowand, W. P. Mockett, and Henry Whitall cannot be
identified other than by the information given here.
274. Hattie, Mont & Elmer are Mannahatta Whitman, Montgomery Stafford, and Elmer
Stafford, of course; I cannot identify W. S. Fullerton (of Greeley, Colorado?). Papers that
Whitman sent could be his Philadelphia *Times,* or something else by or about him.
275.  See footnote 249.
276.  Edward Cattell was a Stafford farm hand, mentioned above.

Feb 11 – Mr Williams call'd – took his book – is
      going to Para, Brazil.[277]

Feb 11 – Monday – Harry here – put r on his hand again
     — had picture taken at Morand's cor Arch &
  9th  Phil: for Michener, cor Arch & 10th

Feb 12 – call'd on Mr Zimmerman (not in) [278]

"   letter from G  W  Foote, 12 Gower st
     London  W  C – (says he will write soon &
       send the £3 — ) <u>fraud</u> [279]     [last word in pencil]

"  13 – talk at Mrs G's at supper ab't the Eng: in the
     Russian & Turkish war

"  14 – George and Lou at Mrs G's to dinner[280]

16th to 23[d] inclusive – down at White Horse

24 Sunday breakfast at J  M  S [281]

      Sunday
24th ∧ wrote to John Burroughs (promising N Y lecture) [282]
   "   D  M  Zimmerman
   "   Gen  Sewell
   "   Mrs F R Ritter  63 S Hamilton St Poughkeepsie
   "   Hattie (& papers) [283]

277. Mr Williams could be Francis Howard Williams (1844–1922), poet and dramatist, at whose home in Philadelphia Whitman stayed (see *The Correspondence of Walt Whitman,* III, 360n); it was not likely Talcott Williams (1849–1928), a journalist on the New York *Sun* and *World,* who was on the Springfield *Republican* in 1879 and did not join the Philadelphia *Press* until 1881 (see *ibid.,* III, 296–297n); another unlikely one is Williams of A. Williams & Co., whom Whitman sold three copies of *Leaves of Grass* on 30 November 1877 (see *ibid.,* III, 103–104).

278. D. M. Zimmerman, secretary and treasurer of the Camden & Atlantic Railroad (see footnote 76).

279. See footnote 162.

280. There do not seem to be many occasions when George and Louisa Whitman joined Walt at Mrs Gilchrist's home in Philadelphia.

281. This is a frequent occurrence for Whitman: a week's visit at the Stafford farm at Timber Creek, and a Sunday breakfast with James Matlack Scovel.

282. Whitman did not make his Lincoln lecture in New York in the Spring of 1878, as he was too weak, but he did make it for the first time on 14 April 1879. This letter is in *The Correspondence of Walt Whitman,* III, 108.

283. These four letters, to D. M. Zimmerman (see footnote 278), General William J. Sewell, Mrs Fanny Raymond Ritter (see footnote 139), and Mannahatta Whitman are all now lost.

25ᵗʰ rec'd <u>Eve</u> <u>Post</u>, with piece ab't Aunt Sarah Mead [284] &
Washington — wrote to Priscilla,[285] 92 Bank Street

"    rec'd letter from J  H  Johnston, 150 Bowery[286]

[102]

[On slip of paper:]   Helen E. Price[287] [not in WW's hand]
        Red B~~ank~~, Mon~~mouth~~ Co N.~~J~~. [not in WW's hand]
            Woodside, Queens Co. L  I
                New York

[On a slip of paper, not in WW's hand:]

        My address 445 Lafayette av   and friend
                Brooklyn            Jeannette Wheeler

[On another slip:]    Kate Hillard [288]

        KH    [logo]  186 Remsen St. [not in WW's hand]
                Brooklyn [not in WW's hand]
                Feb. 14th [not in WW's hand]
        1734.I. st Wash

[Another slip:]

    Alexander Boroday[289] [not in WW's hand]    Russian gent, –
                                    on Chestnut st. Feb. '79

[Opposite card of Max Cohen, book and job printer, 613 Seventh St. N.W.,
Washington:]

accosted me

284.   In a letter to Louisa Whitman of 13–14 April (?) 1878, Whitman wrote that he had heard of the death, at the age of 97, of his grand-aunt Sarah Mead; so this New York *Evening Post* article about her seeing Washington must have been before she died (see *The Correspondence of Walt Whitman*, III, 114).

285.   Priscilla Townsend, a cousin of Whitman's mother and a member of Mrs Mead's family (Sarah Mead's grand-daughter) wrote to Whitman on 11 April 1878 about Mrs Sarah Mead's death; a fragment of the letter is in the Feinberg Collection; Priscilla Townsend's last name and this address are given under the entry for 12 July 1880, below.

286.   This letter from the poet's New York jeweler friend is not extant.

287.   Helen E. Price and her mother Mrs Abby H. Price (1814–1878), who was active in social-reform movements, and father Edmund, who operated a pickle factory in Brooklyn, were friends of the poet's mother; the Prices, especially Mrs Price and the children, were intimates of Walt Whitman, who lived with them in the 1860s and frequently corresponded with them (see *The Correspondence of Walt Whitman*, I, II, III, *passim*).

288.   See footnote 10. Whitman apparently visited Miss Hillard on 29 February 1876, when he first met her; he knew her writings in 1871, and she was a friend of the Prices. See *The Correspondence of Walt Whitman*, III, 25, 26, 114 (about Whitman and Miss Hillard visiting Dr S. Weir Mitchell in Philadelphia on 13 April 1878), *et passim*, where she is mentioned in letters by Whitman, but his letter to her of 8 April 1878 is lost.

289.   In a letter to Herbert Gilchrist of 6 February 1879, Whitman says, "I met Mr Borody the Russian in Chestnut st" (*The Correspondence of Walt Whitman*, III, 147).

on Chestnut St.
Jan '79
(came on to the
Jews Convention) [289a]

[103]

'78

Feb 25 – Monday – Read to-day (over in Chestnut st)
 at Central News Store)   the article in Feb: <u>Nineteen</u>
           article by Fleming Jenkin
<u>Century</u> on Mrs Siddons's Lady Macbeth, with notes
  by Mr Bell ∧ — gives my views of acting & reading,
with ᵃpower, proof, & definiteness I had not antici-
pated, or dream'd of. <u>Is it not really the first</u>
<u>clear outline I have ever seen of the theory</u>
<u>of</u> <u>real</u> <u>acting,</u> <u>or</u> <u>reading</u>? [290]

Feb 26 sent papers to Will Tinker, Greeley, Col [291]
 "   "   Jo Baldwin
 "   "   Geo Stafford
 "   "  Kenilworth to Mrs Stafford

 "  sent Letter to Geo: & Mrs Staf: – also to Pete Doyle –

Feb 27 – wrote John Burroughs about lecture (to Scribner & Co) [292]
          N Y

March 2ᵈ, 3ᵈ, & 4ᵗʰ – down at White Horse

March 5th – sent, Scribner, Armstrong & Co    [in blue pencil,
  743 Broadway N Y   two cop's <u>Two</u>   sideways:] recd
  <u>Rivulets</u> – $7           & paid

289a.   Although Max Cohen of Washington (where Whitman may have known him in the early 70s) is not mentioned, the New York *Times* of 27 January 1879 (p. 1) reported the Third General Convention of the Independent Order of the B'nai B'rith opened in Philadelphia on Sunday, 26 January. This is most likely the convention that Cohen was attending when he ran into Whitman on Chestnut Street in Philadelphia. (For this information and other help I am grateful to George A. Masterton, reference librarian at Wayne State University.)

 290.   Fleeming Jenkin, "Mrs. Siddons as Lady Macbeth (from Contemporary Notes by George Joseph Bell)," *The Nineteenth Century*, III (February 1878), 296–313.

 291.   Will Tinker, to whom Whitman sent other items, such as the Philadelphia Sunday *Times* of 26 January 1879, containing his "Winter Sunshine: A Trip from Camden to the Coast," I cannot otherwise identify; of the others below, Joseph C. Baldwin (see footnote 164) lived in Elliottstown, Effingham County, Illinois; George and Mrs Stafford were his friends of Timber Creek; and Peter Doyle was one of his closest associates, the Washington ex-Confederate and horsecar conductor.

 292.   This letter to Burroughs is lost, but Whitman's letter of 5 March 1878 (in the T. E. Hanley Collection, University of Texas) is in *The Correspondence of Walt Whitman*, III, 109.

"    "  papers to Hattie ⎰ Wesley Stafford [293]
                           ⎱ Dixie Rickreal p o
                           ⎰ Polk Co  Oregon

"    "  to Sister Hannah

"    "  John Burroughs to Scribner's care – also postal
                                  card to Esopus

"  ⎛(to W  H  Stennett)⎞[294] RR agent, Chicago  letter of
   ⎜Gen'l Pass'r Agent ⎟thanks & "  Memoranda (rec'd
   ⎝Ch: & N W RR Co   ⎠                       answer)
          letter from Ed: Cattell –[295]


March 9th & 10 – Saturday & Sunday – down at
     White Horse – two fine summery days —
       Horner, Ben Pease, Will Brown –[296]
     (Wm Stillé, young man at  Coley's, cor 3ᵈ & Fed'l)[297]


                                                        [104]
Wᵐ Stillé, young man formerly at Coley's grocery 3ᵈ & Federal


     John M  Rogers[298]
       Arredondo     Florida


[On slip of paper:]

               Damon Y. Kilgore[299]  [not in WW's hand]
                 517 Preston St   [not in WW's hand]
                between 40 & 41ˢᵗ Sts
                  a few doors above
                 Lancaster  Ave —
               Baring St. Car on Market


293.  Harry Stafford's cousin; see footnote 253.
294.  Whitman's letter to W. H. Stennett, the railroad agent, is lost.
295.  The Stafford farm hand, a frequent Whitman correspondent; but this letter is not extant.
296.  Horner was Harry Stafford's cousin (see footnote 169); Ben Pease also visited Whitman at White Horse on 18 March 1878 (see below); Whitman's letter to him of 20 March 1878 is lost; Will Brown obviously was a friend of Horner Stafford and Ben Pease.
297.  Writing down William Stillé's name here and on the next page — and then neither seeing the young man again, nor writing to him, nor apparently hearing from him — is somewhat similar to other name-writing compulsions in the *Daybook*; one may speculate on why Whitman did this.
298.  See footnote 260.
299.  See footnote 91.

Lancaster Ave. Car on Walnut
          or Vine St. Car      [all lines not in WW's hand]
[In left margin, in blue pencil, sideways:]     April '80
[In right margin, sideways:]       took
                    Thanksgiving dinner
                    there Nov 26 '80

[On another slip:]

    <u>Columbia Av.</u>
    110 – Charles Saunders[300]
    120 – Harry Cooper
       boards – father dead
    128 –
    131  Edw'd Jeffries
    Hudson Greenleaf [in blue pencil]

[On small yellow slip:]
                    Rob't McKelvey,
                         Market st. driver
                    young, blackeyed, affectionate

_____

          John Flinn – driver – Market st
          widower, one boy, 4 yr's old

                                             [105]

'78
March 11 – sent papers to Jessie.[301]

   "   "   " novel &c to Lizzie Stafford[302]

   "   " wrote to John Burroughs at Esopus[303]

   12 – papers to Jo: Baldwin — Geo Stafford[304]
   /owner Geo: bo't his farm of Mrs Smythe \
            25 acres 4400 )

---

300. The names of Charles Saunders and those below of Harry Cooper, Edward Jeffries, Hudson Greenleaf, Robert McKelvey, and John Flinn may well be in the category of William Stillé (see footnote 297 above).
301. Jessie Whitman (1863–1957) was the last surviving member of the immediate Whitman family: she was Jeff's daughter and just short of her 15th birthday at this time.
302. Lizzie Stafford was the wife-to-be of Wesley, Harry's cousin; see footnote 253.
303. This letter is printed in *The Correspondence of Walt Whitman,* III, 110–111.
304. George Stafford, Harry's father and head of the family, either bought a new farm (see next entry) or added to his at Kirkwood (or Timber Creek, or White Horse).

\Bill Edwards[305] — man who is to work it /

"    14 wrote to John M Rogers, Arredondo  Fla[306]
& sent papers

"  papers to Hattie — postal to Dr Bucke[307]

"    15, 16th, & 17th down at White Horse – the severe
rheumatism in right shoulder – Ben Pease
Will Fox, Will & Rachel Morgan – Lizzie Hider[308]

18 – Papers to Hattie[309]
"  rec't to Scribner & Co:  N  Y.
"  letter to Herbert G [310]

"    19 wrote to Susan & Geo Stafford [311]

"    "  papers to Wesley Stafford

"    17th 18th, 19th         rheumatism (& neuralgia?) in
right shoulder, arm, & wrist – bad, restless nights

"    19th    good letter from John Newton Johnson[312]

& sent
"    wrote card∧papers to    "          "

"    19th – sent Whitney & Adams, "old corner book-    [in blue pencil,
store" Springfield, Mass, 1 L  of  G, $2    sideways:] recd

"  postal card to Mrs Gilchrist

---

305.  In a letter to Susan Stafford, George's wife, on 6 August 1883, Whitman refers to a
Mr Edwards, one of Mrs Stafford's boarders; this may be Bill Edwards, "the man who is to
work it [the farm]." See *The Correspondence of Walt Whitman*, III, 346.
306.  See footnote 260.
307.  This post card is lost.
308.  Ben Pease, Will Fox, Will and Rachel Morgan, and Lizzie Hider (who was to marry
Wesley Stafford on 9 February 1881) were the "lots of Company" Whitman referred to in his
letter to Herbert Gilchrist on 18 March 1878; see *The Correspondence of Walt Whitman*, III,
112.
309.  It is impossible to identify the "papers" Whitman sent to Mannahatta Whitman, his
niece, on 14 and 18 March 1878.
310.  This letter (in the University of Pennsylvania Library) is in *The Correspondence of
Walt Whitman*, III, 111–112.
311.  This letter is lost.
312.  See footnote 9a. John Newton Johnson's letters are in the Feinberg Collection, but
Whitman's letters to him are lost.

20<sup>th</sup> wrote to Ben Pease

"    "  Mrs Johnston[313]

[106]

[In pencil, on a slip of notebook paper and two calling cards:]

Amos G Cooper

Oxford

Chester Co.

Penn.

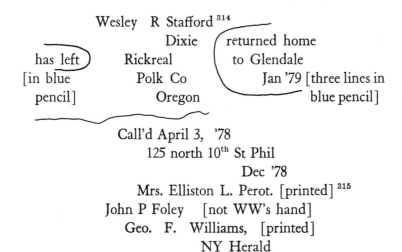

Wesley  R Stafford [314]

Dixie

has left  Rickreal

[in blue  Polk Co

pencil]  Oregon

returned home

to Glendale

Jan '79 [three lines in

blue pencil]

Call'd April 3, '78

125 north 10<sup>th</sup> St Phil

Dec '78

Mrs. Elliston L. Perot. [printed] [315]

John P Foley  [not WW's hand]

Geo.  F.  Williams,  [printed]

NY Herald

[107]

'78 – March

17<sup>th</sup> 18, 19<sup>th</sup>, & 20<sup>th</sup> – bad days – rheumatism

— bad <u>nights</u> — (the spell morning of 20<sup>th</sup>)

"  to 25<sup>th</sup> inclusive  much suffering

from rheumatism & prostration[316]

---

313.  The three letters, to Mrs Anne Gilchrist on 19 March, Ben Pease on 20 March, and Mrs [Alma?] Johnston on 20 March 1878, are all lost.

314.  See footnote 253; Glendale is the area of the Stafford Farm, also referred to as Kirkwood, White Horse, and Timber Creek.

315.  Mrs Elliston L. Perot, who called on Whitman on 3 April 1878, went with Katharine Hillard and the poet to dinner at Mrs Perot's home in Philadelphia, and Whitman wrote "Mrs P brought me home in the coupé" (*The Correspondence of Walt Whitman*, III, 114).

316.  In a letter to Herbert Gilchrist, on 23 March 1878, Whitman painted a less gloomy picture of his health: "Last night the best night for a week & I count on getting better now — only weakness very pronounced & general, & a little sickish — rheumatic pains in shoulder & wrist still present, but much modified" (*The Correspondence of Walt Whitman*, III, 112–113).

"    23$^d$ Harry here the evening

24 Herbert's visits evening $\left(\begin{array}{c}\text{I don't go out}\\\text{too weak}\end{array}\right)$

"    25$^{th}$    papers to Jessie
   "  "  Scotty Fullerton

26$^{th}$    Mrs Stafford   here to dinner

"    27$^{th}$ Mrs G   here to supper

28   sent circ: to Mrs A  S  French   152 A
   st   north east   Washington   D   C

30$^{th}$    sent circ: to Micah Howell   80 West 8$^{th}$ st
     Oswego   New York

"   Harry up here with me[317]

April 1 – sent Mrs A  S  French   152 A street  [in blue pencil, √x
   north east – Washington, D C, a set  sideways:]   recd
   two Vols – pay rec'd

"    John Burroughs here – Herbert G [318]

April 2$^d$ sent papers to Jessie
   "  "  Geo Stafford
   "  "  Jo: Baldwin[319]

3$^d$ – sent <u>Two Riv</u>:  also circ:  also postal card – to [in blue pencil,
   Thomas Dixon,[320] 15 Sunderland st.  sideways:]   recd
   Sunderland, Eng:

---

317.  During this week, between visits from Harry Stafford, Whitman seems to have entertained Mrs Susan Stafford on one night and Mrs Gilchrist on the next; Scotty Fullerton, referred to on 26 March, apparently is the W. S. Fullerton of footnote 274.

318.  Whitman had written John Burroughs two days before, on 29 March 1878, still hoping to give his Lincoln lecture in May (it had to be postponed) and about the Gilchrists leaving Philadelphia.

319.  These "papers" to Whitman's niece Jessie (in St Louis, Missouri), his Timber Creek friends the Staffords (including Harry's cousin Wesley on 3 April below), and to Joseph Baldwin seem too frequent to be the poet's writings alone.

320.  The post card to Thomas Dixon (see footnote 13) is lost.

3    sent papers to Wesley Stafford

5th    letter from Mrs Stafford [321]

7th    (Sunday)   Herbert and Bee[322] down at White
        Horse — both call'd here, evening, on return
        Debbie is to be married in 5 weeks ( I suppose
                                            June 13) [323]

                                                                    [108]

Frederick George (age abt 18) carrier Post
Albert Peterson    (   "    6 or 7) 4th st. n Bridge[324]
                                                        av

[In pencil on slip of lined notebook paper:]

        fine scenery
            High Falls Hotel
                Dingman's Ferry
            Pike Co: Penn:
                go to Port Jervis:
                (J   M Scovel's place) [325]

[On two calling cards:]

                Care Marshal Oliver Esq.   [not WW's hand]
                        Annapolis     [not WW's hand]
                    Miss Hillard. [printed]
                            186 Remsen St. [printed]

    x        Dr S. Weir Mitchell.[326] [printed]
        9 to 12 [scribble not in WW's hand]
                            1524 Walnut Street. [printed]


321.    Mrs Stafford's letter is in the Feinberg Collection.
322.    Mrs Gilchrist's son and daughter were soon to leave Philadelphia with their mother
after 18 months; see *The Correspondence of Walt Whitman*, III, 113.
323.    Deborah Stafford married Joseph Browning on 13 June 1878; see *The Correspondence
of Walt Whitman*, III, 126, and the entry for that date below.
324.    Another example of Whitman's jotting down the name, age, and address of young
boys, yet one may ask: why that of a 6-year-old?
325.    These are apparently directions of Whitman's to himself on how to get to James
Matlack Scovel's for his usual Sunday breakfast.
326.    Kate Hillard (see footnote 10 and at many places in this *Daybook*) went with Whitman to see the physician and novelist Dr S. Weir Mitchell on 13 April 1878 (see *The Correspondence of Walt Whitman*, III, 114).

[109]

'78

April 8 (Monday) Note to Kate Hillard, 710 Washington Sq
                                                    Phil

"    " postal to Pete Doyle

"    " papers to John M Rogers – Will Nice –
                Hattie – Geo. Stafford,
            Amos Cooper

"    " letter to Geo: & Susan Stafford

"    " postal to John Burroughs[327]


9th    papers to Tom Freeman[328] – John Burroughs

9th (evening) Mr Belisle call'd this evening.  Said
        that G  W  Childs desired him to call & say to me
        he would assist me in bringing out a new
        edition of my poems, leaving out the objec-
        tionable passages — said it could be arranged
        on that condition —    I told him to thank
        Mr C from me very deeply for his kindness
        & liberality — (decided at once to decline on any such
                        condition)[329]

9th    Herbert bro't over the Crayon — [330]


10th (Wednesday) rainy day – visit from Debbie & Jo[331]
        Lou away at Norwich, Conn:


11th    to Lou: letter & papers[332]


13 (Saturday)   Miss Hillard came in the coupé
            & took me over to Phila:  pleasant drive —


    327.  All four of these letters of 8 April 1878, to Katharine Hillard, Peter Doyle, George
and Susan Stafford, and John Burroughs, are lost; nor do we know what papers he sent to
John M. Rogers, Mannahatta Whitman, and George Stafford; nor do we even know who Will
Nice and Amos Cooper are.
    328.  See footnote 165.
    329.  See footnote 11 and *The Correspondence of Walt Whitman*, III, 146n.
    330.  This black-and-white portrait of Whitman, drawn by Herbert Gilchrist, is referred to
in two letters from the poet to the artist, 8 and 23 March 1878; see *The Correspondence of Walt
Whitman*, III, 110, 112–113.
    331.  Deborah Stafford and Joseph Browning, who were to be married on 13 June 1878;
see footnote 323.
    332.  Louisa Orr Whitman, George's wife, with whom Whitman was living in Camden
at the time, was visiting the Dowe family, her relatives, in Norwich, Connecticut (see line

went to see Dr. S Weir Mitchell   1524
Walnut   st – gave him some memoranda of
my case – am to go again — Visit to Mrs
Perot   710 Washington square, & lunch
there — Mrs P. bro't me home in the coupé – [333]

13 — Harry here – [334]

[110]

[On a card:]
call'd April 16, '78
spoke of Joaquin Miller in London
invited me to his house in Still
River, Worcester Co.   Mass
    Wᵐ M. F. Round.[335]
a journalist and an
old friend of Joaquin Miller   [these two lines not in WW's hand]
                        [three lines and hand in blue pencil:]
                            Interview
                            with
                            Dr Mitchell [336]
                            ☞

22ᵈ April '78 – Saw Mr. Lippincott[337] – his description
    of Tennyson

[111]

'78
April   postal
13 — ~~letter~~ to John Burroughs

    "        John  Newton  Johnson

    "        Sister  Hannah

above); this letter is lost.

333.  This same information, in almost the same words, is in Whitman's letter to Louisa Whitman, 13–14 April 1878 (*The Correspondence of Walt Whitman,* III, 114); see footnotes 315 and 326.

334.  Another visit to Stevens Street, Camden, by Whitman's young friend, Harry Stafford.

335.  For Joaquin Miller, see footnote 24; William M. F. Round unidentified, except, as Whitman says, he was a journalist and friend of Miller's.

336.  See *The Correspondence of Walt Whitman,* III, 114.

337.  This undoubtedly is J. B. Lippincott the publisher; *Lippincott's Magazine* published a few Whitman poems and prose pieces, but not until several years later, 1887–1891. Whitman's letter to Lippincott, 25 July 1880, is lost.

14 (Sunday) letter to Lou[338]

15 paper to Jo Baldwin
    papers to Lou — also to Hugh Harrop
    letter to Geo & Susan Stafford – papers do:

16 Wm M F Round, call'd —[339]

18th interview (2d) with Dr S Weir Mitchell
    at 1524 Che Walnut st. Phila:  He said my
    trouble (paralysis ℞ commencing Jan 23, '73) was
    undoubtedly from a small rupture of a blood-
    vessel in          of the brain, & its effusion
    ?on the nerves that control the left side —
        that the weight of that seems to have pass'd over —
examined eyes by opthalmascope
∧ — examined my heart by aus[cultation] – pronounced its state
                    pronounced
normal & healthy — the ∧ — bad spells he tho't
recurrences by habit ( ? sort of automatic) —
— gave some medicine – prescriptions –
– prognosis hopeful & cheery —
– spoke of Camden as malarial – advised
        me to get into mountain air this summer[340]

20th Lou return'd from Conn:

20th & 21st – Sat & Sunday   down at White Horse

22d Two Vols – L  of  G & T  R  to –                           recd
        J  B  Lippincott's Phil:[341]     [in blue pencil, sideways:]   paid
    recd Letter from Hannah – wrote to H [342]                        $7

                                                                    [112]

Jeff – Office Water Commissioners
    City Hall – St Louis

338. Of these four letters, only the last one, to Louisa Orr Whitman, is extant; see *The Correspondence of Walt Whitman,* III, 114–115. The letter to the Staffords of 15 April 1878, below, is also lost. I cannot identify Hugh Harrop, below.
    339. See footnote 335.
    340. Such details in the *Daybook* are infrequent: they usually are concerned with Whitman's health or the weather; see footnotes 326 and 336.
    341. See footnote 337.
    342. Both the letters to Hannah Heyde, Whitman's sister, and from her are lost.

[Clipping:]

Mr. Wyatt Eaton has completed a remark-
able crayon head of Mr. Bryant, which will be engraved
by Cole for an early number of *Scribner's Monthly*.[343]

[On slip of paper:]

E.ᵈ Schaeffer   [not WW's hand (in pencil)]

——|——

John Smith[344]   [not WW's hand (in pencil)]

[Three lines in pencil:]

Phil: Sept 7, '78
Adams' Ex: wagon
     Market St:

Round Hill Hotel
     Northampton  Mass[345]

[113]

'78
April 22 – Granular Salts – (Keasbey, Mattison &
                              Rutter, Phil:)

"       letter to Geo: & Susan Stafford [346]

"    "  Pete Doyle

"    "  Jeff at St Louis

"    ~~paper to~~ to S Wesley Stafford
evening of 22ᵈ at Mrs G's, 22ᵈ st

"       23ᵈ – ditto[347] – met young Mr Brainerd [348]

343. Wyatt Eaton (1849–1896) and Walt Whitman met at a reception given by Richard W. Gilder on 14 June 1878; see *The Correspondence of Walt Whitman,* III, 118, 144, 157. Timothy Cole, who made the wood engraving of William Cullen Bryant, was employed by *Scribner's Magazine.*

344. Ed Schaeffer and John Smith may be drivers for Adams' Express.

345. This is Anne Gilchrist's address after she left Philadelphia late in April 1878; Whitman visited her and her daughter Beatrice in Philadelphia for the last time on 23 April 1878 (see entry for that date). The poet's first extant letter to Mrs Gilchrist in Northampton is dated 10 May 1878 (*The Correspondence of Walt Whitman,* III, 117); Herbert Gilchrist, the son, whom Whitman saw many times later, went to Brooklyn.

346. This letter is lost, as are those below to Peter Doyle and Jeff Whitman.

347. This was Whitman's last meeting with the Gilchrist family.

348. Mr Brainerd on this line and Erastus Brainerd two lines below are surely the same

24th paid  80[cts] for N Y Sun, up to date –

"   Erastus Brainerd called with Mr Richardson
              bo't a set of books

x       paid L $20

25th, 26th & 27th Down at White Horse

28th (Sunday)   papers to Hattie
              "    Hugh Harrop
              "    John Rogers
              "    Amos Cooper
              "    Geo: Stafford
29[t]h – papers to Ed Cattell
              Geo Stafford [349]
          letter to Geo & Susan S [350]

sent cir: &c to Henry Festing Jones   1 Craven Hill Gardens
          W.  London   Eng:/June 2 – rec'd letter that the
                        \books hadn't come – sent card
                              that I hadn't sent copies[351]

30  letter to Priscilla Townsend [352]

"   rec'd list of N Y names from Watson Gilder[353]

May 1  Letter from Jeff –

1st & 2[d]  Down at White Horse   May 1st & 2[d]

person; on 9 December 1879 Whitman wrote to Erastus Brainerd (letter now lost) and sent a poem, "What Best I See in Thee," published in the Philadelphia *Press,* 17 December 1879 (the poem deals with General U. S. Grant's return from his world tour), included in the 1881 *Leaves*; see Comprehensive Reader's Edition, p. 485, and *Prose Works 1892*, I, 226–227. Brainerd most likely was on the Philadelphia *Press* staff.

349. Hattie (Mannahatta Whitman) and George Stafford often received various papers from Whitman; Hugh Harrop, who was sent papers for the first time on 15 April (see entry above), and Amos Cooper, sent papers also on 8 April and 20 May, I cannot identify; John Rogers (see footnote 260) was a Brooklyn driver who moved to Florida.

350. Letter now lost.

351. Henry Festing Jones (1851–1928), editor and biographer of Samuel Butler, was sent a letter on this same date but apparently not the books, sent 12 July 1878, as noted below (they are now in the Feinberg Collection); see *The Correspondence of Walt Whitman*, III, 116, 119–120.

352. Priscilla Townsend's letters from Whitman, 25 February 1878, and 13 July 1880, as well as this one, are lost; she lived with her husband James Townsend at 92 Bank Street, New York. See footnote 285.

353. For [Richard] Watson Gilder, see footnote 81.

3ᵈ   Wrote to Beatrice[354] & sent papers
"       Jeff – ~~Geo~~   Mrs Stafford

6ᵗʰ & 7ᵗʰ   Down at White Horse – Monday & Tuesday
two fine days

[114]

14 Cortlandt
Asa K Butts – ~~14 Courtland~~ st N   Y [355]
W J Linton   p o box 489 [356]

[Clipping on Philadelphia street directory, with names of streets running east and west north of Market Street and south of Market Street.]

[Clipping:]      June 4 '78 – [in WW's hand]

— Changes in our Railroad time table went
into effect on Monday. Trains now leave
Yorketown for Phila. at 8.03 A. M. and 3.18
P. M. Leave Philadelphia at 8.10 A. M. and
3.30 P. M. A Sunday train leaves Yorketown
at 7.43 A. M.; Philad'a at 6 P. M.

Watson Crackers &c, 157 North Front
Soda – 8ᶜᵗˢ – Honey 12
Sugar 12 – Graham waf: 14   Phila:

Stroup, Fish, 24 North Wharves
(Delaware Av)

Currant crackers a p        12cts[357]

[115]

'78

May 8 – wrote to W J Linton[358]
Beatrice (postal card & papers)

354.   This letter to Beatrice Gilchrist, and those to Jeff Whitman and Susan Stafford (next entry) are all lost.
355.   See footnote 110; 14 Cortland Street is a new address for Asa K. Butts, and Whitman may have jotted it down in keeping track of one of the book dealers who cheated him.
356.   See footnote 39.
357.   This clipping about railroad time tables and the notes on crackers are examples of the use to which Whitman put the left hand pages of his *Daybook*.
358.   This letter to William J. Linton (see footnote 39) is in *The Correspondence of Walt Whitman*, III, 116–117.

"    postal to Thos: Dixon, England [359]

"  <u>Dem Vistas</u> to W<sup>m</sup> Duncan    144 5<sup>th</sup>   Av   N Y

"  <u>Mem</u>: <u>War</u> to Mrs Jane Ann Chilton, 47<sup>th</sup> St
        & Wentworth av:   Chicago   Ill [360]

10 – wrote Mrs G — Herbert[361] – J   Newton Johnson
letter (dated April 25) [362] from Mrs Fanny
Raymond Ritter , 63 South Hamilton Street,
Poughkeepsie N. Y. (wife of Prof: Ritter, musician)
– kind letter — inviting me to visit them – (asking me
to give notice) [363]

11   sent papers to Jack Rogers, Arredondo[364]

"      Dr Bucke call'd – (bo't books)

12   (Sunday) down at White Horse —

13   letter to Broadbent & Taylor[365]

"   Papers to Mrs Gilchrist

14   paid Broadbent & Taylor $5

15   papers to Mrs Gilchrist — Jo: Baldwin

"  Hattie's photo: to sister Han — also postal card
      (remember hat rec'd from Chas: F   Bender)

16, 17, 18 down at White Horse

19 (Sunday) breakfast at Mr Scovel's

---

359.   The post cards to Beatrice Gilchrist and to Thomas Dixon (see footnote 13) are lost.

360.   It is not known through whom Duncan and Mrs Chilton ordered copies of *Democratic Vistas* and *Memoranda During the War*; nor can I identify them.

361.   The letters to Anne Gilchrist and Herbert Gilchrist are in *The Correspondence of Walt Whitman*, III, 117 and 118; the former to Northampton, Mass., the latter to Brooklyn.

362.   There is a John Newton Johnson (see footnote 9a) letter of 5 May 1878 in the Feinberg Collection, but none for 25 April.

363.   See footnote 139; see also Gay Wilson Allen, *The Solitary Singer*, p. 485.

364.   See footnote 260 for John Rogers.

365.   This letter is lost; but as Broadbent & Taylor were the photographers who had the "butterfly" photograph of Whitman, it may be assumed that the $5 below was for copies of this portrait.

"    "    wrote to Mrs Gilchrist[366] — Mr & Mrs Stafford

"    papers to Beatrice and Herbert

20    papers to Geo: Stafford — Amos Cooper

23$^d$ & 24$^{th}$    down at White Horse

26$^{th}$ (Sunday) down at White Horse    (Ed: Cattell

27$^{th}$    sent L of G (paid) to Sidney Lanier,[367] 33 Denment
                        Baltimore    Md    [sideways:]    recd

[116]

[Letterheads, cards, other slips of paper; the only writing is a signature of Ella Farman Pratt (not in WW's hand), editor of *Wide Awake,* Boston.[368] Cards contain names and addresses of Horace Howard Furness,[369] 222 West Washington Square, Phila.; Stoy's Camden & Philadelphia Express; and John Stroup & Co., wholesale dealers in fish, 24 No. Wharves, Phila.]

[117]

'78

May 30 & 31 ⎱ down at White Horse – dark rainy
& June 1 & 2 ⎰    four days

366.    In this letter to Anne Gilchrist (*The Correspondence of Walt Whitman*, III, 119) Whitman mentions his three-day visit with the Staffords and the usual breakfast with James Matlack Scovel.

367.    Sidney Lanier (1842–1881), American poet, wrote Whitman on 5 May 1878 (*With Walt Whitman in Camden*, I, 208) that he spent "a night of glory and delight" upon *Leaves of Grass,* and "in sending the enclosed bill to purchase a copy . . . I cannot resist the temptation to render you also my grateful thanks for such large and substantial thoughts uttered in a time when there are, as you say in another connection, so many 'little plentiful mannikins skipping about in collars and tailed coats.' . . . It is not known to me where I can find another modern song at once so large and so naive. . . . I beg you to count me among your most earnest lovers, and to believe that it would make me very happy to be of the least humble service to you at any time." Lanier also wrote Bayard Taylor that same year that *Leaves* was "worth at least a million of Among my Books and Atalanta in Calydon," and the book "was a real refreshment to me — like rude salt spray in your face — in spite of its enormous fundamental error that a thing is good because it is natural" (see William Sloan Kennedy's *The Fight of a Book for the World,* pp. 59–60). However, Lanier later attacked Whitman in *The English Novel* (New York, 1883) and Kennedy quotes him elsewhere as saying: "Whitman is poetry's butcher. Huge raw collops slashed from the rump of poetry, and never mind gristle — is what Whitman feeds our souls with. . . . His argument seems to be that because a prairie is wide therefore debauchery is admirable." (Kennedy, *ibid.,* p. 59.)

368.    See footnotes 214 and 254.

369.    Horace Howard Furness (1833–1912), Shakespearean editor who was to be an honorary pallbearer at Whitman funeral; see *The Correspondence of Walt Whitman*, III, 150, 175, 176; IV, 15n, 25n; V, 35, 44; and *Walt Whitman Review,* XVIII (December 1972), 141.

4   sent circ: &c to A   Brentano Jr. 39 Union Sq N Y

5<sup>th</sup> sent papers
to
} Sister Hannah       Wesley Stafford
Hattie               Scott Fullerton
John Rogers          Jo Baldwin[370]
Mem: to Edward Bettle

"   letter to Debbie – also to Geo: & Susan Staf:

6<sup>th</sup> sent to August Brentano,[371] 39 Union Square
N Y
six copies of L  of  G @ $3 – ($18)   [in blue pencil,
(by Adams's Ex:)      sideways:] recd & paid

8th & 9th   down at White Horse
10<sup>th</sup> paid Jas Arnold [372] $58.50 in full
bookbinding
$40.50 in check, & check on Brentano for $18 [in pencil]

12   to   Warren Chapman, College
Hanover, N  H.  both Vols, to                    recd
be paid for.          [in blue pencil, sideways:]  & paid

13th Debbie and Jo: Browning married – [373]
Hattie and Jess came on to Camden
go to N  Y

13<sup>th</sup>  June to July 10<sup>th</sup> in New York[374]

370.  All of these recipients of papers from Whitman have been commented on previously, if not fully identified, such as Joseph C. Baldwin and W. Scott Fullerton; nor can Edward Bettle on the next line be identified.

371.  August Brentano — the same person as A Brentano, Jr mentioned in the entry for 4 June 1878 — is the Brentano of the still functioning book store.

372.  The book-binder; see footnote 22.

373.  See footnote 323.

374.  In *Walt Whitman's Diary in Canada* (Boston, 1904), pp. 54–55, is the following entry in the section "From Other Journals of Walt Whitman":

NEW YORK VISIT. Came on to N. Y. June 13, '78, to 1309 Fifth Ave. 2d door south of 86th street. — At Mr. Bryant's funeral [the poet Bryant] at the church in 4th Ave. June 14, '78. — Up the Hudson River to West Point to Mr. and Mrs. Bigelow's, Sunday, June 16th.

(Wm. H. Taylor, policeman, 959 Fifth Ave.; house south of 85th St. — Alonzo Sprague, 33 years of age — western — been two years with Frank Aiken, the actor.) [The editor of the *Diary*, William Sloane Kennedy, has here added a footnote: "Sprinkled through all Whitman's pocket-book diaries are names of men to whom he was attracted, *e. g.*, a Pullman-car conductor, a policeman, a 'bus driver, a great poet. His magnetic love always drew him hungeringly toward manly men."]

Visit to Watson Gilder's, evening of June 14. Mojeska, Wyatt Eaton, Charles De Kay.
*20–24th June* (*inclusive*). Visit at John Burroughs's, Esopus (Smith Caswell).
*25th June.* Down the bay with Sorosis party.
*July 3, '78.* Visited the *Tribune* newspaper office; read proof [of a letter they printed]. Up,

(see letter in <u>Tribune</u> July 4)
in New York — [374a]          [in blue pencil]
[Four lines in pencil:]

July 11 – wrote to John Burroughs

    "      "      Mrs Gilchrist[375]

    "  Memoranda to Smith Caswell [376]

    "  postal card & paper to Pete Doyle

    "  drew postal money orders, one of $24 from
        Rosetti, $10 from Warren Chapman,[377] & one
        of $9.70 from H  F  Jones[378]    England

                    J  W  England [379]
July 12   sent a set, Two Vols to Mr. English[380]   [in blue pencil,
      publisher  Sun newspaper, New York          sideways:] rec &
                                     paid

\*  "  handed L[381] $12

    "  Hattie & Jessie here

up, up, in the elevator some eight or nine stories, to the top of the tall tower. Then the most wonderful expanse and views! A living map indeed, — all New York, and Brooklyn, and all the waters and lands adjacent for twenty miles, every direction. My thoughts of the beauty and amplitude of these bay and river surroundings confirmed. Other thoughts also confirmed, — that of a fitter name; for instance, Mannahatta, "the place around which there are hurried and joyous waters, continually" — (that's the sense of the old aboriginal word). — Was treated with much courtesy by Whitelaw Reid, the editor who placed his cab at my disposal. [Kennedy's footnote: "Perhaps to make up for his long years of lending the *Tribune* to insulting attacks on Whitman."] Had a pleasant evening drive through the Park [Central Park], it being on my way home.

    374a.  As Whitman says in his article, "A Poet's Recreation," New York *Tribune*, 4 July 1878 (reprinted mainly in *Specimen Days*), he made an impromptu decision to go to New York, where he attended the funeral of William Cullen Bryant on 14 June, went to a reception the same day at Watson Gilder's, took a trip to the Hudson River to Esopus to visit John Burroughs, after a brief stay with John H. Johnston and his family on Fifth Avenue, then came back to the Johnston's before returning to Camden. See *Prose Works 1892*, I, 165–172, 329–330; and letters he wrote to George and Louisa Whitman, Hattie, Anne Gilchrist, Harry Stafford, and John and Ursula Burroughs about his short trip, in *The Correspondence of Walt Whitman*, III, 120–128.

    375.  Both letters are in *The Correspondence of Walt Whitman*, III, 127–128.

    376.  Smith Caswell (see footnote 81), one of Burrough's hired hands; see Walt Whitman's "Real Summer Openings," New York *Tribune*, 17 May 1879 (reprinted in *Prose Works 1892*, I, 340 ("from My Bay-Window"), "My friend S. C. out in the raspberry field carefully plough-ing with one horse between the rows . . ." He is often mentioned in Whitman's letters to Burroughs in *The Correspondence of Walt Whitman*, III, 141, 144, 149, 158, 160, 162, 170, 173, 179; Whitman's letters to Caswell are lost.

    377.  This money is obviously for copies of *Leaves of Grass* and *Two Rivulets* to sent to England, and to Dartmouth College (Chapman).

    378.  Copies sent to Henry Festing Jones; see Whitman letter to him, 12 July 1878, *The Correspondence of Walt Whitman*, III, 128.

    379.  Isaac W. England (1832–1885), publisher of the New York *Sun* from 1868 until his death in 1885.

    380.  "English" is written in error for England (corrected above).

    381.  Louisa Whitman, to whom Whitman paid $12 for his board on Stevens Street.

[118]

July. '78

) 114 north 32ᵈ
Mrs Mingle    } ~~1717 Rittenhouse Street~~
Evelyn Mingle)    Phila
Union Tel. office, 10th & Chestnut
[On calling card:]    Spoke to me at Mr Bryant's funeral [382]
— strong invitation — June '78
Mrs. Elizabeth T. Porter-Beach   [printed in script]
51 W. 33ᵈ   [not WW's hand]

[Calling card: John T. Wilson & Co., ship bread and cracker bakers, Fulton St., New York.] [383]

[119]

'78

July 12 – sent a set Two Vols: to Henry Festing
Jones,   X   Craven Hill Gardens W.        [in blue pencil,
London W. Eng: [384]                  sideways:] recd

"    sent Whitelaw Reid  "Passage to India" – also       [in blue pencil,
letter[385]    sideways:] recd

"    "  Bertha & Grace J.  "Wide Awake" [386]

"    "  postal card to Rossetti[387]

"   "Mem War" to W H Taylor   N   Y.[388]

"   postal card to Dr Bucke[389]

382.  See footnote 374.
383.  This seems a strange card for Whitman to keep, but perhaps no stranger than that of a wholesale fish dealer, above.
384.  See footnote 351.
385.  Whitelaw Reid (1837–1912), publisher and editor of the New York *Tribune*, 1872–1905, met Whitman in the hospitals during the Civil War, admired first his character and then, after reading the Lincoln poems, said the poet "conquered me completely"; they wrote each other several times: see *The Correspondence of Walt Whitman*, II, 317; III, 23, 53, 129, 137, 140, 152, 153–154, 181, 281. This letter of 12 July 1878 is in III, 129, it refers in part to Whitman's 4 July piece in the *Tribune*, "A Poet's Recreation," for which he received $20 (see footnote 374, above, and the entry for 19 July below).
386.  For the *Wide Awake* article, see footnote 214; Bertha and Grace J. are members of the family of John H. Johnston, the New York jeweler.
387.  This card, referring to the $24 which Rossetti sent Whitman (see entry above for 11 July), is in *The Correspondence of Walt Whitman*, III, 129.
388.  This William H. Taylor, to whom Whitman sent *Memoranda During the War*, lived at 201 Elm Street, Newark, New Jersey, and on 18 December 1877 invited Whitman for a visit (see the letter in the Library of Congress); Whitman's letter to him, 24 November 1878, is lost; William Taylor, editor of the Woodstown (New Jersey) *Constitution* (see footnote 207), was another man with the same name, as Woodstown is in South Jersey, a considerable distance from Newark.
389.  This card is lost.

13   sent a set Two Vols. to Dr T   K   Holmes     [in blue pencil,
          Chatham, Ont: Canada              sideways:] recd


14th 15, 16 & 17 – Down at White Horse
                (old Mr Morgan died June 13th '78) [390]
Debbie & Jo married June 13 [391]


19th   sent <u>Two Riv</u>: to W   J   Linton   box 489   [in blue pencil,
                New   Haven, Conn: [392]            sideways:] recd

"  rec'd pay for T. letter from W   R [393]


10th to 20th — <u>hot</u> — <u>hot</u> — <u>hot</u> weather[394]
20th to 24th (Saturday to Wednesday)   down at White Horse


July 28   [four lines in pencil:]   W   M   Rossetti   56 Euston Square
sent             London   W – Four Vols   Two
                                                sets[395]

                              paid


July 26 – sent
      Oscar Tottie[396]              x
            paid   [in pencil]         [in blue pencil, sideways:]   recd
      64 Seymour St

                              London   [in pencil]
                              W

      Edgeware Rd South
            a set   [in pencil] – Two Vols


July 27 – Sent Circ's &c to Geo: Chinn, Marblehead
                              Mass: [397]

"      "      Tribune letter, "Sun" & W J Press of Jan 16 to Dowden[398]


390.  This is Will Morgan, husband of Rachel Morgan, among those who saw Whitman
at White Horse on 15–17 March 1878 (see above); he is also mentioned in Whitman's letter
of 5 August to Herbert Gilchrist (*The Correspondence of Walt Whitman*, III, 131).
391.  Repeated from two pages previously.
392.  See footnote 39.
393.  This is a reference to Whitman's piece in the 4 July 1878 New York *Tribune*, "A
Poet's Recreation," for which Whitelaw Reid paid the poet $20 (see footnote 385).
394.  Two subjects on which Whitman made the most comments: the weather and his
health.
395.  William Michael Rossetti continued to be one of Whitman's best "salesmen." Whitman also wrote him on this date (*The Correspondence of Walt Whitman*, III, 130).
396.  Whitman also wrote a brief note to Oscar Tottie on this date (*The Correspondence
of Walt Whitman*, III, 129); on 11 August 1878 Tottie acknowledged receipt of the two volumes
(letter in the Library of Congress).
397.  I cannot identify George Chinn of Marblehead, Mass.
398.  For Dowden, see footnote 9; the Tribune letter was Whitman's "A Poet's Recrea-

[On slip:]

July 23rd / 1878.

Mrs Gilchrist & Herbert

Care of Geo: W. Rogers
Chesterfield, Mass:[399]

[On another slip:]

| | | |
|---|---|---|
| H. Buxton Forman | | (remember |
| Secretary's office | July | Dr Bucke's |
| General Post Office | '78 | letters |
| | [two lines in pencil:] | about) |
| London | (46 Marlborough hill | him ) |
| England | St John's Wood [400] | |

Sarony, 37 Union Sq: N   Y [401]

Andrew
Frazee[402]
Young fellow, 20,
on the ferry
(right leg
paralyzed)

Oliver Pancoast[403]
512 Benson Street   Camden

tion," New York *Tribune,* 4 July 1878 (see footnote 374); W J Press was "Walt Whitman for 1878," *West Jersey Press,* 16 January 1878; "Sun" may be Whitman's "Abraham Lincoln's Death," New York *Sun,* 12 February 1876, although Whitman did not usually take two years to send his friends clippings and off-prints which he had written, or newspaper items about himself; so a more likely possibility is a clipping of an account of William Cullen Bryant's funeral in the New York *Sun,* 15 June 1878, with the paragraph beginning, "The man most looked at was the white-haired poet, Walt Whitman, who presented a Homeric picture, in which were combined the easy good nature of Grandfather Whitehead and the heroic build of an antique statue." Whitman sent a copy of this clipping to George and Louisa Whitman from New York on 17 June 1878; see *The Correspondence of Walt Whitman,* III, 120. (Whitman's *Tribune* piece is also, in part, on the Bryant funeral. See "Death of William Cullen Bryant," *Prose Works 1892,* I, 165–167.)

399. Herbert Gilchrist must have joined his mother in Chesterfield, Mass.

400. This was Forman's London address; for Forman, see footnote 248.

401. According to Whitman's letter to Harry Stafford, 6 July 1878, Sarony's was "the great photographic establishment, where I was invited to come & sit for my picture — had a real pleasant time" (*The Correspondence of Walt Whitman,* III, 126).

402. Andrew Blair Frazee was a Camden ferryboat captain (see footnote 85), but may not be this Andrew Frazee.

403. I cannot identify Oliver Pancoast.

[121]

'78

July 28 – (Sunday) sent Circ's to Miles A Davis   care
        Ontario County Journal, Canandaigua, Ontario   [in blue pencil,
        County, N. Y. at his request & letter from him[404]    sideways:] recd

   "  papers to Smith Caswell [405]

   "  Trib: of July 4 to Rob't Buchanan, Oban S [406]

   "  rhubarb to Harry[407]

Aug 1 – sent to Geo: P Rowell   10 Spruce
      St. N   Y. a set, ordered & paid for
      by J   W   England,[408] Sun office –   [in blue pencil, sideways:]   recd

Aug 2 – sent Sarony   37 Union Sq: N  Y      [in blue pencil,
      three sets books (and Mem War for Joe)   sideways:]   recd
      by Adams Express[409]

Aug 1   paid for Sunday "Herald" and "Sun"
        up to date[410]

3d 4th 5th & 6th – at White Horse
    wrote to Herbert[411]

7th   sent to Benj Gurney
      at Sarony's   N   Y   a set Two Vols[412]   [in blue pencil, sideways:]   recd

---

404. This letter to Miles A. Davis, Canandaigua, New York, newspaperman, is lost.

405. Smith Caswell, John Burrough's hired hand; see footnote 376.

406. For "Trib: of July 4," see footnote 374; for Rob't Buchanan, see footnote 34a.

407. It seems strange that Whitman should send Harry Stafford some rhubarb: wasn't the young man on a farm, where rhubarb was plentiful?

408. Unidentifiable, except that J. W. England was an admirer who was on the staff of the New York *Sun*: see footnote 379.

409. Benjamin Gurney (?) acknowledged receipt of books for Mr Sarony on 3 August 1878: letter in the T. E. Hanley Collection, University of Texas.

410. These were for subscriptions to the New York *Herald* and New York *Sun*: as is obvious from this and other such entries, Whitman used the *Daybook*, not only to record his health, the weather, trips to White Horse and elsewhere, funerals, deaths, papers and letters which he sent to friends and relatives, but also as an account book.

411. Whitman's letter to Herbert Gilchrist, 3–5 August 1878, is in *The Correspondence of Walt Whitman*, III, 130–131.

412. See footnote 409.

" papers to Wesley Stafford
    "    "    Mont [413]
    "    "    Jo: Baldwin[414]

9  to Tennyson letter "Aldworth  Blackdown
      Haslemerè (or elsewhere) England" [415]

"  letter & <u>Two Rivl</u>  to Josiah Child, care
    of Trübner & Co: 57 & 59 Ludgate Hill London [416]

8th–9th–& 10th — <u>hot</u> – sudden heavy storms different
                           places

[122]

J H  Johnston  Mott av & 149th st[417]
~~1309 Fifth av. 2d house south of~~
~~86th street~~
_____  N Y
Jerry Robbins, driver Stevens st cars[418]
Wm Rauch, ferry night – ("Fred")
Mr Frazee, night bridgeman, Camden side
Geo: "    ass't  pilot
Andy "    deck hand[419]

---

413. Wesley Stafford was Harry's cousin (see footnote 253); Mont was Montgomery Stafford, another member of the Stafford family (see footnote 231).

414. For Joseph Baldwin, who frequently was sent papers by the poet, see footnote 164.

415. Alfred, Lord Tennyson's letter from Whitman is in *The Correspondence of Walt Whitman*, III, 133; and Tennyson's reply, III, 134–135.

416. Josiah Child's letter from Whitman is in *The Correspondence of Walt Whitman*, III, 132.

417. Whitman usually wrote to John H. Johnston at his jewelry shop at 150 Bowery, at the corner of Broome Street, New York City; Johnston moved to 1309 Fifth Avenue after his marriage to Alma Calder on 21 April 1878, and Whitman visited them there in June 1878; these cancelled lines must indicate a move to Mott Avenue and 149th Street; in 1885 the Johnstons were living at 305 East 17th Street.

418. Another of the several notations by Whitman, simply giving the name of a horsecar driver.

419. It is not always clear who was who in the Frazee family, as several of them were connected with the Camden-Philadelphia ferry: in *Specimen Days,* under the date of 5 April 1879, Whitman refers to "captain Frazee the superintendent" (*Prose Works 1892,* I, 183); Whitman sent "Capt Frazee" a copy of the Philadelphia *Times* for 26 January 1879 (see footnote 80, above); with the date "Jan '79" Whitman records the name Andrew Blair Frazee by itself (see footnote 85); and above Whitman says that Andrew Frazee is 20 years old, on the ferry and has a right leg paralyzed. As 20 is too young for even a ferry captain, the Andrew Frazee and Andy, the deck hand, are the same person; and the Captain Frazee may well be the

Beatrice C  Gilchrist  M  D [420]
N  E  Hospital for Women
Codman  av
Boston   Mass

S  H  Morse[421]
66 Pleasant Street  Boston

Charles Johnson[422]
RR man , on train with Pete Doyle   6 mos
I met on Federal st ferry boat  Aug 28
'78

Herbert Gilchrist            Aug 29 '78
care Thos: Smith
Leeds' Point, Atlantic Co   N  J [423]

Miss M  P  Janes[424]
34 West  30th St  N  Y

Dan'l Garwood
drives Soull's wagon

father or an older relative, the Captain A. B. Frazee to whom Whitman wrote on 6 January 1880 (letter now lost).

420.  Beatrice Gilchrist, Anne's daughter, received a letter from Whitman in December 1877, when she was a medical student in Philadelphia, warning her about "crowding too much & too intense study into too short a time," saying that a Mrs Needham, who had gone to the same school, had died in a lunatic asylum "just from sheer overwork, & too intense concentration, ardor, & continued strain" (*The Correspondence of Walt Whitman*, III, 105); after she became an M.D., Beatrice wrote Whitman in August 1878 (letter in the Library of Congress) about her activities in the New England Hospital for Women (*ibid.*, III, 135); in 1881 she committed suicide (see *ibid.*, III, 240; and entry below for 9 September 1881).

421.  Sidney Morse, who was sculpting a bust of Whitman, who received it on 16 February 1879, and entered his comment in the *Daybook* (see below): "head rec'd / bad — wretchedly bad." Whitman's letter to Morse, of that date, is lost; Morse's earlier letter (9 August ?) to Whitman is in the Feinberg Collection. (See *Walt Whitman Review*, XV [September 1969], 197.)

422.  Whitman wrote to Peter Doyle, 1 September 1878, "Saw your friend Ch: Johnson a few evenings since on the ferry — had quite a talk about you, &c" (*The Correspondence of Walt Whitman*, III, 136).

423.  Whitman wrote Edward Carpenter on 1 September 1878 that Herbert Gilchrist "is here in New Jersey": he was in Kirkwood on 22 August, in Camden on 24 August, then back in Kirkwood, and at Atlantic City on 29 August (see *The Correspondence of Walt Whitman*, III, 135).

424.  I cannot identify Miss M. P. Janes, nor (in the entry below) Daniel Garwood.

'78

Aug 10 – Circ's to John W Breese   Lynn   Mass[425]

+   "   gave L $7 in a purse[426]

"   Mrs Stafford quite sick[427]
from 10th to 13th   down at White Horse

14th paid Hunt Photo's, 4.5 for 30 photos to be rec'd

"   applied to Bart Bonsall, for a sit. for Harry[428]

17th to 20th – at White Horse

"   Harry commenced work at Haddonfield [429]

20th rec'd letter from Dr Bucke, London, Ontario, Canada
enclosing one from H Buxton Forman, ab't new
edition of L of G. in England – [430]

22 Herbert here – down at White Horse

24th "   "   three hours visit – (went back to W H)

25th (Sunday) sent papers to Beatrice Gilchrist[431]
"   "   Geo: Stafford
"   "   W S Fullerton[432]
"   "   Amos Cooper

425. Unidentifiable.
426. The usual Whitman money to his sister-in-law Louisa for his board.
427. Whitman wrote Herbert Gilchrist on 5 August 1878: "Mrs S[tafford] is much better to-day — She is about seeing to things somewhat as usual — (A great part of her illness is some peculiar trouble, or breakage or rupture to which *women* only are liable — in her case aggravated by overwork)" (*The Correspondence of Walt Whitman,* III, 131).
428. Whitman wrote Harry Stafford on 15 August 1878: "I wrote Bart Bonsall [co-editor of the Camden *Daily Post* with his father, Henry Lummis Bonsall] a note yesterday about getting you a situation, & stopt there ab't noon to see him to-day — but they told me he was away & would not be back to-day" (*The Correspondence of Walt Whitman,* III, 133–134).
429. Whitman told Edward Carpenter on 1 September: "Harry S[tafford] is back at printing" (*The Correspondence of Walt Whitman,* III, 136), confirmed by the entry below for 17 August 1878.
430. These two letters are apparently lost; Whitman had referred to Forman and Dr Bucke in July 1878 (see above; also see 248); I don't know of this "new" edition of *Leaves of Grass* in England — William Michael Rossetti's selections, *Poems by Walt Whitman,* was published by J. C. Hotten & Co. in 1868; and Hotten issued the 1871–72 Washington edition in London "as near like it as he could make it" (William Sloane Kennedy, *The Fight of a Book for the World,* p. 245). Not until David Bogue issued sheets of the Osgood edition in

rec'd
26th postal card from  Marvin, Wash'n[433]

27th papers to John M   Rogers[434]
   "    "  Jos S  Fullerton, Greeley

29  letter from Harry – [435]

30th recd
  ∧ letters from Edw: Carpenter – also Herbert G [436]
  "    sent letter to Beatrice[437] — papers to Herbert

Sept 1 (Sunday)   wrote letter to Jeff

  "      "      "      "      Geo & Susan Stafford

  "   "  postals to Sister Han & Sister Mary
      "     "  Pete Doyle – Smith Caswell
      "     "  Edw'd Carpenter[438]
    papers to Geo Stafford

  "   tea at Col: Johnston's[439] – met Mr Bartlett [440] (the hour at
        his house, Penn street – the cider – Mrs B. Mr Wright)
        – Mr Cox[441]

---

1881 was there another edition of Whitman in England.
   431.  Whitman continued on very close terms with Herbert Gilchrist, who visited Whitman in Camden (from White Horse), and with Beatrice, who was now an M. D. in Boston (see footnote 420).
   432.  See footnote 370; W. Scott Fullerton and Joseph S. Fullerton both being from Greeley, Colorado (see entry for 27 August 1878, below) were most likely brothers.
   433.  Joseph B. Marvin, the Washington editor (see near the end of footnote 81).
   434.  See footnote 260.
   435.  Harry Stafford's letter of 26 August 1878 is in the Feinberg Collection.
   436.  These two letters from Edward Carpenter, Whitman's English friend, and Herbert Gilchrist are lost.
   437.  This short letter is in *The Correspondence of Walt Whitman,* III, 135.
   438.  Of these six letters Whitman wrote on 1 September 1878, to his brother Jeff, George and Susan Stafford, his sister Hannah Heyde, his sister Mary (who married a mechanic Ansel Van Nostrand, and the poet did not often write to her), Peter Doyle, Smith Caswell (John Burroughs's hired man), and Edward Carpenter the Englishman, only two survive: the letter to Carpenter is in *The Correspondence of Walt Whitman,* III, 135–136, and the one to Peter Doyle, III, 136.
   439.  Colonel John R. Johnston was a Camden artist (see footnote 76).
   440.  Professor Edwin Haviland Miller (*The Correspondence of Walt Whitman,* III, 354n) identifies Bartlett as Truman Howe Bartlett (1835–1923), an instructor at modeling in the Massachusetts Institute of Technology, who made a cast of Whitman's hand (now in the Feinberg Collection).
   441.  Mr Wright and Mr Cox cannot be identified; Mrs B is probably Mrs Truman Howe Bartlett (see footnote 440).

Sept 1ˢᵗ, 2ᵈ    hot – hot –

"    2   ride up from ferry night with O   W ⁴⁴²

[124]

[Clipping of classified ad:]

THE SOCIETY OF FRIENDS IN THE NINE-
teenth Century, by William Hodgson, vol. 2d
just published. For sale by SMITH, ENGLISH &
CO., 710 Arch street, and by the Author, 103 North
Tenth street, Phila.        eod3t*51

Sarah Avery   152 Henry st   N   Y
John Avery⁴⁴³

[On printed slip with name and address of law offices of James M. Scovel,
Camden:]

Harry Sidney Scovel ⁴⁴⁴

[Printed slip of B. Westermann & Co., New York; two classified ads of eye-
glasses, H. E. Mulligan, 29 S. Eighth, and Cooper & Brother, 35 S. Fourth,
Phila. (pointing finger in blue pencil on each side of Cooper ad). On calling
card of D. R. Ashton, 1202 Mt. Vernon St.:]

Trübner & Co:
57 & 59 Ludgate Hill
London   E   C
Eng:⁴⁴⁵

Spectacles    35 S 4ᵗʰ St    Phila:
Bob   417
Cooper
?Bowen⁴⁴⁶

Mrs Sarah E   Brown
Woodside  L  I  ⎛infant
N  Y  ⎝little Walter⎠

442.  Who is O W?
443.  Sarah Avery was Walt Whitman's cousin; her husband John was a New York
merchant; see *The Correspondence of Walt Whitman*, II, 215n.
444.  James Matlack Scovel's son; Whitman often breakfasted with the father on Sunday
mornings (see footnote 71).
445.  This was the name and address of the London publishing house where Josiah Child
handled dealings for Whitman; see *The Correspondence of Walt Whitman*, III, 137, for Whitman's letter of Trübner of 1 October 1878.
446.  There is a letter to Whitman from Sarah E. Brown (or Bowen), a friend of Amelia
Johnston, of New York City, in the Library of Congress, dated 6 April 1877.

1878

Sept 3  "Old Curiosity Shop" to Hannah

"      papers to Herbert

"      "    "    Will Tinker, Greeley[447]

4  lent Bro. G  200 by check – (returned) [448]

"  walk on Chestnut st – call'd at Col. J's[449]

5th   sent "Two Orphans" to ~~Hannah~~ Mary[450]

"    "    papers to Geo Staf: and Herbert

"  rec'd letter from Mrs Gil:[451]

8th  papers to Wesley Stafford

"      "    John Rogers[452]

"  rec'd letter from Josiah Child, London[453]
Sunday – breakfast at J M S's & Supper at Col. J's[454]

9th  rec'd London Times, "London" &c from Josiah Child [455]

"  sent B Westerman & Co: Booksellers, 524 Broadway N  Y
                                                   letters & Circ: [456]

11th to 18th   down at White Horse

18th rec'd 250 photos from Sarony (all paid) [457]

447.  Will Tinker, from Greeley, Colorado, as were the Fullertons, was often sent papers by Whitman (see footnotes 267 and 291).
448.  If this means anything, it at least indicates that Whitman had $200 to lend and was hardly a starving poet.
449.  Colonel John R. Johnston, the Camden artist, had a studio in Philadelphia.
450.  *The Old Curiosity Shop,* which Whitman sent to his sister Hannah Heyde on 3 September 1878, was of course Dickens's novel (1841); and *The Two Orphans,* sent to his sister Mary Van Nostrand, was a French play (1875) by D'Ennery and Cormon, a very popular melodrama at this time.
451.  This letter from Anne Gilchrist, dated 3 September 1878, is in Thomas B. Harned's edition of *The Letters of Anne Gilchrist and Walt Whitman,* pp. 159–160.
452.  See footnote 260.
453.  Dealing with the sale of Whitman's books to Trübner & Company, perhaps; see *The Correspondence of Walt Whitman,* III, 137–138.
454.  Whitman's Sunday pattern: breakfast at James M. Scovel's and supper at Colonel John R. Johnston's.
455.  See footnotes 445 and 453.
456.  This letter is lost.

20 — postal cards to Sarony

"        "        "      Ed Stafford [458]

"        "        "      & papers to   John Burroughs[459]

"        "                Sister  Hannah

"    papers to Mary

"    Photo (Sarony) to Smith Caswell

"    papers to Herbert

23 postal Card to Jo: Baldwin


26th–30th  down at White Horse   rec'd letter
                                 from Mrs Gil [460]


30 rec'd from Trubner & Co: (Josiah Child)
    order for Two Sets – rec'd $14 [461]


Oct 1 – John Burroughs's letter ab't the death of
    Chas Caswell [462]

"    "    sent J  B   the Sarony photo


[126]

[Card of Jeneco M'Mullin, boot and shoe manufacturer, Phila. On slip of
paper on top of another address:]

    Mrs Gilchrist – Herbert[463]

        ~~315 West 19th St   N  Y~~

        112 Madison Av:

    39 Somerset St   Boston


457.  See footnote 401; Whitman's post card to Sarony, the photographer, of 20 September
1878, is lost.
458.  This letter to Edwin Stafford (1856-1906), Harry's brother, is lost, as is the letter
of this same date, to Hannah Heyde, and the 23 September post card to Joseph Baldwin.
459.  This very short letter says he is well, has visited the Staffords, and asks for the
return of the London *Times* (sent him by Child — see above); see *The Correspondence of
Walt Whitman*, III, 136.
460.  The letter referred to in footnote 451.
461.  See Whitman's letter, *The Correspondence of Walt Whitman*, III, 137–138.
462.  The Burroughs letter is lost; Charles Caswell was the younger brother of Smith
Caswell, who worked for Burroughs. See "Three Young Men's Deaths" in *Specimen Days*
(*Prose Works 1892*, I, 155-158). If Whitman wrote to John Burroughs the same day, when
he sent the Sarony photograph (see entry below), the letter does not survive.
463.  Herbert Gilchrist was living at 315 West 19th Street, New York City, as late as 25

Edward Carpenter[464] ~~17 Highland Terrace~~

~~Highfield~~

45 Brunswick Square          ~~Sheffield~~

Oct '81   Broadway near Sheffield          ~~Dec '78~~

~~June 1~~ '81   [red ink]   ~~Brighton   Eng:~~   [in red ink]

Sent 3 L   of   G   [in red ink]

[Six lines in pencil, on slip of paper:]

Charles Van Meter[465]
new driver on S st cars

fruit butter &c
120 Delaware av

Lust Factory   } Seamless
135 Race       } Shoe
               } 614 Arch

[127]

Oct '78

1ˢᵗ   sent Twelve Sets (24 Vols) to John Wiley   [sideways:]
      & sons, for Trübner & Co — The latter are to   rec'd
      acc't to me for ten sets, at $7 a set             by
           went to T & co Oct 4 [466]                   Wiley
                                                        rec'd [in blue pencil]
                                                        by Tr [in blue pencil]

2   sent Mem &c to Mr Douglass & Mr Kirkby
    Children's Aid Soc. 61 Poplar st   Brooklyn

"   Circs to R   Clarke & Co: 65 west 4th St Cincinnati

December 1878; and Whitman wrote him at 112 Madison Avenue on 6 February 1879, so he moved between those dates, and Whitman made the note here. 39 Somerset Street is Anne Gilchrist's Boston address (see entry for 10 November 1878).

464. Whitman wrote to Edward Carpenter at 45 Brunswick Square, Brighton, England, on 28 September 1880, and to him at Broadway near Sheffield [England] on 30 May 1881. No December 1878 letter to Carpenter is known.

465. Charles Van Meter was, like many other horsecar drivers, someone Whitman met, wrote down his address and perhaps never saw again; but Van Meter, a driver on a Stevens Street car, does appear again, above footnote 676.

466. Whitman mentioned these 12 sets in his letter to Trübner & Company, 1 October 1878: see *The Correspondence of Walt Whitman,* III, 137–138.

"   sent novel to Sister Han
    "    "   "   " Mary
"   postal card to Geo & Susan S
"   papers to Harry
    "    "   " Herbert[467]

                         appeared

3 sent "Gathering the Corn" to Tribune    Oct 24th [468]

"   papers to Wesley Stafford (Wesley has left)

"   "   " Pete Doyle – postal card also[469]

"   "   Smith  Caswell

Oct 7 (Monday) been down at White Horse the last
         three days

"   papers to Herbert – Lou's letter to Hat[470]

"   rec'd letter from Joe Baldwin   leaves there last of
                                   Oct[471]

Oct 8 – paid Mr Miller for Herald and Sun
        up to date, & stopt Herald —[472]

9  wrote to Mr Taylor, Woodstown about Harry
                      Harry rec'd answer[473]

467.  In this list of nine for 2 October 1878, Whitman's sisters Hannah Heyde and Mary Van Nostrand, George and Susan Stafford, Harry Stafford, and Herbert Gilchrist are easily identifiable, but Mr Douglass, Mr Kirkby (of the Children's Aid Society of Brooklyn) and R Clarke & Co (of Cincinnati) are not otherwise identifiable.

468.  "Gathering the Corn," a prose piece by Whitman, first appeared in the New York *Tribune* on 24 October 1878; Whitman sent it to Whitelaw Reid to be used as an editorial (see two letters in *The Correspondence of Walt Whitman*, III, 137) on 21 September, but does not mention it in the *Daybook*; Reid wanted Whitman to sign it, so Whitman made changes and sent it back. He was paid $10. It was reprinted in *Good-Bye My Fancy* (1891) from two newspaper clippings — not the *Tribune* — with some changes, and again in *Prose Works 1892*, II, 669–671.

469.  The post card to Peter Doyle is lost; once again, as so often with the word "papers," we don't know what Whitman means, but it was not the *Tribune* with his piece, "Gathering the Corn," which wouldn't be published for three weeks.

470.  This letter from Louisa Orr Whitman, his sister-in-law, which Whitman sent to his niece, Mannahatta, in St Louis is lost.

471.  Joseph Baldwin had left Effingham County, Illinois, but his letter to Whitman is lost; see entry below for 29 October 1878.

472.  These payments are for subscriptions to the New York *Sun* and the New York *Herald*; it is not known why he stopped reading the *Herald*, but ten years later, when Julius Chambers became managing editor, Whitman became a regular contributor for several months.

473.  See footnote 207 and *The Correspondence of Walt Whitman*, III, 133n.

10, 11, 12 – down at White Horse

12  –  paper to Bee[474]

"    sent "The Wandering Heir" to Mrs Johnston[475]

Barrymore
13th Sunday – breakfast at J M S's – met Mr Barsmore[476]

"        papers & postal card to Mrs Gilchrist[477]

14th   sent 8 [?] to Mrs S –[478]

15th at theatre "Diplomacy" [479]

16th to 21st inclusive – down at White Horse

21st rec'd letter from Tennyson[480]

24th to 28th inclusive down at White Horse

23[d] (Wednesday morning)   the furious gale & storm

[128]

[On slip of paper:]

send to Trübner & co: (books &c) through
John Wiley  & Sons[481] [not WW's hand]
No. 15 Astor Place, New York [not WW's hand]

Tennyson
Aldworth, Haslemere
Surrey – Eng —[482]

474.   Beatrice Gilchrist was now an M. D. and connected with the New England Hospital for Women, Boston (see footnote 420).
475.   Of the several Mrs Johnstons, my guess is that this is Mrs Alma Johnston, wife of the New York jeweler; *The Wandering Heir* is a novel by Charles Reade (1814–1884), published in 1872.
476.   I cannot identify James M. Scovel's guest, Mr Barsmore (or Barrymore), but it was not the theatrical family (Lionel Barrymore was born that year, 1878).
477.   This letter is lost.
478.   Undoubtedly Mrs Susan Stafford at White Horse.
479.   "Diplomacy" was written by the French playright Victorian Sardou (1831–1908), called the most successful dramatist and master of stage technique of his day.
480.   This letter, dated 24 August 1878, is in *The Correspondence of Walt Whitman,* III, 134–135.
481.   See entry above for 1 October 1878 and footnote 466.
482.   See footnote 480.

G  P  Putnam's Sons
182 Fifth Av  N  Y [483]

Sent "Gathering the Corn" [484]

Wash Eve Star[485]                    Mrs Gilchrist
Wm Taylor, Woodstown                  Mrs Odenheimer
Mr English – Atlantic City            John Johnston
Jeff                                  Edw Carpenter Eng
Mary                                  Smith Caswell
Han                                   Dr Bucke
Jessie                                J  B  Marvin[486]
John Lucas

[129]

'78 Oct.

28th  Sent papers to Herbert

24 ~~Oct~~

"Gathering the Corn" article in Tribune 24 Oct[487]

29th   visit from Jo Baldwin ⌠ return'd from Effingham Co ⌡
                              ⌡ Ill: work'd for Dr Dewey[488] ⌠

30th letter to Jeff [489]

 "    papers to Mont [490]

 "      "    John Rogers[491]

483. G. P. Putnam's Sons, the publishing house, wrote Whitman on 17 July 1879 (letter in the Library of Congress), but Whitman's reply, shortly after that date, is lost. Whitman sent his *Leaves of Grass* and *Two Rivulets* to them on 31 October 1878 (see entry below).

484. Walt Whitman, "Gathering the Corn," New York *Tribune,* 24 October 1878 (see footnote 468, above).

485. Whitman's article may have been reprinted in the Washington *Evening Star* (or in William Taylor's Woodstown, New Jersey, *Constitution*), and clippings from this paper may have served for Whitman's source for reprinting in *Good-Bye My Fancy* (1891).

486. In this rather short list (for Whitman) of 13 people, easily identifiable are his brother in St Louis, Jeff, his sister Mary Van Nostrand, his sister Hannah Heyde, his niece Jessie, John Lucas (a Philadelphia paint manufacturer with a plant near Kirkwood), Mrs Anne Gilchrist, Colonel John P. Johnston, the Camden artist (or his son John, Jr), Edward Carpenter, the English friend, Smith Caswell (John Burroughs's employee), Dr Richard Maurice Bucke, and John B. Marvin, the Washington editor and Treasury Department employee; Mr English was on the *Review* and of Atlantic City (Whitman visited him there on 3 November 1878); and Mrs Odenheimer I cannot identify.

487. See footnotes 468, 484, 486; the "papers" sent to Herbert Gilchrist in New York City most likely included this piece by Whitman in the *Tribune.*

488. See footnote 471.

489. This letter is lost, but Jeff Whitman's letter of 27 October 1878, to which Whitman surely replied, is in the Feinberg Collection.

490. Montgomery Stafford (see footnote 231).

491. See footnote 260.

31st sent a Set 2 Vols to G   P   Putnam's Sons[492]
    182 Fifth av.   N   Y – ($7 due)    [in blue pencil, sideways:]   recd
                                                   paid

Nov 3 – (Sunday) trip to Atlantic City & back –
    Drive on the seashore – Wm Biddle – Mr En-
    glish of the <u>Review</u> – Mr Wittbank[493]

"   postal cards to Beatrice Gilchrist

"    "    "    Sister  Hannah

"    "    "    Sister  Mary

"    "    "    Pete  Doyle

"    "    "    Harry  Stafford [494]

4th to 8th down at White Horse[495]

8th return'd rec't for $7 to G   P   Putnams Sons, N Y [496]

" over to Col Forney's to see proof "Man-of-War-Bird" [497]

" rec'd letter from Josiah Child, with Trüb-
    ner & Co:   They are to acc't to me

    for ten (10) sets of my books 2 Vols
    each,   at $7 a set[498] – also something
    due me for <u>Dem:</u>  <u>Vistas:</u>

" rec'd letter dated Oct 26, from Jos: Child [499]

" Joe Baldwin here[500]

---

492.  See footnote 483.
493.  For Mr English see footnote 486; William Biddle and Mr Wittbank I cannot identify.
494.  All five of these post cards, though probably of little importance, are lost.
495.  For Whitman's account of this visit, see his letter to Anne Gilchrist of 10 November 1878 in *The Correspondence of Walt Whitman,* III, 138–139.
496.  See entry above for 31 October 1878 and footnote 483.
497.  This poem, later called "To the Man-of-War Bird," first appeared in the London *Athenaeum,* 1 April 1876; then as an intercalation in some copies of the 1876 *Leaves of Grass*; and now in Colonel John W. Forney's Philadelphia *Progress,* 16 November 1878, as "Thou who has slept all night upon the storm." For Forney, see footnote 193, above; for data on the poem, see *The Correspondence of Walt Whitman,* III, 23, 52, 56; and the Comprehensive Reader's Edition of *Leaves of Grass,* pp. 257–258, which of course includes the text.
498.  See entry above for 1 October 1878, and *The Correspondence of Walt Whitman,* III, 137–138, and 140–141.
499.  This letter is lost.
500.  Baldwin also visited Whitman on 29 October (see entry above).

[130]

John Lucas    1028 Race St Phila[501]
                Tuesday evenings

[Slips with addresses of G. P. Putnam's Sons, and Little, Brown, & Co.] [502]
Wm H Taylor    201 Elm St
                Newark    N    J [503]


            112 Madison av: N   Y
Dec 7 – Mrs Gilchrist, ~~177 Romsen st   Brooklyn~~[504]
John Siter    4209 Haverford    av    Phil [505]
[Card of R. J. Morrell, rattan furniture manufacturer, Newfield, N. J., with
notation:]    28 miles from Camden (Mr Judson[506]
Joseph L Browning    )⟨[507]
            Haddonfield    N    J


                                                        [131]

'78 – Nov                                    [in blue pencil,
10$^{th}$ – (Sunday) sent a set 2 Vols to B    Westermann[508]    sideways:]
    & Co:    524 Broadway    N Y ($ due)              recd
                                                        paid

"    sent letter to Mrs Gilchrist    39 Somerset st    Boston
        inc: Tennyson's, & John Bur: letters (to be ret)
                                        also Gath: Corn[509]

"    papers to John Lucas[510]

---

501. This is the address of Lucas's Philadelphia store; see footnotes 81 and 486, and
*The Correspondence of Walt Whitman,* III, 102 and 103n.

502. See footnote 483 for Putnam, who bought two volumes from Whitman; the reason
Whitman has the Little, Brown, & Co., Publishers, address here is that he sent circulars to
them on 24 November 1878 (see entry below).

503. This is not the same William Taylor mentioned in footnotes 207 and 485; for William
H. Taylor, see footnote 388.

504. Anne Gilchrist's letter from Whitman, sent to her at 177 Remsen Street, Brooklyn,
Professor Edwin Haviland Miller dates 6 December 1878 (see *The Correspondence of Walt
Whitman,* III, 140); 112 Madison Avenue, New York City, was Herbert Gilchrist's address (see
*ibid.,* III, 147n and 150–151).

505. Unidentifiable.

506. Whitman ordered a work-basket for Louisa Orr Whitman (see the poet's letter,
*The Correspondence of Walt Whitman,* III, 143); Mr Judson was an employee.

507. Joseph Browning married Harry Stafford's sister Deborah; see footnote 323.

508. Whitman's letter to B. Westerman & Co., perhaps having to do with this order, of
9 September 1878, is lost.

509. Whitman's letter to Anne Gilchrist is in *The Correspondence of Walt Whitman,*
III, 138–139; Tennyson's letter to Whitman, III, 134–135; and I cannot find Burroughs's letter.
"Gath: Corn" refers to Walt Whitman, "Gathering the Corn," New York *Tribune,* 24 October
1878 (see footnote 468, above).

510. See footnote 501.

"  letter & piece ("Roaming in Thought") to Geo W Waters,[511]
          Elmira   N   Y


13th to 23[d] inclusive – Down at White horse
        Harry at Atco[512]

✗  13th  $20 to Lou[513]


                                              ⎛ all paid ⎞ $5 more
"  $15 to Mr Twoes[514] for on acc't clothes – ⎜ $17 due ⎟  paid
                                              ⎝ in full ⎠  Jan 2
    saw Fred: Vaughan[515] in Chestnut street Phil:    $12 due [cancelled in
                                                              blue pencil]

Nov 24 (Sunday)   letters to Mrs Stafford [516]


"          buttons & riband to Ruthey[517]


"          papers to Geo: S [518]


"          circ: to Little & Brown, Boston


"          postal cart to Wm H Taylor[519]


"          circ to E   G   Appleget   563 Walnut st   Camden[520]


"          postal to J   B   Marvin   Wash'n[521]


"    two little oil paintings recd – one by Mr Dyke, one Col J [522]

511.  Whitman's letter to George W. Waters is in *The Correspondence of Walt Whitman*, III, 139; "Roaming in Thought" is a two-line poem, published in the 1881 *Leaves of Grass* (see the Comprehensive Reader's Edition, p. 274).
512.  See the note on Harry Stafford in *The Correspondence of Walt Whitman*, III, 133.
513.  Whitman's board payment to his sister-in-law.
514.  Whitman's tailor: see footnote 145.
515.  A New York driver: see footnote 66.
516.  These are lost.
517.  Mrs Susan Stafford's daughter Ruth (1866–1939), later Mrs William Goldy.
518.  George Stafford, the father of the large family.
519.  See footnotes 388 and 503; this post card is lost.
520.  Unidentifiable.
521.  Joseph B. Marvin was in the Internal Revenue Service in March 1879; he visited Whitman on 24 February 1879 (see entry below). They were old Washington friends (see footnote 81).
522.  Colonel John R. Johnston was a Camden artist with a studio in Philadelphia, whom Whitman called "the jolliest man I ever met, an artist, a great talker, but real, first-rate, off-hand cheerfulness & *comical-sensible* talk — a man of good information, too, travelled in Europe — an hour or two does me real good." (See *The Correspondence of Walt Whitman*, II, 256, 322; III, *passim*. He and his wife and children Jack (John, Jr) and Ida were among Whitman's earliest Camden friends and he often went there on Sunday, as seen in this *Daybook*.

Nov 25  sent "Progress" [523] (2 nos) to

      Mary      Pete Doyle         Jeff
      Hannah    Herbert
      Hattie     Beatrice G

"  Harry here evening[524]

26    postal card to John Newton Johnson[525]

         asking
27    letter to  W Reid   for pay for "Gathering Corn" article $10 [526]
                         [in blue pencil, sideways:]   paid

"    sent piece "Three Young Men's Deaths" $12
       to Mr John Frazer, Tobacco Plant,
       Liverpool — thro Josiah Child [527]

"    "  wrote to Josiah Child [528]

                                    [132]

[On slips of paper, pasted on page:]

    Trubner & Co: [529]    [in blue pencil]        [in blue pencil,
      June 27 '79 – acc't with Trübner & Co   now    sideways:]  paid
    ————————————————————— stands          all

They owe me, (acc't to me for)
37 Vols. at $3.50 – (36 Vols went June 27 '79 by J   B
                  Lippincott)
& 46 Dem. Vistas at 37 cts (all previous dues paid
                     me up to June '79)
    —————————————

    March 4, 1880 – rec'd to-day from T & Co:    [in blue pencil,
      draft for $37.22 – which leaves now in their hands    sideways:]  paid
      to be acct'd on,   27 Vols. at $3.50 — & 40 Dem Vistas @ 37
    ———————————— [rule in blue pencil]

523. "Thou who has slept all night upon the storm" (later called "To the Man-of-War Bird") was published in Philadelphia *Progress,* 16 November 1878 (see footnote 497, above). Whitman sent copies to his sisters Mary Van Nostrand, Hannah Heyde, his niece Mannahatta, his brother Jeff, and his friends Peter Doyle, Herbert Gilchrist, and Beatrice Gilchrist.
524. Harry Stafford was Whitman's closest friend during this period.
525. This card to Whitman's correspondent in Mid, Alabama (see footnote 9a) is lost.
526. See *The Correspondence of Walt Whitman,* III, 140, for the letter to Whitelaw Reid of the New York *Tribune.*
527. Whitman's "Three Young Men's Deaths" (later in *Specimen Days* — see *Prose Works 1892,* I, 155–158) was published in *Cope's Tobacco Plant,* II (April 1879), 318–319. See *The Correspondence of Walt Whitman,* III, 140–141n.
528. This letter is lost.
529. These notations of British sales of *Leaves of Grass, Two Rivulets,* and *Democratic*

July 22, '80 – (at London, Canada) – Rec'd to-day $80.50
  from Trübner & Co — leaves the acc't now – he has to
  acc't to me for. 4 Vols (T  R ) – at $3.50 & 40 Dem Vistas

                              order'd from Canada through Harpers
July 26 '80     Has now to acc't to me for 20 Vols L   of G ∧ &
  14 Vols T   R – 34 Vols. altogether at $3.50 @ Vol: also 40
  Dem Vistas @ 37 cts

                                                      March 4 '81
March 4, 1881 — Rec'd from Trübner & Co: $105.37          due me
    which leaves due (4 copies bound books & 39 Vistas   $28.43
also I send     through Lippincott 20 Vols, 13   L       70.00
    of G. & 7 T R.   at $3.50 —$.70 ———————
                        due me from all these $98.43

ab't Oct 1 '81 sent letter from Boston – ab't copyright for new ed'n[530]

Dec 8th 81 – Rec'd from T & Co. $80.50
              Dec. '81
☞ leaving now ∧ due me     39 Dem Vistas (@ 37cts – $14.43)[531]
                              ⟍ all paid in full ⟋

[Calling card, pasted in, of Model Photograph Parlors, Nos. 52 and 54 N.
Eighth St., Philadelphia.]
[Only line on *Daybook* page itself:]

Express Office – 314 E
            1324 Federal

                                                            [133]

'78 [in pencil]
Nov 29 – to – Dec 6 – down at White Horse

Dec 6 – sent postal card to Mrs Gil: Brooklyn[532]

*Vistas* show how closely Whitman kept up with his book sales and how relatively complete
his records were. See *The Correspondence of Walt Whitman,* III, 137n.
    530.   See Whitman's letter to Trübner & Company, 5 October 1881, in *The Correspondence
of Walt Whitman,* III, 247–248.
    531.   Trübner & Company ceased being Whitman's London publishers or agents and
were replaced by David Bogue; see Whitman letter to James R. Osgood & Company, 8 December 1881, in *The Correspondence of Walt Whitman,* III, 255.
    532.   This is in *The Correspondence of Walt Whitman,* III, 140.

Dec 6 – rec'd draft $47:55   from Trübner & Co. (through
      Josiah Child) – this pays for 6 of the ten sets I
      sent Oct 1 — & leaves 4 sets pay ($28) due me –
      — also 46 Dem: Vistas @$^{cts}$ 37 —— [533]
  "   rec'd pay $10 from Whitelaw Reid for "Gathering Corn" article[534]

8th   paper to Mont – (breakfast at J  M  S ) [535]

  "   postal to J  H  Johnston[536]

9th   letter to Dr & Mrs Bucke, N  Y  Hotel [537]

10th   photos to Josiah Child – letter also – [538]

    "     Cecil C Brooks

    "     W  J  Ham Smith[539]

  "   paper to Mrs Gilchrist[540]

  "   "   " Beatrice[541]

11th  evening with Dr and Mrs Bucke at Conti-
      nental hotel  Phil:  Dr's book "Moral
      Nature of Man" — dedication to me – [542]
  (bro't a set of books for Dr Beemer)

12th  note to G  W  C.   (ans. retd 50) [543]

---

533.  See Whitman to Josiah Child, *The Correspondence of Walt Whitman*, III, 140.
534.  See footnote 468.
535.  Mont is Montgomery Stafford (see footnote 231); J M S is James Matlack Scovel (see footnote 71), Whitman's usual Sunday host.
536.  This letter to Whitman's New York friend is lost.
537.  This letter is lost.
538.  Whitman's letter, thanking Child for the Trübner & Company payment and saying he was sending photographs, is in *The Correspondence of Walt Whitman*, III, 140–141.
539.  The photos to Cecil C. Brooks and W. J. Ham Smith apparently were requested by Josiah Child (see *The Correspondence of Walt Whitman*, III, 141).
540.  Whitman had sent her a post card on 6 December and a letter on 12 December — both listed here in the *Daybook* and quoted in full in *The Correspondence of Walt Whitman*, III, 140 and 142 — and must have sent her his "Gathering Corn" piece in the 24 October New York *Tribune* or the "Man-of-War Bird" poem in the Philadelphia *Progress* of 16 November.
541.  Probably the same papers went to Dr Beatrice Gilchrist as Whitman sent her mother (see footnote 540).
542.  Whitman told Anne Gilchrist about his evening with the Bucke's; see *The Correspondence of Walt Whitman*, III, 142, where Professor Edwin Haviland Miller also cites the dedication to the poet.
543.  An incomplete draft of this note to George W. Childs, co-owner of the Philadelphia *Public Ledger*, is in *The Correspondence of Walt Whitman*, III, 142; see entry below for 17

"     "     to Mrs Gilchrist [544]

"   letter to John Burroughs enc: Tennyson's letter[545]

"   also criticism of New Quart: Mag: London[546]

[134]

Jos: C   Baldwin   (his folks too) Louella Del: Co: Penn[547]

---

Edw'd Carpenter, 17 Holland Terrace                    [two lines, underneath, in
        Highfields                                                WW's hand:]
           Sheffield, Eng     Mrs Barrow ("Aunt Fanny")
[In pencil, on slip of paper, pasted on top of                    30 East 35th Street
  other writing:]
        [?]
    J   W   Whilldin   [not WW's hand]
  Wm Riggans   Captain   [not WW's hand]
        John More, the druggist   [WW's hand, in ink]
  Thos Ford      Engineer [not WW's hand]      [sideways in margin:]
     Howard       [WW's hand in ink]           breakfast again
  J  H  Wilson     Purser [not WW's hand]           Apr 18, '80
    No 34 S. Delaware Ave       [not WW's hand]
        Phila., Pa   [not WW's hand]

Dec 22 '78 [548]

George   Coffman[549]
    177 Edwards Street, 16th Ward   Phila

---

December 1878 about the 50 pair of gloves Childs sent.
    544.  See footnote 540.
    545.  See this letter in *The Correspondence of Walt Whitman*, III, 141–142; Tennyson's letter, *ibid.*, III, 134–135.
    546.  Josiah Child had sent Whitman the *New Quarterly Magazine* (London), which the poet described as "a muddled sort of criticism in a late English magazine, of no particular interest" (*The Correspondence of Walt Whitman*, III, 141), and he sent the magazine to Burroughs.
    547.  See footnote 471; Joseph C. Baldwin and his family apparently lived in Louella, Delaware County, Pennsylvania.
    548.  During a Sunday breakfast which Whitman had on the Baltimore steamboat, "Whilldin" on 22 December 1878 (see entry for that date) with Johnny Wilson, the purser, he must have asked the captain of the ship and others in the crew to sign a slip, which he later pasted in his *Daybook;* when he got home Whitman sent Wilson his photograph and a copy of *Memoranda During the War.* About a year and a half later, on 18 April 1880, he had breakfast again with Johnny Wilson on board the same boat (see notation in the margin here, and the entry for 18 April 1880, below).
    549.  Whitman wrote to George Coffman on 15 December 1878 (see entry that date) and sent a photograph, but the letter is lost.

Gloves[550]

| | |
|---|---|
| Charley Saunders | John Burroughs |
| Harry Cooper | Smith Caswell |
| Taylor Willans | Andy Sweetin (express) |
| Ansel Van Nostrand | Charley Wood |
| Wilson Bray | Wm Wood |
| Aaron Watson | Tommy Jackson |
| Jo Kline | John Williamson (on cars |
| Peter Doyle    recd | John                    (on stage |
|              [in blue | |
| Jerry              pencil] | Francis Warren |
| John Chew              on cars | Geo Jackson |
|              [in pencil] | |
| ?                     on cars | John                on stage |
| | Hudson Greenleaf |
| | Wm Edwards (George's farm) |

Bill Williams [in red ink] ─────

1881 – Charley Van Mater          1881– G  W   Jackson
    John Davis                                   Charley  Wood
    Sam
    Jack  McLaughlin
    Pete Davis?
      Ol Wood

[135]

Dec '78

13th   papers to Sister Hannah

"          "     Herbert

"          "     Hattie

"          "     Geo: Stafford [551]

15th sent Geo: Coffman letter & photo:[552]

550. These 25 pairs of gloves, which Whitman got from George W. Childs (see footnote 543), he gave as Christmas presents to his brother-in-law, Ansel Van Nostrand, old friends, John Burroughs, Peter Doyle, Smith Caswell (Burroughs's hired man), and horse car drivers or other relatively casual friends. Of all the rest here named, William Edwards boarded at the Stafford farm, and Charley Woods and William Woods got letters from Whitman on his Western trip in 1879. Again in 1881, as listed here, he gave horse car drivers eight more pairs (at Christmas?), and the only person even partly identifiable is Charley Woods, who got a pair in 1878 and whom Whitman knew well enough to send a card or letter to on his 1879 trip to the West and St Louis.

551. These "papers" Whitman sent his sister Hannah Heyde, niece Mannahatta, and friends Herbert Gilchrist and George Stafford may have been those mentioned in footnote 540, above.

552. See footnote 549.

17<sup>th</sup> rec'd 50 from G   W   C for the drivers' gloves[553]

18 recd letter from John Burroughs[554]

20<sup>th</sup>   sent Mary the big Bible – gloves to Ans:        [in blue pencil, sideways,
      – portrait of father,      & 6 or 7 photos of self        across three lines:]
         – with Mem: of War, for the girls, & George[555]            recd
         – wrote letter

"   wrote to Miss J   L   Gilder, 148 East 18<sup>th</sup> St   N   Y.

22   wrote to Miss Gilder[556]

"   Christian Union to Hattie

"   Progress to Han[557]

"   papers to Mr & Mrs Stafford

22 Sunday breakfast with Johnny Wilson
      on the "Whildin"   Baltimore   Steamboat[558]

"   Photo & Mem: of War to Johnny Wilson
      34 s Delaware av.   [in blue pencil, sideways:]   recd

23 papers to John M   Rogers

"      "   to Mont[559]

"   evening at Col. Johnstons   Charles Peterson   and
         Milliard   Shute –[560]

"   letter to Sister Han[561] — (purse & $ 2)   [in blue pencil, sideways:] recd

---

553.  See footnotes 543 and 550.
554.  This letter is lost, but Whitman's reply of 23–25 December 1878 is in *The Correspondence of Walt Whitman,* III, 143–144.
555.  These were Christmas presents to members of Whitman's family, Mary Van Nostrand (his sister), Ansel Van Nostrand (her husband), their daughters, and Whitman's brother George; Whitman's letter of this date is lost. The Bible that Whitman gave Mary contained a record of the family and the source for Katharine Molinoff's *Some Notes on Whitman's Family* (Brooklyn, 1941).
556.  This letter is lost, as well as the one to Jeannette L. Gilder on 20 December 1878, though Whitman refers to the letter in his 23–25 December Burroughs letter.
557.  Whitman's sister Hannah apparently had not yet been sent his poem on "The Man-of-War Bird" in the Philadelphia *Progress,* 16 November 1878.
558.  See footnote 548, and the next entry below for 22 December 1878.
559.  For Montgomery Stafford, see footnote 231; for John M. Rogers, see footnote 260.
560.  See footnote 522; I cannot identify these two friends of Colonel Johnston's, although Shute is mentioned below as a "banjoist at Johnny Johnson's."
561.  This letter to Hannah Heyde is missing.

[136]

Baggesen's gade
Rudolf Schmidt   Baggesen's ~~Gate~~   No 3   [in red ink]
    16 Klareboderne
        Copenhagen   Denmark[562]

---

Roden Noel
    Maybury   Woking Station
        Surrey   Eng:[563]

---

S  W   Green   Printer[564]   (? his son has the
    18 Jacob Street — NY                business now)

---

James Berry   porter, old, one wooden leg – Pen RR Phil[565]

---

Jesse E Baker
    Bower's Hill   Norfolk   Co:   Va:
        "old dominion   Burgundy"[566]

---

J. O'B. Inman, Stamford, Conn:[567]

---

Illman Bros:   Steel plate printers
    605 Arch   Phila

---

        John L   Wilson[568]
purser "Whilldin" steamer      34 S Delaware av
                                    Phil

---

            his brother Porley
Edward Chamberlain     (young man   that went to "Diplomacy"
            with the Scovels & self)[569]

562.  See the beginning of footnote 81.
563.  Roden Noel, English poet and critic, to whom Whitman sent *Leaves of Grass* and *Two Rivulets* on 5 September 1876 (see footnote 77, above, and *The Correspondence of Walt Whitman,* III, 60n). See also *Walt Whitman Review,* XX (September 1974), 117.
564.  Samuel W. Green printed 600 copies of *Leaves of Grass* in May 1876; see Whitman's letter to him, *The Correspondence of Walt Whitman,* III, 43; Green's letter is in the Feinberg Collection.
565.  This is an unusual entry, inasmuch as most of the names and addresses in this *Daybook* are of friends, relatives, buyers of Whitman's books, and young men, not old ones.
566.  In an advertisement, nationally distributed in 1962, of Old Crow Kentucky Bourbon, Whitman is pictured with a gift of Old Crow in 1891; Whitman certainly liked champagne, and this entry in the *Daybook* suggests an interest in Old Dominion Burgundy.
567.  John O'B. Inman was a painter who did a portrait of Whitman's father (see entry below for 30–31 December 1878).
568.  See footnote 548 for Whitman's Sunday breakfast on the "Whilldin."
569.  Whitman saw "Diplomacy" on 15 October 1878 (see footnote 479); Edward and

Adin Millard   young man   at   The: Bear (deep bass voice)
Milliard Shute      "         "      banjoist at Johnny Johnson's[570]
Jesse Bassett, little 7 year old boy – Stevens & Fifth St

---

tanner
Jos'C   Reed, 22ᵈ st.        born 1819 too[571]

[137]

Dec. '78
25th   letter from Herbert – sent him postal card[572]        [in blue pencil, sideways:]   recd

"      wrote to John Burroughs   Roxbury   Del   Co   N Y[573]

27   wrote to Mrs Pratt   (Wide Awake) with corrections
         on Mrs Fs "Poets Homes"[574]   [sideways:]   recd
      cold spell   24ᵗʰ 5, 6ᵗʰ, 7ᵗʰ & 8ᵗʰ & 9ᵗʰ        [in blue pencil]

29ᵗʰ (Sunday)   breakfast & dinner at J   M   S's
         papers to Mont:[575]

30th   postal to Herbert G

"      "      Jenny Gilder[576]

31   visit from Harry – has left Atco[577]

30th, 31st &c.   John Inman paints portrait
                              of father for me[578]
      letter from Sister Mary — also Han[579]

x1879 – Jan. paid   J   F   Baker for the Sunday
      paid in full   [in blue pencil]

Porley Chamberlain cannot be otherwise identified.
    570.  Whitman met Milliard Shute at Colonel Johnston's (see footnote 560).
    571.  Another of Whitman's notations of people he saw on the streets and, for some strange reason or compulsion, got their addresses and some brief information; he might well ask a boy how old he is, but a 59-year-old man?
    572.  Herbert Gilchrist's letter to Whitman is lost, but the poet's post card is in *The Correspondence of Walt Whitman*, III, 144.
    573.  See footnote 554.
    574.  Mrs Mary E. Wager-Fisher's "Poet's Homes: Walt Whitman" appeared in *Wide Awake Pleasure Book*, February 1878 (see footnote 214); Whitman's letter to Mrs Charles Stuart Pratt, editor of *Wide Awake Pleasure Book*, is lost.
    575.  This time Whitman added dinner to his usual breakfast at James Matlack Scovel's; the papers went to Montgomery Stafford.
    576.  Both post cards, to Herbert Gilchrist and Jeannette L. Gilder, are lost.
    577.  See footnote 512.
    578.  Inman is mentioned above, footnote 567.
    579.  Both of these letters are lost.

Jan:        papers (79^{cts}) up to date —

x 2   paid Mr Twoes (Harry) $5 – (leaves $12 due) [580]

[in blue pencil, sideways:]  paid in full

"   pleasant supper   Mr & Mrs Scovel (splendid wood
fire)

"   bright, very cold night – gale all night

Jan 2, 3 & 4, 5, 6     bitter cold – continuous gales     [in blue pencil]
rec'd postal card from John Bur:   gloves arrived [581]     [in pencil]

3  return'd bad letter to C  L  H.[582]     [in pencil]

[in blue pencil, sideways:]  retd

4  letter to Mrs Scovel, enclosing Tennyson's[583]
& slips

10th   Hunter hung for murder[583a]

"   papers to Elmer & Mont [583b]

[138]

[On large slip, with smaller slip and clipping on top:]
Dec 24 '78 – gave the post office
men (carriers &c) each a copy of
"War Memoranda" [584]
Wm  Dorman
John  Klopper
          Cowan
Robt  McGown   delivery clerk
Charles  Parker
John  Smith

[Rest of this sheet cannot be read, as it is covered by two slips:]

580.  As H. B. Twoes was Whitman's tailor, this $17 was for clothes for Harry Stafford.
581.  These were among the 25 pairs of gloves (from George W. Childs) which Whitman gave as Christmas presents (see footnote 550).
582.  Charles L. Heyde, married to Whitman's sister Hannah; Whitman had little use for him. Hannah's letter to Whitman, 2 January 1879, is in the Library of Congress.
583.  Whitman sent this letter, printed in *The Correspondence of Walt Whitman*, III, 134–135, to a number of his friends; it is now in the University of Texas Library.
583a.  Benjamin Hunter had been convicted on 3 July 1878 of the murder of John Armstrong; Whitman had written Harry Stafford on 6 July 1878, "Well, I see Hunter was convicted

[On a slip about C. H. Sholes, short-hand reporter, Council Bluffs, Iowa, WW has four lines in pencil:]

> admirer of L  of  G – bo't the book
> (ardent letter
>          from him March '80)
>                    Des Moines and
>          another letter June '80 [585]

[On larger slip, to which above is attached, is name (not in WW's hand) and address, in pencil:]

> Jerome E. Sharp,
> 27. Nth 6th St.
> Philada

[Sideways:]    Sunday – Feb 2 – at J M S's[586]
[At bottom:]    Edward Conners (humpty – dumpty)
[On page itself:]    Geo: W Waters    artist
                Elmira  N  Y [587]

[139]

Jan: 1879

12 (Sunday)   papers to Sister Hannah
    "        Ed: Cattell
    "        John  Burroughs
    "        W  S  Fullerton
    "        Jo Baldwin
    "        Mont[588]

13th    sent photo to Cathcart Taylor[589]
postal card to Mrs Gilchrist[590]

— we will see now whether he is hung" (*The Correspondence of Walt Whitman*, III, 127).

583b.  Elmer E. Stafford (see footnote 232); Montgomery Stafford (see footnote 231).

584.  Whitman's short-title for, of course, *Memorandum During the War*.

585.  This letter prompted a reply from Whitman: see *The Correspondence of Walt Whitman*, III, 181. C. H. Sholes's letters to Whitman are lost.

586.  Breakfast, as usual, with James Matlack Scovel.

587.  See footnote 151.

588.  Of these six people, Whitman's sister Hannah Heyde, John Burroughs, Montgomery Stafford (see footnote 231), and Joseph C. Baldwin (see footnotes 471 and 547) often received these papers; Edward Cattell (see *The Correspondence of Walt Whitman*, III, 77n) and W. S. Fullerton of Greeley, Colorado (see footnote 432) did not hear from Whitman so often.

589.  Unidentifiable.

590.  Although Professor Edwin Haviland Miller (*The Correspondence of Walt Whitman*, III, 147n) says Whitman did not write Anne Gilchrist until 27 March 1879, he lists a lost letter of 13 January 1879, which is this post card.

x  "   paid Lou $10 [591]

19th papers to Sister Han — Elmer S [592]

22   Harry here[593]

"   wrote to Nancy[594] — sent $5    [in blue pencil, sideways:] recd

26 wrote to John Burroughs[595]

27 – papers to Scotty Fullerton – also to Will Tinker[596]

"   visit from Hugh Harrop
          Howard  Rupert
      &     Will Cannon[597]

paper to John M Rogers[598]

Feb 1 .   Saturday night reception at Mr.
          Childs's  Phila[599]

2  Sunday – breakfast at J   M   S [600]
          Jerome Sharp[601]
               paid
George's picture      Spieler $3 – Johnston $4 – frame 1.30 [602]

---

591.   To Louisa Orr Whitman for Whitman's board.
592.   The fact that Whitman had sent papers to his sister Hannah Heyde just one week before shows how often he was in touch with her; Elmer E. Stafford also got papers nine days previously.
593.   Another visit from Harry Stafford, Whitman's closest friend at this time.
594.   This letter is lost; Nancy most likely is Nancy Whitman, who was married to the poet's brother Andrew (who died in 1863 at the age of 36); she was a whore and an alcoholic; see *The Correspondence of Walt Whitman*, II, 42n.
595.   A letter to Burroughs, dated 25 January 1879 is in *The Correspondence of Walt Whitman*, III, 146; it must be this letter.
596.   Scotty Fullerton is the same W. S. Fullerton whom Whitman sent papers to on 12 January 1879; for Will Tinker, also of Greeley, Colorado, see footnotes 267, 291, and 447.
597.   Hugh Harrop, whom Whitman sent papers to on 15 and 28 April 1878 (see entries above) and is not identifiable, apparently visited the poet in Camden with two friends; Whitman wrote to William Cannon (of Stevens Street Dredging Company) on 29 April 1879, but this letter is lost; Howard B. Rupert (see below) was an iron weigher from Kaign's Point.
598.   See footnote 260.
599.   Whitman's letter to George W. Childs, publisher of the Philadelphia *Public Ledger*, 31 January 1879, accepting the invitation to the reception, is in *The Correspondence of Walt Whitman*, III, 146.
600.   As usual, with James Matlack Scovel.
601.   Jerome E. Sharp, whom Whitman apparently met at Scovel's, wrote his name and address on a slip of paper, and Whitman inserted it in his *Daybook*, opposite this entry.
602.   Jake Spieler took pictures of Mannahatta Whitman (see end of footnote 76) and also of Whitman (see footnote 201); here it is difficult to know if "George's picture" means a

|   |   | [in blue | | [in ink:] |
|---|---|---|---|---|
|   |   | pencil and | paid recd | good letter |
| 6 | sent <u>Two</u> <u>Riv</u>: to John Hardie | pencil, | all | from J Hardie |
|   | 6 Finnart st.   Greenock   Scotland | sideways:] | recd | recd in St L[603] |

9th (Sunday) evening at Mrs Odenheimer's[604]
  papers to Sister Hannah

    "    "  Mrs Gilchrist

    "       Mont[605]

                                            [140]

[On small slip at top of page:]
~~Bolger~~ Bolger,[606] (also reporter Times)

---

   Morgan    "

Louis N. Megargee  [not in WW's hand]

Dec: '78 )
      Philada "Times"  [not in WW's hand]
    Dr Lambdin, <u>the</u> <u>cad</u> [607]

[Rest of material on page itself:]
   Young man called Jan 27
   Hugh L Harrop[608]

photograph of George Whitman, or (most likely) one of Walt for George; it is also not clear which Johnston was paid $4 — it may have been to John H. Johnston for a gold or silver frame; if so, what is the $1.30 for a frame?

603. Both Whitman's letter from John Hardie, 3 November 1879, and Whitman's to Hardie are lost.

604. Whitman sent Mrs Odenheimer a copy of his "Gathering the Corn" (see footnotes 484, 485, 486), but I cannot identify her, except that she is obviously someone living near Camden or Philadelphia.

605. Montgomery Stafford.

606. This may well be Peter Bolger, a reporter on the Philadelphia *Times,* to whom Whitman sent a note on 29 May 1884; see *The Correspondence of Walt Whitman,* III, 371; Morgan and Louis N. Megargee also are *Times* reporters, most likely.

607. A. C. Lambdin was a managing editor of the Philadelphia *Times* who opposed *Leaves of Grass* bitterly and malignantly; Whitman said to Horace Traubel: "Have you ever experienced the rankest enmity of one who opposed you with all weapons honest and dishonest without seeming to know why: with no square reason opposed you: you, you, just you — foull, bitterly, you: men who find a stab in the back none too good to use in furthering their malicious designs? I have always regarded Lambdin as that kind of an enemy. . . . [His] is downright personal vituperation and assault . . . of the offensive personal order" (*With Walt Whitman in Camden,* II, 508–509).

608. See footnote 597; Whitman gives only three visitors there, here he adds a fourth, Walter Baxter, an iron weigher of Kaign's Point.

Howard B Rupert, Kaign's Point (iron weigher)
Walter Baxter          "          "
William  Cannon  Stevens St.  Dredging Co:

---

Walter Rowand, ("Schooner")
John R  Rowand, Kirkwood, S's brother[609]

---

Mrs  Cooper, 107  Lexington av  N  Y[610]
                    Feb '79

---

pulverized charcoal
Sam'l Thackara,  ∧ Medford, Burlington  Co  N  J
(bro: Dan'l T.  Mullica Hill – Lima beans)

---

202  2N  Race
Mr Bender, hatter     308 Cherry St.   Phil
           1126 1928  Columbia av  Phil[611]
                [in red ink]
————————————————————————  [rule in red ink]
           Lucy
Mrs Hine ∧ 432 Chapel St   New Haven[612]

[141]

Feb. 1879

10 – Harry here[613]

   pieces sent Mr Alden, Harpers — sent back[614]

14 papers to Harry Stafford

609. Walter ("Schooner") and John R. Rowand are obviously two brothers whom Whitman met on one of his visits to the Stafford farm at White Horse, near Kirkwood.
610. Whitman may have met Mrs Cooper at the George W. Childs reception on 1 February 1879.
611. As Whitman used the *Daybook* to list people whom he met, well-known friends, and merchants and workers to remind himself of things he had to buy or services needed doing, it isn't clear whether these three, Samuel Thackara, Daniel Thackara, and Mr Bender are acquaintances or otherwise.
612. Mrs Lucy Hine was the wife of the artist, Charles W. Hine, who died on 4 August 1871. Hine painted a portrait of Whitman in 1860, now in Brooklyn College.
613. Whitman referred to Harry Stafford's visits in his letter to Beatrice Gilchrist, 21 February 1879 — *The Correspondence of Walt Whitman,* III, 148.
614. The pieces that were rejected by Henry M. Alden, editor of *Harper's Monthly,* could have been "Three Young Men's Deaths," published in *Cope's Tobacco Plant,* II (April 1879), 318–319, reprinted in *Specimen Days* (see footnote 462, above), or some other articles, such as "February Days," which went into *Specimen Days* in 1881; the only other article for 1879 is "These May Afternoons," in the New York *Tribune,* 23 May 1879, which certainly could not have been written in February.

"        Prof Dowden (Shakspere)

"        Sister  Hannah

"        Sister  Mary

        Amos Cooper

"        John Burroughs[615]

(Valentines to Amy Dowe, WW Connelly
        A B Frazee, Walter Lee[616]  )

16    wrote to S H Morse,[617] Boston    ⎰ head rec'd⎱
"    papers to Jeff, John Rogers[618]    ⎰ bad – wretchedly bad⎱

18    wrote to Jas   Vick   florist Rochester   N Y[619]
        paper to Harry[620]
        – met J H J and Mr. Burbank – hour at Guy's[621]

19    papers to Sister Mary

21    papers to Harry – wrote to Beatrice[622]

24th   visit from J B Marvin of Wash'n[623]

25    "L of G" and "Mem War" to Jas Vick Jr Rochester[624]    [in blue pencil,
                        N Y     sideways:]   recd

615.    The newcomer to this list of six is Professor Edward Dowden of the University of Dublin (see footnote 9), and the papers Whitman sent him (having to do with Shakespeare) must have been different from those to Harry Stafford, his two sisters, Burroughs, and Amos Cooper (who had not heard from Whitman since August 1878).

616.    Of these three men and one girl, to whom Whitman sent Valentines, Amy Dowe (see footnote 245) was the 5-year-old daughter of Emma Dowe, sister of Louisa Orr Whitman; A. B. Frazee was most likely the 20-year-old deck hand on the Camden-Philadelphia ferry (see footnote 419); W. W. Connelly and Walter Lee I do not know.

617.    For Sidney H. Morse, the sculptor, see footnote 421.

618.    For John Rogers, mentioned often in the *Daybook*, see footnote 260.

619.    This letter is lost.

620.    Harry Stafford, to whom Whitman sent papers on 14 February 1879, was most likely down at White Horse with his parents.

621.    John H. Johnston, the New York jeweler, knew many important people, but I doubt if this Mr Burbank was Luther Burbank, who was born in Massachusetts and would have been 29 years old at this time, as he was making his experiments in California after 1875.

622.    This letter to Dr Beatrice Gilchrist, replying to hers of 16 February 1879, is in *The Correspondence of Walt Whitman*, III, 148; it is short and says little — about his health, the weather, and the Staffords.

623.    See footnotes 81 and 521.

624.    Other than Whitman wrote to James Vick, Jr, of Rochester, New York, on 18

" sent both Vols to Mrs Hine[625]   [in blue pencil, sideways:] recd

                                   [in blue pencil,

"McLeod of Dare"[626] to Mrs Johnston   sideways:] recd

27  papers to Sister Hannah

     "       Mrs Odenheimer[627]

     "       Grace Gilchrist[628]

     "       W S Fullerton[629]

x28 $10 to Lou[630]

                                          [142]

Hudson Greenleaf  31st & Page Streets  Phila[631]

Mrs Archer's school  1401 Massachusetts av.[632]
        Ed. Mac. Harg,
        1304 South 17th Street,
          Philadelphia.   [these three lines above printed
                        on slip of paper]      Al Swearinger

Clinton Townsend[633]                        1810 Chestnut st
Townsends Inlet                            Mr M Crary's
Cape May C[o]                           go to Cape May in
    N J  [This name and address,          summer
           not in WW's hand, on slip]

March 13 – Met Dr Frank Taylor ⎱
  "      also – Miss Gibbons ⎰ at Forney's[634]

February 1879, and sent him *Leaves of Grass* and *Memoranda During the War* on 25 February, we know no more about him.

    625.  See footnote 612; "both Vols" must mean *Leaves of Grass* and *Memoranda* (not *Two Rivulets*).

    626.  *McLeod of Dare* (London, 1878) was a novel by William Black (1841–1898).

    627.  See footnote 604.

    628.  Grace Gilchrist, whom Whitman called "Giddy," was Anne's younger daughter; although we have no letter from Whitman to her, she is often mentioned in his letters to other Gilchrists — 25 references in *The Correspondence of Walt Whitman*, III.

    629.  See footnote 432.

    630.  Whitman's board money to Louisa Orr Whitman.

    631.  Unidentifiable.

    632.  Whitman's nieces, Mannahatta and Jessie, were at Mrs Archer's Patapsco Seminary, Ellicott City, Maryland, in October 1877; this may be the same Mrs Archer.

    633.  Captain Vandoren Townsend was married to George Stafford's sister, and Clinton Townsend may well be related to him; see footnote 352.

    634.  Colonel John W. Forney was Whitman's Philadelphia publisher friend who accompanied him later this year on his Western trip (see footnote 193).

12th   Dinner at Finelli's – Horace Furness[635]
          — Roberts, the sculptor[636]

---

Lewis More[637]                     [Printed card:] E. D. Carpenter[638]
RR man I meet on the ferry              Grain Broker
     friend of Pete's                    39 Pearl Street,
                                                New York.

---

                                    gade
Rudolf Schmidt[639]  ⋎  Baggesen's g̶a̶t̶e̶   No 3
                   N̶o̶ ̶3̶   Nowdao   C̶o̶p̶Copenhagen
[Two lines in red ink:]                 Den
Mr & Mrs Vanderslice (where Nat Jones is)[640]
      hakkim  (doctor)

                                                                    [143]

1879 – March

 2ᵈ   papers to Hatta[641]

 "     Saml Cox, boy 18, born at Wilmington – (met at RR depot
                Sunday morning) looks – Johnny Gaul   newsboy
                              3ᵈ & Market
                              Phila:[642]

4th   Harry here[643]

6th sent <u>Progress</u> to Han, Mary, Jeff, Hatta,
      Grace Gilchrist, Dr Bucke, John Burroughs,[644]
      Emma & family here[645]

---

635.  Horace Howard Furness was a Shakespearean editor (see footnote 369).
636.  Howard Roberts (1843–1900) met Whitman at this dinner, and on 15 April 1880 the poet sent him *Leaves of Grass*; see *The Correspondence of Walt Whitman*, III, 175.
637.  One often meets this sort of name in the *Daybook*, but at least this man knew a good friend of Whitman's, Peter Doyle.
638.  Why would Whitman keep the card of a grain broker?
639.  For Rudolph Schmidt see the beginning of footnote 81.
640.  Nathaniel G. Jones was one of the many friends to whom Whitman wrote on his Western trip late in 1879, but this letter (or post card) is lost.
641.  Mannahatta Whitman, Walt's niece and Jeff's daughter, as seen in the *Daybook*, is referred to as Hattie, Hatty, and Hatta.
642.  Another of the numerous instances in Whitman's *Daybook*, where he writes the name, and sometimes a very brief description, of boys he meets in various places; almost never do their names turn up again.
643.  Harry Stafford.
644.  To his sisters Hannah Heyde and Mary Van Nostrand, his brother Jeff, his niece Mannahatta, and his friends Grace Gilchrist (Anne's youngest daughter), Dr Richard Maurice Bucke, and John Burroughs, Whitman sent copies of the Philadelphia *Progress* for 16 November 1878, containing his poem, "To the Man-of-War Bird" (see footnote 497, above).
645.  This was the family of Louisa Orr Whitman's sister, Mrs Emma Dowe; for Amy

9th – papers to Clinton Townsend [646] – (again 12th $\Big)$
                                                     again 16 $\Big/$

14th Letter from Harry – papers to him[647]

"     paper to Hannah – 18th letter to her[648]

18    sent L of  G, also two Photos to
          Wm Harrison Riley,[649] St George's Farm
               Totley, near Sheffield, Eng:
                    for John Ruskin
          Ed Cattell here[650]

19    sent L of  G  & T  R  to Wm O'Connor[651]

24   X  Lou   20 [652]

27th   wrote to Johnston[653] N Y, papers to Hannah
               Marvin   Wash      "   Clinton Townsend [654]
          J Burroughs[655]   "
          Mrs Gilchrist[656]
          D L Proudfit  box 1124  N  Y[657]

Dowe, Emma's daughter, to whom Whitman sent a Valentine on 14 February 1879, see foot-note 245.

646.  See footnote 633.

647.  This letter from Harry Stafford to Whitman is lost.

648.  This letter to Hannah Heyde is lost.

649.  See Whitman's letter to William Harrison Riley, who addressed the poet as "My dear Friend and Master," *The Correspondence of Walt Whitman*, III, 148–149.

650.  Edward Cattell lived on the Stafford farm; he had not seen Whitman for some time; see *The Correspondence of Walt Whitman*, III, 77, for a letter Whitman wrote him on 24 January 1877.

651.  This is the *Daybook's* first mention, with sending *Leaves of Grass* and *Two Rivulets*, of William Douglas O'Connor (1832–1889), author of *The Good Gray Poet* and one of Whitman's greatest friends; Whitman and O'Connor had a quarrel in 1872, which led to a ten-year estrangement, and hence on 19 March 1879 they were not speaking. See Florence B. Freedman, "New Light on an Old Quarrel: Walt Whitman and William Douglas O'Connor 1872," *Walt Whitman Review*, XI (June 1965), 27–52.

652.  The usual board money from Whitman to his sister-in-law Louisa Orr Whitman.

653.  This letter to John H. Johnston is lost, as is the one on the next line to Joseph B. Marvin.

654.  See footnote 633.

655.  The letter to John Burroughs, sent to Washington in care of Joseph B. Marvin, is in *The Correspondence of Walt Whitman*, III, 150.

656.  This letter to Anne Gilchrist, Whitman's first reply to five letters from her, is in *The Correspondence of Walt Whitman*, III, 150–151.

657.  This letter to Daniel L. Proudfit is lost; a letter from him to Whitman, ordering books, 14 March 1883, is in the Feinberg Collection.

28th   sent L   of   G   to J Wm Thompson $5 due   [sideways:] rec'd
    Goldsmith Building   Temple   London[658]      paid

"   slips to D   M   Zimmerman   R R [659]

"   papers to Harry[660]

[144]

Harry White   Adams Ex   Phil – (in Race st)[661]
Edward P   Cattell   Glenolden   Del Co   Pa[662]   [in pencil]

. Drivers – &c[663]
Jo Cline, on Stevens St and all – been a RR man, 21 accidents
Phil — Market st —— Aug 20 '79 — open car driver — Thos Collins
                           Del:man Vangezells wife his
                                         sister
Walter Day   Stevens st                      dead
Phila: Market st.   28th to 32d – hill boy – Alfred Childs   Aug
                                        '79

658. James William Thompson, to whom Whitman sent *Leaves of Grass*, paid $5.00 for the book on 16 June; Whitman wrote to him on 28 November 1879, 4 February, and 18 March 1880, but all letters are lost; his letter to Whitman, ordering books, 20 January 1880, is in the Feinberg Collection.

659. See middle of footnote 76: D. M. Zimmerman issued Whitman his railway passes.

660. Harry Stafford. This is the last entry for March 1879 in the *Daybook*, but in *Walt Whitman's Diary in Canada* (Boston, 1904), pp. 59–60, is the following paragraph in the section "From Other Journals of Walt Whitman":

THE ENGLISH SPARROWS. *March 30, '79, Sunday forenoon, 10, 11, etc.* The window where I sit (after a good breakfast with my hospitable friends Mr. and Mrs. J. M. S[covel] and their family, who have all gone off to church, leaving me to myself) opens on a spacious side-yard exhibiting near-at-hand views of an old extensive Ivy Vine, with thick-matted, yet-green foliage, nearly covering the east gable wall of the adjoining house (fifty feet square, I should guess), alive at this moment, in its sunny exposure, with the darting, flirting, twittering, of scores, hundreds, of English sparrows, busily engaged, with much loquacity, pulling old nests to pieces and building new ones. I had before in my walks noticed this grand Ivy, with its flocks of sparrows; but now alone here, comfortable, I note leisurely the little drama, taking it all in and enjoying it. (What a noble and verdant vine yet — a lesson to old age.) What tireless, vehement noisy tit-bits the birds are! What a rollicking time! Evidently what fun! Sometimes, at a spirt of wind coming, the whole swarm of them, as if frightened, emerge instantaneously from the recesses of the vast vine, and slant and radiate off like flashes; but it is all affectation, for presently they return, and operations are renewed and carried on as actively as ever. It is a hurried, whirling, crossing, chattering, most intense and interested scene, for an hour. (As many have said or thought, who knows but what there are beings of superior spheres, invisible, looking on the chattering activity and affectations of man, with the same critical top-loftical air? Echo — who knows?)

661. Harry White was a driver or clerk for the Adams Express Company, Philadelphia.

662. Edward P. Cattell, the Stafford farm hand who saw Whitman last on 18 March 1879, must have been visiting in Pennsylvania.

663. These 16 names of drivers and other workmen on the horse cars in Philadelphia are one more listing by Whitman in the *Daybook*; some of the data given here are curious — one man has been driving for 10 years and works 17½ hours a day, another has married a widow with three children, another is tall, new on the line, and had "the butter & cheese business" — and apparently Whitman made the list first in 1879 and kept adding names to it until 1882.

Johnston Love McFetridge, conductor.[663a]

Amer Devan, 53 Haddington (13)   May 11 '80   been driving
                                                    10 years
                                        works 17½ hours
D. John Parker, 104 car Market st. Yankee          a day
George Jennings   45 Haddington
Jacob Bohrer, (Jan: '81) new driver on Stevens St – married a young
                                        widow with 3 children

James Jones, 110 car Market st   Phil
<u>Mac</u> (<u>Mac</u> Clure) first name Tall   new, on Stevens Apr '81, had "the
                                        butter & cheese business"
W<u>m</u> Clayton boy 13 or 14 on the cars nights – (gets out at Stevens & 2<sup>d</sup>) Apr '81
John Mollan, cor Front and Market, born & brot up
        thereabout – bro:in-law of the keeper of the house
                        ?
May 20 '82 – Harry Rich, (54 Market st) tall – has been a soldier –
                        R
Jo Watson, son-in-law, Capt Wiggins,   Whilldin[664]

[On slip of paper:]

---

young Irishman, on the boat
        Matthew   Kelly[665]   [in pencil]
works at night on the Phil: freight
                        wharf

---

                                                        [145]

1879

April 4 – <u>Progress</u> to England – to sisters –   Dr Bucke
                                            Newton  Johnson
        papers to Harry – Pr to Mrs S [667]   J  H  J
                                            Mrs Scovel
                                            Mrs Johnston[666]

---

663a.  Johnston Love McFetridge is also listed above (see footnote 107).
    664.  The Whilldin was the steamer on which Whitman had breakfast on 28 December 1878, and again on 18 April 1880 (see footnote 548); but the captain's name there is spelled Riggans. The "?" above "54" in the previous line is Whitman's.
    665.  This young man's name appears on a slip by itself, not in a list.
    666.  Whitman had sent, on 6 March 1879, the Progress with his poem (see footnote 644); so why send it again to his sisters and Dr Bucke? John Newton Johnson (see footnote 9a), John H. Johnston (New York jeweler), Mrs James Matlack Scovel (wife of his Camden friend), and Mrs John R. Johnston (wife of the Colonel, rather than Mrs Alma Johnston, wife of John H. Johnston) had not received copies of the Progress.

4 – circl's to Mrs Chas Fobes, Sparta, Wis. in ans to requests[668]

April 8 or 9     $10 to Lou     [except for date, in blue pencil]

April 9 went to New York[669]
   14   Lecture at Steck Hall[670]
      (returned from N  Y. June 14)

667. The papers to Harry Stafford could be anything; "Pr to Mrs S" most likely means a copy of the 16 November 1878 *Progress* to Mrs George Stafford of White Horse.

668. Circulars were promotion pieces which Whitman sent from time to time to those who asked about his books; Mrs Charles Fobes of Sparta, Wisconsin is otherwise unidentified, and her request is lost.

669. Whitman wrote to Herbert Gilchrist, 8 April 1879, that he was leaving at 2 p. m. the next day for New York to stay with John H. Johnston (see *The Correspondence of Walt Whitman*, III, 151); Whitman's account of his visit is in *Specimen Days* — see *Prose Works 1892*, I, 190–202.

In the Feinberg Collection are three MSS, all having to do with the trip to New York and to Esopus. The first is on one sheet of paper, torn from a notebook:

*New York visit April '79*
[C]ame on from Camden to N Y Wednesday   April 9 '79

the beauty animation & individuality of the north river, crossing
at 5 p m from Jersey City to Desbrosses Street N Y

in N Y the sight of the steam L's running — they seem to me a great
nuisance-convenience

deliver'd lecture at Steck Hall, 14th St. Monday evening April 14
                                   '79

Mrs A M Mosher
        Cambridge   Mass
Songs "O wert thou in the cauld blast"
           Bay of Dublin (with the Irish croon)
           Doon the burn

at Miss both's reception
    59th st.   April 12th

The second MS is a notebook of six sheets, folded, sewn and joined with a pin, to make 12 pages, with another sheet pasted in; writing occurs on pp. [1], [3], [5], [7], [9–10] (pasted in), and [11]:

                                               [1]

Mr & Mrs Botta
    25 West 37th street
Send photo & auto.
      & Dem Vistas —

16th April – sent
    Putnam & Davis
      Worcester Mass
  circ: (in ans to request)

Swinton 124 East 38th st
    dinner   Sunday   April 20th

John M Rogers          sent
    Battonville  Fla:   papers from
                    N Y
                    May 22
                     '79

Miss Fanny L. Lenheim
    Care Miss Life, Seminary
      Rye, Westchester Co
send photo          New York

Wm $^H$ Taylor policeman
    (Abraham, broth, 18 or 20)
5$^{th}$ av: bet: 84$^{th}$ & 85$^{th}$ Sts
        N Y

Edward P Cattell (sent paper May 21
Glenalden Delaware Co: Penn   NY)
    (?Darby p o)

175                                                                    [2]
  3
—
5.25

[3]

Friday April 18 – sent L of G & T R to
    John W Britton              Brewster & Co:
cor 47$^{th}$ st & Broadway          wagon making
                        establishment
    to pay [written over:] $10 paid

Wrote to Fred Rauch (sent paper)

Wrote to J P Miller 101 South 8th Phil
          sent $5
    "   to Hanna   and to Mary

Mr & Mrs Bigelow
23$^d$ St bet: 4$^{th}$ av: & Madison
same side as Academy – no stoop

composition ornaments – 204 Centre

David L Proudfit (called)
    American Bank Note Co.
53 142 Broadway N Y.

    Miss Kate Hillard
      33 West 37$^{th}$ st N Y

Christopher Collins, Park Police
    at 90$^{th}$ st entrance
April 21, '79

April 23 – sent C T Dillingham 678 B'dway
             L of G (3.50 to pay) paid

April 23 – (evening) came up on the
Kingston boat James W Baldwin to
    Esopus – arrived about 10.20 p m

[4]

[On the bottom of a card of Mrs C. W. Romney, Boston Post, Buffalo Courier, Indian-
apolis, not in WW's hand:]
The Arlington Fifth Ave. Hotel

[5]

Wyatt Eaton – 10 west 13<sup>th</sup> st N Y

Horace Howard Furness
     222 West Washington Square – Phila

A J Bloor architect [Whitman's eye-witness of Lincoln's funeral in Washington]
     128 Broadway N Y

26<sup>th</sup> April – rec'd letter from Harry Stafford
               from Esopus
April 29 – wrote     to
                         Jack Johnston
     Forney          Hiskey
     Herbert         Eugene Crosby
                         Sister Mary
     Al Johnston     Peter Doyle
     W<sup>m</sup> Cannon     Mr Bloor

paper to Clint Townsend
up at John Burroughs's from
Wednesday
     April 23<sup>d</sup> to May 3<sup>d</sup> '79
went up in the steamer Jas W Baldwin

Send Prof & Mrs F R Ritter
     photos      Poughkeepsie

Thurber & Co New York
     best Canned Goods

[6]

[Blank.]

[7]

May 14 '79 – New York
Albert Decker, cond     Madison
David Kolyer driver     av: Cars
     Met Bob: Cooper –
says Fred: Vaughan is running
     elevator N Y Life Ins: Building
     cor: Broadway & Leonard

Fred Fox, 5<sup>th</sup> av. driver yet
     May 14 '79 – ride down Broadway

[On letterhead of Charles T. Dillingham / Successor to / Lee, Shepard & Dillingham, /
Publishers, Booksellers & Importers / 678 Broadway, / New York.:]
     p o box
     5428
[On card of G. P. Putnam's Sons / 182 Fifth Avenue, / New York:]
A Thorndike Rice (is right)

direct to Hon John Bigelow's folks
     at Highland Falls, (West Point) N Y

[8]

[Blank.]

    Miss Thomas  [not WW's hand]
      32 West 26.  [not WW's hand]

visit to the U S School-Ship Minnesota
      N Y. May 15 '79
Jos W. Daley  Pay Clerk  [not WW's hand]
W^m Little  Lieutenant  [not WW's hand]
W^m S. Moore  T. Ass^t Engineer  [not WW's hand]
Jos. J. Somerby M D.  [not WW's hand]
Paul St. C. Murphy,
    Lieut Marines  [not WW's hand]

    Pay Master Pritchard
    Chaplain Rawson
    Capt Luce

[10]

[Written sideways:]
    I find a large class of the our thoughtful
people – perhaps the largest class – always talking
as though plenty of active manufactures, financial
matters, and foreign markets — were the only
themes worthy of politics and business attention

[11]

[On a printed slip of John Conrad / No. 7 Ann Street, / Makes to order, and keeps constantly on hand, a large as- / sortment of the finest French / Patent Leather Boots, Shoes and Gaiters [etc.]. . . :]
    George Storms [a horse car conductor in New York who named his son Walt Whitman Storms]
      Schroder's Restaurant
      35 West 43rd Street
        [N Y City]

    May F Johnston
    Albert E    "

[12, 13, 14]

[Blank.]
[The third MS is on three pages, a first draft of "Central Park Walks and Talks" in *Specimen Days*; see *Prose Works 1892,* I, 197–198;]

N Y  '79
      19 to 24
    May 12 to 18. I visit Central park every day, sometimes and have for the last three weeks, off and on taking observations, or short rambles, and sometimes riding around, always enjoying happy in this magnificent ground. Perhaps it I think it the Grounds presents its their very best appearance this current month, especially the latter half, of May. The first full flush of the trees — the plentiful white and pink of the blossoms — the pure green of the grass, every-where & yellow-dotted with dandelions — the miracle and reliable of our skies and atmosphere, three days out of four a week at a stretch, this season, — the speciality of gray rocks cropping out everywhere are enough, of themselves. — all please, comfort, nourish strengthen me. Why then am I going to fault-find a little with the Park? Two Three beautiful perfect days, of late, I have spent from 10 to 1 in about the Park, it, enjoying myself capitally, but with the irritating question resting remaining at last on my mind, Why is not it not a for more popular, free, average resort? I suppose the Commissioners will say, Because the Populace don't choose to come. Perhaps they will say, They *do* come. My two But those three lovely days, from 10 to 1, I saw only a few dozens, or scores of visitors — over the common, and along the numerous paths, only sparse figures or groups. Nobody even stopping to scan the browse Shake-

from April 23ᵈ ⎱ up at John Burroughs's ⎱
to May 3ᵈ     ⎰     at Esopus – [671]

In N  Y   from April 9 to June 14 / [in blue pencil]
                          inclusive / [in pencil]

[three lines in pencil and blue pencil:]

June 9 the Gilchrists sail'd from N  Y
                  for Glasgow[672]


X May, from N Y. $10 to Lou for Ed [673]

spere, or Humboldt, or Webster, or the Youth and hawk. — or Nor anything le else. Considering the perfect days, and the leisure and idleness of this our million-headed city — the people out of work, the women and children, the half-invalids, &c. — I would might have expected, to see, any of those times, a hundred thousand at least there! I am told that Saturday is a real rush day in the Park, for the People — and Sunday partially so. (When, considering the perfect weather, and the leisure, idleness, and the need of recreation in our million-headed city, I should have expected a hun troops of hundreds, and troops of thousands — aye, many tens of thousands — people out of work, women and children, half-invalids, &c.) — I found only a few dozens of visitors — over the Common and along the paths, only a few sparse figures or meagre groups. at a intervals. run in) Nobody stopping to scan Shakspere, or Humboldt, or Webster, or the Youth and Falcon. I am told that Saturday is a real rush day — and Sunday partially so. But the [MS breaks off here.]

In *Walt Whitman's Diary in Canada* (Boston, 1904), pp. 56–57, is the following entry in the section "From Other Journals of Walt Whitman":

[*New York*], *Sunday*, '79. Took a slow walk forenoon to-day (Easter Sunday: the chick is breaking the egg) along Fifth Avenue where it flanks the Park, from 85th to 90th street. I rest my note-book, to write this, on the roof-shaped coping of the wall. All round this vast pleasure-ground has been built a costly, grim, forbidding stone fence, some parts of it seven feet high, others lower, capped with heavy bevelled rough marble, — in my judgment a nuisance, the whole thing. There ought to be no such fence; the grounds ought to be open all round (both the spirit of the matter and the visible fact and convenience are important and require it).

Perhaps (though I am not sure) the general planning, designing, and carrying out of this Park, from its original state to the present, are successes and the results good. But the same ideas, theories (by the same person, I understand), applied to Prospect Park, Brooklyn, have in my opinion done their best to spoil that incomparable hill and ground, — in some respects the grandest site for a park in the world. The same error in Capitol Hill at Washington, — exploiting the designs of ingrain carpets, with sprawling and meaningless lines.

670.  This was Whitman's first lecture on the death of Lincoln, a lecture he was to repeat for several years; for this occasion and others on the New York trip, see Gay Wilson Allen, *The Solitary Singer,* pp. 483–486; and Roy P. Basler's edition of Walt Whitman's *Memoranda During the War* [*&*] *Death of Abraham Lincoln* (Bloomington, Indiana, 1962).

671.  Whitman's last visit to Esopus-on-Hudson: see "Real Summer Openings," New York *Tribune,* 17 May 1879; and *Prose Works 1892,* I, 190–196, 339–341; and *The Correspondence of Walt Whitman,* III, 152–160, which includes letters he wrote in Esopus and New York.

672.  The Gilchrists sailed on the Circassia and arrived in Glasgow on 20 June 1879, when Mrs Anne Gilchrist wrote Whitman, and again on 2 August 1879 from Durham; see Thomas B. Harned, *The Letters of Anne Gilchrist and Walt Whitman* (Garden- City, New York, 1918), pp. 181–185; and *The Correspondence of Walt Whitman,* III, 161–162.

673.  The $10 to Louisa Orr Whitman was for the board of Edward Whitman (1835–

[146]

[Slip (pasted on page) with printed name in script of Wm H. Taylor, M. P. of N. Y.] [674]

John V. Sears    Inquirer office[675]
Chestnut & Third – Phila:

Chas. F. Leyman.[676]          [in pencil:]
No. 195.   [Printed on slip]   Charley Van Meter
4th Police District.           new car driver – Stevens st car
                                         June '79

[Four lines in pencil:]

21
Frank Buckman ∧ in feed store    Fed st n   Front, north
                                                      side

Frank Oakley, deck hand on Camden, blonde, (one eye def:)

("Charley Ross")
Thos. Colston, ∧ young, on 122 car Union Line   Phil

Thos: Woolston, young (19) cashier at Ridgeway House

Harry Garrison, my R R young man, sandy compl: at Ferry

[On slip of paper. five lines not in WW's hand:]

Please direct,
            Jennie J. Hastings,[677]
                Harford,
                    Susquehanna Co,
Care C. S. Johnstone.           Penn.

---

1892), the youngest of Walt's brothers and sisters, institutionalized most of his adult life, much of it paid for by the poet.

674. This was the William H. Taylor who, on 18 December 1877, invited Whitman to visit him (letter in the Library of Congress); see footnote 388, above.

675. The *Inquirer,* founded in 1829, was one of the oldest Philadelphia newspapers, but it had little association with Whitman.

676. Here we have, once more, a list of young men: a policeman, a car driver, feed store worker, deck hand, a young man on a car, a cashier, and a young railroad man.

677. Otherwise unidentifiable.

[Three lines in pencil:]

now (Sept. '85) Judge[678]

June 21 – int: to young Mr <u>Westcott</u>, ∧ lawyer
  J Hewitt) ~~has~~ was a glass blower – was a
  Yale student

[147]

1879

June 16

[Nine lines written on tan piece of paper pasted on page:]

| $15.30 paid me | :recd   June 15, '79 | rec'd |
|---|---|---|
|  John Frazer | 10 Lord Nelson St: | $15.30 |
| | | for "Three |
| Liverpool – 15:30   paid | | Young Men's[679] |
| | | Deaths" |

| E   D   Mansfield[680] 11 Worcester | [in blue pencil | sent the |
|---|---|---|
| Terrace, Clifton, Bristol | sideways:] | <u>Two</u> <u>Vols</u> |
| rec'd $9.72 rec'd – <u>Vols</u> <u>sent</u> – paid – | recd | June 16 |

| rec'd    J   W   Thompson[681] Goldsmith | [sideways:] | book |
|---|---|---|
| from | | recd |
| $5  Building   London   E C   paid | | & $5 paid |
| | | me |

14th   papers to Clint Townsend[682]

---

678. John W. Westcott, whom Whitman met in June 1879, became a prominent lawyer and district judge, and the poet returned to his *Daybook* in September 1885 to record this; a native of Camden County who studied in New England, he admired Whitman as a poet and man, often called on him and (recalled his son) "was fond of declaiming *Leaves of Grass* at home and regarded Whitman almost as a saint." (Gay Wilson Allen, *The Solitary Singer*, pp. 505–506.)

679. Walt Whitman's "Three Young Men's Deaths" appeared in *Cope's Tobacco Plant*, II (April 1879), 318–319; the article was sent to John Fraser on 27 November 1878 (see above for that date, and footnote 527); Whitman had asked $12 but received $15.30. His poem, "The Dalliance of the Eagles," was to appear in *Cope's Tobacco Plant*, II (November 1880), 552. See *The Correspondence of Walt Whitman*, III, 157–158; and III, 159 (Whitman's acknowledgement to John Fraser; other letters to the editor, 27 November 1879, 3 May and 9 October 1880, are lost).

680. Whitman mentioned in a letter to Burroughs, 20 June 1879, "I get a stray order now & then from England" (*The Correspondence of Walt Whitman*, III, 159), which referred to these from E. D. Mansfield and J. W. Thompson, just below (see also footnote 658).

681. See footnote 680.

682. See footnotes 633 and 352.

June 15   wrote postal to J  H  Johnston  N  Y  city[683]

16th postal to Pete Doyle also "Three Young Men's D"[684]

17th  L  of  G  and photo to S  W  Green[685]   [in blue pencil,      recd
                                                          sideways:]
        photo to E  D  Williams, 1309 Fifth av.[686]  [in blue pencil,      recd
                                                          sideways:]

20th    sent 2 Vols L  of  G and T R to W G Brooke[687]  [in blue pencil,  paid
                          paid   $10 due             sideways:]   recd
        14 Herbert Street   Dublin Ireland                       recd

"   wrote to John Burroughs – (returned baby's photo)[688]


23[d]   Monday evening – Clarence B Whitaker[689]

25th sent Trübner & Co.  59 Ludgate Hill, London
       18 sets, (36 Vols) per J B Lippincott & Co
       715 Market st. Phil: (at 3.50   $126)[690]

                                                                      [148]

        Jaunt down the Delaware in the Illinois
           to see Coleman[691] off – & return in the Stokely
                                        July 19
                                        Jn  '79

[Clipping, headed "Some of Those Participating", from a newspaper, listing
53 people, beginning with Walt Whitman, mainly newspaper men, 23 of them
from the Philadelphia *Public Ledger*. WW has underlined 11 names: J. M. W.
Geist, Thompson Westcott, Eugene H. Munday, A. M. Spangler, H. B. Ben-

---

683.  This letter is lost.
684.  This letter is in *The Correspondence of Walt Whitman*, III, 158–159; for "Three
Young Men's Deaths," see footnote 679, above.
685.  Samuel W. Green was a New York printer (see footnote 564).
686.  Unidentifiable.
687.  See footnote 680.
688.  This letter is in *The Correspondence of Walt Whitman*, III, 159–160; the baby is
Burroughs's son Julian.
689.  Unidentifiable.
690.  In a letter to Josiah Child, 9 June 1879, written from New York, Whitman acknowledged this order (see *The Correspondence of Walt Whitman*, III, 157–158, and also III,
137n).
691.  I cannot identify a "Coleman" (either with such a last name or a given name),
although he must be someone Whitman knew well enough to see him off on a trip.

ners, Joel Cook, M. Richards Muckle, James H. Alexander, Charles A. Dougherty, Robert M. McWade, and Charles S. Spangler.] [692]

[Four names below in blue pencil:]

Aug 1   Kate Evelyn Mingle[693] sent Photo & Lecture

Aug 1   '79   [in blue pencil, sideways:]   recd

"      Bell Mingle   (Hebe)

"      Nelly      3327 Walnut st
                (Darby road car)

"      Josephine

[149]

1879

June 25 – wrote to Dr Bucke – sent "Three Y M Deaths" – [694]

27 – wrote to Trübner & Co: informing them the 36 Vols.
        have been sent through Lippincott[695]

"     "    a note enclosed to Josiah Child

X July 2 $10 to Lou[696] [in blue pencil,
                        except date]

                        2$^d$, 3$^d$ & 4th   [in pencil]
July 2    went down to Glendale[697]      h o t [in blue pencil]
        staid a week   [in pencil]

2$^d$ to 9$^{th}$ down at Geo: S's at Glendale   N   J[698]

    692. These 11 names which Whitman underlined do not turn up in his letters, or in Traubel, but do turn up below: could he have known these men?
    693. The name Mingle occurs several times in the *Daybook*, among those to whom Whitman sent various items; Kate Evelyn, Belle, Nelly, and Josephine apparently belong to the same family, living in West Philadelphia (?), at 114 North 32$^{nd}$ Street.
    694. Whitman's "Three Young Men's Deaths," *Cope's Tobacco Plant*, April 1879 (see footnote 527, above).
    695. See entry above for June 25; both the letter to Trübner & Co., and Josiah Child are lost.
    696. For Whitman's board to his sister-in-law Louisa.
    697. Another term for the Stafford farm, at White Horse, near Timber Creek, not far from Camden; Whitman's comment on the weather, "hot," was most likely made when he returned to Stevens Street; "staid" is not a misspelling but an archaic (now) variation for "stayed", and it is remarkable how seldom Whitman ever misspelled a word, in this rough and informal *Daybook* or in his many MS drafts.
    698. As far as I know, Whitman kept no notes for this period on one week; he had

– 10<sup>Th</sup>   Col: Forney call'd [699]

14th   sent G   P   Putnam's Sons 182 Fifth av    [in blue pencil,      recd
                 N Y – one set – 2 Vols  $7 due         sideways:]       paid

19<sup>th</sup>   went down Delaware in <u>Illinois</u>  & back
                  in <u>Stokely</u>[700]

20th   Sunday letters & George's picture to
                  Hannah and Mary[701]

–      Photo and <u>Dem</u> <u>Vistas</u> to Mrs Botta[702]    [in blue pencil, sideways:]  recd
                  25 West 37<sup>th</sup> st   N   Y –

27<sup>th</sup>  paid  Mr Buckle, carrier (his son in "Irwin")   [in blue pencil,   paid up
       ~~paid~~                   Aug 1. '79                      sideways:]
                  39<sup>cts</sup> in full up to date, ∧ for <u>Times</u> – both mine &           to Aug
                  <u>paid</u>      paid  [in blue pencil]          Ida's[703]
            owe Jim Baker 38cts  (23 weeks from Jan 1 to June 8                       1 (both)
                        $1 paid) in full)

31st   Evening at Exposition Building, at National
                  Teachers' Reception
            saw the <u>phonograph</u> and <u>telephone</u>[704]

written Mrs Stafford on 24 June 1879 (not recorded above) that he was coming to see them
soon (see *The Correspondence of Walt Whitman*, III, 160).
    699.  See footnote 193.
    700.  Repeated from the opposite page.
    701.  These letters, indeed all letters of July 1879, are lost. George is George Whitman.
    702.  Anne C. Lynch Botta (1815–1891), teacher, poet, sculptor, and author of the *Hand-book of Universal Literature* (revised edition, Boston [etc.], 1902), who wrote her original editions in 1860, 1880 and 1884, had this to say of Whitman (p. 523): "In connection with Poe it is most convenient to speak of Walt Whitman, though the only point they have in common is their uncommonness. Whitman, too, has been lauded by foreign voices; and it may readily be admitted, if we admit that he wrote poetry at all, that he was the poet of democracy. With the exception of a very few bits of verse, however, he scorned metrical restraint, and produced in consequence an amorphous hybrid medium, neither prose nor verse, by means of which he expressed most forcibly, at least, his peculiar doctrine of individualism. We find a certain provocation for his rebellion against form in the insipid 'Correctness' of many of his contemporaries of the 'Knickerbocker school.' Whitman's first volume of verse was written in the same year of the publication of the 'Knickerbocker Gallery.' The verse of [N. P.] Willis and his friends is dead enough now, while Whitman will long be a power." (See *The Correspondence of Walt Whitman*, II, 121, 121n.)
    703.  Ida Johnston, daughter of Colonel John R. Johnston of Camden.
    704.  Although dated here 31 July 1879, Whitman writes briefly in *Specimen Days* under 26 August of a visit to the Exposition Building in West Philadelphia; the July occasion was a teachers' reception, the August of a ball; see *Prose Works 1892*, I, 203. (The *Daybook* does not mention the August visit.)

[Two lines in blue pencil:]
X   Aug 1   $10 to L          Aug 1   & 2 & 3     hot[705]
                             4th 5   6th


[On piece of paper, covering whole page, written mainly in pencil:]     [150]
        Leonard
James Lennon, age 21   Spanish looking –
     I met on the ferry – night Aug 16 –
     – lives toward Cooper's Point – learning machinists' trade
     – "fond of music, poetry & flowers" [706]

Col:
Forney          618 Locust[707]

sent    Jansen, McClurg & Co.,          [name and address      Booksellers
circ:                                      printed on slip]      Chicago
to      Nos. 117 & 119 State Street.                            Aug 2 '79 [three
                                                                        lines
             Robert M Mc Wade[708]                                   in ink]
             Reporter,
                  Ledger   [these three lines not in WW's hand]
[On calling card of P. Arunachalam,[709] Christs College, Cambridge:]   books
                                                                        sent
                                                                    pay rec'd
                                                                      19.44
Hatta, 2316 Pine st   St L[710]   [in blue pencil]
———————————————— [rule in blue pencil]
     Capt. Harry Laughlin
     House of Corrections   [these two lines not in WW's hand]
———————————————— [rule in blue pencil]
Walter S. Crispin    young man 21 [711]   [in ink]
———————————————————— [rule in blue pencil]


705.  Whitman's recording of his $10 for board to sister-in-law Louisa and the hot
weather coincide again, as on 2 July 1879.
     706.  Once again, Whitman comments in his *Daybook* on a young man he met on a
ferry trip.
     707.  See entry above for 10 July 1879 and footnote 193.
     708.  Robert M. McWade was one of the 11 men whose name Whitman underlined in
the piece, "Some of Those Participating," Whitman clipped from a newspaper, pasted in the
*Daybook* above.
     709.  Armachalain, the "Hindoo," wrote to Whitman on 25 August 1879 (letter in the
Feinberg Collection); Whitman's letter to him is lost.
     710.  This is Mannahatta Whitman, Jeff's eldest daughter, 19 years old at this time (1879);
she was to live but nine more years.
     711.  Someone, apparently, in the same category as James Lennon (Leonard) above.

M. Richards Muckle[712]
Business Manager
    Ledger       [These three lines not in WW's hand]
Mr. Sailor        [in ink]
    money articles[713]    [in ink]

                                                [151]

1879

Aug: 5 – sent two sets, (four Vols) to
        P Arunachalam,[714] 45 Brunswick Sq:    [in blue pencil,   recd
        Brighton, Eng: also two photos & circs    sideways:]   paid
            paid – rec'd $19.44

9 [714a] – sent Two Riv:  to Mrs J Alexander, the    [in blue pencil,  recd
        Palace, Derry, Ireland – (letter from    sideways:]   &
        T W H Rolleston)[715] (p o order  £1.1 sent June   paid
             '78 – never recd by me)  [in pencil]

"  wrote to T W H Rolleston (14th aug: wrote again
                      sent p.o. letters)
    glasshouse Shinrone   Kings Co: Ireland
      (sent lecture in Tribune)[716]
    sent Progress to Han, Mary, Jeff, Evey Mingle, Mrs Botta,    [in pencil]
        Mrs Johnston[717]   [in pencil]

---

712. Like Robert M. McWade, above, M. Richard Muckle was one of the 11 men whose name Whitman underlined (see footnotes 692 and 708).

713. "Money articles"? Mr Sailor's pieces, in the Philadelphia *Public Ledger* having to do with the stock market, or financial affairs? James Gordon Bennett wrote such "money articles" in the New York *Herald* in 1835.

714. See footnote 709.

714a. In *Walt Whitman's Diary in Canada* (Boston, 1904), p. 57, is the following paragraph in the section "From Other Journals of Walt Whitman":

*Aug. 9, '79.* GORGEOUS FLOWERS. As I walk the suburbs of a town where I am temporarily staying, great sunflowers bend their tall and stately discs in full bloom in silent salute to the day-orb. Many other gorgeous blossoms. Roses of Sharon are out, both the white ones and the red. Then the tawny trumpet-flower, its rich-deep orange-yellow on copious vines in back yards and on the gables of old houses. Great balls of the blue hydrangeas are not uncommon. I stop long before a tall clump of the Japanese sunflowers.

As Whitman does not record any trip in the *Daybook*, for 9 August 1879, one cannot be certain what "town" he refers to; although in *Specimen Days* he mentions under the date of 4 August 1879 that he "retreated down in the country again," he most likely was in Glendale, New Jersey (see *Prose Works 1892*, I, 202).

715. For T. W. H. Rolleston, see footnote 50; these two letters to him from Whitman, 9 and 14 August 1879, are lost; one from him to the poet, dated July 1879, is in the John Rylands Library, Manchester, England.

716. This was an account, with the full text, of Whitman's lecture in the death of Abraham Lincoln, in the New York *Tribune* for 15 April 1879.

717. Colonel Forney's Philadelphia *Progress* contained an account of the Lincoln lecture, which Whitman sent to his two sisters Hannah Heyde, Mary Van Nostrand, brother Jeff, Evey Mingle, Mrs Anne C. Lynch Botta (see footnote 702), and Mrs John H. (?) Johnston of New York City.

13<sup>th</sup>   Met at Col: Forney's[718]   Mr Sailor of the Ledger   [in pencil]
                    &           Mr Purvis   [in pencil]
   Hatt and Jessie return'd to St Louis[719]
     I and Lou went over to West Phil: & saw
     them off in the cars at 9.10 p m

16<sup>th</sup>, 17<sup>th</sup>, & 18   rainy days & nights   [in pencil]

18th   Address Mrs Gilchrist — Lower Shincliffe   [in pencil]
  (wrote letter to Mrs G)   Durham   Eng[720]   [last two words in pencil]
  [Three lines in pencil:]
  Mr Watkins tells of West Creek N   J   (not
  far from Tuckerton) & "Uncle Joes" [721]
   at (he thinks) $5 a week

20th   two copies L   of   G . to Claxton, R & H – $6 [722]

26th   Dinner with Col F at Guy's[723]   [in pencil]

27<sup>th</sup>   met Geo: Stafford and little George in 4<sup>th</sup> st
               near Pine – all well [724]
     all last of August
Blurrs – 24<sup>th</sup>, 25<sup>th</sup>, 6 &c / was it a bad cold ? [725]   [in pencil]

[152]
[Letterhead cut from Charles T. Dillingham, wholesale bookseller, 678 Broadway, New York, with date, not in WW's hand, Sept 3<sup>rd</sup> 1879.]
Mrs Fannie L Taylor, 1810 Olive st.   St L[726]

---

718.  See footnote 193; Mr Sailor, mentioned above (footnote 713), wrote on the stock market and finances; I cannot identify Mr Purvis.
719.  Mannahatta and Jessie Whitman, Whitman's nieces and daughters of Walt's favorite brother Jeff, visited Camden almost every year, to see both George and the poet.
720.  This letter is in *The Correspondence of Walt Whitman*, III, 161–162.
721.  "Uncle Joes" refers either to a large boarding house in Camden or to Joe Cox, a prominent citizen of West Creek, who furnished room and board for $5.00 a week.
722.  Claxton, Remsen, & Haffelfinger, booksellers, wrote to Whitman on 3 October 1877 and 5 January 1878: letters in the Library of Congress, but not this order, which is lost.
723.  Whitman had been seeing Colonel John W. Forney, the publisher (see footnote 193), fairly often, 10 July 1879, 13 August 1879, and was to make a Western trip with him later in the year.
724.  George Stafford was the father of Harry, Whitman's closest friend at this time, and little George (1869–1924) was his 10-year-old brother.
725.  Whitman's health, following his 1873 stroke, varied in condition: too poor for him to give his Lincoln lecture in 1878, it was good enough in 1879, for he not only gave the lecture in April, but went to Colorado in September; however, illness in October caused him to remain in St Louis until January 1880.
726.  Mrs Taylor (see footnote 129) apparently came to Camden to take Mannahatta and Jessie Louisa Whitman, Walt's nieces, back home to St Louis.

run

P Arohachalam   Ceylon civil service[727]
        Colombo   Ceylon

---

Edward Ettle, age 30, Berlin, stereoptican man, I met
       at Federal st ferry house, Jan '80 [728]

---

Wm A Bryan   1321 north 7th Phila
      I met in Chestnut st. Jan.   (he ask'd me for photo)

---

Hon John G Schumaker   Brooklyn   N Y [729]

---

Tommy Moore, little 6 or 7 boy, black eyed, West & Bridge

---

[153]

1879–August

28th A   N   Brown   6 Ripley Court   Springfield Mass )
     sent circ to, in ans to letter

"   sent Wm H Kelly,[730] with Powers & Weightman   [sideways:]   sold
                                                   him
       cor 9th & Parrish sts, L of G                    L of G
                                                     paid

30th sent circ: to Thos: B Mosher, care of Dresser, Mc
      Lellan & Co:   Portland, Maine[731]

"   wrote to Leavitt & Co. N. Y. abt plates of 60 ed'n[732]

727.  See footnotes 709 and 714.
728.  Edward Ettle, William A. Bryan, and Tommy Moore (the last two listed below) are the sort of people's names Whitman wrote on these right-hand pages of the *Daybook* from time to time, singly or in groups, occasionally with a comment.
729.  John G. Schumaker is described by Bliss Perry (*Walt Whitman: His Life and Work,* Boston, 1906, p. 28) as a lifelong acquaintance of the poet; Schumaker, who wrote about Whitman in the New York *Tribune,* 4 April 1892, recalled having introduced Whitman to General (President-to-be) James A. Garfield on a Washington streetcar.
730.  William H. Kelly's letter, 27 August 1879, ordering *Leaves of Grass,* is in the Library of Congress.
731.  Thomas Bird Mosher (1852–1923), only 27 years old at this time, was to begin publishing his series of attractive but inexpensive Mosher Books in 1891 and his *The Bibelot* monthly reprints in 1895; he also issued Whitman's *Memories of President Lincoln and Other Lyrics of the War* in 1904 (reprinted 1906, 1912); a facsimile edition of the 1855 *Leaves of Grass* in a printing of 400 copies in 1919 and a second impression (500 copies) in 1920; and other collections of Whitman.
732.  See Whitman's account of this whole business, involving Richard Worthington, in addition to Leavitt, the auctioneer, *The Correspondence of Walt Whitman,* III, 195–198, 199–200.

1879 - August

28th A N Brown 6 Ripley Court Springfield Mass
    sent Circ to, in ans to letter

" sent Wm H Kelly with Powers & Weightman
    cor 9th & Parrish st, L of G

30th sent cirs: to Thos: B Mosher, care of Dresser, Mc
    Lellan & Co: Portland, Maine

" wrote to Leavitt & Co. N. Y. abt Plates of '61 edn

Sept 3 sent ??

  papers frequently to John Burrows, Roxbury

5th sent Charles T Dillingham. 1 L of G. 3.50
                        due me

0 sent L of G to Alice R Alexander
    5 Durham Place Chelsea gardens
    St Louis London Eng:
    and Colorade Trip.

Started for St Louis, Missouri abt 9 p m

2th in St Louis (only one night)

3 on through Missouri to Kansas city, & on
    to Lawrence to Judge Ushers

5th, 16th Topeka, Kansas

" on to Denver Colorado
    Rocky Mountain trip. South park
  over the Santa Fe road - Pueblo. Spanish
  Peaks - the Great Plains - the Arkansas
  River - Sterling - Southern Kansas -

Sept 3 – Lou $20    [in blue pencil]
    papers frequently to John Burroughs, Roxbury[733]

5th    sent Charles T Dillingham[734] 1 L   of   G.    3.50    [in blue pencil,
                                        due me    sideways:]        paid

10    sent L   of   G   to Alice R   Alexander        [in blue
            5 Durham Place   Chelsea Gardens        pencil, sideways:]    recd
                        London   Eng:                        paid
            St Louis and Colorado Trip[735] [in red ink]

---

733. Whitman also wrote letters to Burroughs, 20 and 29 August 1879 (see *The Correspondence of Walt Whitman*, III, 162, 163).

734. See Dillingham's letterhead, opposite page.

735. Whitman wrote at considerable length about this trip in *Specimen Days* under such titles as "Begin a Long Jaunt West," "Denver Impressions," "Mississippi Valley Literature," "St. Louis Memoranda," and "Upon Our Own Land": see *Prose Works 1892*, I, 205–230. During the trip, which lasted from 10 September 1879 to 5 January 1880, he wrote to his sister-in-law Louisa on 12 and 19 September on the way west — they are the only letters extant — and from St Louis on 11 October; all but six other letters — see *The Correspondence of Walt Whitman*, III, 166–171 — written from 2316 Pine Street, St Louis, Missouri (Jeff's home) in 1879 are lost. As Whitman's record of these months in the *Daybook* covers only a few lines, which most likely were written after his return to Camden, he apparently did not take the *Daybook* with him; he did take a crudely fashioned 6½-by-4½ inch notebook, and made entries on 16 of its pages, including the front cover. See Rena V. Grant, "The Livezey-Whitman Manuscripts," *Walt Whitman Review*, VII (March 1961), 3–14, for a fairly complete transcription (with a few errors) of the travel notebook, now in the University of California at Berkeley, and some related material.

In this collection, on an 8-by-11 inch sheet, Whitman has written:
        Trip to Kansas &c
left West Phila depot at 9.10 p m Sept
        10 '79
    that night all through Pennsylvania
from east to west — Harrisburgh
    at Pittsburgh Thursday morning to breakfast
    Pretty good view of Pittsburgh and
Birmingham, — fog and damp, smoke, coke,
furnaces, flames, h wooden houses, discolored
& grim – vast collections of Coal barges
    presently a fine region through the
West Va – the Pan Handle
        Then crossing the Ohio
        Yellow flowers thick every where clear
        light yellow. What are they?
                Sept 11
        hills, woods, rocks, – trains meeting
                us everywhere

the Nights in the Sleeper
    [On the verso, letterhead: "Progress, John W. Forney, Editor and Proprietor, S. W. corner of 9th and Chestnut Sts., Philadelphia, Pa." And in Whitman's hand:]
            travelers, merchants, Leadville-folk. [Sideways]

| | | |
|---|---|---|
| G W Childs  x | Boston | Capt A B Frazee  x |
| | Baltimore | |
| N. Y. Tribune  x | Phila | Dr Zimmerman  x |
| | Wa | |

Phil Times  x
St L Globe-Dem  x
Cin: Com:  x
Boston Herald  x
Col Forney  x
Camden Post  x
Lou & Geo  x
Han  x
Mary  x
J Mrs John  x

Harry Gasprell  x
Mrs Johnston N Y.  x
Fred Rauch  x
Til Eugene C  x
Macpherson  x
Jeff:  x
Thos Newton Johnson  x
   Hilliard Store
Pete Doyle  x
John P. Usher Jr  x
Linton Usher  x
Dr Bucke
M H Case  x
Mrs Scovel  x
John Bur  x

New Orleans
Washington
Cincinnati
Chicago
t [?] my own
Brooklyn
of the hills

My own New
York, the
not only the
New Worlds,
but the worlds
   surrounded by
City, with   its
glittering and
beautiful bays.

Gen W J Sewell  x
  Smart
Joseph Adams  x
Ed Cattell  x
Clarence Whittaker
Thos J Hall  x
C S Moyes  x
Smith Caswell  x

[A preliminary draft for "An Egotistical 'Find'" (see *Prose Works 1892*, I, 210–211), beginning, "traveling the Rocky mountains Sept. '79. Here are my Poems!" and a fragment, considerably reworked and cancelled:]

St Louis

To the Editor

Let me give you some flying impromptu notes, confessedly all too meager, a hiatus everywhere, of my journey over three months since . . . . from the Atlantic coast . . . . to Denver for a few days, then by the southern road to Pueblo, over the Plains, to Kansas City, stopping there a while. Then through Missouri again to St Louis, where I have been spending a month . . . . [The 30-odd pp. notebook reads:]

[Front cover]

Kansas &
Colorado
   Trip    '79


*St. Louis*
*Mems:*                 [See *Prose Works 1892*, I, 228.]
Oct & Nov '79
A Kenosha
   Memorandum        [See "An Hour on Kenosha Summit," *Prose Works 1892*,
☞ Started from Phila                                         I, 210.]
      Sept 10 – '79
– returned Jan 9 – '80
      gone not quite
               4 months.                              [Inside front cover]
[On a piece of paper, pasted down:]
Charles
x C. W. Post     [This and next 4 lines not in WW's hand]
   With
   B. D. Buford & Co.
      Kansas City
         Mo.
[On another piece, pasted down:]
Herman Beckurts – prop: Denver *Tribune*

      fare $22.75

leaves in morning 7.30
   "      evening  6.45

36 hours run

Bender, hatter
211 Race St. Phil

[1]

Mems from St Louis
  sent the two Vols. from Camden
  X by Express C o d
  to Nestor Sanborn bank of North
                 America
  $10 due    44 Wall St N Y City

+ + L of G. to Charles      about
           Scribner's Sons Oct 25
                      '79
returned
        $3$^{50}$ due     743 Broadway N Y

       Alice R. Alexander    the Palace
x the P O order from Derry
                Ireland
    $10 due

ans F. Leypoldt – catalogue [*Correspondence of Walt Whitman*, III, 92]

Oct 24 – wrote to Hannah [Heyde]
  "  25    "        Mrs 7 Jim Scovel
             ans by J M S
Oct 30 wrote to Robt U Johnson [*Correspondence of Walt Whitman*, III, 167]
        Ed: Room S Mag 743 B'dway N Y

       "        Fred Rauch
              Lock box 2419

address Thos J Hall, care Cell & Hall
  Jos: W Hall      Fruit dealers Leadville, Col

Oct 31 wrote to W R Wood 443 Kaigh's Pt av. Cam
Nov. 1   "    "  Ed Cattell Glenolden Delaware
                          Co:
  "    "    "  Lou & George [Whitman]
  " ——      Hannah [Hyde]
  " ——      Mary [Van Nostrand]
  " ——      Clarry Whittaker

[2]
  [On card of Stephen F. Smart, Kansas Pacific Railway, General Traveling Agent:]
Joe Hall says gone to Europe
  [On card of Ed. Lindsey:]
        Sterling
           Rice Co: Kansas.
  [On the page:]
rec'd letter from Alice R Alexander
    the Palace, Derry, Ireland
      (p o order for me $10 – at Camden)
  [Card of W. T. Harris, Sup't Public Schools, St. Louis. Office, Cor. Seventh & Chestnut Sts.]

[3]

☞ remember to
    Send book to Dr Bucke for
+        Alfred Withers

    ($5 pay received by me in St Louis)

Wrote to John Hardie, 6 Finnart St
        Greenock Scotland

Nov 4 – Wrote to Smith Caswell
"  5    "    Pete Doyle [*Correspondence of Walt Whitman*, III, 167–169]
"  "    "    Ed: Lindell
"  "    "    Nat Jones
"  "    "    Charley Wood

Nov 6 (Thursday) visit to Crystal City
    Plate Glass Works, (by Iron
    Mountain RR) – Swash creek

"  8th wrote to Mrs Gilchrist – sent map [*Correspondence of Walt Whitman* III, 169–
                                                        170]

remember to send *Dem Vistas &*
             *Memoranda to*
[side-     Joseph Wm. Thompson          [sideways:]
ways:]
             Goldsmith Building        book
Sent
from Camden      Temple  London  Eng:     sent
        p o order
          sent

Nov 12 sent letter to Marvin – Wash'n [Joseph B. Marvin]
        with piece to Noyes – sent map [*Correspondence of Walt Whitman*, III,
                                          170n]

"  rec'd letter from Ed: Lindell
"  sent letter to Dr Bucke declining
    his kind offer of $100
16th sent letter to G W C[ilds] (rec'd ans Nov 24)
17th rec'd letter from Chas Heyde
20th letter postal to Lou & paper, with map
"  letter & piece to H L Bonsall [Camden *Daily Post*]
"  Papers to Han[nah Heyde]

[4]

[On card of R. H. Holland:]
swell
Episcopal Minister   St Louis
[Just below same card:]
Hegelian – going to Chicago
[Below card of Isaac Sharp, Attorney at Law, Council Grove, Kansas:]
J C O'Connor      – the Indian agent
  care of Lands-      I met with the Sioux
  berger & Co:      Chief in Washington
                     8 or 9 years ago
    Wine Merchants – San Francisco

Geo: F. Neale    (the Superintendent)
    Plate Glass Works
      Crystal City — Missouri

[On card with autograph of Henry C. Brokmeyer:]
                    the Lieut Governor
                    St Louis        Mo
[Card of Horace Howard Furness, 222 West Washington Square, Philadelphia.]

[5]

Nov 20 (Thursday) Snow in N Y City
                    & London
Nov 21 – letter & piece to J B M'C
remember to send
x Copy of L of G to Heyde [see entry below for 25 January 1880]
22ᵈ visit to Anhauser's Brewery

23ᵈ Sunday letter to John Burroughs with
        Mrs G[ilchrist]'s & Gilder's letter & map [*Correspondence of Walt Whitman*, III,
                                                                    170–171]

    "  Papers to Mary [Van Nostrand]

24th sent L of G. through Lou [isa Whitman]
X   to Honora E. Thompson      [sideways:]
            Redlands                      rec'd
p o order
            on Bridgewater              paid
in Camden
            Somersetshire      England

24 to G W C[hilds] in acknowledgment

    "  Joe Hall here at 2316 [Pine Street, St. Louis] to see me
            sent a few lines to Tom [Thomas J. Hall, Leadville, Colorado]

                                                        book as
    "  letter to Geo & Lou[isa Whitman] asking to send      above

27th on St L[ouis] Bridge

28th Sent (by request to Lou[isa Whitman],) – by express
                                                    c. o. d.
        L of G. & T R      $7 to –
X      E. Steiger 25 Park Place      [sideways:]
                    N Y City              rec'd
                                          paid

Sent card to Honora E Thompson Eng:
                    See above

    also to Jos Wm Thompson    Eng
            promising books

29th cards & books to Ida Johnston [Camden]
    "          "        Fred Rauch

[6]

Michael Healy Olive st cars
        Cincinnati (Maryland by birth)
        been with shows – (left home at 14)

Mrs Fanny Raymond Ritter [*Correspondence of Walt Whitman*, III, 174]
        103 S Hamilton street
Kind    Poughkeepsie, N Y
letter Nov 23 – (I sent no answer) [See footnote 139, above]

Order from G P Putnam's sons
  to send L of G to
    R F Wilkinson
        Poughkeepsie N Y
& bill to Putnam


      L
Mrs Fannie Taylor
    1810 Olive street
          St Louis Missouri [See footnotes 129 and 726, above]


     E
James H Mills
 room    cor 5th & Olive streets
         St Louis


Dec 2 – get Haswell's
    Engineers' & Mechanics Pocket Book
        Harpers 1868
      680 pp bound in flaps —


Dec 4 p card & papers to Han[nah Heyde ] with map
  "   "   "   "     Mary [Van Nostrand] " "


X Dr Hunt bo't two Vols of Lou[isa Whitman]
         $10


Dec 9 – sent "The best I see in thee"    [See "What Best I See in Thee,"
    to Erastus Brainerd for *Press*    *Leaves of Grass,* Comprehensive
    also ¶ for Personal       Reader's Edition, p. 485]
      in answer to request


      '79
Dec 7, 8, 9 10, 11 *Very bad spells,*
    unable sometimes to walk a block.
    (sometimes tho't it all nearing the end)
             J B's
11th letter to Lou[isa Whitman] (baby's picture)
 "   "  & paper to Han[nah Heyde]


15th rec'd letter from Herbert [Gilchrist]
    wrote postal c to  "  [*Correspondence of Walt Whitman,* III, 171]


17th Wrote to T & J W Johnston & Co
    535 Chestnut St Phila
  to Hannah [Heyde] $5 (rec'd)
  Mary [Van Nostrand] 5


18 wrote to Lou[isa Whitman] — rec'd letter from Mrs Gil[christ]


17th Piece in Phil: Press "What best I see" &c


19th letter to Harry Bons[all] — [?] st to Dr Bucke

                          [8 blank]

                          [9]

Dec 27 – rec'd letter from Dr Bucke
    $45 – send books (*books sent*


                        [26]
[Post card pasted on page, not in WW's hand: "Bee comfortably settled at/Bern. /Dear

Friend / Settled for / the winter I hope/in very comfortable / quarters – / 1 Elm villas / Elm Row / Heath St. / Hampstead / London. XX / Love from us all / A. Gilchrist /." On a slip, not in WW's hand: Nathaniel G. Jones / No. 512 Bridge ave / Camden, N. J.]

[27]

Money due when I get back
    to Camden
$10 Express C. o. d. from Nestor    [sideways:] paid
    Sanborn 44 Wall St                paid
10.20 p o order from Alice R Alex    [sideways:]
    ander, the Palace, Derry, Ireland       paid
5.10 p o order from Honora E. Thomp    [sideways:]
    son, Redlands, Bridgewater         paid
        Somersetshire Eng
7 Express c. o. d. E. Steiger    [sideways:]
    25 Park Place N Y City            paid
2.67 p o order from J. W. Thompson    [sideways:]
    Goldsmith Building Temple        paid
       London Eng:
10 from Dr Hunt, friend of    [sideways:] paid
    Dr Bucke's, for a set              paid
  remember Dr Bucke's books
             seven
    two T R – seven L of G – one besides    [sideways:] Sent
  "       orders from G P Putnam's        Sent
       Sons N Y
  "       T W & J W Johnston & Co
      535 Chestnut Phila
$5 from Phil Press    [sideways:] paid

[28]
[On slip, not in WW's hand: G. L. McKean / with / Hickman Trunk M'f'g Co. / 309 N 3d St / Room / Cor 11th & Olive /.]

[On calling card:]
      Dec 12 '79
    Willie T. Elder   [printed]
    3303 Olive     [not in WW's hand]
      Street City   [not in WW's hand]
   St Louis Missouri

[Clipped from printed envelope: T. & J. W. JOHNSTON & CO. / 535 Chestnut Street, PHILADELPHIA, Pa./.]

[29]

    John P. Usher [not in WW's hand]
    John P Usher Jr   [not in WW's hand]
    Arthur P Usher   [not in WW's hand]
    Linton J Usher   [not in WW's hand]
    Fairmount, Leavenworth Co
    Samuel C. Usher [not in WW's hand]
       Lawrence
         Douglas Co:
       Kansas
        Sept 14, 15 & 16
          '79

  O H Rothacker
    Ed Tribune newspaper
    Denver Col:

[Rest of page, ten lines, in pencil:]

"   Started for St Louis, Missouri abt 9 p m

12ᵗʰ   in St Louis (only one night)⁷³⁶

13   on through Missouri, to Kansas City, & so
      to Lawrence, to Judge Ushers⁷³⁷

15ᵗʰ, 16th   Topeka, Kansas
      on to Denver, Colorado
         Rocky Mountain trip. South park
         over the Santa Fe road – Pueblo – Spanish
         Peaks – the Great Plains – the Arkansas
         River – Sterling – Southern Kansas –⁷³⁸

|  |  | [154] |
|---|---|---|
|  | [in pencil:] |  |
| Sent <u>Post</u> Jan 7 '80 to⁷³⁹ | Sent <u>Critic</u>⁷⁴⁰ |  |
| Hannah | Dr Bucke |  |
| Mary | Jessie |  |
| Smith Caswell | Mary |  |
| Pete Doyle |  |  |
| John Newton Johnson |  |  |
| Dr Bucke | <u>Phil Press</u> – March 3 ⁷⁴¹ |  |
| Warren & Amy Dowe | Dr Bucke |  |
| W J Linton | Al Johnston [in pencil] |  |

736.  Whitman had meant to spend 36 hours but was delayed by a railroad collision (see Gay Wilson Allen, *The Solitary Singer,* pp. 486–489, for this and other details of the western trip).

737.  Whitman was supposed to deliver a poem at a meeting in Topeka; however, as he had none ready, he wrote out a short speech (see the text in *Prose Works 1892,* I, 207–208) but got so interested in talking to Judge John P. Usher's sons, he forgot to go and give the lecture. Usher was the Mayor of Lawrence and former Secretary of the Interior under President Lincoln.

738.  See Robert R. Hubach, "Walt Whitman in Kansas," *Kansas Historical Quarterly,* X (May 1941), 150–154; "Three Uncollected St. Louis Interviews of Walt Whitman," *American Literature,* XIV (May 1942), 141–147; and "Western Newspaper Accounts of Whitman's 1879 Trip to the West," *Walt Whitman Review,* XVIII (June 1972), 56–62.

739.  On 20 November 1879 Whitman recorded (see footnote 735) that he sent to Henry Lummis Bonsall a "letter & piece"; as Bonsall was editor of the Camden *Daily Post,* this may be the article (which Whitman may have sent out on 7 January 1880) and not the date of the piece to his two sisters and ten friends (for John Newton Johnson, see footnote 9a; for William J. Linton, see footnote 39; for Warren and Amy Dowe, see footnote 245; Albert Johnston was the son of J. H. Johnston, the New York jeweler; the others need no identification).

740.  This issue of *The Critic,* which Whitman sent to Dr R. M. Bucke, his niece Jessie in St Louis, and his sister Mary Van Nostrand, cannot be identified; *The Critic* edited by Jeannette L. Gilder did not begin until January 1881.

741.  "What Best I See in Thee" (a poem on U. S. Grant) appeared in the Philadelphia

Mrs Gilchrist
    also Denver <u>Trib</u>
Ed Cattell [in pencil]
Al Johnston

[155]

1879

St Louis & Colorado Trip   [in red ink]
[Most of page, ten lines, in pencil]
St Louis[741a]

*Press* on 17 December 1879; Albert Johnston was J. H. Johnston's son; Dr Bucke was the only one who received all three of Whitman's mailings, and his own piece on Whitman, the first of several, was to be published in the Philadelphia *Press* on 7 May 1880.
    741a. In *Faint Clews & Indirections: Manuscripts of Walt Whitman and His Family,* edited by Clarence Gohdes and Rollo G. Silver (Durham, North Carolina, 1949), pp. 58–60, are the following travel notes from the Trent Collection, Duke University:
    the RR we go on (Sept 13 '79 from St Louis to Lawrence) is *the* (northern) *St Louis and Kansas City RR,* 275 miles (from St L to K C) right through the (northern) centre and natural beauty and richness of this great State. Cross'g the Missouri river on the bridge at the pretty town of St Charles, we enter upon the finest soil, show (on a loose, slip-shod scale) trees, beauty, eligibility for tillage of crops, and general look of open air health, picturesqueness that I ever saw, and continue all day on the same enchant'g nearly three hundred miles — ahead of any thing in Pennsylvania or New York states good as those are

they raise a good deal of tobacco in these counties of Missouri, you see the light greenish-gray leaves pulled and now (Sept 13, '79) in great patches on rows of sticks or frame-works, hanging out to dry — looking like leaves of the mullein, familiar to eastern eyes. [See *Prose Works 1892*, I, 206–207, for a revised version of these passages.]
    Yet, fine as it is, it isn't the finest part of the State. (There a bed of impervious clay and hard pan every where down below on this line, that holds the water — "drowns the land in wet weather, and bakes it in dry," as some one harshly said.) South are some rich counties; but the beauty spots of Missouri are the north-western portions

Missouri
mules (first) oxen, horses — products on the largest scale — everything all varieties and no stint — cattle, wheat, maize, hay, hemp, tobacco, corn wine wool fruits, —
Kansas
— every where products and people and energy and practical ? — every where towns go-ing up, provided or be'g provided with the best, pavements water, gas, parks, police print'g office — everywhere the Railroad, equipped with the best

Wednesday
Sept 17 '79
Topeka Kansas

the ride about Topeka (driven by William Muroe) — fine hard smooth roads miles and miles of them — over a flat & unbroken surface, stretching in every direction as far as the eye could see — the Capitol, (only one fine wing of it, the rest to be) — the Governor — Chief Judge Horton, other Judges
abt Sept 20 '79
How inexpressibly magnificent and ample it is! The contrast — the alternation! After these easy-peaceful and fertile prairies of a thousand miles area, corn & wheat & h start up the grandest mountains of the globe, with many a savage canon, and cloud pierc'g peaks by hundreds! — and spots of terror & sublimity Dante and Angelo never knew

going east, after we leave Sterling, Kansas the sun is up about half an hour — every th'g

Two Vols. to Nestor Sanborn, 44 Wall st.      Bank of
    North America – paid $10 [742]

Nov 24.   Sent L  of  G (through Lou)   L  of  G to    [in blue pencil, paid
    Honora E Thompson, Redlands, Bridgewater,      sideways:]      recd
    Somersetshire, Eng.   Paid

Jan 3ᵈ  [in ink]
return'd – left St Louis, Sunday morning 8 o'c.
    for the east – got in West Phila.  7. 20
    Monday evening – Jan 5. 1880 – (absent from
Sept 10, '79)
nearly four months[743] [in ink]

[156]

wholesale grain & seed
Wᵐ P Evans, gent (Quaker stock) age 35 – ∧Malvern Flour &c
Mills
    introduced himself to me at Ferry house, Phila: side, Jan '80 [744]

George Coffman, 117 Edwards st.   16ᵗʰ Ward, Phila[745]   [in pencil]

Joe's Sisters – 616 n 36ᵗʰ street – go up in Baring St   [in pencil]
    car & get off at 36ᵗʰ [746]   [in pencil]

Maps – Smith – 25 S 6th st   [in pencil]

fresh and beautiful — the immense area flat as a house floor, visible for 20 miles in every direction in the clear air. The grass all autumn yellow and reddish tawny. Little houses, farms, enclosures, stacks of hay, dotting the landscape — the prevail'g hue a rich

In *Walt Whitman's Diary in Canada* (Boston, 1904), p. 56, is the following paragraph in the section "From Other Journals of Walt Whitman":
    *Oct., Nov., etc., '79.* NOTES IN ST. LOUIS. In the Mercantile Library on Fourth Street (where I used to go for an hour daily to read the New York and Philadelphia papers by courtesy of Mr. Dyer) they have a very good photograph from the life of Edgar Poe and a bust of Thomas H. Benton, the best life likeness. Also a colossal clay figure, very good, of Mr. Shaw, a rich philanthropist here, and donor of a handsome park and botanical garden to the city.

    742.  Sending Nestor Sanborn and Honora E. Thompson (below) copies of his books was part of the "business" details Whitman cleared up on his arrival in Camden; they ordered books while he was in the West (see footnote 735).
    743.  See footnote 735.
    744.  William P. Evans apparently did not follow up this introduction; he does not appear again in these pages or in Whitman's correspondence.
    745.  Whitman had written to George Coffman on 15 December 1878 (letter now lost).
    746.  Joe's Sisters could be the sisters of Joe Hall, or of Joseph Browning (Harry Stafford's brother-in-law) or of Joseph Elverson, Jr (assistant editor of the Philadelphia *Saturday Night*), or the name of a place.

[On slip with printed name and address and date (in a hand not WW's) of E. Steiger,[747] German news-agent, wholesale and export bookseller, 25 Park Place, New York, Nov. 25th 1879, three lines in blue pencil:]

> books sent
> recd
> paid

[On a calling card of F. Gutekunst,[748] 712 Arch St., Philadelphia, photographer, is written, not in WW's hand:]

> Dr:

Presented by    F  H  Babbit[749]
  Mr Walt Whitman –

[157]

1880 – After Colorado & St Louis trip [in pencil]

Jan 6 – Sent G  P  Putnam's Sons 182 Fifth av. N Y [750]  [in pencil]   [in blue
                                                                     pencil, sideways:]
                                          [in pencil:]  paid    recd
  (by express) Two Sets – 4 Vols – $14 due – (sent back  rect'd )
                                                         bill  )       paid

            ferry pass rec'd
  " wrote to Capt Frazee,∧Jeff, Bonsall, Trib., Ledg:[751]  [in pencil]

Jan 7.   sent to Dr R  M  Bucke, Asylum for the   [in blue pencil,
                                                    sideways:]         all
          Insane, London, Ontario, Canada (by express)  [these lines   paid
              14 Vols altogether –            in blue pencil:]  recd
  10 Vols – paid for —                           recd            paid
              paid                              paid
    4 (or is it 4?) to be accounted for[752]      all

9th   sent Mem:  and Vistas  to Jos Wm Thompson[753]
       Goldsmith Building, Temple, London, E  [in blue pencil,
                                                sideways:]    recd

---

747. E. Steiger ordered books from Whitman when he was in the West (see footnote 735).
748. F. Gutekunst made numerous photographs of Whitman, used in *Leaves of Grass.*
749. Unidentified; Whitman met in March 1880 at F. Gutekunst's studio (see below).
750. More of Whitman's unfinished business (see footnote 735).
751. All five of these letters are lost; for Captain Frazee see footnote 419.
752. Still more unfinished business, delayed by the trip to the West.
753. Also ordered while the poet was in Colorado and Missouri (see footnote 735).

recd

9th   got 50 Two Riv: from Arnold, cor 6th
          & Minor sts. (paid $20) (as I estimate
          there are 150 Vols. yet due me)[754]

10th   sent circ to C  P  Farrell   1421 New York av:
          Washington   D C (at his request)[755]

"   paid Carrier for <u>Sunday Times</u>, (both) up to date

"   sent circ & note to T  & J  W  Johnson & Co[756]
          535 Chestnut St  Phil (ans: recd)   [in blue pencil,
                                        sideways:]    recd

11   papers to Clint Townsend [757]   [in pencil]

13   sent photos, to Pat Hartnet, Frank Elder [?], Bill Elder,
          & Mike Healy, 3301 Olive St.  St. Louis   [in blue pencil,
          Missouri  City  R R [758]         sideways:]   recd

"   rec'd pass from Camden & Atl: R R for 1880
          acknowledged it[759]

"   papers to W S Fullerton  Greeley  Col [760]

14   sent circ (by request) to Fred K  Gillette  Garrettsville
                                              Ohio

"   sent John P Usher Jr, Lawrence, Kansas, <u>Mem</u>: of War   [in blue pencil,
          & two photos – one for Linton[761]          sideways:] recd

[158]

[Calling card of James E. Mills, consulting geologist and metallurgist, St Louis; and one of D. M. Zimmerman, secretary and treasurer of the Camden & Atlantic RR.] [762]

---

754.  James Arnold was the binder, at 531 Chestnut Street, Philadelphia, of *Two Rivulets*.
755.  Unidentifiable.
756.  Whitman wrote to the company on 17 December 1879 from St Louis (see footnote 735); the letter is lost.
757.  An in-law of the Stafford's?
758.  These four men Whitman obviously met in St Louis, in much the same way he met workmen on the ferry in Camden and Philadelphia.
759.  Through D. M. Zimmerman; see *The Correspondence of Walt Whitman*, III, 207, acknowledging the 1881 pass; the 1880 letter is lost.
760.  See footnote 432 for Scotty Fullerton, of whom little is known.
761.  John P. Usher, Jr is one of the sons of the Mayor of Lawrence (see footnote 737);

Mrs Gilchrist ~~1 Elm Villas, Elm Row~~
~~Heath St   Hampstead London~~
  5 Mount Vernon   Hampstead   London[763]
John P Usher, Jr   Lawrence, Douglass Co: Kansas[764]
Linton J   Usher, Fairmount   Leavenworth Co   Kans[765] [in blue pencil,
O  H   Rothacker, Daily Tribune, Denver, Col[766]          sideways:]     recd
Harry J Gasprell, Tefft House, Topeka   Kans[767]
M  H   Case, Mayor, Topeka   K
Thos J Hall   box 2419 Leadville   Col[768]
E  C   Devereaux, Topeka   K
Chas W Post,[769] with B   D Buford & Co: Kansas City, Mo [in blue pencil,
                                                sideways:]   recd
                                                             letter
Stephen F Smart, gone to Europe [last three words in blue pencil]          May
Ed Lindsey, Sterling, Rice Co:   Kansas[770]                               8
W  T   Harris, Supt Schools, cor 7th & Chestnut St L[771]                 '80

Geo: F Neale, Plate Glass Works, Crystal City   Mo
H  C Brokmeyer   Lieut Gov.  St Louis
Pat Hartnett   Missouri R R Co office, 3301 Olive st   [in pencil]
                                     St Louis   [in pencil]

Linton J. Usher is probably the brother of Judge John P. Linton; see Whitman's letter (a transcript of it) in *The Correspondence of Walt Whitman*, III, 173.
    762.  See footnote 759.
    763.  Mrs Anne Gilchrist had written Whitman a card (see footnote 735) about her winter quarters at 1 Elm Villas, the address on her letter of 5 December 1879 (see *The Letters of Anne Gilchrist and Walt Whitman*, edited by Thomas B. Harned, pp. 187–189); but by 5 January 1880, she was at 5 Mount Vernon, Hampstead (*ibid.*, pp. 190–192).
    764.  See footnote 761.
    765.  See footnote 761.
    766.  O. H. Rothacker, editor of the Denver *Tribune* (listed in the notes Whitman kept of his trip west — see footnote 735), met the poet in Colorado.
    767.  These 11 men (below) were all among those Whitman met on his trip to Colorado, Kansas and Missouri, and most of them are listed in the notes he kept in the memorandum book (see footnote 735); he does not appear to have kept in touch with most of them — the exceptions are Thomas J. Hall, Charles W. Post, and William Torrey Harris.
    768.  Whitman's letter to Thomas J. Hall, 17 January 1880, is lost.
    769.  Whitman's letter to Charles W. Post, 8 February 1880, and Post's letter to Whitman, about 8 May 1880, are both lost.
    770.  Ed Lindsey is mentioned in Whitman's letter to Peter Doyle, 5 November 1879: "I stopt some days at a town right in the middle of those Plains, in Kansas, on the Santa Fe road — found a soldier there who had known me in the war 15 years ago — was married & running a hotel there — I had hard work to get away from him — he wanted me to stay all winter" (*The Correspondence of Walt Whitman*, III, 168). He is also the "E. L." in *Specimen Days*: "Remembrances to E. L., my old-young soldier friend of war times, and his wife and boy at S[terling, Kansas]" (*Prose Works, 1892*, I, 219).
    771.  William Torrey Harris (1835–1909) was also a philosopher and editor of *The Journal of Speculative Philosophy*; see Whitman's letters to him, 27 October 1879, from St Louis, and 28 September 1880, from Niagara Falls, *The Correspondence of Walt Whitman*, III, 166–167, 187–188; see also III, 171 and *With Walt Whitman in Camden*, I, 191.
    772.  See bottom of p. 6 of St Louis notebook (footnote 735, above).

[159]

1880 — January –

15<u>th</u>  sent a set 2 Vols to James E Mills,[772] room 37    [in blue pencil,
           Lucas Building, 506 Olive st cor 5th    sideways:]    recd
                St Louis    Missouri    paid

17  sent Charles Pope   St Louis,   the two Vols:   [in blue pencil,
                letter with circulars[773]    sideways:] recd

"   sent photos to Mayor Case, & Harry Gasprell, Topeka[774]

"       "   also to Ed: Lindsey[775]

"   — postal card to Tom Hall[776]

                              [in blue pencil,    rec'd
22  sent Willie Mills,[776a] <u>Mem</u>: <u>War</u> & photo:    sideways:]    paid

"   Fred K Gillette, Garrettsville, Portage Co: Ohio   [sideways:]  paid
        Mem:, Vistas, & <u>Strong Bird</u>[777]
                        answ'd   recd   [in blue pencil]

"   sent postal card to Trübner & Co. asking ab't books sent[778]

"   "   "   "   J H  Johnston, declining dinner[779]

25th  Scribners for Dec to Mary[780]

"   L  of  G  to Heyde[781]

"   papers to Ed: Lindsey[782]

---

773.  Letter lost.
774.  See footnote 767.
775.  See footnote 770.
776.  Post card lost.
776a.  James E. Mill's letter in acknowledgment, 15 February 1880, is in the Feinberg
Collection.
777.  The three books which Whitman sent Gillette were *Memoranda During the War*
(Camden, 1875–'76), *Democratic Vistas* (Washington, 1871), and *As a Strong Bird on Pinions
Free, and Other Poems* (Washington, 1872).
778.  These letters to and from Trübner & Company are lost.
779.  Letter lost.
780.  Mary Van Nostrand, Whitman's sister. John Burroughs's "Nature and the Poets" in
*Scribner's* quoted J. A. Symonds on Whitman as "more thoroughly Greek than any man of
modern times!"
781.  Charles L. Heyde, married to Whitman's sister Hannah, was no favorite of the
poet's, who referred to Heyde as a "wretched cur."
782.  See footnote 770.

"      "      " Will Tinker[783]

26    postal to Dr Bucke[784]

&  postal & papers to Al Johnston[785]

28    letter from Tom Hall, Leadville[786]

"     sent papers to Smith Caswell

30    postal to Dr Bucke

"      " Gutekunst[787]

Feb 1    papers to Linton J Usher, Fairmount[788]

4th    sent Two Riv to Ethel Thompson care Charles Thompson
Esq: Preswylfa, near Cardiff, England – & postal card to
Jos: W  Thompson, Goldsmith Building, Temple, London[789]

[in blue
pencil,
sideways:]
paid
recd

5th    sent Notes on WW to J  W  Thompson (above)

[in blue pencil,
sideways:]
paid
recd

7th    sent   James E Mills, St L.   4 copies Mem of War[790]

[in blue pencil,
sideways:]
paid

"      pictures to Tommy Hall

---

783.  See footnote 291.
784.  This and the post card of 30 January are lost.
785.  Post card to the son of J. H. Johnston, New York City, is lost.
786.  One of the few men Whitman met out west who kept in touch, but the letter is lost.
787.  The photographer (see footnote 748).
788.  See footnote 761.
789.  Whitman wrote a note to himself, 8 November 1879, to send *Democratic Vistas* and *Memoranda During the War* to Thompson (see p. 3 of western notebook, footnote 735, above), and he here is sending *Two Rivulets* to members of the Thompson family, and *Notes on Walt Whitman as Poet and Person* by John Burroughs to Thompson (see entry just below); the post card to Thompson is lost.
790.  I cannot identify James E. Mills, except that Whitman met him in St Louis in the Fall (see footnote 772), sent him *Leaves* and *Two Rivulets,* and here sends him four copies of *Memoranda During the War.*

8th   letter & photo to Chas W Post   care of B D Buford & Co     [in blue
pencil, sideways:]
Kansas City  Mo[791]                                               recd

---

"     papers to Will Tinker[792]

---

"     "     " Clint Townsend[793]

[160]

1540   North 15th   st Phila:[794]

p

Isaac R Pennybacker   "Press" writer

poet

---

[Slips of paper, clipped from larger pieces, on which are printed names and
addresses of Charles J. Wood,[795] 4082½ Lancaster Avenue, taxidermist;
Edwin C. Sparks, 427 So. 5th Street, Camden, umbrellas; and Jas. H. Dewey,
city agent, The Hektograph.[796]]

---

Hall

H  J  Bathgate  Oakenholt  ~~Discard~~ Cheshire
Nr  Flint  England[797]

---

[Five lines in pencil:]
Robt Wolf, boy of 10 or 12   rough     at the ferry
lives cor 4th & Market

---

Wm C Pine – "Walt Whitman sociable"

---

791. See footnotes 767 and 769.
792. See footnote 291.
793. See footnote 757, also 633.
794. The Philadelphia *Press* published Whitman's poem "What Best I See in Thee" on
17 December 1879, mentioned the poet at the Robert G. Ingersoll lecture on 26 May 1880,
and Whitman sent copies of his Lincoln lecture on 15 April; Isaac Pennypacker may have had
something to do with these; see entries also for 13 February and 3 March 1880, below.
795. This may be the Charley Woods to whom Whitman wrote from St Louis on 5
November 1879, but the letter is lost.
796. The Hektograph is unidentifiable, through regular sources, as a newspaper or
magazine; it may have been a duplicating or printing device. (See Rigby Graham, "The Hektograph," *American Notes & Queries,* XI [March 1973], 104–105.)
797. Herbert J. Bathgate, author of a piece on Whitman in *The Times,* London, in
1879 (reprinted in *Papers from The Times,* London, 1879, II, 155–164), was a friend of
Ruskin's, and Whitman named him in 1885 among "friends (or used to be friends) of L of G.
and W. W." (see *The Correspondence of Walt Whitman,* III, 405; see also III, 174n and 305n).
Whitman's letters to him, 17 February, 14 and 18 March 1880, are lost; Bathgate's to Whitman, 31 January 1880, is in the Feinberg Collection, and 2 July 1880, in the John Rylands
Library, Manchester.

Robert Norris    144 car – Market st   Phil –
28 yrs old – stair maker – widower[798]

~~Rob~~ Mr Whiteing, Republican, Springfield, Mass.
Talcott Williams[799]    "          "

Peter Bayne's article   Contemporary Review
December 1875   London[800]

| | |
|---|---|
| F. H. Babbit M D [801] [not WW's hand]<br>at Gutekunst's<br>712 Arch<br>March 1880 | W  W  Nevin<br>129 South 13th st Phila<br>March 13  '80 |
| W   S   Kennedy[803]<br>college<br>man        14 Kirkland Place<br>poetry<br>letter from        Cambridge<br>March '80<br><br>Mass: | Mrs Ellen E  Dickinson<br>317 West 28th st<br>N   Y [802] |

[161]

1880   sent two sets (4 Vols) to Mrs Jenny C Croly[804]   [in blue pencil,
sideways:]  recd

798.   These three people, Robert Wolf, William C. Pine, and Robert Norris, are similar to others Whitman met casually in Philadelphia; I'm not quite sure what "Walt Whitman sociable" as recorded here means.

799.   Talcott Williams (1849–1928), on the New York *Sun* and *World*, a Springfield *Republican* editorial writer in 1879, who joined the Philadelphia *Press* in 1881 (see *The Correspondence of Walt Whitman*, III, 297, 378–380, 383); Whitman told O'Connor in 1882 that Williams was an ardent friend, and he told Traubel that Williams "has original talent of no common order — but I guess it will never get out: a man tied up as Talcott is with a great newspaper in a big city has little chance to make the best of himself" (*With Walt Whitman in Camden*, I, 202). Whiteing apparently was a fellow-writer on the *Republican* who came with Williams to see the poet.

800.   Peter Bayne wrote "Walt Whitman's Poems," *Contemporary Review*, XXVIII (December 1875), 49–69. See *The Correspondence of Walt Whitman*, III, 21, 27.

801.   See opposite footnote 749.

802.   See entry below for 13 March 1880.

803.   William Sloane Kennedy (1850–1929), who was then on the *Saturday Evening Post* staff and was to become one of the warmest admirers of Whitman and *Leaves of Grass*, author of *Reminiscences of Walt Whitman* (London, 1896), and *The Fight of a Book for the World: A Companion Volume to Leaves of Grass* (West Yarmouth, Mass., 1926), and at least 10 articles on Whitman, beginning in February 1881, is here first mentioned by Whitman: "college man poetry letter from March '80," and his address. His extensive correspondence with the poet began on 25 February 1881; see *The Correspondence of Walt Whitman*, III, 214 *et passim*. There are 198 Whitman letters to Kennedy in Vols. III–V.

804.   Jenny C. Croly's letter to Whitman, 21 May 1882, requesting a poem for *Demorest's Illustrated* (apparently never sent), is in the Library of Congress.

Feb 11    162 East 38th st N Y City,    one for Wm Black              paid
          to be paid for ($7) & one as a present to Mrs C. [roly]

13    Isaac R   Pennybacker called [805]

15    sent one copy <u>Memoranda</u> to Jas E Mills, St Louis,    [in blue pencil,
          & one do: to Hiram F Mills, office of Essex Co: sideways:]    paid
          Lawrence, Mass[806]

"    papers to Clint Townsend [807] – <u>Herald</u>  to Jeff

16    recd check from Ruskin ₤ 70    England [808]  5 sets to go)  [in blue pencil,
                                                                    sideways:]    all
"    sent postal card to H J Bathgate[809]  (two sets sent 19th Feb)              sent

19    sent Dr Bucke Two Sets    4 vols (3 L of G & 1 T R)[810]  [in blue pencil,
                                                                sideways:]  paid

                                                             [in blue pencil,
"    sent H   J. Bathgate (for Mr Ruskin) [811]   (all 5     sideways:]    recd
                                                   sets sent)

      Oakenholt, Liscard, Cheshire, England –                           paid
                                    five sets
          Two sets, 4 vols    (3 sets to go)    sent

20    sent circ:  to C  H  Sholes   416 4th st
                  Des Moines  Iowa[812]

"    rec'd letter from John Burroughs, (check $25) [813]

805.  Pennybacker, apparently a reporter, had a piece on Whitman in the Philadelphia
*Press* on 3 March 1880 (see below).
806.  Hiram F. Mills is obviously related to James E. Mills (see footnote 790).
807.  See footnotes 352 and 633.
808.  John Ruskin (1819–1900), the famous British essayist and critic, first got a copy of
Whitman through William Harrison Riley (see *The Correspondence of Walt Whitman*, III,
149), and here he orders through Herbert J. Bathgate (see *ibid.*, III, 174n, and footnote 797,
above).
809.  This post card is lost.
810.  Dr Richard Maurice Bucke, who must have been giving friends copies of *Leaves
of Grass* and *Two Rivulets*, was, at this time, writing his *Walt Whitman*, published in 1883,
the first full biography of the poet, who edited and wrote part of it (see *The Correspondence
of Walt Whitman*, III, 174).
811.  See footnote 808.
812.  See Whitman's letter to Sholes, a shorthand reporter, who wrote the poet an
"ardent letter," in *The Correspondence of Walt Whitman*, III, 181.
813.  Whitman's reply is in *The Correspondence of Walt Whitman*, III, 173–174.

29th   papers to Jeff and Mary     [in pencil]

---

March 1 – sent a set, two Vols, to Talcott Williams,      [in blue pencil,
      office Republican newspaper Springfield, Mass[814]      sideways:]   recd
                                                                            paid

3[d]—Pennypacker's piece about W W in <u>Phil Press</u>[815]

---

4th   sent a set Two Vols  to R  H  Ewart, 3 East 41st      [in blue pencil,
      Street N  Y  City                                          sideways:]   recd
                                                                              paid

"    rec'd draft from Trübner & Co: $37.22 – up to
      Dec 31. '79 – (wrote to them acknowledging rec't)[816]

---

6th to 12th   down at Glendale[817]

---

12th   sent the Two Vols: to C  H  Sholes               [in blue pencil,
      Glenwood, Mills Co: Iowa[818]                      sideways:]  paid
                                                                     recd

13th   rec'd $1.45 from J  W  Thompson, London, Eng:

---

"    sent Mrs Ellen E Dickinson   317 West
      28th St   N  Y – slips & postal card [819]

---

"    sent slips to W  S  Kennedy   14 Kirkland Place
      Cambridge  Mass: [820]

[162]

                              sent steel engs[821]
B  W  Hubbard, 218 Middle St  Portland  Maine     [in pencil]
      ~~letter from him March 1880  college man  poetry~~[822]

---

814.  See footnote 799.
815.  Isaac R. Pennypacker visited Whitman on 13 February 1880 (see above).
816.  Letter lost.
817.  This seems to be Whitman's first visit to the Stafford farm at White Horse since 9 July 1879; see "Loafing in the Woods," dated 8 March 1880, and written "down in the country" — i. e., Glendale — in *Specimen Days: Prose Works 1892*, I, 234–235.
818.  See footnote 812.
819.  Letter lost.
820.  See footnote 803.
821.  It is not clear what these steel engravings were for, but Whitman had used some in his books.
822.  This cancelled line refers to William Sloane Kennedy, and was rewritten on the opposite page.

Wm M Rossetti   5 Endsleigh Gardens
      Euston Road   London   N W [823]

John Johnston Jr, Ziegler & Swearingen   36 north 4th Phil [824]   [in pencil]

John Battles (makes the "potato chips")   38 yrs of age
               been 4 years soldiering [825]

☞ paid $31.50 May 27, '80

April 11 '80 – Dr Bucke is to acc't to me   [in blue pencil, sideways:]   all
    paid all [in blue pencil]   paid
for Five Vols:   3 L of G and 2 T R, at $3.50 a vol [826]
             17.50 altogeth

[On calling card of M. W. Gridley, 9 Duke Street, London Bridge:]

Mr & Mrs Gridley called on me    J  L  Brotherton
   May 6, '80, bo't Two Sets    553 North 16th St
for son Chas Oscar Gridley [827]    Phila
           the Quaker that came upon   [in pencil]
           the Atlantic in Phila   [in pencil]

[On slip of paper with printed address of a photographer. 54 North Eighth St., Phil.:]

Geo: C   Potier

[On slip of paper:]   Jas. Huneker [828]
         1029 Walnut st

---

823.  William Michael Rossetti's name and address are here perhaps because about this time Whitman had received a request from him to send *Two Rivulets* to Frederick Locker-Lampson in London (see *The Correspondence of Walt Whitman*, III, 174).

824.  John R. (Jack) Johnston, Jr was the son of Colonel Johnston, the Camden and Philadelphia artist friend of Whitman; young Johnston was employed by Ziegler & Swearingen, sellers of notions in Philadelphia.

825.  More interesting than the name of John Battles, another casual acquaintance Whitman lists, is "potato chips," here mentioned at an early time in its history; Mitford M. Mathews, *A Dictionary of Americanisms* (Chicago, 1951), p. 1295, cites its first appearance in print as 1878 in the *American Home Cook Book*, p. 67.

826.  Evidence of Dr Bucke's promotion of Whitman in Canada.

827.  Charles Oscar Gridley, who may have been introduced to *Leaves of Grass* here, became the secretary of the Carlyle Society and called on Whitman himself in 1884; he was listed in 1885 as a friend of L. of G. and W. W. (see *The Correspondence of Walt Whitman*, III, 405).

828.  James Gibbons Huneker (1857–1921), critic and author, who wrote an essay, "A Visit to Walt Whitman," in his *Ivory Apes and Peacocks* (1915, pp. 22–31).

Geo: Wehn at Schwartz & Graffs   Wood & Willow Ware
(Clinton Townsend) [829] Store, 516 Market

[Calling card of Scholl, photographer, 112 and 114 N. Ninth Street, Phil.]

[163]

1880   March                              [in blue pencil,
    Sent the Two Vols: to Titus Munson Coan[830]    sideways:]   paid

13th     110 East 56th street   N Y City
            enclosed
        also ~~letter with~~ slips –

                                            [in blue pencil,
    "     sent the Two Vols to J   A Mackenzie     sideways:]   paid
            Sarnia, County of Lambton, Ontario, Canada         recd

    "   sent B W Hubbard, 218 Middle st   Portland   Maine
            steel engraving[831]

    "   sent postal card to Dr Bucke[832]

14 – wrote postal to H J Bathgate, England [833]

15   rec'd photos from Gutekunst (Dr Babbitt) [834]

16   sent "the Prairie States" (7 or 8 lines) to Arthur B Tur-
        nure, 140 Nassau St   N Y. for Art Autograph
        for Irish Famine Relief [835]

    "   sent photo to Tennyson, Haslemere   Eng

        "      "      "  J A Symonds, Bristol   Eng[836]

---

829.   See footnotes 352 and 633.
830.   Titus Munson Coan's later letter, 22 November 1880, from the Century Club, ordering books, is in the Library of Congress.
831.   See footnote 821.
832.   Post card lost.
833.   As with the post card of 16 February 1880, this one is also lost.
834.   Gutekunst, of course, took numerous photographs of Whitman, but I cannot identify Dr Babbitt in connection with the photographer.
835.   Whitman's poem "The Prairie States" was published in facsimile in *The Art Autograph,* May 1880, collected in the 1881 *Leaves of Grass,* and is in the Comprehensive Reader's Edition of *Leaves,* p. 402.
836.   These photographs, and perhaps the one to Frederick Locker-Lampson, were among those Whitman got from F. Gutekunst on 15 March 1880.

"    sent letter to Jeff – (rec'd one from him)[837]

17   sent Dr Bucke Two copies L of G. on sale

18   sent three sets (6 Vols) to Herbert J Bathgate   [in blue pencil,     all
     Oakenholt, Sandrock Park, Liscard, Cheshire,     sideways:]     recd
     England, for Mr Ruskin – 5 sets sent altogether[838]   [last four words in
                                                              blue pencil]

"    papers to Clint Townsend

"    postal (& Tribune April 15,[839] with slips) to J   W Thompson[840]
                                                        Eng

"    postal to H J Bathgate[841]

"    letter to John Gilmer-Speed, World office N Y [842]

                                                    [in blue pencil:]
20th   Sold Edward S Ziegler,[843] 36 north 4th st Phil — a set –     paid

21st Sunday – dinner at Mr Dudley's – Curtin, Dougherty

"    sent the copy of "Riddle Song" to A   C   Wheeler   [in blue pencil,
     "Sunnyside Press"   Tarrytown   N Y ($20)[844]       sideways:]   recd
                                                                        paid
                                                                        10

"    circ to W   R   Shipman   College Hill, Mass[845]

837.   Both the letter to Jefferson Whitman, and the letter from him, are lost.
838.   Herbert J. Bathgate seems to have joined others in promoting Whitman in Europe (see footnote 808, also).
839.   This note on the [Chicago] "Tribune April 15" must have been added later: the paper contained Whitman's Lincoln lecture material.
840.   James W. Thompson purchased, in June 1879, a two-volume edition of Whitman; his correspondence with the poet is lost.
841.   Post card lost, most likely having to do with the sets sent the same day.
842.   This letter, lost, must have been personal, as I know of nothing by Whitman, either poetry or prose, or about him in the New York *World*, edited at this time by William Henry Hurlbert and owned by Jay Gould.
843.   As Edward S. Ziegler was in the firm of Ziegler & Swearingen, which employed Jack Johnston (see footnote 824), Ziegler must have learned about *Leaves of Grass* from Johnston.
844.   "A Riddle Song" appeared in the Tarrytown (New York) *Sunnyside Press* on 3 April 1880, then in Colonel Forney's *Progress,* 17 April 1880, in the 1881 *Leaves* (see Comprehensive Reader's Edition, pp. 476–478).
845.   Unidentified.

sent <u>Two Riv</u>: to Frederick Locker, 25 Chesham    [in blue pencil,    paid

sideways:]    recd

St London S W – (by request of Rossetti) also photo[846]

[164]

Sent Comp: <u>Tickets to Lecture</u>[847] to⌋          Wm Taylor

| Mrs Gilchrist (in | My friends the | Woodstown |
|---|---|---|
| "Sunnyside Press" [848]) | Staffords[849] | Mr   English, Atlantic City |
| J Ad'n Symonds | Elmer,  Ed. &c | Mr Siegfried – Atco |
| (in ditto) | Mr Whitall | Peter Doyle |
| Dr Bucke (in ditto) | Col Hamilton | |
| (See list back 👉) | ?Olive Harper | |
| [in blue pencil] | Col Johnston | |
| | J  H  Johnston | |
| | Al:       " | |

Y M C A. Phila, Thos Marshall   Financial Secy

Chas A Wevyl    Ass't     "

<u>Sent Camden Post 16th of April</u> [850] to:    | Al Johnston

| Mary  t | Pat Hartnet  t | J Hubley Ashton |
|---|---|---|
| Hannah t | Wm M Rossetti ⌐t | Pete Doyle |
| Jessie t | ⌐and⌐ | A C Wheeler |
| John 'Burroughs | Thomas Dixon | ⌐Rudolf Schmidt |
| Moncure Conway | W J Linton | ⌐both Press & Star |

846.  See Whitman's letters to Frederick Locker-Lampson (1821–1895), an English poet and related to Tennyson by marriage, *The Correspondence of Walt Whitman*, III, 174–175, 179–180, 188.

847.  Whitman's lecture on the death of Lincoln, Association Hall, Philadelphia, 15 April 1880; see Roy P. Basler's edition of *Memoranda During the War* [&] *Death of Abraham Lincoln*, pp. 29–33.

848.  See footnote 844. These three people, Mrs Anne Gilchrist, John Addington Symonds, and Dr Richard Maurice Bucke, were not sent lecture tickets, but copies of the *Sunnyside Press* containing Whitman's poem.

849.  The page in the *Daybook* containing this list is reproduced in Roy P. Basler's book (see footnote 847); it is not known how many of those to whom Whitman sent tickets actually went to Association Hall, probably George, Susan, Elmer, and Edwin Stafford (Harry Stafford did not need a ticket, as he assisted at the lecture — see *The Correspondence of Walt Whitman*, III, 176), Colonel John R. Johnston, and John H. Johnston and his son Albert may well have come from New York; William Taylor was the editor of the Woodstown (New Jersey) *Constitution*; Mr Siegfried, a printer or publisher at Atco?, and Mr English of Atlantic City both could be newspapermen; Peter Doyle may have come up from Washington, but I know of no evidence one way or the other; the two YMCA administrators could very easily have heard the lecture.

850.  This issue of the Camden *Daily Post* contained an account of Whitman's lecture on Lincoln; he wrote the news account, and it was printed with a few minor omissions (see Roy P. Basler, as in footnote 847). Whitman also sent other newspapers copies of the lecture, which he had set in type, so the Camden *Press, Star, Herald,* and *Progress* may well have contained similar news stories.

| Addington Symonds | Mrs Gilchrist | W S Fullerton |
| Mrs Stafford | John P Usher Jr | with Herald |
| Ed Cattell | | John Hay |
| | | Frederick Locker[851] |

Sent Dr Bucke the <u>Press</u> of April 16 [852]

Send   Progress with Riddle Song[853] to

| J W Thompson \ | R Buchanan \ |
| Ed'wd Carpenter \ | H J Bathgate[854] \ |

also Press on
lecture T Harris \ St L[855]
Prof Dowden \
Rodolf Schmidt —

[165]

1880 – March

21 – postal card to Rossetti[856]

26   sent Dr Bucke three Vols: two T R and one L of G.    5 Vols in all to be acc'td for $3.50 each

"   rec'd cordial, flattering, affectionate letter from Col Ingersoll
Washington[857]

"   sent papers to Scott Fullerton, Greeley Col [858]

27 (Saturday night) Reception, Penn Club, Phila:

851. Of the 22 people listed here, 16 received papers on previous occasions and need not be further identified (for many of them, see footnote 81); for Thomas Dixon, see footnote 13; William J. Linton, footnote 39; John Hay, footnote 65; John P. Usher, Jr, footnote 761; J. Hubley Ashton was Assistant Attorney General in Washington when Whitman was in that office; W. S. Fullerton, who received the *Herald* as well as the Camden *Post,* was in Greeley, Colorado; for Frederick Locker [-Lampson], see footnote 846.

852. The *Progress,* Colonel Forney's paper, contained the account of Whitman's talk on Lincoln also.

853. This was the *Progress* for 17 April 1880 (see footnote 844, above).

854. The paper with "A Riddle Song" here went to admirers abroad, Schmidt in Denmark; Thompson, Carpenter, Buchanan, and Bathgate in England; and Dowden in Ireland.

855. T. Harrie, to whom Whitman sent the Camden *Press,* with an account of the Lincoln lecture, may well have been someone he had met in St Louis in 1879.

856. Post card lost.

857. For Whitman's brief reply, 2 April 1880, see *The Correspondence of Walt Whitman,* III, 175; also the text of Ingersoll's letter, now in the John Rylands Library, Manchester.

858. Whitman also sent Fullerton a copy of the Camden *Post* of 16 April 1880.

1880 – March

21 – postal card to Rossetti

26 sent Dr Bucke three Vols: two T R and one L of G. 5 Vols all to be asked for 3 etc

" rec'd cordial, flattery, affectionate letter from Col Ingersoll Washington

" sent papers to Scott Fullerton, Greeley Col

27 (Saturday night) Reception Penn Club, Phila

29 papers to sister Mary, Clint Townsend, John Burroughs

30 – A set, Two Vols: to H H Furness 222 Wash: sq. Phila

April 5th to 8th Down at Glendale

8th sent "Sunnyside Press" to Mrs Gilchrist, J A. Symonds & Dr Bucke (tickets enclosed)

12th rec'd letter from H J Bathgate – also Mrs Gilchrist

13th sent Lecture to Chicago Tribune & Cincinnati Com.

15 – sent a set, two Vols Charles F. anxious Tongue & Upper Park Place Richmond Hill Surrey England

" Lecture ("Death of L") Association Hall – Phila

send Vols to Roberts artist to Horace Furness & A. Atherton Blight

papers to Will Tinker Greeley

18 Sunday – Breakfast on the Whillden at Arch St wharf with Johnny Wilson.

April 23 to May 4 – down at Glendale

May 6 – sold Two Sets (4 Vols) to Mr Gridley
– Mrs & Mr Gridley called
" wrote to Sister Hannah (enclosed Jessie's letter)
" " Gen: Sewell (enclosed Photo)
gave Photo & c to Pratt House

Sat to Scholl photo: 5th st Phila

5th Letter to John Burroughs (enc: Herbert's D G Rossetti letter)
papers to Clint Townsend

29    papers to Sister Mary, Clint Townsend, John Burroughs  [in pencil]

30 – A set, Two Vols: to H H Furness    222 Wash'n Sq.    [in blue pencil, recd
                                        Phila[859]    sideways:]      paid

April
    5th to 8th   Down at Glendale[860]

8th    sent "Sunnyside Press" to Mrs Gilchrist, J Ad: Symonds
        & Dr Bucke (tickets enclosed)[861]   [last two words in pencil]

12th   rec'd letter from H J Bathgate – also Mrs Gilchrist[862] [in pencil]

13th   sent Lecture to Chicago Tribune & Cincinnati Com[863] [in pencil]

15 – sent a set, two Vols to Charles Francis Tonge      [in blue pencil,    recd
      8 Upper Park Place   Richmond Hill Surrey          sideways:]        paid
                              England

"  Lecture ("Death of L") Association Hall – Phila[864]

[Three lines in pencil:]                      [in blue pencil,
send Vols to   Roberts[865] artist ⎫ to         sideways:] paid
    &  " Atherton Blight ⎬ Horace
                          ⎭ Furness

papers to Will Tinker, Greeley[866]

18 <u>Sunday</u> – Breakfast on the <u>Whillden</u> at Arch St wharf
      with Johnny Wilson – [867]

859.  See the two letters from Whitman to Horace Howard Furness, 8 and 13 April
1880, *The Correspondence of Walt Whitman*, III, 175 and 176.
    860.  Whitman made several visits to the Staffords this Spring.
    861.  The Tarrytown *Sunnyside Press* for 3 April 1880 with Whitman's "A Riddle
Song" (see footnote 844, above); the tickets for Whitman's Lincoln talk could hardly be
used by these three friends, who were a long way from Philadelphia on 15 April 1880.
    862.  Mrs Anne Gilchrist's letter, 28 March 1880, is in the John Rylands Library, Man-
chester.
    863.  See *The Correspondence of Walt Whitman*, III, 177; Roy P. Basler's edition of
*Memoranda During the War [&] Death of Abraham Lincoln*, pp. 30–33.
    864.  See previous note.
    865.  Howard Roberts (1843–1900), a sculptor Whitman met 12 March 1879 (see *The
Correspondence of Walt Whitman*, III, 175n).
    866.  See footnote 291.
    867.  A few more details are given in his letter to Harry Stafford, *The Correspondence
of Walt Whitman*, III, 177.

April 23ᵈ to May 4 – down at Glendale[868]

May 6 – sold Two Sets (4 Vols) to Mr Gridley[869]
    ⁻ Mrs & Mr Gridley called

"   wrote to Sister Hannah – (enclosed Jessie's letter)[870]  [in pencil]
 "   "   Gen: Sewell (enclosed Photo)   [in pencil]

    gave Photo & eng: to Pratt Hoops   [in pencil]

Sat to Scholl, photo: 9th st Phila[871]

9th   letter to John Burroughs[872] (enc: Herberts D G Rosetti letter)

    papers to Clint Townsend[873]

[166]

Smith Caswell            J L Brotherton [not WW's hand]
        Roxbury         (Quaker gentleman that came up to
Arkville   Delaware Co N Y[874]  \me on the platform to my lecture
                          Sarah P. Brotherton[875] [printed]

W T Harris    moved [in blue
                     pencil]    J L B   real estate agent
    Concord Mass:               wrote to me about Leaves
    p o box 2398 St Louis Mo    of Grass in '75[876]

868.  See Whitman's letter to Herbert Gilchrist, *The Correspondence of Walt Whitman,* III, 177–178.
869.  Mr and Mrs M. W. Gridley, of 9 Duke Street, London Bridge (see footnote 827).
870.  Both Whitman's letter to Hannah Heyde and Jessie Whitman's letter are lost, as is the letter to General William J. Sewell, below.
871.  Emil Scholl, whose calling card is above in the *Daybook,* does not seem however to have taken any of the photographs in Henry S. Saunders's *Whitman Portraits* (Toronto, 1923), a hand-made collection of 400 portraits: copy in the Feinberg Collection.
872.  Whitman's letter is in *The Correspondence of Walt Whitman,* III, 178–179.
873.  See footnote 633.
874.  John Burroughs's employee at Esopus-on-Hudson.
875.  In *With Walt Whitman in Camden,* III, 209, Whitman spoke of a Quaker lady from Philadelphia named Brotherton, who could be this Sarah P. Brotherton, who had picked up *November Boughs* at a friend's house, had "been attracted chiefly, I suppose, by the Hicks piece: said that simply seeing that much had created in her the desire to see more"; she "thee'd" and "thou'd" the poet when she visited Whitman in Camden in November 1888. "When she came to go she took my hand, put into it a little folded piece of paper — so — indicating: said, 'Don't open it till I'm gone — this is not for thee alone but for me': passed out. When I looked, lo! she had left me a two dollar and a half gold piece. The whole manner of it was characteristic: much the way of the Friends."
876.  John L. Brotherton's letter is not extant.

Frederick Locker
25 Chesham Street
Belgrave Square
London   S W   Eng:[877]

Wm D O'Connor[878]
U S Life Saving Service
Treasury Dept:
Washington   D C

Literary World     Boston
Edward Abbott[880]
E H Haines   p o box 1183

James & Priscilla Townsend [881]
92 Bank St
N Y

No. 553 North Sixteenth Street
[printed]

Sent Emerson article in Lit: World [879]
Symonds, \           W T Harris \
Mrs Gil \            Frederick Locker
Bathgate \           W D O'Connor
John Bur: \
Ed Carpenter \
Wm M Rossetti \

sent Dr Bucke's letter in Post
                    May 28 [882]
Smith Caswell
Mr Whiteing          J H Johnston
       Springfield Rep:   Sister Hannah
Whitelaw Reid            "   Mary
Mr Abbott Lit: World    Jessie
Crosby S Noyes          Peter Doyle
Prof: Dowden            R J Hinton
(& all above marked \ ) [883]
Mrs Stafford            A C Wheeler[884]
Elmer

877.  See footnote 846.
878.  See footnote 651; Whitman was still, in May 1880, estranged from O'Connor, and their correspondence did not resume until May 1882.
879.  Whitman's "Emerson's Books (the Shadows of Them)" was published in *The Literary World,* XI (22 May 1880), 177–178; reprinted in the New York *Tribune,* 15 May 1882 before *Specimen Days*; see *Prose Works 1892,* II, 514–518. The nine friends to whom he sent copies are among those who received the Lincoln lecture accounts or "A Riddle Song" (see notes above), with the exception of William Douglas O'Connor, with whom Whitman was now trying to reestablish a relationship (see footnote 651 and 878).
880.  Edward Abbott, associated with the Boston *Literary World,* had asked Whitman for a poem for the "Emerson Number" of 22 May 1880; instead the poet sent him the essay noted above.
881.  For the Townsends see footnotes 285 and 352.
882.  Dr Bucke had a piece, "The Good Gray Poet," in the Philadelphia *Press* on 7 May 1880; and a Letter-to-the-Editor, dealing with Colonel Robert G. Ingersoll's lecture and Whitman, in the *Press* on 26 May 1880, and it is likely that this last letter was reprinted in the Camden *Daily Post* on 28 May, 22 copies of which Whitman sent out.
883.  Those marked — above are John Addinton Symonds, Mrs Anne Gilchrist, Herbert J. Bathgate, John Burroughs, Edward Carpenter, William Michael Rossetti, and William Torrey Harris (see footnote 771 for Harris).
884.  Of the 15 people listed here, Whitman's sisters Hannah Heyde, Mary Van Nostrand,

May – 1880

9th   Sunday – Breakfast at J M S [885]

13th Thursday – at Quaker meeting – cor 15$^{th}$ & Arch – Phila

"    papers to Smith Caswell, (Lincoln lect: & ticket) –also 23$^{d}$ [886]

19$^{th}$ to 23$^{d}$   down at Glendale – 21st p m with Elmer[887]

asked Literary World (criticism on <u>Emerson</u>   May 22)
24
to send paper to Symonds, Mrs. Gil:, Bathgate, & John Bur:[888]

25   <u>meeting with Dr Bucke</u>, Sterry Hunt, & Dr Metcalf [889]

"    – dinner at Girard House

niece Jessie Whitman, and his friends Smith Caswell, Mrs Susan Stafford, Elmer Stafford, John H. Johnston, and Peter Doyle need no further identification; Mr Whiteing was obviously on the staff of the Springfield (Mass.) *Republican*; Whitelaw Reid was publisher of the New York *Tribune* (see footnote 385); for Edward Abbott, see footnote 880; Crosby Stuart Noyes (1825–1908) was editor of the Washington *Star* from 1867 until 1908 (see *The Correspondence of Walt Whitman*, II, 57n, III, 88, 170n, 280n); Edward Dowden was Professor of English in the University of Dublin (see footnote 9); for Colonel Richard J. Hinton, writer and newspaperman, see footnote 249; A. C. Wheeler was on the staff of the Tarrytown (New York) *Sunnyside Press*, in which Whitman's "A Riddle Song" appeared on 3 April 1880.

885.   This was the first time since 2 February 1879 that Whitman recorded a Sunday breakfast with James Matlack Scovel, with whom he frequently breakfasted Sunday mornings. That evening he was with Mrs John R. Johnston, Ida, and John, Jr (Jack) in Camden: see *Specimen Days, Prose Works 1892*, I, 235.

886.   Although it was obviously impossible for Smith Caswell to use his ticket to Whitman's lecture on the death of Lincoln, given on 15 April 1880, the poet kept a number of them and gave them to friends as souvenirs, also signing them. A ticket is reproduced in Bliss Perry's *Walt Whitman* (Boston, 1906), opp. p. 224; and in Roy P. Basler's *Memoranda During the War*, p. [32].

887.   Elmer E. Stafford, then 19 years old, was the cousin of Harry Stafford of White Horse, on Timber Creek, near Glendale, New Jersey.

888.   *The Literary World* (Boston), which Whitman sent to Mrs Anne Gilchrist, Herbert J. Bathgate, and John Burroughs, contained the poet's essay, "Emerson's Books (the Shadows of Them)," in its 22 May 1880 issue; see footnote 879, above.

889.   Dr Richard Maurice Bucke, who was at this time gathering material for a book on Whitman (this is why Whitman sent him the two scrapbooks the next day), came to Philadelphia and Camden, and on 3 June 1880 accompanied Whitman to London, Ontario; Whitman was away from Camden until 29 September 1880. With Dr Bucke were Dr T. Sterry Hunt, who first brought Whitman's writings to the attention of Dr Bucke (see Richard Maurice Bucke, "Memories of Walt Whitman," *Walt Whitman Fellowship Papers*, I [September 1894], 35–45), was a minerologist to the Geological Survey of Canada, and was Whitman's host in Montreal, on 4 August 1880, as described in *Walt Whitman's Diary in Canada*, p. 26; Dr W. G. Metcalf, of Kingston, Ontario, on whose "handsome little steam yacht" [Whitman spent] some days cruising around" the Lakes of the Thousand Islands and St Lawrence River on the same August trip to Canada; see the *Diary in Canada*, pp. 17, 22–26, and *The Correspondence of Walt Whitman*, III, 185–186.

"   heard Col: Ingersoll lecture – talked afterward
    with him a few minutes[890]

26  sent Dr Bucke the two large Scrap Books
    also Rough Draft in MS of Riddle Song & Ox Tamer[891]

"   sent Horace Furness two copies   Two Riv    they came [cancel marks in
                                       back[892]         blue pencil]

27th  sent letter to Frederick Locker[893]

28  visit from Dr Theodore F Wolfe   Jersey City
    (writer for Scribner's)[893a] he bo't L of G.

30 (Sunday) visit from Moses Ainsworth Walsh, chemist
    & engineer, 921 Parrish st: Phila – works as chemist
    at Powers & Weightman – been in India – told me
    much about India – bo't 2 Vols – (came with Mr.
    Ingram[894]) – Is a Lancashire, England, man

890. This was apparently the first time Whitman had heard Colonel Robert G. Ingersoll (1833–1899), famous American lawyer and agnostic, lecture or had met him, though Ingersoll had written the poet on 25 March 1880 (see above); see *The Correspondence of Walt Whitman*, III, 175, 175n, and 207; and Ingersoll's book, *Liberty in Literature: Testimonial to Walt Whitman* (New York, 1890), and his "Address at the Funeral of Whitman," *In Re Walt Whitman* (Philadelphia, 1893), pp. 449–452 (also reprints "Liberty in Literature," pp. 253–283). Ingersoll, who became one of Whitman's most enthusiastic friends after John H. Johnston's insistence that he read *Leaves of Grass* carefully, lectured on the poet at Whitman's birthday dinner in 1890, gave a benefit speech for Whitman in October 1890 ("Liberty in Literature"), with the poet on the stage, and spoke at Whitman's funeral and was a pallbearer on 30 March 1892. See Gay Wilson Allen, *The Solitary Singer*, pp. 528, 535, 536–537, 541, 543, 544, 594.

891. "A Riddle Song" was in the Tarrytown (New York) *Sunnyside Press* (see footnote 844); "The Ox-Tamer" was in the New York *Daily Graphic*, December 1874, in *Two Rivulets* (1876), and the 1881 *Leaves of Grass* (see Comprehensive Reader's Edition, pp. 397–398).

892. Furness was living at 222 West Washington Square, Philadelphia at that time; it is not known why the two copies of *Two Rivulets* were returned.

893. This letter, dated 26 May 1880, is in *The Correspondence of Walt Whitman*, III, 179–180.

893a. Theodore F. Wolfe, M.D. wrote three factual pieces, "A Day with the Good Gray Poet," *Literary Shrines* (London, 1895), pp. 201–217; "Bryant, Whitman, etc.: A Long Island Ramble," *Literary Haunts and Homes* (Philadelphia, 1898), 143–147; and "The Haunts of Walt Whitman," *Literary Rambles* (Philadelphia, 1900), pp. 85–99.

894. Mr Ingram was most likely William Ingram, an old Quaker who kept a tea store in Philadelphia and, out of philanthropic motives, often visited prisons; he dropped in to see Whitman from time to time, and Traubel reported that Ingram "sorely tries W.'s patience sometimes. Yet W. loves him. Very kind — generous: sends W. coffees, teas, fruits, home-made wines, &c. W. always grateful, 'seeing the beautiful heart below his peculiarities'" (*With Walt Whitman in Camden*, III, 341; see also I, 182, 185; II, 47, 320, 322, 323, 416; IV, 94, 264, 449; V, 216). See also *The Correspondence of Walt Whitman*, II, 231–232.

"   Sent letter (in answer to his May 3) to Thomas
     Gibbons, 119 Pentonville Road, London, N.
     with Thomas Paine piece of '77, & circ:[895]

June 3 – Started for Canada with Dr Bucke[896]

[168]

Adv of 20 to x   [in blue pencil]          J. L. Payne[900]   [Three lines
[List below on slips, pasted on page]                            printed]
               In Canada[897]              City Editor's Staff:
                          or postals[899]   "Free Press," London, Ont.

Sent London        letters ∧ to
  papers June 5 [898] to Lou         | Mrs Elisa L. Leggett[901]
– Geo Stafford   x   Elmer           |            x
– Elmer   "   x   Geo & Susan Stafford| 169 E Elizabeth st
– Smith Caswell   x   Daily Herald [Boston]| Detroit   Mich:
– W C Pine         Louis Magargee    |

895.  Whitman's "In Memory of Thomas Paine" (*Specimen Days: Prose Works 1892*, I, 140–142) was set from "Walt Whitman and Thomas Paine," New York *Tribune*, 29 January 1877 (see footnote 106, above).

896.  For accounts of Whitman's trip to Canada, 3 June–29 September 1880, see *Specimen Days: Prose Works 1892*, I, 236–246; *Walt Whitman's Diary in Canada* (Boston, 1904), reprinted at the end of this edition of the *Daybook*; *The Correspondence of Walt Whitman*, III, 181–188; Gay Wilson Allen, *The Solitary Singer*, pp. 489–490.

897.  This enormous list, the longest one in the *Daybook*, seems to be four or five lists: London, Ontario, papers on 5 June 1880, 41 names; an undated list, 29 names; post cards and letters from Sarnia, Ontario, 20 June 1880, 15 names; 24 June, 1 name; 1 August, 1 name; undated, 1 name — 88 in all, with a few of them repeated. Whitman certainly kept in touch with his relatives and friends.

898.  Lengthy interviews with Whitman upon his arrival in Ontario appeared in the London *Advertiser* and the London *Free Press* of 5 June 1880. Of the 41 who apparently were sent one or both papers, those not previously identified include: W C Pine, Wm Dorman, Morgan (NY *Times*), John Battles, Geo Wehn, Chas Leyman, Frank Oakley, The: Bear, Ed Dodimead, Mr Walsh, Tobasco Flint, and Wm Clark, none of whom can be identified or seem to have been important in Whitman's life; Mrs M E Van Nostrand, coming as it does after Mrs H L Heyde (Whitman's sister Hannah), must be Mrs Mary Elizabeth Van Nostrand, Whitman's sister; Lyndell may be Captain Respigius Edward Lindell, of the Camden ferries; Hiskey was also on the ferries, Tilghman Hiskey (see *The Correspondence of Walt Whitman*, III, 182–183, 185, for Whitman's letters to him); C. H. Sholes was a shorthand reporter in Des Moines, Iowa (see *The Correspondence of Walt Whitman*, III, 181, for Whitman's letter to him, 9 June 1880); Jo at Sarony's was an employee of the photographic studio in New York; and John Frazer may well be John Fraser, editor of *Cope's Tobacco Plant* (Liverpool).

899.  Of the 10 listed here, the following letters are in *The Correspondence of Walt Whitman*, III: Whitelaw Reid, 17 June 1880, p. 181; George and Susan Stafford, 13 July 1880, pp. 183–184; the others are apparently lost.

900.  J. L. Payne may well have been the man who interviewed Whitman when he got to London, or he may have written the story in the London *Free Press*, 5 June 1880.

901.  Mrs Leggett wrote to Whitman on 19 July 1880 (letter now in the John Rylands Library, Manchester) and on 19 December 1882 (see Thomas Donaldson, *Walt Whitman the Man* [New York, 1896], pp. 246–248); see *The Correspondence of Walt Whitman*, III, 239n; and *Prose Works 1892*, I, 239; Whitman's letters to her, 8 June 1880 and 27 December 1880, are lost.

902.  Richardson's letter to Whitman, 8 September 1880, is in the Library of Congress; see

– John Burroughs   x   Whitelaw Reid

– Mrs Gilchrist   x   Harry Bonsall

– J H Johnston   x   E S Noyes

– H L Bonsall   x   E B Byington    R R Pas Agent Mauch Chunk    Pa

– Scholl, photo     Robt H Sayre   RR Eng: &c    Bethlehem Pa

– Mrs Louisa     [on scrap of paper, pasted on page:]
  Whitman x

|  |  |  |
|---|---|---|
| Aug 21ᵗ sent a big bundle papers | | |
| John Richardson[902] Battery st | | |
| Citadel   Quebec | | |

– Thos J Whitman x

x Mrs H L Heyde   x

          postals &c sent from

          Sarnia, Sunday June 20 '80 [903]

– Mrs M E Van     postals to          letter to Geo &
  Nostrand        George & Lou          Susan Stafford

– Rudolf Schmidt  x  Hannah          postal to Ed Cattell

– W M Rossetti  x   Elmer Stafford       John Burroughs

– H J Bathgate  x   Jeff             Wm Clark

– Edward Carpenter x  Mary            Pete Doyle

– D M Zimmerman x  Smith Caswell      Hiskey

– Ed Cattell   x    Harry Scovel       J H Johnston
  Wm Dorman                        Jo at Sarony's

Morgan (Times)      to Harry Stafford, from Sarnia, June 24 [904]

John Battles      C A J Imeckburnen [ ? ] [905] (Joe)   R J Hinton x

Edward Abbott     ~~Ed    Stafford~~    – Jas E Mills   room 37   x

Peter Doyle       James Scovel [in          506 Olive st St Louis

Geo Wehn              blue pencil] ————————

Lyndell          W T Harris x 2398    – Isaac R Pennypacker   x

Chas Leyman         [in blue pencil]    1540 N   15ᵗʰ   St Phila

Hiskey     x      C W Stoddard  Adv ————————

Frank Oakley   –     [in blue pencil]  Charles Wood   x

The: Bear          616 Harrison St ————————

Ed Dodimead      ————— San   F   – Mr Gutekunst

Harry S Scovel  x   C H Sholes           712 Arch St   Phila –

– C H Sholes      Johnny Johnston    ————————

– Jo at Sarony's   – Mary Wager Fisher  Patrick   Hartnett      x
  37 Union Sq:              x         Missouri RR of:   3301 Olive

– Mr Walsh   x     – Mrs Eliza L Legget     St Louis              st

– Edwin Stafford

*L'Âne d'Or*, V (1926), 44–45.

903. Of the 15 post cards and letters Whitman sent from Sarnia, Ontario, on Lake Huron 60 miles west of London and where Dr Bucke was a practising physician for ten years, only two postals survive: to Tilghman Hiskey and to John H. Johnston, *The Correspondence of Walt Whitman*, III, 182–183. Letters to the Staffords, 13 July 1880, and to Peter Doyle, 24 July 1880, are extant (*ibid.*, III, 183–185) and may be these.

904. Letter lost.

905. This letter, sent about 23 June 1880, is lost; Hueckberny's[?] to Whitman, 24 June 1880, effusively acknowledging a note, is in the John Rylands Library, Manchester.

| | | | |
|---|---|---|---|
| - Josiah Child   x | Detroit   x | | |
| - Col Forney | Thos: Dixon   – [in | John Klopper[906] | |
| John Frazer | pencil] | | |
| Tobacco Plant | Prof: Dowden – x | | |
| Wm Clark | [in pencil] | | |
| | F Locker – x [in pencil] | | |
| | G W Childs x [in pencil] | | |
| | – W J Linton   x 489 | | |

[169]

June, 1880 – In Canada, Canada Trip [last two words in red ink]

4 – 5 – At London, Ontario, with Dr and Mrs Bucke[907]

6th (Sunday) at the Insane Asylum Church, London[908]

7    a copy of L  of  G , also T R to George Eyvel      paid

8 – a ride to & through London

8 – sent a letter to Mrs Leggett    thanks for her letter & for the print of E H [909]

"    "   postal card to Mary Wager Fisher[910]

9   "        "    "     Pete Doyle[911]

letter to Johnny Johnston[912]

---

906. These 19 names, some with addresses, plus two names (Ed Stafford and Thomas Dixon) cancelled, may have been people Whitman wrote to, or more likely, those who wrote to him, for such letters survive: from Hueckberny (see footnote 905); from John H. Johnston, 26 June 1880 (John Rylands Library, Manchester); from Frederick Locker-Lampson, 3 July 1880 (John Rylands); from Charles Warren Stoddard, 7 July 1880 (John Rylands); from Mrs Elisa S. Leggett, 19 July 1880 (John Rylands).

907. Leaving Philadelphia "on a first-class sleeper," Whitman wrote briefly of his 22-hour trip to London, where "I am domiciled at the hospitable house of my friends Dr. and Mrs. Bucke, in an ample and charming garden and lawns of the asylum" (*Prose Works 1892*, I, 237).

908. Described in *Specimen Days* under the title "Sunday with the Insane," *Prose Works 1892*, I, 237-239.

909. This letter is lost, but Whitman has a note concerning the engraved head of Elias Hicks, *Prose Works 1892*, I, 239.

910. For Mrs Wager-Fisher, see footnote 214; this letter to her is lost.

911. Post card lost.

912. Letter lost.

June, 1880 — In Canada    Canada Trip

4 – 5 – At London, Ontario, with Dr and Mrs Bucke

6th (Sunday) at the Insane Asylum church, London

7 a copy of L of G, also J R to George Eyvel [Reid]

8 – a ride to & through London

8 – sent a letter to Mrs Leggett   thanks for her letter & for the print of E H
    "   "   postal card to Mary Wagon Fisher
    "   "   "   "   Pete Doyle

9   letter to Johnny Johnston
"   postal to C H Sholes, Des Moines, Iowa
"   note to Whitelaw Reid — note to Harry Bonsall

10 postal to Col. Forney — Geo & Susan Stafford
    "   "   George & Lou — Mary   (went through the Insane Asylum "the refractory")
"   Papers to Smith Caswell

12 postal to sister Hannah
    "   "   Hattie — Mrs Scovel —

14   "   Wm Reidel — Progress to Hannah

15 sent J R to Wm Hamilton [Paid] Sandusky, Ohio
    "   postal card to W H also
    "   "   "   to John L Peck, Vineland
    "   papers to "Smith Caswell

16 ride through London — Call at Dufferin Coll: letter from Pete Doyle
17 sent off first letter "Summer Days in Canada"
    various Canada and U S papers, (see next page)

19th went to Sarnia   St Clair river & Lake Huron
    Staid from Saturday 19th to Thursday 24th at the
    house of Hon: Timothy Blair Pardee, (Commissioner
    of Crown Lands)   Mr Pardee bo't the two Vols:

26th from London, Canada.
    sent L of G to Miss Macdonald, Care of Prof:
    Blaskie. Oban. Scotland (sent postal also)

"   sent a set L of G and J R to Chas Warren
    Stoddard, 616 Harrison Street, San Fran-
    cisco, California. (10 due) sent postal card
    don't forget the [——]

"    postal to C H Sholes, Des Moines, Iowa[913]

"    note to Whitelaw Reid – note to Harry Bonsall – [914]

10   postal to Col: Forney – Geo & Susan Stafford

"      George & Lou – Mary          went through the

"    papers to Smith Caswell         Insane Asylum

12   postal to Sister Hannah          "the refractory"

"      Hattie – Mrs Scovel –

14   "    Wm Reidel – Progress to Hannah

                          paid
15   sent T R to W^m Hamilton      Sandusky   Ohio   [in blue pencil,
                                              sideways:]      recd
"       postal card to W H also

"      "    "    to John L Peck, Vineland

"    papers to Smith Caswell

16   ride through London – call at Duffering Coll: letter from
                                              Pete Doyle[915]

17   sent off first letter "Summer Days in Canada"
        various Canada and U S papers, (see next page)[916]

19th  went to Sarnia   St Clair river & Lake Huron,[917]
        Staid from Saturday 19th to Thursday 24th at the
        house of Hon: Timothy Blair Pardee, (Commissioner
        of Crown Lands)   Mr Pardee bo't the two Vols:

---

913.  Printed in *The Correspondence of Walt Whitman*, III, 181.
914.  These two notes are lost, as are all the others through 15 June 1880.
915.  Letter from Peter Doyle lost.
916.  "Summer Days in Canada," sent to 15 newspapers (listed in the *Daybook*, below), was published in the Camden *Daily Post* (free) and in the Philadelphia *Press* ($10); see *The Correspondence of Walt Whitman*, III, 181–182. Parts of it were used by Whitman in *Specimen Days*: see *Prose Works 1892*, I, 236–241, 345–346.
917.  Described very briefly in Whitman's letters to Tilghman Hiskey, and John H. Johnston, *The Correspondence of Walt Whitman*, III, 182–183; and in greater detail in *Walt Whitman's Diary in Canada*, pp. 3–10; see below at the end of the *Daybook*.

from London, Canada

26ᵗʰ  sent ʌ L  of  G to Miss Macdonald, care of Prof:    [in blue pencil,
                                                          sideways:]    paid

   Blackie, Oban, Scotland (sent postal also)⁹¹⁸

---

"   sent a set of L of G and T R to Chas Warren        [in blue pencil,
    Stoddard, 616 Harrison Street San Fran            sideways:]    paid
    cisco, California, ($10 due)  sent postal card                  recd
                          don't forget the lingo⁹¹⁹

[170]

|              | London, Ontario                        |                     |
|--------------|----------------------------------------|---------------------|
| Dr Bemer     | Wm Kittermaster                        | Mrs. Way            |
| Archie Bremner | Richard Flynn⁹²⁰                      | Miss Forsyth        |
| Lilla        | W Mafer, Advertiser office⁹²¹          | Miss Mary D'Ervians |
| Mrs.ʌGosling |                                        | Mary Ettie Lorenzen |
| Clifford Riggs. [not WW's hand] |                     | Miss Flora Cottle   |

918. Whitman's post card to Miss Katie Macdonald is lost, but hers, ordering *Leaves of Grass,* 5 and 9 June 1880, are in the John Rylands Library, Manchester.

919. Charles Warren Stoddard (1843–1909), California writer and traveler, who had written at this time his *Poems* (edited by Bret Harte, 1867), *South-Sea Idyls* (based on a trip to Hawaii and Tahiti, 1873), and *Mashallah!* (from a voyage to Egypt and the Holy Land, 1880); he later lived in Hawaii, was converted to Catholicism, wrote numerous travel books, served as professor at the University of Notre Dame and the Catholic University of America before spending his last years in California. Stoddard's first letter to Whitman, 8 February 1867 (now in the Feinberg Collection), asked for an autograph; the second, 2 March 1869 (Feinberg, printed in *With Walt Whitman in Camden,* IV, 267–268), from Honolulu, begged for "a few lines from your pen [and] your photograph," and wrote of his meeting a native boy — "He speaks [my name] over and over, manipulating my body unconsciously, as it were, with bountiful and unconstrained love. I go to his grass house, eat with him his simple food, sleep with him upon his mats, and at night sometimes waken to find him watching me with earnest, patient looks, his arm over my breast and around me" — to which Whitman replied briefly, 12 June 1869 (*The Correspondence of Walt Whitman,* II, 81–82), "Those tender & primitive personal relations off there in the Pacific Islands, as described by you, touched me deeply": and Whitman also told Traubel that "occidental people, for the most part, would not only not understand but would likewise condemn the sort of thing about which Stoddard centers his letter." In his next letter, 2 April 1870 (Feinberg; printed in *With Walt Whitman in Camden,* III, 444–445), Stoddard began, "In the name of CALAMUS listen to me!" and said, "I think of sailing toward Tahiti. . . . I know there is but one hope for me. I must be in amongst people who are not afraid of instincts and who scorn hypocrisy. I am numbed with the frigid manners of the Christians; barbarism has given me the fullest joy of my life and I long to return to it and be satisfied." He sent Whitman his "South-Sea Idyl," *Overland Monthly,* III (September 1869), 257–264, of which Whitman wrote him, 23 April 1870 (*The Correspondence of Walt Whitman,* II, 97) that he found it "soothing & nourishing. . . . As to you, I do not of course object to your emotional & adhesive nature, & the outlet thereof, but warmly approve them," yet the poet did say that the worldly experiences and qualities of American practical life did "prevent extravagant sentimentalism" and are not without "their own great value & even joy." Stoddard's letter of 14 June 1880, ordering the two Whitman books, is in the John Rylands Library, Manchester; Whitman's reply of 26 June 1880, with this phrase, "don't forget the lingo" (?), in the *Daybook,* is lost; Stoddard's of 7 July 1880 is also in the John Rylands Library.

920. Richard Flynn, 24 years old in 1880, was an employee in Dr Bucke's asylum,

June 17 & 18 – Sent "Summer Days" to following: [922]

| | |
|---|---|
| – Tribune, Denver | 10 |
| – Boston Herald | 10 |
| – New York Tribune | 12 |
| – Phil Press | 10 |
| – Cin Commercial | 10 |
| – Chic Tribune | 10 |
| – Louisville Courier Journal | 10 |
| ~~New Era~~  Lancaster Pa | |
| — 3 Washington Post ——————— | |
| ~~Eve Star~~, Washington [cancelled in | |
| blue pencil] | 10 |
| – Free Press   Detroit | 10 |
| / Globe, St Johns   New Brunswick | 10 |
| – Chronicle, Halifax  N S  ——— | 10 |
| – John C Dent, Globe newspaper, Toronto | 10 |
| – Witness, Montreal. | 10 |
| – Register, Woodstown N J | 7 |
| – Post   Camden, free | free |

[171]

June 1880 – in Canada        Canada Trip [in red ink]

27 – (Sunday) – papers to Sister Hannah

28   sent letter & Circ: to Wm Erving 121 Fourth Av: N Y.[923]

29th rec'd letters from Mrs Gilchrist, Frederick Locker, Harry
        Scovel [924]

"   sent postal and paper to T W H Rolleston[925]

which leads one to assume some of the others named here were connected with the hospital; the list is unusual in the number of women here.

921. The *Advertiser* was a London, Ontario, newspaper in which an interview with Whitman appeared the day after he arrived in the city.

922. According to Edwin Haviland Miller, only two of these 15 newspapers, the Camden *Post* and the Philadelphia *Press,* published Whitman's piece; see footnote 916, above, and *The Correspondence of Walt Whitman,* III, 181n. The "10" in the right-hand column indicates that Whitman was asking each paper to pay $10 for his article.

923. Letter lost.

924. Mrs Ann Gilchrist's letter, 15 June 1880, is in the Whitman House, Camden; Frederick Locker-Lampson's letter, 15 June 1880, and Harry Scovel's, 22 June 1880, are in the John Rylands Library, Manchester.

925. Letter lost; for T. W. H. Rolleston, see footnote 50.

30    letter rec'd from Elmer – one from Norman[926]

"    C H Sholes called [927]    saw Dr Baud myself in Dr B's
library – London

July 4 – letter to Geo: & Susan Stafford [928] – _Progress_ to Sister Hannah

"        papers to Smith Caswell – letter to Norman McKenzie

7    sent letter to Lou (rec'd one from her)[929]

"    _Woodstown Register_ to Ed: Cattell

10    paper to Mont[930]

12    letter to Lou (enc: Mrs Gilchrists & Carpenters – )[931]

"        papers to James & Priscilla Townsend, 92 Bank st[932]

"        _Progress_ to Hannah[933]

13th    letters to Geo & Susan Stafford & to Elmer[934]

"    postal to James & Priscilla Townsend [935]

16th    postal (recp't) to Chas Warren Stoddard  616 Harrison St. San F [936]

926.  Elmer is Elmer Stafford, and his letter is lost; Norman is Norman McKenzie, a Canadian schoolboy (see _The Correspondence of Walt Whitman,_ III, 182n), and his letter is in the John Rylands Library, Manchester.

927.  For C. H. Sholes, see footnotes 812 and 898; he had apparently come to London from Des Moines, Iowa.

928.  The letters to the Staffords, Norman McKenzie (see footnote 926), Louisa Orr Whitman, and Ed Cattell, below, are all lost.

929.  Louisa Orr Whitman's letter is in the John Rylands Library.

930.  Montgomery Stafford, George's brother (see footnote 231), who has not been noted in Whitman's _Daybook_ for some time.

931.  The letter to Louisa Orr Whitman is lost, but the enclosures from Mrs Anne Gilchrist, 15 June 1880, and Edward Carpenter, 1 July 1880, are in the Whitman House, Camden, and the John Rylands Library.

932.  See footnotes 285 and 352.

933.  Whitman sent his sister Hannah Heyde the Philadelphia _Progress_ on 14 June and 4 July 1880, as well as on 12 July, so one need not assume the _Progress_ necessarily carried news of Whitman in every issue; Whitman had the paper sent to him in Canada, and sent copies to his sister simply as reading matter.

934.  The letter to the Staffords, longer than most of the others he wrote in London, is in _The Corerspondence of Walt Whitman,_ III, 183–184; the one to Elmer Stafford is lost.

935.  Post card lost.

936.  See footnote 919.

22  rec'd draft from Trübner & Co: $80.50 [937]

---

recd
letter from Mrs Stafford – one from Debbie[938] [in pencil]

---

recd
24  letter from Lou – one from Elmer – [in pencil]

---

"    sent postal cards to Lou, Hannah, Mary, Harry, Pete Doyle[939]

---

25 – postals to F B Sanborn,[940] Lou, & (with papers) to
                                    Chas S Gleed

"   letter to J B Lippincott
    wrs sent 20 L of G & 10 T R          R R agent Kansas City
                        to Trübner[941]         Mo

---

paper to John Newton Johnson[942]

---

[Three lines in blue pencil]
26th   trip to Toronto   Kingston, Thousand
        Islands, Montreal, Quebec & the
        Saguenay river –[943]

937. Whitman, in his list of those to whom he wrote about 5 June 1880, included Josiah Child, who was acting for Whitman in London, England, and thus Trübner & Company sent Whitman's draft to Canada, through Child (letter in the John Rylands Library).
938. Whitman had complained, in his letter of 13 July 1880, that he had not heard from any of the Staffords, so 22 and 24 July he received letters from Mrs Susan Stafford, her daughter Deborah Browning, and her nephew Elmer Stafford (all are now in the John Rylands Library).
939. The post card to Peter Doyle is in *The Correspondence of Walt Whitman,* III, 184–185, but those to Whitman's sisters Hannah Heyde and Mary Van Nostrand, and to Harry Stafford, are lost.
940. A transcript of the post card to Franklin Benjamin Sanborn is in *The Correspondence of Walt Whitman,* III, 185; it is a reply to Sanborn's invitation (which is in the John Rylands Library). The post cards to Louisa Orr Whitman, J. B. Lippincott, the publisher, and Charles Gleed are lost. Gleed is mentioned, with a clipping, in one of the earliest pages of the *Daybook* (see footnote 25).
941. As his own publisher, Whitman may well have taken a number of copies of *Leaves of Grass* and *Two Rivulets* to Canada with him; apparently there would have been no one back in Camden to send copies to Trübner & Company in England for him.
942. It is remarkable how Whitman kept in touch with those, such as Johnson (see footnote 9a), whom he did not know particularly well.
943. As seen below, 23 August 1880, Whitman sent accounts of his trip to the Philadelphia *Press,* the Washington *Sunday Herald,* and the Camden *Daily Post* after his return; the *Press* and the *Post,* as well as the London, Ontario, *Advertiser* published his "Letter from Walt Whitman" on 26 August 1880, and he used the material in *Specimen Days* — see *Prose Works 1892,* I, 241–245, 346–347 — and it is also in *Walt Whitman's Diary in Canada,* pp. 16–40, and in this *Daybook,* below.

Aug 14 — return'd to London[943a] [in pencil]

[172]

<u>Tennyson</u>    Farringford, Freshwater, Isle[944]
of Wight, "about seven months
in the year – the winter especially ["]
address 1882 [in blue pencil]

943a. In *Notes and Fragments,* edited by Richard Maurice Bucke (London, Ontario, 1899), pp. 65–66, is the following, with a footnote by the editor ("Must have been written in 1880, but I did not know until I found this fragment in 1899 that Whitman ever had at that or any other time any thought of lecturing at Ottawa."):
For Ottawa lecture.
For thousands of years in the history of the masses of humanity why does it seem as if that history was all dominated by one word — war? All too necessary to the progress, civilization, the . . . . . . .
Now, *Business* does it all — opens up China, Japan, Africa, colonizes, builds roads, penetrates, communicates . . . . . . . .
Is there going to be but one heart to the world?
If I should dare confess to you to-night my friends I should perhaps, rude as it might seem, own up that it is more with the wish to put in shape, for my own sake, the brief experiences of a late trip on the line of the St Lawrence and the Lakes [the trip with Dr Bucke from London to Chicoutimi] and touches at the great cities with some thoughts arising out of them, than from any hope of pleasing you, that I am now speaking. I shall certainly not only be unable to tell you anything new, but it may very likely prove that I have only caught surface and present surface impressions. Still as the Frenchman Taine says in premising his fine ensemble of the letter and spirit of English Literature it is worth something to see how these things seem to a new comer and a stranger.

In *Faint Clews & Indirections* (Durham, North Carolina, 1949), pp. 60–63, is a section which the editors, Clarence Gohdes and Rollo G. Silver, say Whitman may have also intended for the Ottawa lecture, notes from which I have quoted above:

London — 1880
Then about drinking habits.
My observations and goings around here pretty freely, indoors and out, note, so far, a singular scarcity of cases of intemperance; I have seen no drunken man (nor drunken woman.) — have run across no besotted or low or filthy quarters of the town either. I should say it was an unusually temperate city. Here for a thousand people at the Insane Asylum, no alcohol-beverage is used — not a pint in a week. The head physician, Dr Bucke, never prescribes it; some of the assistants at rare intervals. Dr B. tells me he thinks it needless, and can get along just as well without it, or even better, under any circumstances.
London Canada June 1880
for London
Dufferin College
Huron College for theology
a good high school
the Savings and Investment Society offers money to farmers & others at 7 and 7½ per cent, with privilege of paying interest or principal in instalments
— a good yellow brick, made here is plentiful and cheap — many fine mansions with

944. The few words here about 1882 must have been added later by Whitman, who heard about Tennyson's travels from Frederick Locker-Lampson on 15 June and 3 July 1880 (letters in the John Rylands Library — see *The Correspondence of Walt Whitman,* III, 179n); Whitman had asked Locker on 26 May 1880 for Tennyson's address (*ibid.,* III, 180).

gardens, some of exceptional size and elegance — on Dundas and Richmond — streets, the principal rows of shops, offices, banks

— Queen's and Dufferin avenue for fine residences also Ridout street, old & fine, backing the river
     many handsome churches
— a large and fine Revenue Office building, also Post Office, also several Bank Buildings, also some large Hotels, the Tecumseh House
    and many four-story houses in rows, with stores on the ground story
      Some of the streets
Queen's avenue,
    very wide either their whole length or in part, and agreeably parked with grass and trees
— London stands mainly on high ground in the fork between the north & south branches of the river (Thames)
over the south fork is Westminster
over the north fork is Petersville
    The Thames river winds its twirling and shallow, but very pretty waters to the
?    of the main body of the town, and on the side are clusters of comfortable houses, mostly one or two storied, quite democratic, with now and then a costlier one. I saw on the river several small-sized steamers, neat-looking, hawsered, waiting for passengers, or steaming up or down, with the British colors flying.

Of banks and banking houses there are nine or ten.
some 20 churches
The population is 25,000
There are several lines of horse-railways. I occasionally saw members of the police patrol, with helmets and white gloves — all I saw were fine-looking young fellows.

the pavement question
some concrete

By what I am told London would show finely to my eyes in September, from the great annual fair, when there is a gathering of the farmers and their families, men and women, especially the young people — altogether many thousands, and the streets all alive with them for several days
On this occasion one would get a direct view of the average People, the *humanity* of this part of Canada (the main thing of every country.) By what I am told I am sure this average would please me much, and would be very high

There are two large and live daily papers here. the *Advertiser* and *Free Press*
the R R's

Hellmuth College superior extensive school for young ladies

the Asylum is the show place of London, it and its handsome grounds being always visited by journeyers.
The land all about fertile lying well, hardly any where rocky or with chasms.
a scarcity of black persons
   *Produce*
hay (little or no rye)
wheat little or no flax
oats
barley               *wool* is quite important
potatoes
small-eared corn
    fruits
apples
plums
cherries
all the small fruits in great perfection & plenty

Aldworth, Haslemere, Surrey)[encircled in blue pencil]
        four months of the summer
    (& then a month or five weeks in London)
but probably as good as any address

care of Frederick Locker
        25 Chesham Street
        London   S W
(Tennyson started for Venice ab't
    middle of May, '80, on a visit
    of a month)
(Lionel Tennyson[945] 4 Sussex Place
        Regents' Park – London N W)
(Mrs Gilchrist has been at Locker's house
    to copy old letters of Blake for the
    new ed'n)

[On calling card of Chas. S. Gleed,[946] with W. F. White, G.P.&T.A., Atchison, Topeka & Santa Fe Railroad:]   Topeka   Kansas
        Stephen F Smart[947]            Sept '80
    1 & 2 ~~Qeen~~ Queen Anne Chambers
        Poultry   London   E C

E C Stedman    80 Broadway[948]
71 West 54th street   N   Y

no peaches from the cold
no pears from blight

---

grapes moderate, but they do well

---

Of human stock here in and about London & perhaps through Ontario, English largely preponderates

London is perhaps 50 years old — 40 years ago some twelve or fourteen houses

---

beef
cheese
horses

945. Lionel, Lord Tennyson's son, had married Locker-Lampson's daughter (see *ibid.,* III, 134).
946. See end of footnote 940.
947. Stephen S. Smart, a travel agent, is mentioned in the early pages of the *Daybook*.
948. Edmund Clarence Stedman (1833–1908), critic, poet, anthologist, and also a successful stockbroker, is listed, with others, in footnote 150; Whitman met him in October 1863 in Washington (see *The Correspondence of Walt Whitman,* I, 167), and in June 1875 Stedman asked Whitman for a piece of MS., saying, "I am one of those American writers who always look upon you as a noble, original, and characteristic poet" (*ibid.,* 11, 334n); Stedman's "Walt Whitman" was in the November 1880 *Scribner's Monthly*; the poet thought

R Worthington, 770 Broadway N Y[949]

---

       Glasshouse   Shinrone   Kings Co: Ireland [950]   [correction in
T W H Rolleston, ~~Lange/Strasse 29th~~  ~~Dresden Saxony~~    red ink]

---

Pete Doyle   295 Spring Street   N Y City – June '80 [951]

---

   [173]

August 1880   in Canada      Canada Trip [in red ink]

---

15   papers to Sisters Hannah & Mary – & Smith Caswell

---

   postals to Lou, Jeff, Pete Doyle, Al: Johnston – Mrs Gilchrist[952]

---

   "     John Burroughs[953] – book to Isabel Walker

---

16   letter to W Curtis Taylor   photo. 914 Chestnut st[954]

---

23   sent Saguenay letter (printed slip) to Phil Press, Wash Sunday
     Herald and Camden Post[955]

---

"   letter to Sister Hannah – sent Progress

---

26   Saguenay letter in London Advertiser[956]

---

25   letter to Lou $20 for Ed – p o order[957]

---

it "quite funny," but it infuriated Dr Bucke, and Burroughs felt it would do good (see *ibid.,* III, 193, 198). Stedman is mentioned more than 150 times in Traubel's *With Walt Whitman in Camden.*

949. See Whitman's letter· to Richard Worthington, 21 August 1880, in *The Correspondence of Walt Whitman,* III, 186; and 195–198, where Whitman discusses the whole Worthington affair concerned with electroplates of the 1861 *Leaves of Grass* (see footnote 732, above).

950. Whitman had written T. W. H. Rolleston on 29 June 1880 (letter lost); see footnote 50.

951. Peter Doyle must have been visiting New York City, for Whitman wrote him in Washington on 24 July 1880; Doyle was in Niagara Falls late in September and went back to Philadelphia with the poet.

952. Whitman did not write Mrs Anne Gilchrist until 28 September 1880; of the other four postals mentioned here, only the one to Albert Johnston, John H. Johnston's son, survives: *The Correspondence of Walt Whitman,* III, 186.

953. Post card lost.

954. Whitman's letter to W. Curtis Taylor, Philadelphia photographer, is lost.

955. See footnote 943.

956. See footnote 943.

957. This $20 to Louisa Orr Whitman was to pay the board bill of Walt's youngest brother Edward, now 45 years old and institutionalized.

26    sent Saguenay letter[958] to Mrs R B Johnston. Progress to Hannah

29    rec'd postal from Elmer[959]

31    papers to Thomas Barnes, Wine Mfr, Hamilton[960]

Sept 17    postal to Jack Richardson[961]

19    letter to Worthington, 700 Broadway   N Y (☞ 770 Broadway) [962]

"    "    to John H Ingram   Engineer in Chief's
          office, General Post Office London, Eng. pro-
          posing two Vols, one Poems – one prose[963]

Sept 28 & '9 – returned home – stopt a day
          & night at Niagara – [964]

Back in Camden    [in blue pencil]
Oct 1    sent papers to Sisters Hannah and Mary    [in pencil]
              with "Home again" [965]    [in pencil]

"    "Home again" to London Advertiser    [in pencil]

          paper to Tommy Nicholson[966]    [in pencil]

2    "Home again" to Jessie

958.  For Whitman's letter about his Saguenay trip, see footnote 943; Mrs R. B. Johnston is unidentified.
959.  Elmer E. Stafford (Harry's cousin) wrote more often than the others in the family
Whitman spent so much time with at White Horse on Timber Creek.
960.  Whitman undoubtedly met Thomas Barnes in Hamilton, Ontario, between Toronto and London, where Whitman stopped on 12, 13, and 14 August 1880, during one of
his side trips with Dr Bucke.
961.  Whitman's letter and post card to Richardson, about 7 and 17 September 1880,
are lost (see footnote 902).
962.  This letter is lost, but see footnotes 732 and 949.
963.  John H. Ingram's letter to Whitman, 1 August 1880, is in the Feinberg Collection;
Whitman's reply of 19 September 1880 is lost; Ingram (1848–1916), editor and critic, is
briefly discussed in the poet's letter to Mrs Anne Gilchrist, 14 November 1880, in *The
Correspondence of Walt Whitman,* III, 193; see Herbert Gilchrist's letter in Thomas B.
Harned, *The Letters of Anne Gilchrist and Walt Whitman,* pp. 195–196.
964.  See the list of people, below, to whom Whitman wrote post cards and letters; it
seems strange that Whitman does not mention that Peter Doyle came to Niagara Falls and
they returned to Philadelphia together.
965.  Whitman's "Home Again" was in the Camden *Daily Post,* 30 September 1880;
sent to the London, Ontario, *Advertiser,* it appeared as "Walt Whitman Safe Home," 4
October 1880.
966.  Tommy Nicholson was an attendant at Dr Bucke's asylum in London; see Whitman's letter to him, *The Correspondence of Walt Whitman,* III, 189–190.

" " Mrs Gilchrist

" Clifford Riggs call'd & bo't set of books (2 Vols $10) for
E M Cox (C R, 19 yr's old, printer & reporter)

3 Geo & Susan Stafford papers

Smith Caswell "

[174]

Sent Sun Nov 19 '81 to x
[List of names in pencil:]
Sept 28 – Sent from Niagara[967]
  postal cards                             letters
    – Elmer x                            Mrs Gilchrist
    Geo & Susan Stafford                 T W H Rolleston
    John Newton Johnson                  Edward Carpenter
    J H Johnston                         Chas S Gleed
    Smith Caswell                    [three lines in blue pencil:]
    Jeff x                             at Niagara
    Mary x                             28th & 29th Sept
    Hannah x                                  '80
    Frederick Locker
    Dowden
    Josiah Child            [Clipped name and address, printed on blue scrap:]
    J A Symonds               Charles T. Dillingham,
    W T Harris           Publisher Bookseller & Import[er]
    Rudolf Schmidt                 678 Broadway,
                                    New York.

Wm W Reitzel              Hiskey 513 Arch[968]

John A Fetters Salem N J – Richard A H
            Elsinboro John Thomas

967. Of the 14 post cards and the four letters Whitman wrote at Niagara, five are
extant: see *The Correspondence of Walt Whitman,* III, 186–188, for those to Edward Car-
penter, Mrs Anne Gilchrist, William Torrey Harris (see footnote 771, above), Frederick
Locker-Lampson, and Rudolf Schmidt; the others are lost.
    968. Tilghman Hiskey worked on the Camden ferries, and Whitman wrote him from
Canada, but sent the letters in care of Ed: Lindell, Camden, not to 513 Arch, which was in
Philadelphia.

Cook & Bro: 51 & 53 North 8th – Underwear

---

Mrs Gilchrist, Keats' corner, 12 Well Road
     Hampstead London Eng[969]

---

Mr Michael Nash 813 L street south east
  Mrs Ann [in purple pencil] Washington D C[970]

---

[Clipped name and address, printed, of W. R. Balch, managing editor, The American, Box 1690, Phila., 720 Chestnut Street.] [971]

                     [175]

1880 – <u>In Camden</u>

                   Wide Awake
Oct 5 Letter to Dr Bucke with two scraps for letter ∧ to Jessie B

---

" 8 Letter to Dr B with scraps[972]

---

"  "  W R Balch, with "My Picture Gallery"  [in blue pencil:]
    for <u>American</u> 726 Chestnut St ($5)      paid[973]

---

" paper to Rudolf ~~Sm~~ Schmidt

---

9 sent "<u>Dalliance</u> of <u>Eagles</u>" to <u>Tobacco Plant</u> 10 Lord
    Nelson st Liverpool E. $10 – paid[974]

---

"Patroling Barnegat" to Harper's Monthly $10 [in blue pencil:] paid[975]

---

969. Mrs Anne Gilchrist had moved to this address from 5 Mount Vernon, Hampstead, where she lived earlier in the summer.

970. Mr and Mrs Michael Nash were old friends (Nash was an uncle) of Peter Doyle's; Whitman stayed in their home in 1875 (see *The Correspondence of Walt Whitman*, II, III, *passim,* where they are briefly mentioned in 22 letters to Doyle).

971. Whitman's poem, "My Picture Gallery," was published in *The American*, 30 October 1880; see more data about Whitman, Balch, and *The American* in *The Correspondence of Walt Whitman*, III, 223n.

972. These two letters of 5 and 8 October 1880 are lost, but the scraps may be for use by Dr Bucke in his book on Whitman; *Wide Awake* must refer to Mrs Mary E. Wager-Fisher's "Poets' Homes: Walt Whitman," *Wide Awake Pleasure Book*, VI (February 1878), 109–114. Jessie B refers to Jessie Gurd Bucke, Dr Bucke's wife.

973. See footnote 971.

974. Whitman's "The Dalliance of the Eagles" was first printed in *Cope's Tobacco Plant* (Liverpool), November 1880, and was included in the 1881 *Leaves of Grass*: see the Comprehensive Reader's Edition, pp. 273–274.

975. Whitman's "Patroling Barnegat" was first printed in *The American* (Philadelphia), June 1880; reprinted in *Harper's Monthly*, LXII (April 1881), 701; and was included in the 1881 *Leaves of Grass*: see the Comprehensive Reader's Edition, pp. 262–263.

9th to 13   down at Glendale

"   sent postal card to Herbert Gilchrist[976]

letter to P M Gen'l   Ottawa   Canada   (rec'd ans) [977]

14   letter & paper to Tom Nichelson, Canada[978]          [in blue pencil:]
                                                            rec'd ans

papers (four) to Tom Bradley[979]   "

15   photos to Rev Mr Richardson, Dr Beemer & young
          Wm Saunders, & one for Dr B to Dr Bucke          [in blue pencil,
          London – with postal card – [980]                sideways:]   recd

down at Glendale from 16th to 21st[981]

22   sent both Vols to A P Hitchcock, office  [in blue pencil, sideways:]   recd
                                              [in blue pencil:]             recd
          Morning Bulletin   Norwich   Conn:   paid

"   sent circ: to Isaac Hull Platt   13 William st[982]
                                   N Y

"   "   James Berry Benzel   Lynn   Mass

976.  Whitman's postal, written on his first visit to the Stafford farm at White Horse since his return from Canada, is in *The Correspondence of Walt Whitman*, III, 189.

977.  Letter lost; it is about a missing letter (see *The Correspondence of Walt Whitman*, III, 191).

978.  See footnote 966.

979.  Tom Bradley, to whom Whitman refers in his letter to Thomas Nicholson (*The Correspondence of Walt Whitman*, III, 190), was employed in Dr Bucke's asylum.

980.  These three people were undoubtedly friends of Dr Bucke's whom Whitman met in London during his stay there; the post card to Dr Bucke is lost.

981.  Whitman seems to be spending as much time with the Staffords as staying at 431 Stevens Street, Camden.

982.  Isaac Hull Platt (1853–1917), a New York lawyer, 23 years old at this time, is first mentioned here in the *Daybook*; he was to write four articles on Whitman in the *Conservator* between 1894 and 1906, "Whitman and Shelley," *Poet-Lore*, VIII (June 1896), 332–342; "A Poet Who Could Wait," *Book News*, XXIV (April 1906), 545–549; *Walt Whitman*, Beacon Biographies Series (Boston, 1904); and was called by William Sloane Kennedy, in his *Fight of a Book for the World*, p. 92, "one of the most indefatigable public defenders of W. W." Dr Platt also became one of the early presidents of the Walt Whitman Fellowship, founded in 1894. The poet sent him, on 27 October 1880 (see below), a copy of *Leaves of Grass*; see *The Correspondence of Walt Whitman*, III, 190, for Whitman's letter of 22 October 1880.

"        "Red Court Farm"   to Mrs Stafford [983]

23   sent letter to Dr Bucke   disfavoring the letter[984]

"    sent a set two Vols: to Dr Henry A   Martin   [in blue pencil,   paid
[in blue pencil:]                                        sideways:]      recd
  paid                      25 Dudley street   Boston Mass:              recd

24ᵗʰ   papers to Sister Hannah

    Smith  Caswell

    John A Fetters[985]

[176]
[On calling card of Isaac Hull Platt, attorney-at-law, 13 William Street,
N.Y.C.:]

|  |  |
|---|---|
| Oct 23 – Letter from   <u>very</u> <u>warm ab't poems</u>, & asking" ~~for~~ ab't books – I sent circular[986] | Dr Bucke at Park Avenue Hotel [printed] 4th Ave. 32d and 33d Sts, |
| [four words in blue pencil:] | [printed] |
| bo't | Dec:   New York   [printed] |
| Books | '80 [987] |
| (I sent the letter to Dr Bucke)   paid | |
| recd | |

[Printed name and address of Jno. S. Stott, stationer, printer, 224 State Street,
Chicago. On calling card of Ernest Ingersoll, U. S. Fish Commission, Washington:]

Met him on the Camden ferry

---

983. *The Red Court Farm* was a novel by Mrs Henry (Ellen Price) Wood (1814–1887),
the popular author of *East Lynn*; the edition Whitman sent Mrs Stafford was most likely the
one published by G. Munro, New York, in 1878 in the Seaside Library.
    984. With Whitman's letter to Dr Bucke lost, it is not clear what Whitman means by
"disfavoring the letter."
    985. John A. Fetters is listed on the page in the *Daybook* dealing with Niagara Falls,
28–29 September 1880, with Salem, New Jersey given as his address, so Whitman may have
met him at the Falls.
    986. See footnote 982.
    987. Whitman saw Dr Bucke in Philadelphia on 5 December 1880, so he must have
been in New York shortly before or after this date.

boat Saturday evening Oct 23 '80

[side lines in red ink:]

Rev: John Page Hopps – De Montfort St.   Leicester
    Eng: (is quite an author, religious books –
    – two friendly well written articles ab't me
    in Truth Seeker, Sept. and Oct. 1880)[988]
[Not WW's hand:]          is a unitarian minister
From J. Page Hopps          call'd, Sept. 13, '82
          Leicester
[clipped from letter]

| From Milton | | Due – Oct 26 |
| Pa: at Test's    J. Miller Clark [printed] | | $10 from Dr Martin   Boston |
| Drug Store | | 7 "    Putnam's Sons |
| Mrs Mingle | 114 | 10 "    C L Ehrenfield |
| (Mrs | North 32ᵈ | 10 "    Paymaster Browne |
| Belle Archer) | West Phil | 8 "    Phil: Press[989] |
| Nelly   Nov '80 | | |

Fred Vaughan[990] [not WW's hand]

[Clipping of name and address: New-York Life Insurance Co., 346 & 348 Broadway, NYC.]

[177]

Oct 1880
    send
25   a set to E C Cheever[991] office   Lathrop       [in blue pencil,    paid
[in blue pencil:]   sent                              sideways:]    recd
    Coal Mining Co:  Kewanee   Illinois

988. John Page Hopps, the English author, whose reputation does not seem to have survived; he wrote these two pieces on Whitman in the *Truth Seeker* and visited the poet in Camden.

989. These sums were either for copies of *Leaves of Grass* or for pieces by Whitman, and cancelations undoubtedly meant that they were paid; see book orders below.

990. Fred Vaughan was a friend of Whitman's; his letters to the poet, 1860–1862, and 11 August 1874, are in the Feinberg Collection; see footnote 66.

991. E. C. Cheever ordered a set of Whitman's *Leaves of Grass* and *Two Rivulets* on 20 October 1880; the letter is in the Feinberg Collection.

[in blue pencil:]
  sent     sent    – G P Putnam's sons
  booksellers   182 Fifth avenue  [in blue pencil:]     [in blue pencil,
                                  recd           sideways:]   sent
                                    paid

---

       also to  W J Forbes  p o box  4141  [in blue pencil,    paid
[in blue pencil:]             [in blue pencil:]  sideways:]    recd
  sent        New York City      paid             recd

---

[in blue pencil:]                                [in blue pencil,
  sent — James T Fields[992] 148 Charles     sideways:]     sent
                         [in blue pencil:]       paid
    street  Boston         recd   paid        recd

---

"   circ: to Jno: S Stott   stationer &c
      224 State street  Chicago  Ill[993]

---

  sent
"  ∧ Rev Mr Hopps's "Truth Seeker" Oct.  Sent to Dr Bucke

---

[in blue pencil:]
    sent   C L Ehrenfield  State Librarian   [in blue pencil,    recd
    &                               sideways:]    paid
    paid       Pennsylvania  Harrisburg  Pa[994]       recd

---

     Paymaster Samuel T Browne  USN
[in blue pencil:]             [in blue pencil,
    sent     U S S Powhatan    sideways:]  paid   recd
    Norfolk  Va

---

[in blue pencil:]
Sent     George Heard,[995] Petroleum Broker
[in blue pencil:]               recd         paid [in blue pencil]
    sent    Oil City   Penna  a set     [in blue pencil,
                                  sideways:]    recd

---

992. James T. Fields (1817–1881), editor of *The Atlantic Monthly,* who published "Proud Music of the Sea-Storm" in February 1869 ("Sea" was dropped from the title in *Leaves of Grass*); see *The Correspondence of Walt Whitman,* II, 73.

993. John S. Stott's letter to Whitman, 10 November 1880, is in the Feinberg Collection.

994. C. L. Ehrenfield's letter to Whitman, 25 October 1880, is in the Feinberg Collection.

995. George Heard's letter to Whitman, 25 October 1880, is in the Feinberg Collection.

27    sent affectionate letter to Sister Hannah[996]

"  postal to Geo and Susan Stafford – to Dr Bucke[997]

"  pictures to Geo:  England  London  Canada
                                    Cambridge
        to Charlotte Fiske Bates ~~acknowled~~
        Mass:  acknowledging "Risk" [998]

Sent   Frederic Almy[999]   151 Pawtucket St       [in blue pencil,
        the two    [in blue pencil:]              sideways:]  sent
Lowell   Mass: Vols     paid  recd

Sent   H C Bunner   330 East 17 street       [in blue pencil,
                        [in blue pencil:]    sideways:] sent
        New York City   the two      paid

Sent   Isaac Hull Platt[1000]   Attorney at Law, 13 Wil-  [in blue pencil,
                        [in blue pencil:]      sideways:]   sent
        liam Street  New York  Two     paid                  recd

[178]

[Three slips, with names and addresses, printed, of G. P. Putnam's Sons, 182
Fifth Avenue, NYC; A. Williams & Co., 283 Washington Street, Boston,
booksellers; and James Arnold, 6 & Minor St., Phila., book binder.]

M  D  Conway  1008 Clinton Street

                                avenue
Jeff  2511 Second Carondelet ~~street~~ St L[1001]

R Worthington   770 Broadway[1002]

H M Alden   Editor   Harpers'  Franklin Square  N Y [1003]

---

996.  Letter lost.
997.  Both post cards, to the Staffords and to Dr Bucke, are lost.
998.  Charlotte Fiske Bates and "Risk" not identifiable; letter lost.
999.  See Whitman's letter to Frederic Almy, 30 October 1880, in *The Correspondence
of Walt Whitman,* III, 190–191.
1000.  See footnote 982.
1001.  Thomas Jefferson Whitman's new address in St Louis, Missouri.
1002.  See footnotes 732 and 949.
1003.  Whitman's poem, "Patroling Barnegat," was published in *Harper's,* April 1881
(see footnote 975, above).

Charles W Eldridge   U S Revenue Agent [1004]
         Park Hotel   4th av & 32$^d$ street
    Post Office Building   Boston   Mass:

---

Will E
Wm Saunders   188 Dundas St   London Ont Canada[1005]

---

Potter, Photo's,     5 North 8th Street

---

Geo: A Leavitt & Co: Auctioneers,[1006] 817 Broadway
                                          N Y

---

Richard E. Labar   [not WW's hand]         box 274, Ann
         Public Ledger Office [not WW's hand]     Arbor
Sunday Dec 12 '80)                                Mich
Friday    " 24 ( Philadelphia, Pa. [not WW's hand]

---

A and P
   Mrs Elisa Seaman Legget   169 East Elizabeth St. Detroit   Mich[1007]

---

Albert E Johnston   Mott av & 149th street[1008]

---

W S Kennedy   ~~110~~ 7 Waterhouse St   Cambridge Mass[1009]

---

Jeannette L Gilder   20 ~~Lafayette~~ Place N Y City[1010]
                          Astor

---

Percy Ives, care Academy of Arts , Broad st & Cherry
         Phila: [1011]

---

1004. Charles W. Eldridge was a longtime Whitman friend and co-publisher of the 1860 *Leaves of Grass*; he had moved from Washington to Boston as a U. S. government agent.

1005. William Saunders was one of those Whitman had sent a photograph, through Dr Bucke, on 15 October 1880.

1006. Leavitt, as auctioneer, was connected with the sale of the 1860 *Leaves* electroplates to Worthington (see *The Correspondence of Walt Whitman*, III, 196–197).

1007. Mrs Elisa Seaman Leggett (see footnote 901) was the grandmother of the artist Percy Ives, who drew in 1881, at the age of 17, several pencil sketches of Whitman (one is in the Detroit Public Library), and whose oil painting of the poet is in the Feinberg Collection (see *The Correspondence of Walt Whitman*, III, 239n; and III, opp. p. 202, where the Ives portrait is reproduced). See footnote 1105.

1008. Albert E. Johnston was the son of one of Whitman's best New York friends, John H. Johnston.

1009. See footnote 803.

1010. Jeannette L. Gilder (see footnote 96) was co-founder and editor of *The Critic* (1881–1906).

1011. Percy Ives was the artist mentioned in footnote 1007 (see Whitman's letter to him, 11 August 1885, in *The Correspondence of Walt Whitman*, III, 402–403).

[On printed name & address of The Critic,[1012] Broadway, New York:]

~~30 Lafayette~~ Place
20 Astor
North American Review
~~same building~~
30

[179]

Oct 1880

28 – receipt $7 to G P Putnams Sons   N Y [1013]

sent Dr Bucke "Matador's" criticism[1013a]   [in pencil]

31   letter to Harry[1014] – postals to Jas Arnold & G & S Stafford

cards to John Burroughs – Charlotte F Bates[1015]

slips   a full set to Jas T   Fields[1016]

[in blue pencil:]
    sent Clarence H Pierce, care Alman                    [in blue pencil,
                rec'd            rec'd   [blue pencil]   sideways:]   paid
      H   Fogg & Co:   Houlton   Aroostock Co:   Maine

Nov [in blue pencil:]                                      [in blue pencil,
    1.   sent   William   Brough   Franklin   Penna.   sideways:]   recd
                                                                    paid

---

1012. *The Critic* was founded in 1881 by Joseph L. Gilder and his sister Jeannette (see footnote 96), who served as editor; Whitman was to publish a number of poems and prose pieces in the magazine.

1013. As is obvious from the notations in the *Daybook*, Whitman was selling a number of copies of *Leaves of Grass* and *Two Rivulets*; he says so himself in his letter to Harry Stafford (31 October 1880, see below), also mentioning that he brought two boxes of bound copies of his books home to Stevens Street.

1013a. In New York *Graphic*, 25 November 1873; reprinted in Bucke's *Walt Whitman*, pp. 209–210.

1014. Printed in *The Correspondence of Walt Whitman*, III, 191–192.

1015. The cards to James Arnold (Whitman's book binder), George and Susan Stafford (whom he wrote to say he would be down to White Horse in a week, as he told Harry Stafford the same day), John Burroughs, and Charlotte Fiske Bates (Cambridge, Mass.) are lost.

1016. James T. Fields, who had published a Whitman poem in *The Atlantic* 11 years previously (see footnote 992), is now getting a set of slips, on which Whitman had printed his new poems.

[in blue pencil:]
   sent   A   Williams & Co:   283   Washington st
                            [in blue pencil:]
   Boston , two vols[1017]       paid   ~~$7 due~~   rec'd

2 – sent circ to Geo: E. Dodge   Dodge Meigs & co
            72   Wall   street     N Y

papers ("American") [1018] to Dr Bucke and Sister H — to Richard Fet-
                                             ters[1019]

sent "My Picture Gallery" to London Advertiser[1019]

[in blue pencil:]
4   sent Rev M J Savage   37 West Newton st
               [in blue pencil:]
   Boston, Mass:   paid   rec'd

sent   Leaves of Grass to [Dr] B   A Watson, 124
                          [in blue pencil:]
   York Street   Jersey City   N J   paid   rec'd

[in blue pencil:]   the two Vols:
   sent     Geo.   E Dodge, ∧ care   Dodge, Meigs & Co
                       [in blue pencil:]
   72 Wall st   N Y City   paid   rec'd

+   from 6th to 16th inclusive
       down at Glendale[1020]

16th   letter to Mrs Gilchrist (written   at Glendale)
                      also
   postal to Dr Bucke[1021]     (Sunday Tribune 7th)

---

1017. Some but not all of those who ordered books from Whitman were sent letters, such as A. Williams & Company; see *The Correspondence of Walt Whitman,* III, 192.

1018. *The American* published Whitman's "My Picture Gallery" on 30 October 1880.

1019. Richard Fetters was undoubtedly related to John A. Fetters of Salem, New Jersey, listed above.

1019a. The Whitman poem, "My Picture Gallery," first published in *The American,* was to be in the 1881 *Leaves* — see Comprehensive Reader's Edition, pp. 401–402.

1020. Yet another visit with the Staffords, which Whitman described in his letter (see next entry) to Mrs Anne Gilchrist, printed in *The Correspondence of Walt Whitman,* III, 192–194.

1021. Post card lost.

17   sent two Sets (four Vols:) to George Tyson
      sent Mrs Tyson letter and phototype by mail
                        [in blue pencil:]
  – Germantown, by Express.    paid

"    sent a set (two Vols:) to R   W   Gilder[1022]
      office Scribner's Mag: 743 Broadway   N Y
      [line in blue pencil:]
      rec'd        a present to Mr & Mrs G

[180]

John P Foley is coming on the staff
[in red ink:]
has left    of the Phila: Times  (he has left)

[cancellation marks in blue pencil:]
Due   Nov 29 et seq[1027]
~~Century Club  N Y~~  ~~10~~
Cope's Tobacco Plant  10
~~A  W  Williams  Boston~~ ~~7~~
~~C  T Dillingham  N Y~~ ~~10.50~~
~~John A Scott (see~~  ~~$10~~
        ahead)

Mr Handy (long on the Times) is
   managing editor of the Press

~~Dr Bucke~~      ~~5~~
~~John Hayes, Corydon Iowa~~ ~~10~~
~~Horace Furness~~    ~~10~~

Johnny Roth, fine boy of 7 or 8 – Stevens st
                Dec: '80

~~Christopher Starr,~~
    Port Williams
    Kings County  } 10
    ~~Nova Scotia~~

Percy Ives, Mrs Legget's grandson,[1023]
  age 16, a student intends to be an
  artist – lives bachelor's hall fashion
  in Philadelphia – reads Emerson,
    Carlyle, &c
  – is a son of Lewis T   Ives, artist –
    [line in red ink:]
    Academy of Fine Arts

Richard Hoe Lawrence
81 Park Av: N Y  $10
books sent March 7

Geo. A . Lung  [name and address
              (in pencil) not in
      Lewisburg    WW's
Union Co.      Penna    hand]

G Wm Harris
Cornell University  } $10
Ithaca  N Y

Jan 11 – Rich: M Ware, lawyer,
           Mullica Hill

C  T  Dillingham
N Y    3.50

---

1022. See Whitman's letter, same date, to Richard Watson Gilder in *The Correspondence of Walt Whitman*, III, 195.

1023. See footnotes 1007 and 1011.

1027. These names and addresses, which also occur in other places in the *Daybook*, have to do with pieces Whitman sent for publication, or with orders of *Leaves of Grass*; cancelation is an indication that the sums were paid.

gent 50, I met at the boat landing
   Camden – said he intended to come
   Jan 12 '81   & see me[1024]

Albert D  Shaw
U S  Consul
Manchester Eng:     10

Mr. Brotherton[1025]
   cor: 16th & Brandywine sts
     (?553 North 16th)

Wm H  Millis   Dover
Jan '81   Kent Co:  Del:[1026]

[181]

Nov: '80 – sent Rev: Frank W Gemsauben   care of
17th                     South
   Ohio Home Journal   108 High st Columbus
     by mail         [in blue pencil:]
     Ohio – a set – 2 Vols    paid

"    sent John S Stott   stationer &c: 224 State Street
                               [in blue pencil:]
     Chicago   a set by mail     paid   rec'd

"    sent C B Foote   Hatch & Foote   Bankers[1028]   12 Wall
                               [in blue pencil:]
   St  N Y City   a set by express    paid   rec'd

sent letter & circ: (by request) to Edward Dakin, Regents
Park College   London N W – Eng:

sent letter & circ. (by request) to Colin MacKenzie[1029] of
Edinburgh Scotland   care   Scottish Union   Ins Co 64
Pearl St.  Hartford   Conn

18    sent a woman's estimate of Leaves of Grass to Whitelaw Reid [1030]

---

1024. Whitman wrote Richard M. Ware on 23 November 1881, but the letter is lost.
1025. The same Brotherton as the one mentioned in footnote 876, J. L. Brotherton?
1026. Whitman wrote to William A. Mills on 26 January 1881, but the letter is lost, see footnote 175.
1028. The people here, and those on the previous page of the *Daybook,* further show what Whitman meant in his remark to Harry Stafford, "I am selling quite a good many of my books now."
1029. Whitman's letter to W. Colin Mackenzie is lost, but Mackenzie's letter, 11 November 1880, is in the Feinberg Collection.
1030. The article which Whitman sent to Whitelaw Reid, editor of the New York

sent one L of G to G   P Putnam's Sons 182 Fifth
                              [in blue pencil:]
    av   N Y City                       paid   recd

---

W S Kennedy call'd [1031]

---

19   Phil Press paid $8 –(has thus paid for both letters) [1032]

---

letter to Mrs Stafford [1033] . . . papers to Mont [1034] . . . papers to
                                                Rich Fetters [1035]

---

21   breakfast at Mr & Mrs Scovel's [1036]

---

[in blue pencil:]       a set 2 Vols
22   sent   Colin MacKenzie ∧ care Scottish Union
                                  [in blue pencil:]
    Ins: Co:   64 Pearl st Hartford Conn:    paid [1037]

---

[in blue pencil:]
    Sent David Hutcheson   152 A street   N E
                             [in blue pencil:]
    Washington   D C   a set two Vols   paid   recd [1038]

---

[in blue pencil:]
23   sent a set Two Vols: by mail to Edw'd G Doggett
                                [in blue pencil:]
    31 Richmond Terrace, Clifton, Bristol, Eng:   paid   rec'd [1039]

---

*Tribune,* must have been Anne Gilchrist's "A Woman's Estimate of Walt Whitman . . . ,"
*The Radical* (Boston), VII (May 1870), 345–359.

1031.  Although Kennedy, in his *Reminiscences of Walt Whitman* (p. 1), gives the date of his first meeting with Whitman as 21 November 1880, the poet records the visit on 18 November; because of the nature of the entry, and the possibility that Whitman wrote the entry on that day, Whitman's date is most likely accurate; see footnote 803, above.

1032.  The Philadelphia *Press* "letters," for which Whitman was paid $8, have not been located.

1033.  Letter lost.

1034.  Montgomery Stafford, Harry's uncle, though only 18 years old at this time.

1035.  See footnote 1018.

1036.  This was Whitman's first visit with the James Matlack Scovels since his return from Canada; for Whitman's account of an earlier breakfast, see footnote 660.

1037.  See footnote 1029.

1038.  David Hutcheson's letter, 20 November 1880, ordering the books, is in the Feinberg Collection.

1039.  Whitman's letter to Edward G. Doggett is in *The Correspondence of Walt Whitman,* III, 195.

[in blue pencil:]

24    sent Titus Munson Coan   Century Club   109

[in blue pencil:]

east 15th St N Y City   a set 2 Vols   paid   recd[1040]

26    paid James Arnold   $20 (192 Vols due, less 40)[1041]

wrote to R   W   Gilder    ⎫ about the
"   "   John Burroughs[1043]   ⎬  Worthington matter[1042]

a set   two Vols:    by mail to A Williams
& Co: booksellers, 283 Washington St   Boston
$7   due

|  | [five lines in pencil:] | [182] |
| Josiah Child | to do – Dec 21 | |
| at Trubner & Co's | send photo to | |
| 57 & 59 Ludgate Hill | Lizzie Westgate[1044] | |
|  | 2123 Larkin St | |
|  | San Francisco   Cal | |

[183]

1880

[in blue pencil:]

Nov. 29   sent a set, two Vols: by mail to A Williams

[in blue pencil:]

& Co:   283   Washington st.   Boston   paid   recd

[in blue pencil:]

Dec: 1   sent   Charles T Dillingham   678 Broadway N Y

[in blue pencil:]

by express three Vols:    paid recd

1040.  Titus Munson Coan's letter, from The Century Club, 20 November 1880, ordering the books, is in the Library of Congress; Whitman had sent him two volumes in March 1880.

1041.  James Arnold was the binder of Whitman's *Leaves of Grass* and other volumes.

1042.  The letter to Richard Watson Gilder, the fullest account of Whitman's difficulty with Worthington over the 1860 plates, is in *The Correspondence of Walt Whitman*, III, 195–198, with Edwin Haviland Miller's notes on the subsequent history of the affair.

1043.  The letter to John Burroughs is in *The Correspondence of Walt Whitman*, III, 198.

1044.  Lizzie Westgate, described as "a fervid young admirer," wrote to Whitman on 28 November 1880 (letter in the Feinberg Collection).

[in blue pencil:]            ne?
"    sent Charles A Martiur   Georgetown   Colorado
    ☞ [in blue pencil]        [in blue pencil:]
    a set Two Vols: by mail      paid   rec'd

---

3   letter to N A Review   promising <u>Tennyson in America</u>[1045]

---

papers to Richard H Fetters, Salem, Elsinboro

---

5th (Sunday) <u>breakfast</u> at Mr & Mrs Scovel's[1046]
    spent the afternoon with Dr Bucke at Girard House
                                            Phila

---

$50 rec'd from R   Worthington (by J M S)[1047]

---

6   sent the following rec't to Worthington:

    Rec'd from R Worthington (thro' Jas M Scovel)
    Fifty Dollars on account of royalty in selling
    my book <u>Leaves</u> of <u>Grass</u>      W. Whitman

    paid Mr Scovel $10 – (he sent for it)

---

7    sent letter to John Burroughs ab't Worthington[1048]
                                        affair

---

7    rec'd postal card from Dr Bucke (Leavitt)[1049]
     sent a copy to John Burroughs

---

9    postals to Gilder – & G & S Stafford [1050]
     papers to Richard Fetters

---

10  Papers to Will Tinker   Greeley Col:

---

1045. Rather than "Tennyson in America," Whitman sent *The North American Review*, which had asked him for a piece and paid him $100 for it, "The Poetry of the Future," *NAR,* CXXXII (February 1881), 195–210; it was reprinted in *Specimen Days and Collect* as "Poetry To-day in America" (see *Prose Works 1892,* II, 474–490); Tennyson comes in for a certain amount of discussion. An early draft of the essay is in the Feinberg Collection, another (?) in the Trent Collection, Duke University.
1046. See footnotes 660 and 1036.
1047. See footnote 1042; J M S is James Matlack Scovel.
1048. See *The Correspondence of Walt Whitman,* III, 199–200.
1049. Leavitt was the auctioneer in the Worthington matter (see footnote 1042).
1050. The post card to Richard Watson Gilder is in *The Correspondence of Walt Whitman,* III, 200; the one to George and Susan Stafford is lost.

11    sent letter & circ: (in response) to Joseph Baron    73
      Audley Range, Blackburn, England [1051]

12    paper to Mont:[1052] visit from Dick Labar[1053]

17    letter to Tom Nichelson[1054] Americans to Harry Scovel [1055]

      papers to Dick Fetters – & to Smith Caswell [1056]

19    postal to Harry – to Jack Richardson[1057]
      "    rec't to Century Club

20th  evening – sent Poetry to-day in America  to N A Rev[1058]
      paper to Tom Bradley

[184]

"Poetry of the future" [1059]                  Gloves – 1880'–81 [1061a]
       article                                 a pair to Hiskey
[In left margin, sideways:]                     "      Ol Wood
names marked x "Death of Carlyle" [1060]  sent  "      Pete
– Dr Bucke      2 x                             "      Charley Woods
– W D O'Connor    x                             "      Sid Jackson
– John Burroughs      x                         "      John Shuman

1051. Letter lost.
1052. Montgomery Stafford.
1053. Richard E. Labar was associated with the Philadelphia *Public Ledger* (see *The Correspondence of Walt Whitman*, III, 240n).
1054. Whitman's letter to Thomas Nicholson, who worked for Dr Bucke in London, Ontario (see footnote 966), is in *The Correspondence of Walt Whitman*, III, 200–201.
1055. Harry was James Matlack Scovel's son; the *Americans* which Whitman sent were most likely the issues of June 1880, containing "Patroling Barnegat," and of 30 October 1880, containing "My Picture Gallery."
1056. Richard Fetters, who was being sent papers often at this time, lived in Salem, New Jersey; and Smith Caswell was of course John Burroughs's hired man at Esopus-on-Hudson, New York.
1057. Both postals, to Harry Stafford and to Jack Richardson (see footnote 902), are lost.
1058. This was not the title used in the magazine, but was the title Whitman used when he included the essay in *Specimen Days and Collect* (see footnote 1045).
1059. In *The North American Review*, February 1881 (see footnote 1045).
1061a. Late in December 1878 Whitman obtained about 50 pairs of gloves from George W. Childs (see footnotes 543 and 550), 25 of which he gave as Christmas presents; the list here is of six more recipients, with some "repeaters," such as Charley Wood (or Woods). Hiskey is Tilghman Hiskey, of the Camden ferries (see also footnote 903), and Pete is not Peter Doyle, but Pete Davis (see earlier list). Most of the men worked on the horse cars or on the ferries.
1060. Whitman's essay, "Death of Carlyle," *The Critic,* I (12 February 1881), 30; reprinted as "The Dead Carlyle," *The Literary World* (Boston), 12 February 1881, and in its original form in *Essays from "The Critic"* (Boston, 1882), pp. 31–37. It was included in *Specimen Days* as "Death of Thomas Carlyle," with some changes (see *Prose Works 1892*, I, 248–253).

Edwd Abbott Lit World
W T Harris
- Moncure Conway
J A Symonds
- Edwd Dowden
- Wm M Rossetti
Tennyson
Frederick Locker
- Mrs Gilchrist
Edwd Carpenter
Rudolf Schmidt
H J Bathgate
W S Kennedy
Josiah Child [1061]

T W H Rolleston Lange Strasse 29[II]    Glasshouse Shinrone
    Dresden    Saxony[1062]    King's County Ireland

Mrs Mary Wager Fisher[1063]
Lord Hougton (Carlyle
       only)[1064]

[On card of J. E. Winner, of J. M. Stoddart & Co., publishers, 727 Chestnut Street, Phila.:]

Met in 9th st: Phila: "representative.
of Stoddart's Review" – ask'd me to
call, &c, &c.

[Printed name and address of J. M. Stoddart[1065] & Co., with address changed (in ink) from 727 to 10 Chestnut Street.]

Hall's Health Syringe    632    Arch

---

1061. The 17 people here, to whom Whitman sent one or both of his pieces, are all identified in various places in the *Daybook*; William Douglas O'Connor (see footnote 651) and Whitman were still not speaking to each other, so his name here is significant; William Sloane Kennedy (see footnote 803) had just shortly before met Whitman; and Moncure D. Conway (see footnote 36) did not often appear in such lists.

1062. T. W. H. Rolleston (see footnote 50) had been writing to Whitman about this time: see his letters to the poet, 16 October and 11 November 1880 in Horst Frenz, editor, *Whitman and Rolleston — A Correspondence* (Bloomington, Indiana, 1951), pp. 15–18, 19–20; and in Horace Traubel, *With Walt Whitman in Camden*, II, 67–69.

1063. See footnote 214.

1064. Lord Houghton, Richard Monckton Milnes (1809–1885), met Whitman in December 1875 in Camden; he was a poet and dilettante, and when Whitman wrote to him in June 1885 he referred to him as "Dear old friend." See *The Correspondence of Walt Whitman*, II, 344n, and III, 395.

1065. Joseph M. Stoddart (1845–1921) established *Stoddart's Review* in 1880, which merged with *The American* (in which Whitman had appeared) in 1882, and he became edi-

[185]

1880 Dec – letters to Hannah and Mary    – (5 cash for Christmas)
21 — letter to Dick Labar[1066]   [in pencil]

/ papers to Dr Bucke – Mrs Gilchrist (Cedar-Plums)[1067] [in pencil]
    circs to Dr H A Martin   Boston   [in pencil]

circ: (by request) to Geo: Willis Warren, Farmington
                                            Conn:

Mr Young (Yonge?) call'd – is on his way to
Tennessee, to the Rugby Colony (Thomas Hughes's)
– about 35 years old – has been at Cambridge,
Mass: teaching & studying – told me ab't Prof:
Elliott, Longfellow, Howells &c – visit two hours

24   Visit from Dick Labar[1068]

25   Christmas dinner & afternoon & evening with Mr
     & Mrs Lung   426 Stevens St – very pleasant – George,
     Emma, Charley, Ed. & Carry – went into Clark's to
     see the Christmas tree & the <u>bears</u> —[1069]

27   paper (taxidermist show, Rochester) to Will Saunders

rec'd   from G W Childs, for benevolent purposes

sent letter to Mrs Legget Detroit (poetry slips)[1070]

rec'd box books from James Arnold – 144 books – $56 due
                                            him[1071]

sent [in blue pencil]
28   sent . . . Two Vols:  to John P Woodbury, Hotel
     Vendome, Boston[1072]       [in blue pencil:] recd   paid

tor of *Lippincott's Monthly* in 1889 (see *The Correspondence of Walt Whitman*, III, 263).
    1066.  Letters to Hannah and Mary lost; letter to Richard Labar lost — see footnote 1053.
    1067.  For "Cedar Plums" as a name for *Specimen Days*, see *Prose Works 1892*, I, 245.
    1068.  See footnote 1053.
    1069.  The Lungs were of course neighbors of George and Louisa Orr Whitman on Stevens Street.
    1070.  See footnote 1007.
    1071.  Whitman needed these books from his binder (see entry for 26 November, above) because of increased sales.
    1072.  A letter, to an unknown correspondent, 28 December 1880, may be to John P. Woodbury: *The Correspondence of Walt Whitman*, III, 201.

31    wrote to Jenny Gilder    148 East 15th St    N Y    promising sketches – (her first number is to be out Jan 15)[1073]

---

sent rect to James Hearne Century Club    N Y.[1074]

---

Jan 1 '81 – postal to Mrs Gilchrist[1075]

---

2 – letters to Mrs Stafford    & to Harry[1076] – paper to Mont

---

5th    sent two "How I get around at 60"    to Jeannette
L Gilder    recd $20 in pay[1077]

---

6    sent circ: (by request) to F H Ransom, of D Ransom, Son & Co: Buffalo N Y

---

†    "    to Lou $23 [1078]

---

"    rec'd pass for '81 over W J R R from Gen: Sewell [1079]

[186]

[On card of Dr. W. H. Webb, 556 N. 16th St., Phila.:]

| Met on Chestnut St. Jan 13 '81 | John Hardie |
| p. m. he was in | 6 Finnart St   Greenock |
| Armory Sq: Hosp: | Scotland |
| Wash: & knew me there[1080] | (fine letter, Sept.   '79 – I sent it |
| | to Dr Bucke Jan '81)[1081] |

1073.  Jeannette Gilder was the editor of *The Critic,* and Whitman sent her the first part of "How I Get Around at 60, and Take Notes," six instalments to appear between 29 January 1881 and 15 July 1882; see *The Correspondence of Walt Whitman,* III, 202, for a transcript of Whitman's letter.

1074.  James Hearne's letter is in the Library of Congress; Whitman's to him is lost.

1075.  The post card, full of information, is in *The Correspondence of Walt Whitman,* III, 203.

1076.  The letter to Harry Stafford, but not the one to his mother, is in *The Correspondence of Walt Whitman,* III, 203–204; Mont is Montgomery Stafford, Harry's uncle, though younger than he was.

1077.  See footnote 1073; see three letters to Jeannette Gilder, 5, 8, and 15 January 1881, in *The Correspondence of Walt Whitman,* 205–206; Whitman's pieces, "How I Get Around at 60, and Take Notes," are scattered through *Specimen Days,* with various changes, including different titles, *Prose Works 1892,* I, 3–4, 118–120, 132–133, 136–139, 142–144, 149–154, 164, 172–178, 233–235, 264–269, 278–282, and (rejected paragraphs) 347–351.

1078.  This $23 to Louisa Orr Whitman was for the poet's board at 431 Stevens Street.

1079.  This annual pass for use on the West Jersey Railroad, given to Whitman by General William J. Sewell, was one of the two the poet received; the other was on the Camden & Atlantic Railroad (see below, 26 January 1880).

1080.  This coincidence did not, naturally, happen often; most of those whom Whitman met in Camden and Philadelphia, and whose names he recorded in the *Daybook,* were workmen, young boys, and strangers.

1081.  This letter from John Hardie, September 1879, is lost.

[Clipped from printed letterhead of Dr. Chas. H. Thomas, 1807 Chestnut St., in WW's hand:]

Met on Ferry, Phil: Jan 13
    he talked much of Judge Tourgee
    & ab't "Fool's Errand"

John Shuman[1082] 417 William st
        [in blue pencil, on slip:]
        Begin here
        Oct. 15  p m

[On card of Theo. T. Crane, piano and organ tuner, with Wm. H. Bonner & Co., Chestnut St., Phila.; residence, 302 Cooper St., Camden:]

musical composer I meet on the
cars & ferry — wants me to
write something that he may
set to music[1083]

[187]

Jan: 1881 – 7th – paper (American) to Mrs. Gilchrist [1084]

6th   note to D M Zimmerman C & A R R [1085]

"    visit (2d) from Percy Ives   3d visit Jan 31 [1085a]

7    sent circ: (by request) to J S Watson 18 State st  Hartford
                                    Conn:  dealer

[first word in blue pencil:]
13th  Sent Two Volumes, to Mrs. Wm C Banning
                                [in blue pencil:]
    204 Fifth Avenue, N. Y. City    paid  rec'd

1082. John Shuman was one of those to whom Whitman gave a pair of gloves for Christmas 1880; he must thus have been a young man on the Camden ferries or on the Philadelphia horse cars.

1083. There are numerous musical settings of Whitman's poems, but I do not know of any by Theo. T. Crane.

1084. This could have been *The American* for June or 30 October 1880, containing Whitman poems, "Patroling Barnegat" and "My Picture Windows."

1085. Perhaps concerning Whitman's annual pass on the Camden & Atlantic Railroad (see entry for 26 January 1881, below).

1085a. Percy Ives was the artist who made several portraits of Whitman (see footnote 1007).

rec'd $12.75 from Dr Bucke for the three Vols: I left

---

15   sent letter to Miss Gilder ab't proof [1086] & Art: in N A <u>Rev</u>:

---

rec'd pay 100 for art in Feb. N A Rev: with
        N A R's special "thanks" for art:[1087]

---

[second word in blue pencil:]
16   Sunday     Sent to John A Scott, Pembridge Villa Southfield
                                                    [in blue pencil:]
        Wandsworth   S W London Eng.   The two Vols:     paid   recd

---

wrote to E H Hames & Co: <u>Literary</u> <u>World</u>   Boston,
declining to write an article on Longfellow & alluding
to the <u>London</u>   <u>Times</u> (June '78) Bryant article[1088]

---

sent letter to George and Susan Stafford.[1089]

---

[first word in blue pencil:]
17   Sent the Two Vols: to Miss Harriet W. Robinson
                                     [in blue pencil:]
        6 Montague Terrace, Brooklyn   N Y   paid   recd

---

[first word in blue pencil:]                 [in blue pencil:]
18   Sent "Leaves of Grass" to C B Burr M D.     recd
        Asylum for the Insane   Pontiac Mich:   paid

---

paid Daughady, 725 Chestnut st.
$34.25 for bill of materials, for John
Newton Johnson, of Meltonsville, Ala: [1090]

---

                                            [in red ink:]
sent Mr Lung a miscellaneous package        ret'd [1091]

1086.   "How I Get Around at 60, and Take Notes," *The Critic*, 29 January 1881 (see footnotes 1073 and 1077, above).
1087.   "The Poetry of the Future," *The North American Review*, February 1881 (see footnote 1045).
1088.   Whitman's last piece in *The Literary World* was "Emerson's Books (the Shadows of Them)," 22 May 1880 (see footnotes 879 and 880, above); and he sent "The Dead Carlyle" for the issue of 12 February 1881 (see footnote 1060, above).
1089.   The letter is in *The Correspondence of Walt Whitman*, III, 206–207.
1090.   For Whitman's eccentric and colorful friend, see footnote 9a; it is not clear what is meant here by "bill of materials."
1091.   Mr Lung was a Stevens Street, Camden, neighbor, with whom Whitman had Christmas 1880 dinner.

20     sent a check 46 to Gutekunst & proposed to him

[in red ink:]

for another thousand          rec'd & receipted [1092]

---

"     paid James Arnold $56 in full for binding

---

[in blue pencil:]

sent Allen Thorndike Rice, photo lith     recd [1093]

---

[first word in blue pencil:]

Sent   a set two Vols to John Hayes, Jr.

[in blue pencil:]

Corydon, Iowa     recd     paid

---

sent back proof of "How I get around at 60"
   to Critic, 757 Broadway   N Y [1094]

[188]

sent "Progress" April 30 – to those marked C ᶜthe Critic also[1095]

| c Sister Han A S Inv: | John Burroughs | May 9 [1096] |
| c T H Bartlett[1097] | Wm R Wood | c |

1092.  F. Gutekunst was the photographer at 712 Arch Street, Philadelphia, whose picture of Whitman the poet first planned to use in the Osgood 1881–82 edition of *Leaves of Grass*, then changed his mind; see *The Correspondence of Walt Whitman*, III, 228 and 243n.

1093.  Charles Allen Thorndike Rice (1851–1889) was the owner of *The North American Review*, who wrote Whitman "the most eulogistic" letter (the term is Whitman's) about the piece in the February 1881 issue — "I hope to be able to afford readers of the Review frequent opportunity of being instructed by you," Rice wrote the poet. (See *The Correspondence of Walt Whitman*, III, 209n.)

1094.  See footnotes 1073 and 1077.

1095.  The Philadelphia *Progress*, 30 April 1881, undoubtedly contained a piece of interest to Whitman, but it cannot now be located. *The Critic*, 29 January 1881, published "How I Get Around at 60, and Take Notes"; and *The American* (Philadelphia), 4 June 1881, published "A Summer's Invocation" ("A SInv" is Whitman's abbreviation, below, for this poem in *The American*), later called "Thou Orb Aloft Full-Dazzling" (Comprehensive Reader's Edition, pp. 462–463) in the 1881 *Leaves of Grass*.

1096.  By 9 May 1881 Whitman had printed three instalments of "How I Get Around at 60, and Take Notes" in *The Critic*, 29 January, 9 April, and 7 May; so Whitman could have sent all three to O'Connor, Henry W. Longfellow, and Clapp. Longfellow (1807–1882), then at the height of his fame, does not often appear in Whitman's lists; he most likely met the poet about June 1876, when he went to Camden with George W. Childs (see *The Correspondence of Walt Whitman*, III, 52n); see entry for 16 January 1881, above, where Whitman declined to write an article about Longfellow; and see Whitman's letter of 20 February 1881, asking for an autograph for a friend of Dr Bucke's (*ibid.*, III, 212–213). For O'Connor, see footnote 651; George Clapp was the brother of Henry Clapp, one of Whitman's friends in the Pfaff days who edited the New York *Saturday Press*; Whitman described George Clapp in 1867 as a "good creature, apparently not shined upon by fortune's bright sun" (*The Correspondence of Walt Whitman*, I, 339).

1097.  Truman Howe Bartlett (see footnote 440), whose plaster cast of Whitman's hand,

c Col Fairchild [1098]

c Mr Shaw   Boston

  Mrs Susan Stafford

  Elmer

c Sister Mary   A S

            Inv:

A   D M Zimmerman

Hattie  St Louis  A  SInv:

c G P Lathrop [1099]

c Charles B Ferrin [1100]

c Boyle OReilly [1101]

c Frank Hill Smith

c Sylvanus Baxter [1102]

Allan Leslie Belleville

      [in red ink:]

A and P   20th & Cherry

S Inv to W J Linton [1103] [in red ink]

Mrs Legget Am May 21 – SInv: [four words in
                   red ink]

Wm D OConnor   c

Longfellow

George Clapp

    only c

    [in red

    ink]

American of May 21 – to

    Mrs Gilchrist

    Dr Bucke

    W W Wilson   Syracuse

    James E Murdock

Rev J P Hopps   Eng [1104]

    Josiah Child   "

    Will Saunders, P and Am: [1105]

               [On slip, not    R.M.Ware  Esq
              in WW's hand:]    Mullica Hill
                                        N. J.

now in the Feinberg Collection and reproduced as Plate No. 3 in *The Correspondence of Walt Whitman*, III, following p. 202, was made in Boston in April 1881.

1098. Colonel Fairchild probably met Whitman in Boston in April 1881 (see *The Correspondence of Walt Whitman*, III, 354–355n).

1099. George Parsons Lathrop (1851–1898), journalist and son-in-law of Nathaniel Hawthorne, wrote Whitman on 20 April 1878 (Feinberg Collection; Traubel's *With Walt Whitman in Camden*, II, 315–316); he invited the poet on 23 March 1881 to make his Lincoln lecture in Boston (letter lost; see *ibid.*, III, 219n), which Whitman made on 15 April 1881. See William White, "Lathrop's Unpublished Letter to Traubel on Whitman," *Renescence*, XX (Spring 1968), 165–166.

1100. Charles B. Ferrin was the proprietor of the Revere House, Boston, where Whitman stayed before and after his lecture on Lincoln; see *The Correspondence of Walt Whitman*, III, 220, 223.

1101. John Boyle O'Reilly, coeditor of the Boston *Pilot*, was an old friend of Whitman's (see footnote 1).

1102. Sylvester Baxter (1850–1927), Boston *Herald* writer, met Whitman on his visit to Boston for the lecture on the death of Lincoln; see *The Correspondence of Walt Whitman*, III, 236, 237n, 251–252, 289, 308–309, 391–392, 394.

1103. William J. Linton, see footnote 39; and Harold W. Blodgett, "Whitman and the Linton Portrait," *Walt Whitman Review*, IV (September 1958), 90–92.

1104. See footnote 988.

1105. "P and Am:" means, obviously, that Whitman sent Will Saunders both the Philadelphia *Progress* of 30 April 1881 and *The American* of 21 May 1881; "A and P" above means the same thing.

[189]

Amelia W

1881 – Jan: 22 – sent Mrs˄Bate, Milwaukee, <u>Lit</u> <u>World</u> — E[m: ?] [1106]

710 Astor st

23 – Tribune criticism on Blake to Mrs Gilchrist also "WW's poetic platform" [1107]

"   sent postal to Dr Bucke – sent Critic No 1 [1108]

25   sent treble letter to Dr B   ~~photos~~ for the book[1109]

paper to Tommy Nichelson[1110]

acknowledged it

26   rec'd '81 pass on Camden & Atlantic RR from Mr Zimmerman[1111]

[first word in blue pencil:]                                      [in red ink:]
sent a set, L of G & T R to H H Furness                          all rec'd
222 <u>West</u> Washington Square (two portraits also)           paid
                                                                  ·10 —

wrote letter to Wm A Millis (sent 1st Canada letter in it) sent 2d [1112]

also

27   letter to Harry – (rec'd one from him) [1113]

30th (Sunday) letter to Mrs Stafford ("wrestling" slip to Harry)

1106.  *Lit World* must refer to Whitman's "Emerson's Books (the Shadows of Them),"
*The Literary World*, 22 May 1880.

1107.  The New York *Tribune* may well have carried a review or some notice of a new
and enlarged edition of *The Life of William Blake* (London, 1880), with a "Memoir of
Alexander Gilchrist," by Anne Gilchrist at the end of Vol. II. (Review not located.)

1108.  *The Critic*, No. 1, contained Whitman's "How I Get Around at 60, and Take
Notes," 29 January 1881; the post card to Dr Bucke is lost.

1109.  Dr Bucke was writing his biography of Whitman, published in 1883; I cannot
identify "treble letter."

1110.  Whitman sometimes spelled the name "Nichelson," one of Dr Bucke's attendants.

1111.  See footnotes 1079 and 1085, and *The Correspondence of Walt Whitman*, III,
207, for Whitman's letter of thanks.

1112.  Both letters lost.

1113.  Whitman's letter to Harry Stafford is in *The Correspondence of Walt Whitman*,
III, 207–208; the letter from Stafford is lost.

[in red ink:]
"Old Curiosity Shop" to Debbie     rec'd [1114]

---

papers (N Y walking match) to Tommy Nichelson [1115]

---

[in blue pencil:]
31   sent paper (Beranger) to W S Kennedey     recd

---

sent papers (two <u>Tribune</u> N Y letters & the Saguenay letter)
[in red ink:]
to Dick Labar     rec'd [1116]

---

Feb. 1 – letter (two cards) to John Burroughs – rec'd letter from him [1117]

---

"     "American," (with crit: on my Rev: art) to Dr Bucke [1118]

---

"Critic" to sister Hannah – same to Mrs Gilchrist

---

"Critic" to Mrs Legget   Detroit – to Hattie   St Louis
– to Sister Mary – Mr Zimmerman C & A R R [1119]

---

[first word in blue pencil:]
2   Sent a set Two Vols: to Frank H Ransom of
     D  Ransom Son & Co:  Medicine Warehouse, Buffalo N Y.
     – He writes (letter rec'd to day), that he sent me a p.o. order for

---

1114.  The letter to Mrs Susan Stafford is in *The Correspondence of Walt Whitman,* III, 208; *The Old Curiosity Shop* is of course Charles Dickens's 1841 novel, which the poet gave Mrs Stafford's daughter Deborah Browning (he gave his sister Hannah Heyde a copy on 3 September 1878); the "wrestling" slip for Harry Stafford seems to be a clipping from a paper on wrestling.

1115.  See footnote 1110.

1116.  See footnote 1053 for Richard E. Labar; the letters from the New York *Tribune* could be almost anything concerning Whtiman, or they might be issues of 17 and 24 May 1879, containing Whitman's "Real Summer Openings" and "These May Afternoons"; the Saguenay letter was Whitman's account of his trip up the river, published in the London *Advertiser,* Philadelphia *Press,* and Camden *Daily Post* on 26 August 1880 (see footnote 943), one of which he sent to Labar.

1117.  Whitman's letter to Burroughs is in *The Correspondence of Walt Whitman,* III, 208–209; but Burrough's letter is lost.

1118.  *The American* (Philadelphia) had a piece about Whitman's article, "The Poetry of the Future," which was in the February 1881 *North American Review;* Whitman sent this *American* to both Dr Bucke and John Burroughs.

1119.  Whitman sent to these six people (he consistently misspelled Mrs "Legget") copies of *The Critic* for 29 January 1881, containing the first instalment of his "How I Get Around at 60, and Take Notes."

$12.50 on Jan: 22 – I write to-day that I have not seen
or heard of any such order, but consider it my loss, & send
[in blue pencil:]
the books — rec'd – paid  (12.50) [1120]

---

[first word in blue pencil:]
"  Sent a set Two Vols: to Louise Chandler Moulton[1121]
[in blue pencil:]
28 Rutland Square, Boston – recd      paid

---

[first word in blue pencil:]
3  Sent Two Riv: (one Vol) to W H Furness   1426 Pine st
[in blue pencil:]
Phila    recd    paid
5th    death of Carlyle    aged 85

---

[in blue pencil:]
6th    evening – sent "Death of Carlyle" to Critic – paid [1122]

---

7th    visit from Harry[1123]

---

sent "the Dead Carlyle" to ~~R E H Hays & Co:~~ ~~L~~Literary World [1124]
box 1183 Boston – printed – paid $5

---

[first word in blue pencil:]
9  Sent Elihu Vedder 68 Capo le Case   Rome Italy a
[in blue pencil:]
set, Two Vols –     paid    recd [1125]

1120.  Whitman's letter to Frank H. Ransom of 2 February 1881 is also lost.
1121.  For Whitman's letter to her, see *The Correspondence of Walt Whitman*, III, 209, and III, 65, for another letter of 11 December 1876.
1122.  See footnote 1060; see also Whitman's letter to Jeannette L. Gilder, 6 February 1881, in *The Correspondence of Walt Whitman*, III, 210.
1123.  Harry Stafford.
1124.  See footnote 1060; see also Whitman's letter to the Editor of *The Literary World*, 16 February 1881, in *The Correspondence of Walt Whitman*, III, 212.
1125.  Elihu Vedder's letter, 25 February 1881, to Whitman is in the Feinberg Collection.

[190]

[On card of Franklin H.
    Hovey:]
    Call'd upon me Sunday
    bot books – lives at
    Beverley – mentioned
    Mr Williams on the
    Springfield Republican[1126]

Rome brothers  printers[1127]
    377 Fulton st
96 Myrtle   Brooklyn
        av

Stedman[1128]
    8 Pine street
    71 West 54th st
        N Y

N   A   Review[1129]
    1 Bond st   N Y
    30 Lafayette Place

[On card of Mr Eustace Conway:]
    D'rt [?] Mr M D. Conway[1130]    [not WW's
        call'd Feb: 21 '81                hand]

address, after March
    163 West 48th Street

(with Bangs & Stetson)  126 East 28 th [not WW's
( 137 Broadway         )          hand]
                New York [not WW's hand]

Benton H Wilson
    lock box 29

Walt Whitman Wilson[1131]
    111 Elbridge street
        Syracuse. N  Y

Wm   R   Wood
    Warsaw  Richmond Co:
            Va

[Card of George P. Williams, engraver on wood,
528 Walnut Street, Phil., residence (in hand not
WW's) 558 Benson St. Camden.]
[Two classified newspaper ads clipped: Charles
R. Street, attorney and counselor at law, 59 Main
St., Huntington, L.I., and C.H.Ritter, proprietor
of The Huntington House, 43 Main St., Hunt-
ington.]

1126.  Whitman referred to Hovey's visit in his letter to Harry Stafford, 28 February
1881; see *The Correspondence of Walt Whitman*, III, 215; for Talcott Williams, see footnote
799.
    1127.  The Rome Brothers printed the first (1855) edition of *Leaves of Grass*.
    1128.  Edmund Clarence Stedman: see footnote 948.
    1129.  *The North American Review*, for which Whitman wrote "The Poetry of the
Future," February 1881.
    1130.  For Moncure D. Conway, an American who had been living in England, see
footnote 36; Eustace Conway, associated with Bangs & Stetson, New York City, was his
uncle; see Whitman's letter to him, 22 February 1881, in *The Correspondence of Walt Whitman*, III, 213.
    1131.  Whitman sent Walt Whitman Wilson a copy of *The American* of 21 May 1881
(see list above), and William R. Wood a copy of the Philadelphia *Progress* of 30 April 1881;

[191]

'81 – Feb: 11 – Mrs Edward Smithson    S Mary's Lodge
   [in blue pencil:]                        [in blue pencil:]
    sent     York   England   The Two Vols   paid   recd

        sent Carlyle Death of
11  letter to Harry – (rec'd one from him)[1132]

[first word in blue pencil:]
12  sent T W H Rolleston, Glasshouse   Shinrone   Kings
                                  [in blue pencil:]
    county   Ireland   one Vol. L of G.   recd   paid[1133]

"    sent photo – lith portrait to Frank H Ransom   Buffalo

13  postal to Dr Bucke   ab't Longfellow's autograph[1134]

    Critic No 2 to Mrs Stafford[1135]

    pp. from old magazine to W S Kennedey[1136]

    picture & "Scattered Seeds" to John Shuman's little girl   recd[1137]
                                            [in blue pencil]

14  sent "Calvin Harlowe"[1138] to W R Balch   <u>American</u>

    paid Miller, 8th st.   Phila. $21 for 12 shirts – took rec't

how close they were to the poet I do not know.

    1132. In his letter to Harry Stafford, in *The Correspondence of Walt Whitman*, III, 211, Whitman described Mrs Smithson as "a big lady in England," and mentions the New York *Critic* piece he wrote on the death of Thomas Carlyle (12 February 1881 issue), who, Whitman said (to Stafford), was "the grandest writer in England."

    1133. See footnotes 50 and 1062.

    1134. See footnote 1096, and entry below for 20 February 1881.

    1135. *The Critic*, edited by Jeannette L. Gilder, contained Whitman's "How I Get Around at 60, and Take Notes" [Part I] in No. 1, 29 January 1881; and "Death of Carlyle" in No. 3, 12 February 1881; but nothing in No. 2, 5 February 1881.

    1136. Kennedy's first piece on Whitman, "A Study of Walt Whitman," was in the *Californian*, III (February 1881), 149–158, so this material "from old magazine" could not have been for that article.

    1137. For John Shuman, see footnote 1082; *Scattered Seeds* undoubtedly refers to the monthly publication of the General Conference of the Society of Friends in Philadelphia (May 1869-December 1935).

    1138. "Calvin Harlow" was a poem by T. W. H. Rolleston, eventually published in *Kottabos* (Trinity College Dublin), IV (No. 1, 1882), 1–2: see Horst Frenz, *Whitman and Rolleston: A Correspondence* (Bloomington, Indiana, 1951), pp. 41, 57.

bro't me:

15  call from Harry – (chicken – strawberries) – Harry's long letter[1139]

16  sent letter to Anson Rider, Wyoming, Wyoming Co: N Y.[1140]
the man I was curious about – brune [?] 50 yrs old, plug hat –
that crosses the ferry, is named Hollis, lives at Woodbury, was
an independent candidate for U. S. Senator

Harry call'd to-day

[first word in blue pencil:]
17  sent J Christopher Starr   Port Williams, Kings
                                        [in blue pencil:]
county, Nova Scotia, the two Vols:    recd   paid

"    wrote to Harry[1141]

my late pieces "Poetry Future," "Carlyle" to Dr Furness[1142]
1426 Pine St – Evening visit from W S Kennedey[1143]

18 – Sent Springfield Rep – & Secular Rev to Dr Bucke[1144]

met a young man on Chestnut St.   he introduced
himself as young Mr Whittier, from Baltimore on the Times[1145]

19  ordered shoes at 229 n 8th – Phil: to be done
                                        Saturday 26th – $6

1139.  It is not quite clear what is meant by "Harry's long letter," as Stafford had visited the poet on 11 February, on this day 15 February, and on 16 February 1881.
1140.  This letter to Anson Ryder, Jr (as Edwin H. Miller spells the name) is lost.
1141.  Letter to Harry Stafford: *The Correspondence of Walt Whitman*, III, 212.
1142.  Whitman's "The Poetry of the Future" was in *The North American Review*, February 1881; and "Death of Carlyle" in *The Critic*, 12 February 1881 (also in *The Literary World*, same date, different title).
1143.  William Sloane Kennedy (see footnotes 803 and 1136) was at this time on the staff of the Philadelphia *American*.
1144.  Without more details it is not possible to identify which issues of the Springfield (Mass.) *Republican* Whitman sent to Dr Bucke, perhaps for use by him on his Whitman book; there were pieces on Whitman in the issues of 18 January and 19 April 1876, but as Talcott Williams was still on the *Republican* at this time (1881), other pieces may have concerned Whitman; W. Hale White's "Genius of Walt Whitman" was in the *Secular Review* on 20 March 1880, most likely the issue Whitman sent his biographer.
1145.  Once again Whitman meets and comments on a young man he meets on Chestnut Street in Philadelphia.

[in blue pencil:]

20 – sent letter to Longfellow for autograph for Sir G W    ansd [1146]

paper to Ed Stafford

21    Eustace Conway called – 22 letter to him    126
                                    sent
        East 28th st    N Y – letter to him[1147]

22    sent letter to Mrs Stafford ("The first spring day" slip) [1148]

23    sent "Johnny Ludlow" to Sister Hannah[1149]

"    "Poetry Future" & "Critic" No 2 – to Dick Labar[1150]

"    papers to Harry Scovel

Springfield Rep: to John Burroughs[1151]

24    circ to Wm A Eddy, 133 East 16th st    N Y

papers to Sister Hannah

[192]

March 1 – driver I gave gloves – big, young, blonde W^m Powers[1152]
                            boy 10 or 11, Eddy Rice    newsboy, Ferry, Phila
                                            ?
            young new driver, sandy, Elias ~~Powers~~

1146.    See *The Correspondence of Walt Whitman*, III, 212–213.
1147.    See footnote 1130.
1148.    Whitman's letter to Susan Stafford is in *The Correspondence of Walt Whitman*, III, 213; Whitman piece, "The First Spring Day on Chestnut Street," appeared in Colonel Forney's Philadelphia *Progress*, 8 March 1879, and is included in *Specimen Days*; see *Prose Works 1892*, I, 188–190.
1149.    *Johnny Ludlow* was a novel by Mrs Henry Wood (see footnote 983), the first two series published in 1874 and 1880.
1150.    Whitman's "Poetry of the Future" was in *The North American Review*, February 1881, but *The Critic*, No. 2, 5 February 1881, contained nothing by Whitman; could Whitman have meant *The Critic* of 12 February 1881, with "Death of Carlyle"? Richard Labar was on the Philadelphia *Public Ledger*.
1151.    The same issue sent to Dr Bucke?
1152.    These gloves could have been some left over from the Christmas gloves of 1878 and 1880 (see footnotes 550 and 1061a). This long list of drivers, workmen, and young boys of various ages is another instance of the many such lists in the *Daybook* which Whitman made. In very few cases do the names or the people turn up again; one exception here is Tasker

Clark Hilton   extra conductor on 105 Market st. – I came down with (age 23–or '4) April 23 '81

Wⁿ Gibbs, umbrella maker – W W Club[1153] – I took him for young Harry Bonsall [1154] – (age 20)

Wⁿ Mosslander, paper hanging, on Federal St. above 5th – is a age 20 – (on the boat April 23 evening) nephew of Delacour, druggist

James E Murdoch (& Fannie Murdoch)
[first word in red ink:]
 Am: Lanesville p o Cape Ann: Mass   for summer
of '81

Sammy Cox   boy, 17 or 18 – Dick Davis's nephew – butter & cheese business in market stand – ice cream – Apr '81

Tasker Lay, boy 15 or 16, with Mr Lee

Harry Read, son of Jo Read, 2ᵈ near Stevens

Montelius Heitter (young man at M Cown's Store Phila)

John Copper   new driver (extra) on Stevens — works for Ben Stafford

little black-eyed Post boy at ferry, Paddy Connelly

Alex: Anderson, cond: on 110 night of June 25

Charles Matson, As'st Pilot on Columbia

Camden driver extra – Benj Roney – July 10

Walter Borton, charcoal driver   young man   Kirkwood

Lay, who was 15 or 16 at this time (1881) when Whitman first met him, and who died on 9 March 1884 (see *The Correspondence of Walt Whitman,* III, 366n). From the dates it can be seen that Whitman did not record all the names at the same time, but wrote them down from time to time: 1 March, 23 April, April, 25 June, 10 July, and 8 December 1881.
    1153.  W W Club: Walt Whitman Club?
    1154. In a letter to Harry Stafford, 28 February 1881 (*The Correspondence of Walt Whitman,* III, 215), Whitman said that Harry Bonsall had been for some time in the Insane Asylum at Blackwoodtown, New Jersey; he died there in 1889, at a time when Whitman's brother Edward was there.

309

Wm        Stein, gun maker, Federal St. (tall young man at ball
                                                        Dec. 8 '81)

Charlie McLean, driver, Stevens st.
    looks like Harry Stafford     [Printed notice:]

> Camden Parlor Orchestra
>
> Edmund R. Watson, Leader.
>
> 1st Violin — M. Smithers.
>     2d Violin — Chas. H. Stein.
>     Viola — Edward Lindell.
>     Bass — Louis E. Stein.
>     Cornet — Chas. D. Bowyer.
>     Clarinet — Wm. Stein, Jr.
>     Flute — Philip C. Bott.
>     Trombone — Benj. Woolman.
>
> The orchestra can be engaged for Receptions, Parties,
>     &c., by applying to
>
> W. Stein, Jr., 309 Federal Street.
>     Capt. Lindell, Federal St. Ferry.

[193]

1881 – Feb: 24 – rec'd $5 from T W H Rolleston[1155]

24 – autograph from Longfellow – sent to Dr Bucke[1156]

letter to Harry –[1157]

25 – postal to W S Kennedey[1158] – rec't to J L Gilder $10
                                        for Carlyle[1159]

[first word in blue pencil:]
27   Sent   Wm   A Eddy, Coombs, Crosly & Eddy, 18 Cliff st

1155.  This letter is in Horst Frenz, editor, *Whitman and Rolleston — A Collection*
(1951), pp. 21–24.
    1156.  See footnotes 1096, 1134, and 1146.
    1157.  The letter is in *The Correspondence of Walt Whitman*, III, 214.
    1158.  This post card, the first of many to Kennedy, is in *The Correspondence of Walt
Whitman*, III, 214.
    1159.  This $10 from Jeannette L. Gilder, editor of *The Critic*, was for "Death of Carlyle"
in the issue of 12 February 1881.

[in blue pencil:]
box 3714 – N Y City – the two Vols & duplicates &c    paid recd [1160]

---

[in blue pencil:]
Franklin H Hovey call'd – bo't a set – paid – is in business
(is a cousin of
in Phila:   lives at Beverly – Mr Williams   Springfield Rep)[1161]

---

× 
+ 28 – paid Lou $30 [1162]

---

letter to Harry (in answer to one rec'd from him)[1163]

---

sent "American" to Rudolf Schmidt[1164] – ret'd Tribune to
W S Kennedey[1165]

---

by express 324 Federal
March 1   sent ∧ Joseph R Rhoads, Attorney at Law, 419
["sent" in blue pencil]            [in blue pencil:]
Locust street a set   Two Vols:   paid   recd

---

2   photo-lith to W A Eddy[1166] – Herald to Tommy Nichelson[1167]

---

3 – rec'd 105.37 from Trübner & Co: by J Child [1168]

---

5   sent 20 Vols: (13 L of G & 7 T R) to Trübner & Co: through
J B Lippincott

---

6   sent rec't to Trübner & Co: also informing them of the 20 Vols. sent

---

1160. William A. Eddy, from apparently his home address, had written Whitman for circulars, which he sent on 24 February 1881 (see above).
1161. See footnote 1126.
1162. Whitman, as usual, paid Louisa Orr Whitman his monthly board bill.
1163. The letter from Whitman is in *The Correspondence of Walt Whitman*, III, 214–216.
1164. Rudolf Schmidt (see footnote 81) was the Dane who introduced *Leaves of Grass* to Scandinavia; *American* could mean the June 1880 or 30 October 1880 issues with Whitman poems, or the February issue with the criticism of Whitman's *North American Review* piece on poetry.
1165. The New York *Tribune* of 21 February 1881 contained excerpts from pieces about Thomas Carlyle.
1166. See footnote 1160.
1167. See footnote 1110.
1168. As is evident from this entry and the two just below, Whitman's books were also selling in England, where Josiah Child was acting for him.

"   sent Dr Bucke old Saturday Press — [1169]

7   letter to Harry[1170] — paid 72 cts for Sunday

[first word in blue pencil:]
8   sent Richard Hoe Lawrence, 81 Park Av.   N Y   a
                                    [in blue pencil:]
        set ordered, 2 Vols:          recd   paid

9   sent letter-card to Ruth Stafford [1171] – papers to Mrs & Harry Scovel

10 – sent circ (by request) to J Spencer, Bew, Spencer & Co:
      Vicker's building, 13 German St. box 842, Baltimore Md

      sent circ (by request) to E D Taylor, Stillwater
         Minnesota

x11th to 14th   down at Glendale[1172]

[first word in blue pencil:]
15   Sent J Spencer, Bew, Spencer & Co.   Vicker's
                              po box 842   2 Vols   [in blue pencil:]
        Building   13 German St.   Baltimore, a set   paid   recd

16   wrote to John Burroughs – (rec'd letter from him – 10)[1173]

"   sent Sister Mary <u>Progress</u> March 19

17   sent Rossetti and Conway, the <u>Barnegat</u> & <u>Dead</u> <u>Carlyle</u> slips[1174]

1169. The New York *Saturday Press*, edited by Henry Clapp, published "A Child's Reminiscence" (now called "Out of the Cradle Endlessly Rocking") in its issue of 24 December 1859 (with a note on the editorial page, perhaps by Whitman), and a defense of the poem, by Whitman, "All About a Mocking-Bird," on 7 January 1860. When the 1860 *Leaves of Grass* appeared, the *Saturday Press* of 19 May 1860 had a long article, "Walt Whitman / Leaves of Grass," with a review on 2 June 1860 and a certain amount of discussion during the following weeks. See Gay Wilson Allen, *The Solitary Singer*, pp. 231–233, 242–244, 260–264; and T. O. Mabbott and R. G. Silver, *A Child's Reminiscence* (Seattle, 1930), a critical edition. See also *The Correspondence of Walt Whitman*, I, 54n, 55.

1170. Letter in *The Correspondence of Walt Whitman*, III, 216.

1171. Letter-card in *The Correspondence of Walt Whitman*, III, 217; Ruth Stafford was Harry's sister.

1172. On the Stafford farm, Kirkwood, Glendale.

1173. Whitman's letter is in *The Correspondence of Walt Whitman*, III, 217–218; Burroughs's (Feinberg Collection) is in Traubel's *With Walt Whitman in Camden*, I, 43–44, and Clara Barrus, *Whitman and Burroughs: Comrades* (Boston, 1931), pp. 199–200.

1174. Whitman must have sent William Michael Rossetti and Moncure D. Conway proofs

[first word in blue pencil:]
Sent T W Nemeyer, 150 Crown St New Haven
[in blue pencil:]
Conn: a set 2 Vols, (for Sarah A Booth)   paid rec'd

---

letter to Tommy Nichelson[1175]

---

18th to 22ᵈ   down at Glendale

[194]

Queens Co:
Helen E Price   Woodside∧Long Island   N Y [1176]

---

Wᵐ V Montgomery   Glen Mills   Delaware Co: Penn:[1177]

[On card of Rev. Henry Scott Jeffreys, 334 N. 31st St.:]

|  |  |
|---|---|
| Son | Heineken[1179] |
| gone to San Mateo | Allan Leslie Belleville[1180] |
| California | 1412 Walnut st.   Phil |

[On card of Howard Challen,
in red ink:]

I met on ferry boat, men's side
June 1 '81

Rev: Mr Furness[1178]
1426 Pine st Phila              The American [printed in script]

[195]

1881 – Camden – March 23 – Ed went to live (board $16 a
   month) at Wm V Montgomery,   Glen Mills. Del: Co: Penn: [1181]

---

or off-prints (which he called "slips") of "Patroling Barnegat" and "The Dead Carlyle," which had appeared in *The American*, June 1880, and *The Literary World*, 12 February 1881, respectively. (*The Critic*, 12 February 1881, also published "Death of Carlyle," the same piece with a different title.) "Patroling Barnegat" was to be reprinted in *Harper's Monthly*, April 1881, and in the 1881 *Leaves*; "Death of Thomas Carlyle" was to be in *Specimen Days and Collect*, 1882.

1175. Letter in *The Correspondence of Walt Whitman*, III, 218–219; see footnote 1110, above.

1176. See footnote 287; see entry for 21 April 1881, below.

1177. William V. Montgomery was sent $16 a month to care for Edward Whitman, the poet's feeble-minded younger brother (see entry for 23 March 1881, below).

1178. For Horace Howard Furness, see footnote 369; this must be his new address.

1179. Theodore Hieniken (whose name Whitman spelled Heineken, Hinieken, and Hieneken) was apparently a friend of the Staffords; see *The Correspondence of Walt Whitman*, III, 194.

1180. Allan Leslie Belleville was one of those to whom Whitman sent the Philadelphia *Progress*, 30 April 1881 (see list above, footnote 1095); I know of no further identification.

1181. See footnote 1177.

23 – Letter from Lathrop, Boston – I am to come on there to
      deliver my Death of Lincoln lecture[1182]

24 – papers to Harry Scovel, Harry Stafford & John Fetters

26th to 30th — down at Glendale[1183]

30th      G W<sup>m</sup> Harris, Ass't Lib: Cornell University
[in blue pencil:]                            [in blue pencil:]
    sent        Ithaca, a set two Vols:      paid   rec'd

April 1 – Library Journal to John Burroug[h]s – <u>Trib</u> to Dr Bucke[1184]
      paper to Richard Fetters

[first word in blue pencil:]
2     sent Chas T Dillingham    678 Broadway    N Y[1185]
                            [in blue pencil:]
      one   <u>Two Rivulets</u> – recd   paid

2<sup>d</sup> to 7th   April   down at Glendale[1186]

[first word in blue pencil:]
8th    sent to   J W Wiggins Jr   187 Prince st Brooklyn
                            [in blue pencil:]
      a set Two Vols –            paid   recd

[first word in blue pencil:]
9   Sent two No's: (3 and 4) of Notes. to J B & J L Gilder
                  [in blue pencil:]
      for Critic     paid $20[1187]

---

1182.   For Lathrop, see footnote 1099; for the lecture, see Gay Wilson Allen, *The Solitary Singer*, pp. 491–492; Roy P. Basler, editor, *Memoranda During the War* [&] *Death of Abraham Lincoln*, pp. 34–35 (which quotes from the Boston *Herald* of 16 April 1881); and *Specimen Days and Collect: Prose Works 1892*, I, 264–265.

1183.   This was Whitman's third visit of the month at the Stafford farm.

1184.   This may well have been the New York *Tribune* of 21 February 1881 with excerpts from articles on Carlyle, though he records having sent this issue back to W. S. Kennedy on 28 February 1881; a number of 1878 and 1879 *Tribunes* contained pieces by Whitman, which Dr Bucke would have wanted to see for his book.

1185.   Charles T. Dillingham was the New York publisher, bookseller and importer who had been buying a number of copies of Whitman's books during the last few months, according to the entries in the *Daybook*.

1186.   Back at the Stafford place with hardly three days in Camden.

1187.   "Notes": third and fourth instalments of "How I Get Around at 60, and Take Notes," which were to appear in *The Critic* on 7 May (pp. 116–117) and 16 July 1881 (pp. 184–185).

1881 – Camden – March 23 – Ed went to live (board $16 a month) at Wm V Montgomery. Glen Mills. Del: Co: Penn:

23 – Letter from Lathrop, Boston – I am to come on there to deliver my Death of Lincoln lecture

24 – papers to Harry Scovel, Harry Stafford & John Fetters

26th to 30th down at Glendale

30th G Wm Harris, Ast Lib: Cornell University, Ithaca, a set two Vols: paid recd

April 1 – Library Journal to John Burroughs – Trib to Dr Bucke paper to Richard Fetters

2 sent Chas T Dillingham 678 Broadway N Y one Two Rivulets recd paid

2d to 7th April down at Glendale

8th sent to J W Wiggins Jr 187 Prince st Brooklyn a set Two Vols paid recd

9 sent two Nos: (3 and 4) of Notes to J B & J L Gilder for Critic paid

9 sent Albert D Shaw, U S Consul, Manchester England a set, Two Vols: paid recd

11 Sent Editor Literary World Boston L of G

Sent John Wiggins Brooklyn filled up blank to join old Brooklynites

13 10 from Horace Furness

" Start for Boston Boston Trip

in Boston from 13th to 19th April the Death of Lincoln lecture 185

20th sent postal Card to Dr Bucke
" recd to Chas T Dillingham
papers to Mrs Scovel

21 Letter & papers to Helen Price

22 sent 16 to Wm V Montgomery, Glen Mills, Delaware Co. Pa: for Ed,

24 lent George 100 (makes 250 all together) (3 all paid back

26 sent letter to J W Rolleston

28 – sent Boston notes to Critic recd 15 paid

29 – letter to Ruth postponing visit until I hear from them

" gave Burns's Poems to Fred Rauch

[first word in blue pencil:]

9   sent   Albert D Shaw, U S Consul, Manchester,
England a set, Two Vols:   paid   recd [1188]

11  sent Editor Literary World   Boston L of G [1189]

sent John Wiggins Brooklyn   fill'd up blank to join
Old Brooklynites[1190]

[in red ink:]

13   10 from Horace Furness[1191]        Boston Trip

"    Start for Boston

in Boston from 13th to 19th   April    [in blue pencil]
$
the Death of Lincoln lecture (135[1192])    [in blue pencil]

20th   sent postal card to Dr Bucke[1193]

"     "     "    rec't to Chas T. Dillingham

papers to Mrs Scovel

21   letter & papers to Helen Price[1194]

22   sent $16 to Wm V Montgomery, Glen Mills, Delaware Co:
Pa: for Ed [1195]

1188.   Albert Shaw (1857–1947), founder and editor of the *Review of Reviews* from 1891 until its merger with the *Literary Digest* in 1937, author of *Abraham Lincoln* (1929) and other books, is mentioned once in Horace Traubel's *With Walt Whitman in Camden,* IV, 483: "W. had 'skimmed through' Albert Shaw's tribute to John Bright in today's Press. Shaw quoted Bright's expression of regret that so many millionares got into our Senate. W. said: 'Yes, I read that paragraph — read it all: of course I liked it.' "
1189.   Edward Abbott? (see footnote 880).
1190.   As a long-time Brooklyn resident, editor of Brooklyn newspapers, author of "Brooklyniana," and as Brooklyn was where *Leaves of Grass* was first published, Whitman not surprisingly should join the "Old Brooklynites"; but we don't know that he took any part in such an organization.
1191.   The $10 was undoubtedly for one of his books, though Whitman, who usually recorded these facts, does not here say so.
1192.   See footnote 1182 for sources of details on the lecture, which Whitman told the Staffords in a letter from Boston "went off first rate . . . best I have had yet, better audience (better than New York or Philadelphia)" (*The Correspondence of Walt Whitman,* III, 221).
1193.   Post card lost, as is the one below to Charles T. Dillingham.
1194.   Letter to Helen Price (see footnote 287): *The Correspondence of Walt Whitman,* III, 221–222.
1195.   See footnote 1177.

lent George $100 (makes $250 altogether) ☞ all paid
_____ back[1196]

26   Sent letter to T W H Rolleston[1197]

_____

[in blue pencil:]
28 – Sent Boston notes to Critic   rec'd   $15 paid [1198]
_____

29 – letter to Ruth postponing visit until I hear from them[1199]
_____

"   gave Burns's Poems to Fred Rauch[1200]

[196]

[Letterhead of James R. Osgood & Co., publishers, 211 Tremont Street (James R. Osgood, Edward L. Osgood, Benjamin H. Ticknor, Thomas B. Ticknor); clipping with name and address, printed, of Scholl, portraits, 112 and 114 North 9th Street; Phila.; John P. Foley, wholesale and retail stationery and fancy goods dealer, 21 North 2nd Street, Phila; and in hand not WW's: Geo. G. Clapp / 40 Grove St / Chelsea Mass /.]
[On large slip of paper:]

_____

Drivers – Market st. June '81 [1201]      [in pencil]
[in pencil:]
     Frank – 177 –      ⎧ Rob't Devine
                        ⎪ driver Summer car 148
     Jo Hill   –        ⎨ "gallus" 21 – N Y. style
_____

[in pencil:]
     Al Giberson, bright little newsboy
               Phil Side – ferry
_____

Edward Kelley, boy of 9 or 10, I met on the Boat
_____ June 30

1196. Whitman's books were selling, he was writing pieces for magazines, and he was making his Lincoln lecture; living carefully, he was certainly able to lend $250 to his brother George; he had also lent him $200 (paid back) on 4 September 1878 (see entry of that day, above).

1197. Letter lost.

1198. In a letter to Jeannette L. Gilder, 27 April 1881, Whitman says he will send "a page or more of Boston notes" for *The Critic*; most likely he added these to the material sent on 9 April 1881 (see entry of that day, above) to make up No. 3 of "How I Get Around at 60, and Take Notes" for the issue of 7 May 1881.

1199. Letter: *The Correspondence of Walt Whitman*, III, 222–223.

1200. Fred Rauch, of the Camden ferries, wrote Whitman on 24 June 1880 (letter in the John Rylands Library) about his travels in Germany.

1201. This list of nine young men and boys must have been made on the ferries and horse cars; written on a slip of paper it was later placed in the *Daybook*, along with several other such lists; the last two may have been horse car drivers Whitman met on his Boston trip.

Market st
Drivers &c – Charles Butler –
—— Lewis Wright – his conductor
Denny M'Carty ⎫
Collins Donne  ⎬ Harvard Sq: drivers

[197]

1881 – Camden – May –

[in red ink:]

3ᵈ – Bumble Bees & Bird Music to W R Balch – $30 rec'd $20 [1202]

again   papers to Wm Wood – "Newspaper ballads" to Harry [1203]
May 29

sent to Editor Cope's Tobacco Plant for $10 due me [1204]

[in red ink:]

4   sent proposition to Scholl, photographer,   250 copies   accepted [1205]

trans Vistas
5   Sent Danish papers & magazine to Dr Bucke – also postal [1206]

[in blue pencil:]

"   Sent letter to Harry [1207] – to Critic for 20 copies – rec'd [1208]

sent paper to Theodore Hieniken [1209]

1202. "Bumble-Bees and Bird-Music" was published in W. R. Balch's *American* (Philadelphia), 14 May 1881 and reprinted in *Specimen Days* in five places as "Bumble-Bees," "Birds and Birds and Birds," "A Couple of Old Friends — a Coleridge Bit," "An Unknown," and "Bird-Whistling"; see *Prose Works 1892,* I, 123–126, 146–147, 163, 163–164, 263, 269–270, and 352.

1203. As Whitman explained in his letter to Harry Stafford, 5 May 1881, *Newspaper Ballads* was a little book of poetry by a boy 13 years old, in Pennsylvania, who sent it to Whitman "with a nice letter" which is now lost (*The Correspondence of Walt Whitman,* III, 223).

1204. Whitman's letter to the editor of *Cope's Tobacco Plant* (Liverpool) is lost, but as "The Dalliance of the Eagles" was published in that magazine in November 1880 (Vol. II, p. 552), this must have been the poem Whitman wanted to be paid $10 for.

1205. Letter to Emil Scholl lost.

1206. Post card lost; the Danish papers may well have been pieces by Rudolf Schmidt, who introduced Whitman to Scandinavia. (Dr Bucke helped translate Schmidt's "Walt Whitman, the Poet of American Democracy" for *In Re Walt Whitman* [Philadelphia, 1893], pp. 231–248.)

1207. Letter: *The Correspondence of Walt Whitman,* III, 223–224.

1208. This was the 7 May 1881 issue of *The Critic* with the third part of Whitman's "How I Get Around at 60, and Take Notes."

1209. See footnote 1179; Whitman here spells the name correctly as Hieniken, but in his letter to Ruth Stafford on 29 April 1881 he spelled it Hinieken.

6   Sent to Balch to send proof Tuesday aft: at 3 [1210]

---

Sent letter to Mrs Stafford [1211]

---

8   wrote to J R Osgood, in answer to O'Reilly's note[1212]

---

Sent postal to O'Reilly[1213]

---

[Entries from 13th through 20th in pencil on slip of note paper:]

13th $\dfrac{\text{to 20th}}{\text{x}}$     down at Glendale x  till 17th, then up to C day     12 days  [in red ink]    one

to 20th &c – (18, 19, 20, May rainy & cool) [1214]

                                        for
20th letter to J. R. Osgood, promising copy of book
        & describing ab't the Worthington plates – also stating
        that new Vol: would supercede all others[1215]

"   Cards to Henry A. Beers, New Haven[1216]

1210.   This was a proof of "Bumble-Bees and Bird-Music" in *The American* for 14 May 1881 (see footnote 1202, above).

1211.   Letter to Mrs Susan Stafford lost.

1212.   The letter to James Ripley Osgood (1844–1890), the Boston publisher, about the publication of a new edition of *Leaves of Grass,* is in *The Correspondence of Walt Whitman,* III, 224; for O'Reilly, see *ibid.,* III, 224n. Whitman's letter to Osgood was written on the verso of one to the poet from O'Reilly, 26 April 1881 (in the Henry E. Huntington Library), which said that the publisher wanted to see the material for the complete book of poems.

1213.   Post card lost.

1214.   Before going to the Stafford farm, Whitman wrote to Ruth Stafford on 10 May 1881 that he would be there "Friday afternoon" 13 May (*The Correspondence of Walt Whitman,* III, 225. In *Walt Whitman's Diary in Canada* (Boston, 1904), pp. 58–59, is the following in the section "From Other Journals of Walt Whitman":

> *May* 13 *to* 25, '81. Down in the country, mostly in the woods, enjoying the early summer, the bird music, and the pure air. For interest and occupation I busy myself three or four hours every day, arranging, revising, cohering, here and there slightly rewriting (and sometimes cancelling) a new edition of L. of G. complete in one volume. I do the main part of the work out in the woods. I like to try my pieces by negligent, free, primitive Nature, — the sky, the seashore, the sunshine, the plentiful grass, or dead leaves (as now) under my feet, and the song of some catbird, wren, or russet thrush within hearing; like (as now) the half-shadowed tall-columned trees, with green leaves and branches in relief against the sky. Such is the library, the study where (seated on a big log) I have sifted out and given some finishing touches to this edition (J. R. O[sgood] publisher, 1881). I take a bout at it every day for an hour or two — sometimes twice a day.
>     Received back to-day the MS. of a little piece of "A Summer's Invocation," which I had sent to H.'s [Harper's] magazine. The editor said he returned it because his readers wouldn't understand any meaning to it. (Put in Holland's [Scribner's].)

1215.   Letter: *The Correspondence of Walt Whitman,* III, 225–226; for the Worthington business, see *ibid.,* III, 195–198, 199–200.

1216.   Letter: *The Correspondence of Walt Whitman,* III, 225. Henry A. Beers (1847–1926), poet, English professor at Yale, author of *Four Americans — Roosevelt, Hawthorne,*

"   "   Innes Randolph, Baltimore American[1217]

"   rec't to Albert D Shaw, U S Consul Manchester

[in red ink:]

[two lines in ink:]                                    ret'd        ?    ?
"   "Spirit that form'd this scene" to Mr Rice    N A Rev: $~~20~~   15 [1218]

[in red ink:]
"   "A summer Invocation" to Harpers      ret'd [1219]

2 rec'd 3ᵈ letter from J R Osgood [1220]

27th   sent letter to J R O. promising copy of L of G
       by 30ᵗʰ [1221]

Sent "a summer Invocation" to Balch, American, $12 [1222]

[in red ink,
"   Sent copy of L of G     527 pages to James     sideways:]    rec'd copy
    R Osgood   211 Tremont St. Boston (at                          back
    his request) [1223]                                           June  1
                                                                    1

28 sent "Spirit" &c to Jeanne Gilder    $5 [1224]

29 – papers Progress and Am: to Mrs Scovel

        "       "       "      Pete Doyle[1225]

Emerson, Whitman (New Haven, 1920), of which W. S. Kennedy said in The Fight of a Book for the World (1926), p. 100: "Whitman and the academic Beers were temperamentally antagonistic. A single glance of Walt's penetrating and terrible eyes would probably have chilled the sensitive and delicate Beers to the marrow."

1217.  Post card lost.

1218.  Whitman's poem, "Spirit That Form'd This Scene," rejected by Charles Allen Thorndike Rice of The North American Review (see footnote 1093), was published in The Critic, 10 September 1881; it was included in the 1881 Leaves of Grass — see the Comprehensive Reader's Edition, p. 486.

1219.  Another poem, "A Summer's Invocation," was also rejected, this one by Harper's, but was published in Balch's Philadelphia American on 14 June 1881; retitled "Thou Orb Aloft Full-Dazzling," it was included in the 1881 Leaves of Grass — see the Comprehensive Reader's Edition, pp. 462–463.

1220.  Osgood's letters, 12, 23 and 31 May, and 3, 10, 21, 25 June, 18 July, and 13 September 1881 are all in the Library of Congress; seven of them are printed in The Complete Writings of Walt Whitman (1902), VIII, 277–284.

1221.  Letter to James Ripley Osgood: The Correspondence of Walt Whitman, III, 226.

1222.  See footnote 1219.

1223.  This has come to be regarded by many critics as the outstanding edition of Leaves of Grass.

1224.  Jeannette Gilder was editor of The Critic: see footnote 1218.

1225.  These issues of The American were no doubt those of 14 May 1881, containing Whitman's essay, "Bumble-Bees and Bird-Music," though other numbers had Whitman material.

to Tommy Nicholson – [1226]

letter to Osgood – [1227]

(Americans to friends) [1228]

[198]

[On six small clipped slips:]          [Printed:]

   Walter Lewin, [printed]          PAPERS FOR THE TIMES are in-
4 German Terrace [in red ink]     tended for men and wo [    ] who have a
Price St [in red ink]                     living interest in social, ethical, and reli-
                                          gious questio [    ] their bearing on hu-
   Birkenhead. [printed]          man welfare. They are especially suitable
                                          hi [    ] medium for the spread of Liberal
London    Eng: [in red ink]       Thought and Culture.

Ouida.   By Herbert J. Bathgate.[1229]

     149th Street

J. H. Johnson, [printed] & Mott       | John  Woodhull [1230]
  Jeweler, [printed]  avenue        | Wm       " later [in pencil]
150 Bowery, N. Y. [printed]            | Schuyler  "correct [in pencil]
                                       | Charley  "
Met on the open car – June, '81        | Miss Mary  "
spoke of the (Benj. F. Lee, [printed]
 Trenton          clk Supreme Ct [not WW's hand]
Potteries &      Trenton N J   Trenton N J [not WW's hand]
 M'f's of wire
for Bridge          – the boy also
                 John H Copper \ Mr & Mrs
                 1013 South 6th St \Walker
                    Camden

[199]

["Sent" in blue pencil:]
1881 — May 30 – Sent  Edward Carpenter,[1231] Bradway
                                    [in blue pencil:]
  near Sheffield, Eng, three Leaves of Grass    paid   recd

---

1226.  See footnote 1110, but here Whitman spells the young man's name correctly.
1227.  Letter to the Boston publisher: *The Correspondence of Walt Whitman*, III, 226–227.
1228.  See footnote 1225.
1229.  See footnote 797.
1230.  Whitman's numerous chance acquaintances, whom he met on the horse cars (such as these here), or these five members of the Woodhull family, may be of interest if we knew more about them: why did Whitman write their names down at all, for example? One may

31 – gave James Page letter to the Episcopal Hospital

papers to Mont – Wm Wood – Theo: Heineken[1232]

June 2 – papers to Theodore Heineken

"      1 – letter to J R Osgood – terms 25$^{cts}$ royalty on $2
       book – 30$^{cts}$ on $2.50 [1233]
       ~~letter to~~

                                        [in blue pencil:]
2    proof "Summer Invocation" to Balch    accepted    paid
                                                       $12 [1234]

letter to Mrs Stafford [1235]

4    letter from Osgood, giving me my terms & settling engagement
     letter to Osgood, (see copy) – (mistake about price of lith
                                   corrected next day)[1236]

5    circ: to Israel Betz, Oakville Cumb: Co   Pa

letter to Dr Bucke[1237]

6 Harry call'd – papers to Jessie – Mont[1238]

circ: to Louis G Richardson    17 Western Av: Cambridgeport
                                                          Mass
sent word to Kirkwood I would come Thursday[1239]

speculate, though an answer is impossible.
    1231. Carpenter (see footnote 20) was one of the best of Whitman's English friends, and there were many. See Whitman's letter, 30 May 1881, in *The Correspondence of Walt Whitman*, III, 227.
    1232. Mont was Montgomery Stafford, Harry's young uncle; for Heineken, see footnote 1179; William R. Wood lived in Warsaw, Richmond County, Virginia.
    1233. These same proposals for Whitman's royalty on *Leaves of Grass* by James R. Osgood, the Boston publisher, are in the poet's letter: *The Correspondence of Walt Whitman*, III, 227–228. The terms were accepted: see *ibid.*, III, 228.
    1234. "A Summer's Invocation" is a poem Whitman first sent to *Harper's* (see footnote 1214 and 1219) before publication in Balch's *American*.
    1235. Letter lost.
    1236. Letters to Osgood, 4, 7, and 16 June 1881, are in *The Correspondence of Walt Whitman*, III, 228–230.
    1237. Letter lost.
    1238. Harry is Harry Stafford; Jessie is Jefferson Whitman's daughter in St Louis; and Mont is Montgomery Stafford.
    1239. Letter, undoubtedly to Mrs Susan Stafford, is lost; Whitman was at White Horse, Kirkwood, Glendale, New Jersey 11–15 June 1881 (see entry below).

[first word in blue pencil:]
           attie
7  Sent Miss H∧W Robinson  6 Montague Terrace
                             [in blue pencil:]
    Brooklyn  N Y  the Two Vols:  paid  recd –

sent letter to Osgood asking for two sample pages (rec'd)[1240]

9  letter to Mary, Greenport, $10 p o order – rec'd  [red ink]
    "   Hannah  Burlington $10 "  "   recd [1241] [red ink]

[first word in blue pencil:]
11 Sent John Fraser, 10 Lord Nelson street, Liverpool
                      [in blue pencil]   [in red ink]
    England, the Two Vols:     paid     recd [1242]

11, 12, 13, 14, 15  down at Glendale[1243]

went over to see old Mrs Morgan & help her
she is para
∧lyzed badly, cannot talk or move around [1244]
                                     returned
    Stopt at Wesley and Lizzie's at the old place    15th Evening[1245]

16   receipts to W R Balch (for $12)[1246] – & John Fraser,[1247] Liverpool for
                                             James Thompson's
                                               poems

papers to Wm Wood [1248] – autograph to Mr Bok,N Y. for son[1249]

1240.  A sample page is reproduced in *The Correspondence of Walt Whitman,* III, 229.
1241.  Both letters to Whitman's sisters Mary Van Nostrand and Hannah Heyde, to whom he often sent small sums of money, are not extant.
1242.  John Fraser was the editor of the Liverpool magazine, *Cope's Tobacco Plant,* to which Whitman was contributing.
1243.  As seen above, in entry for 6 June 1881, Whitman also referred to the Stafford farm as Kirkwood.
1244.  Mrs Rachel Morgan and her husband Will were friends of George and Susan Stafford (see footnote 308).
1245.  Other Stafford relatives, Lizzie Hider and Wesley Stafford were married on 9 February 1881. Wesley was Mrs Susan Stafford's nephew.
1246.  This $12 was for Whitman's poem, "A Summer's Invocation," in *The American,* 14 June 1881 (see footnote 1219, above).
1247.  See footnote 1242.
1248.  See footnote 1232.
1249.  Edward Bok (1863–1930), author of *The Americanization of Edward Bok* (1920), was of course 18 years old at this time and could have been Mr Bok's son referred to here;

letter to J R Osgood [1250]

17 – sent letter to John Burroughs – also "Summer Invocation" [1251]

19 – sent letters to Tommy Nicholson & Ed Cattell [1252]

20   paper to Mont – [1253]

[first word in blue pencil:]
22   Sent the two Vols to W J Paulding, 149 Broadway
                                        [in blue pencil:]
        room 11   N Y, by Express c o d    recd    paid

23   rec'd specimen page – sent letter to Osgood & Co: [1254]
        sent $1 to Mrs M by Walter Barton [1255]

                                              [200]

    Sent Boston Globe Aug   26 [1256]
* to
        Sent "A Week at West Hills" Tribune
                        Aug 4 '81 [1257]  Critic of July 16 [1258]

* Lou            Tribune      *Dr Bucke-also L'g I'der [1260]   xEd Lindell [1263]
*Hannah x       Aug 15 *      *John Burroughs x                 Furman Hand
*Mary x         "City Notes   *Henry Lloyd [1261]               Charley Walton
*Jeff  x        in Aug:" [1259]  H L Bonsall [1262]             Sister Hannah
*Chas Velsor    Sent N.Y      *Ed Lindell                        "    Mary
x Lem Carll     Sun 19th      *Mr Zimmerman [1266]
Lawyer Street [1265] Nov to x [1264]  John Chichester
  xMrs Gilchrist              *Helen Price [1267]

Boston Globe [1268] to Critic | W D O'Connor [1269]
also Tommy Nicholson [1270] | Erastus Brainerd [1271]
also Mrs Alma Johnston [1272]
  "   Albert Curtis

the elder Bok died that year (1881); the young Bok became editor of the *Ladies' Home Journal* at the age of 26 in 1889. Whitman is not mentioned in the *Americanization.*
    1250.   See footnote 1236.
    1251.   Letter in *The Correspondence of Walt Whitman*, III, 230–231, mainly about the Osgood edition; "A Summer's Invocation" — see footnote 1219.
    1252.   The letter to Nicholson (whose name Whitman here spells correctly) is in *The Correspondence of Walt Whitman*, III, 231–232; they expected to meet again in London, Ontario, but met in Jersey City, New Jersey, instead on 23 July 1881. The letter to Edward Cattell, Harry Stafford's friend, is lost.
    1253.   Montgomery Stafford.

Trib: of Aug 15 [1273] to) Harry Stafford, Albert Hopper, John Sherman
Ben Doty, Smith Caswell, Mr Nash, x(Mrs M Wager Fisher
John Capper, Wm Wood, Mrs Leggett, Mrs Scovel with Long
Island [er] [1274]

x Henry H Clark, Boston[1275]

x Tom Nicholson

x Mrs Dr Drake

P. Girard [not WW's hand]
_____

Editor of the Graphic [not WW's hand]

39–41 Park Place, New York. [printed]

1254.  Letter: *The Correspondence of Walt Whitman*, III, 232.

1255.  Mrs M may be Mrs Rachel Morgan (see footnote 1244, and entry above for 11–15 June 1881).

1256.  "The Good Gray Poet," a long interview with Whitman, was in the Boston *Globe* on 24 August 1881 (see *The Correspondence of Walt Whitman*, III, 238n).

1257.  Whitman's essay, "A Week at West Hills," was published in the New York *Tribune*, 4 August 1881, reprinted with changes in *Specimen Days* as "The Old Whitman and Van Velsor Cemeteries" and "The Maternal Homestead" (*Prose Works 1892*, I, 5–8, with unreprinted paragraphs, I, 352–354).

1258.  *The Critic* for 16 July 1881 contained the fourth instalment of Whitman's "How I Get Around at 60, and Take Notes" (see footnotes 1073 and 1077).

1259.  "City Notes in August," in the New York *Tribune*, 15 August 1881, was reprinted as "Hot Weather New York" and "'Custer's Last Rally'" in *Specimen Days* (*Prose Works 1892*, I, 273–276, with unreprinted paragraphs, I, 354–355).

1260.  *The Long-Islander*, a weekly newspaper which Whitman founded in 1838 and still in existence in Huntington, New York, published Mrs Mary E. Wager-Fisher's piece (see footnote 214) about the poet on 4 August 1881, and also another feature, "Walt Whitman in Huntington."

1261.  Henry Lloyd is listed among the "friends and relatives" to whom Whitman was indebted for courtesies in connection with "A Week at West Hills"; he most likely lived in Huntington, Long Island (see footnote 1265).

1262.  Henry L. Bonsall was editor of the Camden *Daily Post*.

1263.  Ed Lindell was a friend who worked on the Camden ferries, as a captain; Furman Hand and Charley Walton were also Camden ferry-boat captains.

1264.  The New York *Sun* published on 19 November 1881 a long review, "Walt Whitman and the Poetry of the Future," by E. P. M.

1265.  Like Henry Lloyd (see footnote 1261), Charles Velsor, Lemuel Carll, Lawyer Charles R. Street, and John Chichester, apparently all from the Huntington or Cold Spring Harbor, Long Island, area, were helpful and courteous to Whitman in writing "A Week at West Hills," New York *Tribune*, 4 August 1881; see *Prose Works 1892*, I, 353.

1266.  Secretary and treasurer, Camden & Atlantic Railroad.

1267.  See footnote 287.

1268.  The Boston *Globe* published "The Good Gray Poet" on 24 August 1881 (see footnote 1256, above).

1269.  See footnote 651; O'Connor and Whitman were to make up in 1882.

1270.  See footnote 1252.

1271.  See footnote 348.

1272.  Mrs Alma Johnston was the second wife of the New York jeweler, with whom Whitman was to stay in October 1881.

1273.  "City Notes in August" was in the New York *Tribune*, 15 August 1881 (see footnote 1259).

1274.  Of the 11 people listed here, several are not now identifiable: Harry Stafford was Whitman's closest young friend of that period in his life; Smith Caswell was John Burroughs's employee at Esopus; Michael Nash was a long-time Washington friend; Mrs Mary Wager-Fisher wrote the piece in *The Long-Islander* referred to here (see footnote 1260); William R. Wood was an acquaintance from Warsaw, Virginia; Mrs Eliza L. Leggett of Detroit was the grandmother of Percy Ives, who was to paint Whitman's portrait; and Mrs Harry Scovel was an old Camden friend with whom Whitman breakfasted.

1275.  Henry H. Clark was the superintendent of James R. Osgood & Company's printing

[201]

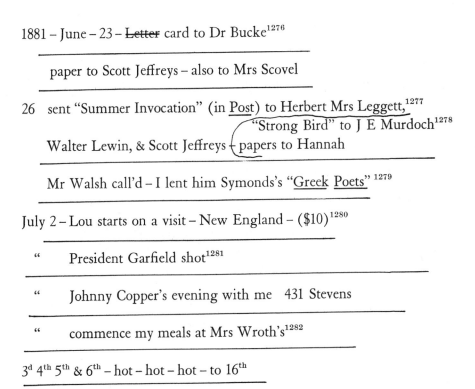

1881 – June – 23 – ~~Letter~~ card to Dr Bucke[1276]

paper to Scott Jeffreys – also to Mrs Scovel

26   sent "Summer Invocation" (in Post) to Herbert Mrs Leggett,[1277]

"Strong Bird" to J E Murdoch[1278]

Walter Lewin, & Scott Jeffreys ⟨ papers to Hannah

Mr Walsh call'd – I lent him Symonds's "Greek Poets"[1279]

July 2 – Lou starts on a visit – New England – ($10)[1280]

"      President Garfield shot[1281]

"      Johnny Copper's evening with me   431 Stevens

"      commence my meals at Mrs Wroth's[1282]

3ᵈ 4ᵗʰ 5ᵗʰ & 6ᵗʰ – hot – hot – hot – to 16ᵗʰ

office in Boston; Mrs Drake lived at 35 G Street South, Boston.

1276.  Post card lost.

1277.  Whitman's poem, "A Summer's Invocation," reprinted from *The American* of 14 June 1881 in the Camden *Daily Post*; Herbert is of course Herbert Gilchrist, who was in London, England with his mother at this time; Mrs James Matlack Scovel, one of the poet's Camden friends, was receiving a number of papers from Whitman recently.

1278.  This most likely was the small book, *As a Strong Bird on Pinions Free and Other Poems,* published by Whitman in Washington, 1872; the main poem is now called "Thou Mother with Thy Equal Brood" (see the Comprehensive Reader's Edition of *Leaves of Grass,* pp. 455–461).

1279.  John Addington Symonds wrote in his *Greek Poets* that Whitman "is more thoroughly Greek than any man of modern times."

1280.  Presumably this $10, which Whitman gave to his sister-in-law Louisa Whitman, was for his room, not his board, as she was on her way to Norwich, Conn., and he was to take his meals (see below) with Mrs Caroline Wroth at 319 Stevens Street, a few houses from George and Louisa Whitman's at 431 Stevens.

1281.  In keeping with most entries in the *Daybook,* this is all that Whitman can say of the assassination of Garfield, who did not die until 19 September 1881. In his letter to Louisa Whitman (see entry for 6 July 1881) he said that "the shooting of President Garfield . . . has depressed me very much, but for the last twenty four hours, his case is so much more favorable"; and when Garfield died, Whitman wrote "The Sobbing of the Bells," which he sent to various papers on 24 September 1881 (see entry below); it was published in the Boston *Daily Globe* on 27 September, included in *The Poets' Tribute to Garfield* (Cambridge, Mass., 1881), p. 71, and in the 1881 *Leaves of Grass* just before the book came off the press in Boston (where Whitman was in September); see Comprehensive Reader's Edition, p. 500; Gay Wilson Allen, *The Solitary Singer,* p. 495; *New England Magazine,* VI (August 1892), 714–721; New York *Daily Tribune,* 4 April 1892, p. 8; *Poet-Lore,* X (1898), 618; and Horace Traubel, *With Walt Whitman in Camden,* I, 324–326, III, 129, 136.

1282.  See footnote 1280.

July 6   letter & papers to Lou at Norwich[1283] – paper to Mrs Scovel

July 15 – Dr Bucke arrives at College Point, L. I., N. Y.
care of Mrs Chase – I wrote postal card [1284]

quite unwell these days – prostrated with the
heat & bad, bad air of the city

busy with the copy of book for Osgood

15   Sent photo: to Mrs A. L. Williams   593 W Jackson St.
Chicago, Ill: for Childrens' Home benefit $1

Sent E & F N Spon ℞ 446 Broome St N Y "Poetry Future" [1285]

[seven lines in pencil:]
rather a bad time the last two weeks – the
fearful heat, night & day – casual things
happening – the President's ~~all~~ assassination , as
supposed for three days – tackling with the
copy of my new & complete edition, for
Osgood, Boston, & not getting it to suit me –
– the comet – sister Lou absent, &c &c[1286]

17th   Sent letter to Osgood, proposing that I come on
to Boston on or before Sept: 1 – [1287]

Note to Dr Bucke stating that I intend coming on
to N Y to Astor House, Thursday[1288]

[202]

Visit to West Hills, Huntington, Cold Spring &c
July 29, 30 & 31, & Aug 1, 1881 [1289]

1283.  Letter: *The Correspondence of Walt Whitman*, III, 232–233.
1284.  Post card lost; but a letter to Harry Stafford of 14 July 1881 (not recorded in the *Daybook*) is in *The Correspondence of Walt Whitman*, III, 233–234.
1285.  "Poetry Future" most likely means Whitman's essay, "The Poetry of the Future," *North American Review*, February 1881 (see footnote 1045, above).
1286.  This is one of the rare occasions on which Whitman made a comment about something rather than just a bare recording such as "President Garfield shot."
1287.  Letter: *The Correspondence of Walt Whitman*, III, 234–235.
1288.  Note to Dr Bucke lost; but Whitman apparently did not go to the Astor House in New York City that day — instead he met Dr. Bucke and Tommy Nicholson in Jersey City (see entry below for 23 July 1881).
1289.  Whitman's account of the visit is in his "A Week at West Hills," New York *Tribune*, 4 August 1881 (see footnote 1257, above).

Huntington L.I. July 29,30,31 & Aug 1, '81

[Names in pencil:]

| | |
|---|---|
| Charles Velsor[1290] | Cold Spring Harbor |
| Lemuel Carll | Huntington |
| John Chichester | Huntington |
| Miss Jane Rome | Huntington |
| Benjamin Doty | Cold Spring |
| *Charles Sheppard | Harbor |
| Smith Sammis | H |
| Henry Boyd | |
| Wm May | |
| Albert Hopper | |
| John Fleet | |
| Thos: Rogers | |
| Atkins, | |

W̶m̶ Misses ∧Wood, Sammis
Roscoe,        Henry Sammis
Fred W Galow
Ezra Prime        Sam Scudder
lawyer Charles R Street [1293]

returned to New York
Aug 1, '81 – to Edgar
M Smith's
5 East 65th Street[1291]

―――――――

went to
J H Johnston's
Mott av: & 149th St
N Y, Aug: 6th to
        Aug 19 '81 [1292]

[On slip of paper:]
    at West Hills
        1881
July 29, 30, 31 &
        Aug 1 — '81

――――――――――――

in New York City
        Edgar M Smith [not WW's hand]
    Mrs Amanda D Smith [not WW's hand]
            5 East 65th   St [not WW's hand]
            Aug 2 to 5 '81 [1294]

[203]

July & August '81 – <u>Long Island & N. Y. visit</u>

        went Eastern Trip    in New York    left Camden[1295]    [line in red ink]
July 23d – on from Camden to Jersey City, where I
                    went
    met Dr Bucke & Tommy Nicholson & so∧on to

1290.  Some of these names of people whom Whitman saw on his trip to Long Island are listed on a previous left-hand page of the *Daybook* (see footnotes 1261 and 1265).

1291.  See *The Correspondence of Walt Whitman*, III, 234n.

1292.  Whitman's left-hand pages in the *Daybook* (for different kinds of entries) sometimes get ahead of the entries on the right-hand pages.

1293.  Like so many other lists of names in the *Daybook,* whether of men or boys in Camden, Philadelphia, London (Ontario), or elsewhere, this one made on Long Island includes people who do not turn up in Whitman's life again — or only again in the *Daybook* once or twice to show him he sent them an article he had written.

1294.  Edgar M. Smith is listed in the New York Directory as a secretary (see footnote 1291, above).

1295.  See footnote 1289.

Woodside, L. I. to Helen & Arthur Price's[1296]
– there till 29th – then on to West Hills &
Huntington – one day at Far Rockaway – another at Long Branch

Huntington     L I     [in red pencil]

July 28th, 29th, 30th, 31st, & Aug 1, in Huntington
West Hills, & Cold Spring – a grand four days – [1297]

1296.  See footnote 287.
1297.  In one of Whitman's envelopes, in the Feinberg Collection (with his name and Camden, New Jersey printed on it), carrying his notation, "Genealogical Notes (original Whitman immigration) written at West Hills L I July 31 1881," are six small pages in his handwriting, as follows:

Robert Whitman of Ipswich Mass came in the Abigail, 1635, aged 20, and had a wife Susannah whom he married 1648, and she died 1664 —

Thomas, eldest son of John first born in England in 1629

☞  one is mentioned as a great linguist interpreter with Indians

—the vessel True Love was the vessel that brought over some of the original Whitman (1640) from London

Whitman in early days often spelt Whiteman

Far back – first of all John Whitman (undoubtedly born in England) died 1692

1639 freeman of Dorchester Mass: soon after goes to Weymouth Mass:

no doubt this was as far back as we can go — he h[ad] nine children by
    1689 *

his (John's) son Zachariah, born 1644 —

☞  in Harvard College 1668

* four or five of these were born in England — Zachariah the youngest,
    (ordained minister 1670) father of John Joseph

— he John deceased 1692, aged little if any short of 90 years, & may well seem to be the ancestor of the thousands bearing the name "of Whitman in America

— (the ministry deacons, clergy &c & a good education, are features of those old Whitman) — also great longevity)

many graduates of
    John
    Zachariah
    Joseph

Graduates in 1834 Whitmans Farmer (1834) notes that the of Whitman graduates

    12 at Harvard
    5 at Yale
    & 9 at other N E Colleges – in times past

                    from New Eng Hist. Reg

from early records of Boston

    Hannah, daughter of John Whitman born 24th 6th Month, 1641

Savage's Genealogical Dict: of New Eng. Vol 4 p 524 says

gets the Whitman family established at Huntington, L. I. per Joseph, probably before 1664 as in that year he was admitted freeman of Connested [?] (registered I suppose as a denizen of Huntington)    he was the son of Rev Zachariah Whitman of Milford, Conn: & Joseph probably died before his father

Mr Lloyd adds — Joseph is probably quite certainly the L I group of

    Whitmans started & radiates from this Joseph son of Rev Zebulon Zachariah (son of John)

    At West Hills L I at Henry Lloyd's July 31 '81          West

on our way we passed the Second Presbyte    Speculations          Hills

11 a.m.

Aug 1  —  back to N Y to 5 East 65th street

to Edgar Smith's, where (3½ p m Aug 1) I

/5

days

am writing  this – was there from 1st to 6th inclusive[1298]

in New York City   [in blue pencil, with in N Y

3 – Called at Tribune office – saw John Hay[1299]      overwritten in ink]

"   "  Critic office – saw Jennie & Jo Gilder[1300]

4  "A Week at West Hills" in Tribune[1301]

5  postals to – Lou – Harry – Dr Bucke – Ed: Lindell[1302]

package of Tribunes to Lou, for self[1303]

[in red ink:]

Sunday      in New York

7th  am now ∧ at Mr & Mrs  Johnston's,[1304] Mott avenue &

149th Street, (p o Station £ ) – having left Mr

& Mrs Smith's in 65th Street, yesterday forenoon

"Long Islander" to Dr Bucke[1305] – paper to Tommy Nicholson

postals to Lou, Dr. Bucke, Postmasters Camden & N Y[1306]

Weymouth Mass is seems to be the American settlement source of the Whitman
  According to N E
  Aabiah Whitman – married Mary Ford
      & John Whitman (his son) of Weymouth Mass: were registered freemen in 1681
    from the same in the early records of Weymouth is found th a memorandum of the
    birth of Experience, daugh[ter] of John & Aabigail W in 1673
      from the New Eng Hist Reg:

1298.  See footnote 1294.

1299.  Whitman's letter to the editor of the *Tribune* is in *The Correspondence of Walt Whitman,* III, 235.

1300.  Jeannette and Joseph Gilder had printed the fourth instalment of "How I Get Around at 60, and Take Notes" in *The Critic* for 16 July 1881 (see footnote 1077).

1301.  See footnote 1257.

1302.  The only post card of these four known is the one to Harry Stafford: *The Correspondence of Walt Whitman,* III, 235–236, and this is printed from a transcript in a Sotheby & Company catalogue, 13 May 1935.

1303.  Those to whom Whitman sent copies of "A Week in West Hills," New York *Tribune,* 4 August 1881, are listed above (see footnote 1257).

1304.  In *Walt Whitman's Diary in Canada* (Boston, 1904), p. 60, is the following paragraph in the section "From Other Journals of Walt Whitman":

*Aug.* 7, '81. How deeply I was touched just now reading in the account of the famed Italian tragedian and manager Modena that he had succeded in "founding a school of acting with *Liberty* as its keystone and motto"! With that inspiration he seems to have brought forward Salvini and Rossi.

1305.  The issue of 4 August 1881 (see footnote 1260, above).

1306.  These four post cards are lost; a letter to Jeannette Gilder, 6 August 1881 (not

                                     ester
8    sent letter to Sylvanus Baxter Boston, to secure boarding place[1307]

---

11 – call'd on R Worthington 770 Broadway N Y & had
      an interview of over half an hour – I told him em-
      phatically he must not print and publish another copy of
      L of G. from the '60–'61 plates – if so it would be at his    [sideways (in red
      peril – he offered $50 down if I would warrant his printing      ink) in left
      a new edition of 500 from said plates, which I peremptorily      margin:]
      declined – Mr Williams & one or two clerks in the store heard    Mr Williams
      the conversation – R. W. paid me $25 due me on back sales       was present
      – I shall not trouble him for anything past – but shall hold
      him to strict account for what is done after this date[1308]

---

16   Mulvany's picture "Custer's Last Rally"[1309]

[204]

Alonzo Van Velsor   581 Broadway   New York[1310]

---

Pfaff's, 9 west 24th St.[1311]

John Mulvany[1312]
     697 Broadway   N Y

---

recorded in the *Daybook*) is in *The Correspondence of Walt Whitman*, III, 236; it gives Whitman's permission to announce Osgood's 1881 edition of *Leaves of Grass* in *The Critic* of 13
August 1881.
      1307.  Sylvester Baxter (see footnote 1102) was the author of "Whitman in Boston,"
*New England Magazine*, VI (August 1892), 714–721; see Whitman's letter to him, 8 August
1881, *The Correspondence of Walt Whitman*, III, 236–237.
      1308.  The Worthington business, which kept coming up from time to time (see footnotes
732, 949, and 1042), did not finish, or get settled at this time; the plates, as is clear from *The
Correspondence of Walt Whitman*, III, 197, were even used by Worthington until some time
after Whitman's death; see *The Complete Writings of Walt Whitman* (1902), VIII, 280.
      1309.  After seeing a painting in New York City by John Mulvany, called "Custer's Last
Rally," Whitman used his brief essay on it as part of his "City Notes in August," New York
*Tribune*, 15 August 1881; see *Prose Works 1892*, I, 275–276.
      1310.  After Whitman's grandmother died, her husband Major Van Velsor remarried
and had a son, Alonzo Van Velsor, who "returned from California with his 'pile,' went into
business in New York, and died in Newark, N. J. July 22, 1883" — Clarence Gohdes and Rollo
G. Silver, editors, *Faint Clews & Indirections* (Durham, N. C., 1949), p. 45.
      1311.  Pfaff's restaurant, which was a center for the "Bohemians" — writers, artists, news-
papermen — of New York, was on Broadway just above Bleeker Street in the 1850s, when
Whitman became one of its habitués. See Albert Parry, *Garrets and Pretenders: A History of
Bohemianism in America* (New York, 1933), pp. 14–48; and Gay Wilson Allen, *The Solitary
Singer*, pp. 228–231, 269–270, 272–273, and 494. There is a brief account of Whitman and Pfaff
in August 1881 talking over the old times at the restaurant in 1859 and 1860 on Broadway, in
"Some Old Acquaintance — Memories," *Specimen Days: Prose Works 1892*, I, 277.
      1312.  See footnote 1309.

26                                                            [205]

"City Notes" in Trib[1313]

August '81 – in New York   ~~on my Boston progress~~   Aug 15

[in red ink]

Excellent   in New York   24th St N Y [1314] — an hour's sit afterward [ ? ]

16 ‸Breakfast at Pfaff's‸ – Col: Seymour then down
     in the 5ᵗʰ ave stage –

Broadway‸ – jaunt to Brooklyn – Call on Mr

                       in open car

Kinsella, Eagle office[1315] – Mr Hersey – jaunt‸ thro

                 old name which is ⎱ better

Myrtle avenue[1316] 'way to Broadway (Division av:) ⎰

and so               old familiar               retain'd

~~then~~ in Reid av: car to‸ Fulton av (pleasant

         and about     A jaunt of two hours, finishing

section, 25ᵗʰ ward   Bedford) – ~~and so~~‸ by Fulton

av: cars back to Fulton ferry.

     with J H J [1317]

– ride up through Central Park (the obelisk)

       through

– and so ‸to the splendid breadth of Seventh av:

to the Boulevard and on home to 149ᵗʰ st

   – seven or eight miles of the most varied, broad, picturesque

              panorama ~~beauty~~ of wealth, humanity, natural

               beauty and "improvement," our land can show

17    letter to P M Camden – also to Sylvester Baxter[1318]

   Left New York ~~for~~ travelled

19   Arrived in Boston – ~~came on~~ by the Shore route

            [in red pencil:]

RR, via Providence –        Boston

1313.  See footnote 1259.

1314.  See footnote 1311.

1315.  Thomas Kinsella became editor, during the Civil War, of the Brooklyn *Eagle,* which Whitman had edited in 1846–1848.

1316.  Whitman lived with his family, his father and mother, on Myrtle Avenue, Brooklyn, beginning in April 1849, and also published the *Freeman* from the same address until 11 September 1849; Whitman sold the house in May 1852.

1317.  John H. Johnston, Whitman's host on this part of the visit.

1318.  Both letters lost; for Baxter, see footnote 1307.

20    letters to Lou, Dr Bucke – P M. Camden[1319]

21 – letters to Phil: <u>Press</u> – to Bonsall – Helen Price – Dick Labar[1320]

to Charles Brown, Vancouver, Clarke County Washington
Territory, informing him of books, $5

to Willard K Clement, Brandon, Vt, informing
him of price, two Vols. $5 – ride to Cambridge

in  Boston  printing  my  book  [line in red pencil, also underlined
in red pencil]

22 – Monday – spent the forenoon at Rand & Avery's[1321]
printing office   Franklin street, outlining
matters of type, size of page, & other details –
– the superintendent Mr Clark very kind & thoughtful – appears as though I was going to have things
⌐in fact a little room,
all my own way – I have a table & nook⌐all to
myself, to read proof, write, &c.[1322]
[two lines in pencil:]
(com. boarding at "Waterston"   evening Friday Aug: at $8
a week)

28 – letter to Lou[1323]

1319.  Although the letters to Louisa Whitman, Dr Bucke, and the Camden Postmaster
are lost, one to Harry Stafford, of this date, is in *The Correspondence of Walt Whitman*, III,
237–238. Whitman expected to stay in Boston "a month or more": he was actually there from
19 August until 22 October 1881.

1320.  All of these letters, to the Philadelphia *Press*, Henry L. Bonsall (editor of the
Camden *Daily Post*), Helen Price (of Woodside, Long Island, where Whitman had just visited),
Richard Labar (of the Philadelphia *Public Ledger*), as well as those, below, to Charles Brown
and Willard K. Clement, are lost.

1321.  Whitman wrote Osgood, about this time, that his mail should be sent to Rand &
Avery's every morning: *The Correspondence of Walt Whitman*, III, 238.

1322.  During Whitman's stay in Boston he made notes on loose scraps of paper during
his walks and rides about the city; and some of these MSS. are in the Library of Congress.
Those published in Clifton Joseph Furness's edition of *Walt Whitman's Workshop: A Collection
of Unpublished Manuscripts* (Cambridge, 1928), pp. 263–265, follow:

With its rich and varied shows of (everything you can mention of the best) goods
and buyers and shoppers and countless human currents of Tremont, Washington, Court,
West, Winter and School Streets and Temple Place, and then the solid commission and
wholesale regions of Summer, Milk, Franklin and Bedford Streets and Post Office Square;
retail, busy: Winter, Temple Place, School; jobbers: Milk, Franklin, Bedford.

The horse-cars form one of the great institutions and puzzles of Boston. I ride in

1323.  Letter to Louisa Orr Whitman: *The Correspondence of Walt Whitman*, III, 238–
239.

August '81 — in New York — on to Boston — "City Notes" in Trib:

16 — Breakfast at Pfaff's — Col. Seymour then down and
Broadway — jaunt to Brooklyn — Call on Mr
Kinsella, Eagle office — Mr Hersey — jaunt thro'
Myrtle avenue way to Broadway — & vision
then in Reid av: Car to & Fulton av: (pleasant
section, 25th ward Bedford) — and so by Fulton
av: cars back to Fulton ferry.
— ride up through Central Park (the Obelisk
— and so to the splendid breadth of Seventh av:
to the Boulevard and on home to 149th st
— seven or eight miles of the most varied, broad, picturesque

17 letter to P M Camden — also to Sylvester Baker

'9 Left New York for — Arrived in Boston — travelled on by the Shore route
RR. via Providence — Boston

20 letters to Lou, & Bucke — P.M. Camden
21 — Letters to Phil: Press — to Bonsall — Helen Price — Dick Labar
to Charles Brown Vancouver, Clarke County Washington
Territory, informing him of books. $5

to Willard K Clement Brandon Vt. informing
— of price, two Vols. $5 — ride to Cambridge

in Boston — printing my book

22 — Monday — spent the forenoon at Rand & Avery's
printing office Franklin street outlining
matters of type, size of page, & other details
— the superintendent Mr Clark very kind & thoughtful
ful — appears as though I was going to have things
all my own way — I have a table & nook all to
myself, to read proof, write &c.

(com: boarding at "Waterston" every Monday Aug: at $8
a week)

28 — letter to Lou

them every day — of course get in the open ones — go out to Harvard Square often.
Aug. 22 '81

I often ride out fine afternoons in the Harvard Square open cars through Cambridge Street across the long stretch of back bay, and go on to the end. The whole route (four miles) is a lively and varied contribution — the sniffs of salt and sedge from the bay, the half-rural dwellings, the plentiful shrubbery and fine elms, the fine old mansions of Cambridge and the College buildings.

There on the red cars, in, out, and around — turning angles and curves — no long monotonous straight lines like Washington and Philadelphia.

"Walk your horses on curves and switches."

"No talking with the driver."

The ride out on the Cambridge cars upon the broad and stately North Avenue, with its old elms and pleasant mansions, embowered in shrubs and vines.

"Do not get off this car while in motion."

"Face to the front when you get off this car."

The old elms on the Common, especially edging Beacon Street, are in full vigor though sedate and a little thin.

The swell streets of Boston residences are Beacon Street and Commonwealth and Columbus Avenues. All the wealth and progress of growing Boston spread out toward the Back Bay. A great Park is in process of formation here — will contain acres.

Brookline is hard to match in its rural beauty, maturity, its great second growth of trees, its picturesque winding roads, everywhere well-kept, hard and smooth.

With all its old people — and they are pretty numerous — Boston looks very young. Take a walk on Saturday evening in some of the most frequented streets, and you will see the brightest, handsomest young men and women in the world, by hundreds and thousands. They are out for a promenade, for a change at the end of the week's work. But indeed I notice the same custom in most of our American cities.

In Boston there is quite an irruption of Chinese, mostly running laundries. You see their signs, Chi Wang or Lui Foo, Ah Quee, or the like, every few blocks — Tong-tong and Kee-kee.

I saw the Chinese professor at Cambridge, dressed in his native costume, walking about the streets.

Boston, Aug. 23 '81

In the printing office (Rand and Avery, 117 Franklin Street) most of the day. I have nearly altogether to myself a nice little room with table and big chair; and the constant kindness of Mr. Clark who has charge of the book-printing department, and whom I find invaluable in his experience, suggestions good nature and patience.

Aug. 24, '81. The first batch of page-proofs of the new volume, to-day. We are compacting the space, no white lines or padding or dashes or leads — all solid matter — all run in. I like the type, long-primer.

I have the good luck here in the printing-office to fall in the hands of Henry H. Clark for putting my "copy" through all the steps and stages that result at last in the finished, and bound, book, ready for all purchasers, at so much a copy. Mr. C. is quite a veteran at making books — not the mental or spiritual but the concrete, the typography of them I mean — which is much more important and difficult than generally supposed.

For many years Mr. C. was principal proof-reader, and afterward in charge of the book-department for such establishments as Riverside Press, Cambridge, and of late years here at Rand and Avery's. Was proof-reader in the Government printing office at Washington.

Mr. Clark has had to do with all the distinguished authors of New England, and has been in quite intimate personal relations with many of them; sometimes, for instance, in his printing office room, Emerson, Longfellow, Mrs. Stowe, and Lowell, being present. If the first named had heard the half-hour's string of respectful and printerial and affectionate eulogism of Emerson as a man among men, I think he would have felt more refreshed than at all the mere literary admiration of the day.

All this is not only to show my obligation to Henry Clark, but in some sort to all proof-readers everywhere, as sort of a tribute to a class of men, seldom mentioned, but to whom all the hundreds of writers, and all the millions of readers, are unspeakably indebted. More than one literary reputation, if not made is certainly saved by no less a person than a good proof-reader. The public that sees these neat and consecutive, fair-printed books on the centre-tables, little knows the mass of chaos, bad spelling and grammar, frightful (corrected) excesses or balks, and frequent masses of illegibility and tautology of which they have been extricated.

My Boston Names

| | [Printed card:] |
|---|---|
| Col Frank E Howe[1324] | Rand, Avery & Co. |
| Capt Milton Haxtun U S N | Printers, |
| Ed Dallin   [in pencil] | No. 117 Franklin St. |
| Harry Godden | Boston. |

Printed Proofs.

| | [Printed slip:] |
|---|---|
| Sylvester Baxter[1325] | From |
| C Crowell, foreman printing office | S. H. Sanborn, |
| Henry H Clark[1326] sup't  " | Bookbinder, |
| Dan Rogers, the boy. | 73 Federal Street, Boston |

M. F. Sweetser, [printed]   Sweetser [not WW's hand]

Manager of Advertising } [not WW's hand]
for James R. Osgood & Co.

Mrs Emma Bourier [?] Childs[1327]
    Walnut & 22ᵈ Streets  Copyright
        [Clipping of a newspaper article:]

"IRISH AMERICAN," Leadville, Col. — We believe that your interests are fully protected by your copyright. The law on the subject is as follows: — It protects you from loss for twenty-eight years, and gives you a right of renewal for fourteen years more. Authors can reserve the right to translate or dramatize their works. The law gives to the author of a dramatic composition the sole liberty of publicly performing or representing, or causing it to be performed or represented by others. A copy of the title of the book or other work must be sent to the Librarian of Congress,

---

1324.  These three men, Howe, Haxtun, or Dallin, do not turn up by name in Whitman's *Correspondence,* but Professor Edwin H. Miller (III, 240n) suggests that one of them may be in mind when Whitman writes "I have a friend here [in Boston], a man of leisure, who has a good horse & phaeton, takes me out riding afternoons or fine evenings." Harry Godden was a bookkeeper on the Boston *Herald.*

1325.  See footnote 1307.

1326.  For Henry H. Clark, C. Crowell, Dan Rogers, connected with Rand, Avery & Co., printing the 1881 *Leaves of Grass* for Osgood, see footnote 1322.

1327.  Mrs Emma Bouvier Childs was the wife of George W. Childs, publisher of the Philadelphia *Public Ledger.*

Washington, D. C., before publication, and two copies of the work ten days after publication. Fifty cents are charged for making the record, and fifty cents for a copy of the entry. A copy of a new edition must also be sent to the Librarian, under a penalty for $25. The fact of entry with the Librarian of Congress must be stated in each copy of the book or work; if not, no action can be taken for an infringement. The penalty for publication of an entry not actually made is $100. For the infringement of a dramatic composition the penalty for the first offence is $100, and $50 for every subsequent one. About the title you had better consult a good lawyer, and see that all the requirements of the law of copyright have been complied with.

[Card of Howard M. Jenkins, "The American," Phila.] [1328]

[207]

<u>Aug: and Sept: 1881 – In Boston, printing the Osgood book</u>
                    Boston    [in blue pencil]
Aug 20 to 30 – the book well under way – I am at the printing
    office some hours every day – health about as usual of late

26   rec'd $10 from <u>Tribune</u> for letter of Aug 15 – I sent for the 10 for Aug
                                                                    4 letter [1329]

    note from Erastus Brainard [1330]

Sept: 1 – Sent long letter to Dr Bucke – with          [encircled in blue pencil]
    proofs up to page 143 [1331]                    Sept 3
                                                Interview with
Sept 3 – Ed Dallin with me   "Bird"        J R Osgood  in
                                            Tremont st. — the
4   sent proofs to p 176 to Dr Bucke       English copyright
                                                question

1328. *The American* (Philadelphia), edited by W. R. Balch, had William Sloane Kennedy on its staff in 1880–1881, which may account for their printing Whitman material; Whitman's letter to Howard M. Jenkins, 14 November 1881, is lost.
1329. Whitman's article, "City Notes in August," was in the New York *Tribune* on 15 August 1881 (see footnote 1259, above); and "A Week in West Hills" was in the 4 August 1881 issue (see footnote 1257, above).
1330. See footnote 348.
1331. This letter to Dr Bucke, who was of course still working on his life of Whitman, is lost. "Bird" in the next line could refer to Ed Dallin (unidentified), or to "As a Strong Bird on Pinions Free" (1872) or to "To the Man-of-War-Bird" (1876), both poems included in the 1881 *Leaves*.

Aug: and Sept 1881 — In Boston, printing the Osgood book.

Boston

Aug 2D to 30 — the book well under way — I am at the printing office some hours every day — health about as usual of late

26 — rec'd $10 from Tribune for letter of Aug 15 — I sent for the 10 for Aug 4
note from Erastus Brainerd

Sept: 1 — sent long letter to Dr Bucke — with proofs up to page 143
                                                                    Sept 3

Sept 3 — Ed Dablin with me "Bird"

Interview with
J R Osgood in
Tremont st — the
English copyright
question

4 — sent proofs to p 176 to Dr Bucke

an hour with Harry Godden in his room — he showed me the ferns of Jamaica — many & nice photos — the curious case-bark of Jamaica &c. (he is here employ'd as book-keeper on the Herald)

Dr Bucke mentions A W Drake of Scribner's in connection with the pictures of the White men and Van Pelser burial hills

4. — Globe and Pilot to Mr. Nash. Washington

7th Wednesday — the hottest yet — (three very hot days)

9th (Friday) Every thing going on satisfactorily — I write this in my room, Hotel Waterston, 8 Bulfinch Place — have just read proof to page 245 of the book — some gloomy news — sad, sad, — the death of Beatrice Gilchrist — as accomplished and noble a young woman as I ever knew —
sent letter to F B Sanborn, Concord, Mass
sent letters to Lou, check for $10 for taxes       also
  "  to Harry Stafford (sent Long Islander & Globe)  Trib: Aug 15

11 sent rec't to Tribune for the $10

12 — sent letter to J R Osgood & Co

14 sent letter to Harry, inc: one to Sec: of War

15 sent letter to J R Osgood & Co —

16 — Interview with J R Osgood & Co: The price of the book is settled at $2. (my royalty 25 cts a copy) The English Copyright
The binding — the Steel Plate (price $40 & 20 books)
                                      Still in Boston

24 — sent letter to John Burroughs
  "    "  Mrs Anna Johnston
  "    "  "the Sobbing of the Bells" to various papers

an hour with Harry Godden in his room – he showed
me the ferns of Jamaica – many la nice photos –
the curious lace-bark of Jamaica &c. (he is
here employ'd as book-keeper on the <u>Herald</u>)

[Three lines in pencil:]
Dr Bucke mentions A W Drake, of Scribner's
in connection with the pictures of the Whitman and Van Velsor burial hills

4. Globe[1332] and Pilot to Mr. Nash, Washington[1333]

7th <u>Wednesday</u> – the hottest yet – (three very hot days)

9th (Friday) Everything going on satisfactorily – I write this
in my room, Hotel Waterston, 8 Bulfinch Place[1334] – have
just read proof to page 245 of the book – some gloomy news –
– sad, sad, – the death of Beatrice Gilchrist – as accomplish'd
and noble a young woman as I ever knew – [1335]

Sent letter to F B Sanborn, Concord, Mass[1336]

Sent letters to Lou, check for $10 for taxes[1337]

1332. "The Good Gray Poet," a long interview with Whitman, was in the Boston *Daily Globe* on 24 August 1881: John Boyle O'Reilly sent Whitman a copy of his article in *The Pilot,* a Catholic magazine O'Reilly edited, on 30 August 1881 (letter: Library of Congress).

1333. Michael Nash and his wife were old Washington friends of Whitman and Peter Doyle.

1334. Bliss Perry, *Walt Whitman* (Boston, 1906), p. 230; William Sloane Kennedy, *Reminiscences of Walt Whitman* (Paisley, 1896), p. 3n; and Sylvester Baxter, "Whitman in Boston," *New England Magazine,* n.s. VI (August 1892), 717, who suggested the place, referred to it as the Hotel Bulfinch; the correct name is Hotel Waterson, according to *The Boston Directory* (Boston, 1881), p. 1143. See *Faint Clews & Indirections,* p. 55n.

1335. Whitman learned about Dr Beatrice Gilchrist's suicide from Mrs Susan Stafford, Herbert Gilchrist (who wrote her) thinking the shock to Whitman would thus be less abrupt: see Mrs Anne Gilchrist's letter to Whitman, 14 December 1881, in Thomas B. Harned, *The Letters of Anne Gilchrist and Walt Whitman,* p. 203. See also footnotes 420, above.

1336. Letter lost.

1337. Although this letter is lost, Whitman probably accepted an invitation to spend the weekend in Concord. This visit is not mentioned in the *Daybook,* which has no entries between 16 and 24 September 1881. Franklin Benjamin Sanborn (1831–1917), newspaperman — on the Springfield *Republican,* 1856–1914 — and literary biographer, whose abolitionist trial Whitman had attended in 1860, came to Boston on 17 September 1881 and took the poet to Concord, where they spent an evening with Ralph Waldo Emerson and had dinner the next day with the Emersons. See *The Correspondence of Walt Whitman,* III, 40n, 244–245, 288; see also "A Visit at the Last, to R. W. Emerson," "Other Concord Notations," and "Boston Common — More of Emerson," all revised in *Specimen Days* from "How I Get Around at 60, and Take Notes," Part V, *The Critic,* 3 December 1881 — *Prose Works 1892,* I, 278–282.

                                                                    also
"   to Harry Stafford (sent <u>Long</u> <u>Islander</u> & G<u>lobe</u>) Trib:
                                                          Aug 15 [1338]

---

11   Sent rec't to Tribune for the $10 [1339]

---

12 – Sent letter to J R Osgood & Co [1340]

---

14   Sent letter to Harry, enc: one to Sec: of War [1341]

---

15   Sent letter to J R Osgood & Co – [1342]

---

16 – Interview with J R Osgood & Co:

The price of the book is settled at $2,   (my royalty
                                           25 cts a copy)

The English Copyright
The binding – the steel plate (price $40 & 20 books) [1343]

---

                         <u>Still in Boston</u> [in red pencil]


24 – sent letter to John Burroughs [1344]

——  "    "       Mrs Alma Johnston [1345]

"   "  "the Sobbing of the Bells" to various papers [1346]

---

1338.  Letter: *The Correspondence of Walt Whitman*, III, 240–241; *The Long-Islander*, 5 August 1881, contained a piece on Whitman by Mrs Mary E. Wager-Fisher; the Boston *Globe*, 24 August 1881 contained "The Good Gray Poet," an interview; and the New York *Tribune*, 15 August 1881, printed Whitman's "City Notes in August" (see footnotes 1256, 1259, and 1260, above).

1339.  This $10 from the New York *Tribune* was for "A Week in West Hills," in the issue of 4 August 1881.

1340.  This letter, with copyright and other details of importance, is in *The Correspondence of Walt Whitman*, III, 241–242.

1341.  Letter to Harry Stafford: *The Correspondence of Walt Whitman*, III, 242–243; the letter to the Secretary of War, to help Harry get in one of the coast lifesaving stations or similar place, is lost.

1342.  Letter, mainly on Whitman's portrait in the book, is in *The Correspondence of Walt Whitman*, III, 243.

1343.  These were matters taken up in the two letters, above.

1344.  Letter: *The Correspondence of Walt Whitman*, III, 245–246. Three other letters, not recorded here, to Louisa Orr Whitman, 18 September 1881; to John Burroughs, 19 September 1881; and to Henry H. Clark, same date, are in *ibid.*, III, 244–245.

1345.  Letter: *The Correspondence of Walt Whitman*, III, 246–247.

1346.  "The Sobbing of the Bells," a poem about President Garfield, who died on 19 September 1881, was published in the Boston *Daily Globe*, 27 September 1881 (see footnote 1281, above). A facsimile of the MS, written on the back of a letter to Whitman from John Boyle O'Reilly, is in Horace Traubel, *With Walt Whitman in Camden*, II, opp. p. 136.

[208]

[Card of the New-England Historic, Genealogical Society, 18 Somerset St., Boston, dated Sept. 28, 1881, and signed: John Ward Dean, Librarian.]

Mrs Dr A B Drake, 35 G street south
                    Boston

| H. E.<br>Mr & Mrs ∧ & little Mildred<br>Fuller, 218 State Street<br>Boston | [Slip with    100 on it and signed:<br>John Barons.] |
| --- | --- |

Mrs K W Lombard
       41 Pinckney Street   Boston

Harry Stafford
care of T B Gibbs – Berlin   N J

[Rubber stamp of T. H. Bartlett,[1347] sculptor, 394 Federal St., Boston; card of W. B. Merrill, The Press, Philadelphia.]

Garitee, Masten & Allen
518 Chestnut

[209]

1881 – Sept:        Still in Boston        [in red ink over red pencil:]
                                            Boston

Sept: 28 – letter to Dr Bucke[1348]
        papers to Smith Caswell – Elmer Stafford
            "   "   Tommy  Nicholson – Hannah  and  Mary[1349]

Visit to the New England Genealogical Society[1350]

30 – Paid Mrs Moffitt's board bill $41.44 , – pays for
                                        paid $21
        six weeks, up to date (8 Bulfinch Place) afterwards[1351]

---

1347.  See footnotes 440 and 1097; Whitman wrote to him at this address on 14 October 1883 (see entry below).

1348.  Letter lost.

1349.  One can never know what papers Whitman sent, for he was always sending papers to someone; but as his pieces, and news stories about him, were appearing in newspapers, the Boston *Daily Globe, The Pilot,* the New York *Tribune,* and *The Long-Islander,* among others, he may well have sent such papers to his two sisters Mrs Hannah Heyde and Mrs Mary Van Nostrand, and to his young friends.

1350.  The Society's librarian, John Ward Dean, signed the card given Whitman (see above).

1351.  This was for Whitman's stay at Hotel Waterson (see footnote 1334).

J R O paid me $40 for the steel plate[1352]

read the last of the proofs, (the six contents
pages) to-day — all cast now, – 382 pages –

Oct: 4 – sent a complete set proofs 382 pp to Dr Bucke
also letter[1353]

1ˢᵗ  signed Agreement with J R Osgood, they
to publish L. of G. for ten years – $2 a copy
– 25ᶜᵗˢ royalty – [1354]

sent letter to Lou[1355]          <u>Still</u> in <u>Boston</u> [in red pencil]

6  wrote to Hannah – quite a long letter – [1356]

11  went to see the Italian Rossi in Romeo – Globe
theatre, Boston – (Sylvester  Baxter) [1357]

1352.  Whitman first suggested, in his letter of 4 June 1881, using a new portrait by F.
Gutekunst, then changed his mind and decided to use an earlier portrait, of which he had
the engraving (see his letter to James R. Osgood & Company, 15 September 1881). William
Sloane Kennedy, *The Fight of a Book for the World* (West Yarmouth, Mass, 1926), p. 248,
quotes Whitman on the McRae shirt-sleeve portrait, "The portrait is required in the text to
face page 29 [of the Osgood edition] — in fact is involved as part of the poem," and, Kennedy
adds, "It is to be hoped, nevertheless, that this repulsive, loaferish portrait, with its sensual
mouth, can be dropped from future editions, or be accompanied by other and better ones that
show the mature man, and not merely the defiant young revolter of thirty-seven, with a very
large chip on his shoulder, no suspenders to his trousers, and his hat very much on one side."
1353.  Letter lost.
1354.  The full agreement with James R. Osgood & Company, now in the Library of
Congress, is in *The Complete Writings of Walt Whitman* (1902), VIII, 285–286:
      The agreement hereby made by and between the undersigned compacts that Walt
Whitman endows James R. Osgood & Company for ten years from this date with the sole
and exclusive privilege of issuing and publishing his, the said Whitman's, poems of *Leaves
of Grass,* in one volume, at the price of Two Dollars — that said Osgood & Company shall
pay for that privilege to said Whitman twenty-five cents royalty on every copy of said
*Leaves of Grass* sold, said payments to be made to said Whitman on the first day of
January and the first day of July of every year — that the copyright remains vested solely
in said Whitman — that said Osgood & Company shall have the privilege of publishing the
said *Leaves of Grass* in any other more costly form by paying said Whitman at the same
rate of royalty before specified — that said Whitman, holding also the British copyright,
endows the said Osgood & Company, as far as he legally can, with the same rights and
privileges in Great Britain, on the like conditions of royalty before specified, and for the
same period of time — that any future points of agreement, or modification of this agreement, may be made at any time by amicable and written consent of both parties — and
finally that at the end of ten years this contract may be continued at the pleasure of the
undersigned — or their heirs or assigns.
      Made and executed this first day of October, A.D. 1881.
                                          WALT WHITMAN.
                                          JAMES R. OSGOOD & CO.
(See Thomas B. Harned's "Walt Whitman and His Second Boston Publishers," *ibid.,* VIII,
275–300.)
1355.  Letter to Louisa Orr Whitman is lost.
1356.  Letter to his sister Mrs Hannah Heyde is lost.
1357.  For Sylvester Baxter, see footnote 1102; Ernesto Rossi, the Italian actor who starred
in "Romeo and Juliet," was on an American tour.

15 – Saturday Night – Boston – Supper &c, with the
  printers & proof readers[1358] – Mrs. Moffitt's[1359]

18th Evening at Mrs A B Drake's, 35 G street [1360]

19 – Boston – City Point – (East Broadway & Q street)
  – four hours at the Point – (Johnny Barons) [1361]

  – paid Mrs Moffit $21, in full up to date ($62.44 altogether) [1362]

22ᵈ  Saturday – Left Boston[1363] – on  to  New  York  by
     day train        in  New  York  [in red pencil]

1358. See "A Poet's Supper to His Printers and Proof-Readers," Boston *Daily Advertiser,* 17 October 1881, most likely written by Whitman himself.
1359. Mrs Moffitt's was the Hotel Waterson, where Whitman stayed in Boston.
1360. Whitman writes Mrs Dr A B Drake's name and address on the opposite page.
1361. A slip on the opposite page has "100" on it and is signed: "John Barons." Meaning is not clear.
1362. See footnotes 1334, 1351, and 1359.
1363. In *Walt Whitman's Diary in Canada* (Boston, 1904), pp. 60–62, is the following paragraph in the section "From Other Journals of Walt Whitman":
    LEAVES OF GRASS FINISHED. *Boston, Oct.* 22, '81, 8.30 A.M. I am pencilling this in the N. E. and N. Y. depot, foot of Summer street, waiting to start west in the 9 o'clock train. Have been in Boston the last two months seeing to the "materialization" of my completed "Leaves of Grass" — first deciding on the kind of type, size of page, head-lines, consecutive arrangement of pieces, etc.; then the composition, proof-reading, electrotyping, etc., which all went on smoothly and with sufficient rapidity. Indeed I quite enjoyed the work (have felt the last few days as though I should like to shoulder a similar job once or twice every year). The printing-office (Rand and Avery's [corner Franklin and Federal streets]) is a fine one, and I had the very genial and competent aid throughout of Henry H. Clark, principal proof-reader and book-superintendent of the concern. [W. S. Kennedy footnote: "Mr. Clark was for many years at the University Press, Cambridge, and used to tell me how he would sometimes induce Longfellow to alter a word at his suggestion, the poet often dropping in from his home on the same street to oversee the work of getting new poems into type."] And so I have put those completed poems in permanent type-form at last. And of the present prose volume [W. S. Kennedy note: what volume? he did not begin to prepare his first and only prose volume, *Specimen Days,* until July, '82; see first page of that work] — are not its items ("ducks and drakes," as the boys term the little pebble-flats they send at random to skip over the surface of the water and sink in its depths) — is not the preceding collection mainly an attempt at specimen samples of the bases and arrieres of those same poems? often unwitting to myself at the time.
    In *Faint Clews & Indirections* (Durham, North Carolina, 1949), pp. 54–55, is a companion-piece to the above memorandum; attached to the MS., in the Trent Collection, Duke University Library, are two newspaper clippings, from the Boston *Daily Advertiser* (see footnote 1358, above) and the Toledo *Journal* (a review of *Leaves of Grass,* January 1882). These notes are similar to material written above in the *Daybook*:
        *Sept:* '81
        Copy of
        *Leaves of Grass*
        Set up, cast, & printed
        Boston
        Aug: 22 – Sept: 29 – '1881
        at office of
        RAND, AVERY & CO.
        PRINTERS,
        No. 117 Franklin St.
        BOSTON.

23ᵈ – Sunday – at Grand Union Hotel – 4ᵗʰ av & 42ᵈ st [1364]
        with Dr Bucke and Matilda Gurd [1365]

24ᵗʰ, '5ᵗʰ &c – at Mr & Mrs Johnson's Mott av. & 149ᵗʰ st [1366]

25 – sent letter to Ruth Stafford (in answer to one rec'd from her) [1367]

[210]

[On long slip of lined paper — all in pencil:]
Vol 4   Savage's Genealogical
Dictionary, 1862, pages 523,
~~524,~~ '24, '25.[1368]
Memoir of John Whitman
& his Descendants, 1832, by
Ezekiel Whitman.

Henry Onderdonk Jr
        Jamaica L I

Charles  B  Moore
Office Genealogical Society ~~Off~~
64 Madison Avenue
        New York[1369]

(1881)

Henry H Clark
        superintendent Book Department

        J R Osgood & Co: 211 Tremont st:
            publishers of book

        is to be $2 retail – & I am to
            have 25cts a copy royalty

        I was in Boston from Aug: 19 to Oct

        Dan Rogers – the boy messenger

        boarding place, Mrs. Moffitt's, Hotel Waterston
                8 Bulfinch place

1364.   Whitman wrote a long letter to his sister-in-law Louisa Orr Whitman, *The Correspondence of Walt Whitman,* III, 249–250.

1365.   Matilda Gurd, Dr Bucke's sister, was in poor health and had come to New York with Dr Bucke to consult a specialist.

1366.   Whitman had written Mrs Alma Calder Johnston, 10 October 1881, that he would come to stay with them "this week"; instead it was in two weeks — *The Correspondence of Walt Whitman,* III, 248.

1367.   Letter: *The Correspondence of Walt Whitman,* III, 250–251.

1368.   This was the source of the genealogical data which Whitman wrote in West Hills, Long Island, 31 July 1881 (see footnote 1297, above, for a transcript of those notes.)

1369.   In addition to the material in footnote 1297, Whitman wrote other notes of a similar nature, which went from Dr Richard Maurice Bucke to the Trent Collection, Duke

University Library, and were printed in *Faint Clews & Indirections* (Durham, North Carolina, 1949), pp. 42–48:

In the Revolution, a squad of British cavalrey, on a raid on their own account, came to Kell Van Velsor's, (mother's father [Major Cornelius Van Velsor (1768–1837)], "Uncle Kell,") then a youth, and went to the barn, and were just tak'g away a very fine young sorrel mare. Amy V. V. [Naomi Williams Van Velsor, wife of Cornelius] and Kell's sisters, prevented him by force for a while from going to interfere, but just as the British soldiers were lead'g the mare out, K. broke away from the women, made a rush, and seized the bridle from the thieves. They drew their sabres, and flourished them round his head, but he was resolute; and demanded to see their authority for press'g his horse. As usual, great courage, will, and coolness, stood him in hand. The swords flourished and flashed around his head — the women were in tears, expect'g he would be killed; but he held on to the mare, and the upshot of it was, the British rode away without her.

Grandmother Whitman, tells that one day a British quartermaster's deputy, with some attendants, came out to her house, (the old house below the hill,) and ordered her to get ready the parlor and adjoin'g bedroom, for an officer of rank, in a few days. She did so, but the officer never came.

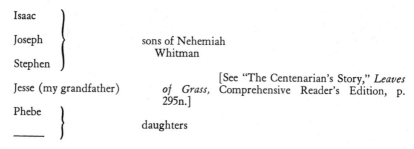

Isaac

Joseph          sons of Nehemiah
                Whitman
Stephen

                                [See "The Centenarian's Story," *Leaves
Jesse (my grandfather)      *of Grass,* Comprehensive Reader's Edition, p.
                                295n.]
Phebe

————          daughters

Hannah Brush, daughter of Tredwell Brush & ———— *Platt* Her parents died when she was quite young, she was adopted by her aunt Vashti Platt — This latter must have been mistress of quite an estate, for grandmother related that she has seen fourteen little niggers, belonging to the family, eat'g their supper at even'g, all at once in the kitchen. Tredwell Brush, her brother, died a young man unmarried.

Hannah Brush, (my grandmother Whitman) had only one brother, who died a young man — (the grave-stones from his grave were among those I saw at the back door.)

And only one sister who married ———— Scudder, father of Tredwel Scudder, (on the South Side,) who was father of Tredwell, Walter Richard, Wilmot, Hannah & Julia Scudder

Portland
avenue

Oct. 29, '62 — Brooklyn
— A visit from Sarah Mead, mother's aunt, her mother's sister. [Obituary, New York *Times,* 12 April 1878; and a clipping with a notation by Whitman: "death of Aunt Sarah Mead early in April '78 — N. Y. Eve Post Feb 22 '78.] — She is 80 years of age, quite smart — lives with her daughter in New York.

*Phoebe Pintard,* another of my mother's aunts, aged 85, lives in New York.
Mrs. Clara Avery, aged about 82, is also living.
Peggy Williams, (another) an old maid died about two years ago.
(The above four of the eight daughters of Capt. Williams, mothers maternal grandfather
*1873. Nov. 20. Camden.*

Just rec'd word from N. from mother's aunt, Mrs. Sarah Mead, (born Williams.) She is now in her 92d year, having been born 24th Sept. 1782. On her 91st birth-day, now just past, she rode in a carriage through Central Park, & took great interest & pleasure in the scenes. Her sister, Mrs. Phebe Pintard, died a few years since in N. Y.; must have been nearly a hundred years old.

Mother's family lived only two or three miles from West Hills — on a solitary picturesque road, that wound up from Cold Spring Harbor. — Her father was Major Van

Velsor, and her mother's name Naomi Williams. — Capt. Williams and his wife, her parents, fine old couple, exceed'g generous. — I remember them both (my mother's parents) very well. She was a mild, gentle, and sweet tempered woman, fond of children — remarkably generous and hospitable in disposition — a good wife and mother. — In dress she was rather Quakerish. — Her mother's (my great grandmother's) maiden name was Mary Wooley, and her father, Capt. Williams, was owner of a vessel that sailed between New York and Florida.

Major Van Velsor was a good specimen of a hearty, solid, fat old gentleman, on good terms with the world, and who liked his ease. — For over forty years, he drove a stage and market wagon from his farm to Brooklyn ferry, where he used to put up at Smith & Wood's old tavern on the west side of the street, near Fulton ferry. — He was wonderfully regular in those weekly trips; and in those old fashioned times, people could almost tell the time of day, by his stage passing along the road — so punctual was he. — I have been up and down with him many times: I well remember how sick the smell of lampblack and oil with which the canvass covering of the stage was painted, would make me. —

?3

After my own grandmother died, in 1826 the old man married again but did not make a very good investment — He had a son Alonzo, by this second marriage — now, (Sept. 1850,) in California. He is a good young man, I think, from what I know of him. — He has since returned from California with his "pile," went into business in New York, and died at Newark, N. J. July 22, 1883 [obituary, Newark *Daily Advertiser,* 23 July 1883]

tomb stones; for on the old hill, at the native place, among all the numerous graves, there is not one inscribed grave stone [see *Prose Works 1892,* I, 5–7], except Mahala Whitman, and I think I have heard that that was put up at the instance of a young man who was to have been married to her. —

The old house in which my father's grand parents lived, (and their parents before them,) is still partly standing — a ponderous frame; it is now turned into a carriage house and granary. — The largest trees near it, that I remember, appear to have been cut down. —

The Whitman were among the earliest settlers of that part of Long Island — West Hills, township of Huntington, county of Suffolk, New York. — They must have originally come from some rural district of England — a stalwart, massive, heavy, long-lived race. — They appear to have been always of democratic and heretical tendencies. — Some of them are yet represented by descendants in New England

My father's grandfather was quite a large territorial owner in that part of Long Island, and also on the southern shore of the town. — They all espoused with ardor the side of the "rebellion" in 76. —

I remember when a boy hearing grandmother Whitman tell about the times of the revolutionary war. — The British had full swing over Long Island, and foraged every where, and committed the most horrible excesses — enough to make one's blood boil even to hear of now. — My father's father I never saw. —

Nov. 23d. 62 Portland av.

Jesse Whitman the youngest of the children (my grandfather) had 2 (or ? 3) brothers, older than himself, Stephen and Isaac; and one sister, Phebe. — She married Zaire Jarvis, (he lived just west of Babylon, on the South road, in 1840)

Isaac had a son *Jacob Whitman* a carpenter, — of this Jacob him my father learnt his trade — the first part of the time about Huntington West Hills, &c. and the last portion of his apprenticeship, (?about — years) in New York city. —

Jacob Whitman, (above mentioned) worked as a sort of foreman for a Venetian blind maker in New York — who died, and J. W. married the widow, and had two children by her — She died, and then J. W. married her daughter, and by her had quite a brood of children

Father finished his apprenticeship in New York city, and then worked for some three years there — I have heard him speak of boarding steady for three years in New York in one place. He then went up around the Hills, and South, Long Island, and took contracts at build'g. He was a first rate carpenter, did solid, substantial, conscientious work. I have heard mother say that he would sometimes lay awake all night plann'g out some unusually difficult plan in his building arrangements. [Verso of page:] ~~Vedder at Brother Jonathan office Beekman st. — ½ past 3 in the rear.~~

Walter Whitman married Louisa Van Velsor June 8, 1816
Mary E. Whitman & Ansel Van Nostrand, married, Jan. 2, 1840.

[211]

<u>1881</u>                                          [in red pencil:]
Oct 29 – Sent "My Long Island Antecedents"   in New York
    to N A Review – returned [1370]              in Mott Avenue

paper to Harry Scovel

John Burroughs (28th & 29th Oct.) in N Y – 28th dined at
    "Oriental" – went to "Century" magazine rooms – saw R.W.Gilder
    – in forenoon I call'd at "Critic" office [1371] – 29th J B with us in
    Mott av. a couple of hours [1372]

30th – Sunday – delightful ride up through Morrisconia – Mrs. J., May,
    Harold, Calder, little Allie. [1373] (Seems to me I should like to live in M.)

31  wrote to J R O & Co: advised 250 tru-calf (or half-calf) binding
    for holiday sales – [1374]          [in red pencil:]  Mott Haven

rec'd (& returned) from Trübner, (Josiah Child) form of

Hannah Louisa Whitman & Charles Louis Heyde, married 16th March 1852 [Van Nostrand
    Bible: 16 April — see Katherine Molinoff, *Some Notes on Whitman's Family* (Brook-
    lyn, 1941), p. 7]
Walter Whitman born July 14th 1789. –died July 11th 1855: aged 66 buried at Evergreen
    Cemetery
Louisa Van Velsor born Sept. 22, 1795
Jesse Whitman born March 2, 1818. [Van Nostrand Bible: 2 April]
Walter Whitman Jr. born May 31, 1819
Mary Elizabeth Whitman born Feb. 3, 1821
Hannah Louisa Whitman born Nov. 28, 1823
Infant born March 2d 1825 [Van Nostrand Bible: 12 April]
Andrew Jackson Whitman, born April 7th 1827
George Washington Whitman born Nov. 28th 1829.
Jefferson Whitman, born July 18th 1833
Edward Whitman born August 9th 1835
Infant died Sept. 14, 1825, aged 6 months & 12 days.

Naomi or Amy Williams was daughter of Capt. Williams and his wife Molly [Mary
    Woolley ?] Williams. — Besides two sons, they had eight daughters, Amy, Sally, Peggy,
    Hannah, Clara, Molly

                                                    —They lived in a
little house high upon the hills at Cold Spring. — Aunt Molly, the mother was easy,
good-natured, and inclined to let thgs go. Capt. Williams followed the sea. —

1370. This piece, "My Long Island Antecedents" (which may well have been based on
the notes in footnote 1369, above), was apparently never published; the whereabouts of the
MS is not known.
1371. Richard Watson Gilder (see footnote 81) was editor of *The Century* from 1881
until 1909, and was brother to Joseph and Jeannette Gilder, for whose *Critic* Whitman was
contributing regularly at this time.
1372. Mott Avenue refers to the home of Mr and Mrs John H. Johnston, who were
Whitman's New York hosts on this stop.
1373. These were members of the John H. Johnston family.
1374. Letter to James R. Osgood & Company lost.

(in New York — Mott Avenue

Oct 29 — Sent "My Long Island Antecedents" returned
to N A Review —
paper to Harry Scovel

John Burroughs (28th & 29th Oct.) in NY — 28th dined at
"Oriental" — went to "Century" magazine rooms — saw R. W. Gilder,
— in forenoon I call'd at "Critic" office — 29th JB with us in
Mott av. a couple of hours

30th — Sunday — Delightful ride up through Morrisania — Mrs. J, Mary
Harold, Calder, little Allie. (Seems to me I should like to live in M.)

31 wrote to J R O & Co: advised 250 tree calf (or half calf) bindings
for holiday sales —
rec'd (& returned) from Trübner, (Josiah Child) form of
entry for English copyright
wrote to all sorts editor Boston Post

Nov: 1 — sent back the fill'd up Copyright blank to
Trübner & Co: England
Robert Colyer up here (Mott av. NY) to tea,
& spent the evening. (Oct 31 '81)
letter to sister Hannah (enclosing Lou's)

Nov 2 — in New York (my last day the visit)

3 on home to Camden in the 1–4 pm train

5 "interview" visit from W B Merrill of the Phil: Press

back in Camden

6 (Sunday) sent back pictures (with autographs) to N A Review
wrote card to Harry — Berlin
sent the two sheets (new poems) to Dr Bucke
to Osgood to send back to Chas E Shepard
to Arthur Leibkeucher, care Krementz & Co
Newark N J
to Chas E Shephard    visit from 'Dick Labar
to J H Johnston

7 sent circulars (enc: slips of the new pieces) with postals to
Rossetti — Conway — Symonds
Nov Scribner to Hannah — L of G to Mary

8 letter to Critic promising Notes by Nov 10
ordered new black overcoat $12
went last night to see Fra Diavolo — Phil:

entry for English copyright [1375]

wrote to All Sorts' editor Boston Post [1376]

Nov: 1 – sent back to the fill'd up copyright blank to
Trübner & Co: England [1377]

Robert Colyer up here (Mott av: N Y) to tea, [1378]
& spent the evening, Oct 31 '81

letter to Sister Hannah (enclosing Lou's) [1379]

Nov 2 — in New York (my last day, this visit) [except date, line in red pencil]

3ᵈ  on home to Camden in the 1 – 4 p m train [1380]

5  "interview" visit from W B Merrill of the Phil: Press [1381]

back in Camden    [line in red pencil]

6 (Sunday) sent back pictures, (with autographs) to N A Review [1382]
wrote card to Harry – Berlin [1383]

1375. See Whitman's letter to Trübner & Company, 5 October 1881, *The Correspondence of Walt Whitman,* III, 247–248; in the end, however, Trübner declined to published the Osgood edition: see entry below for 8 December 1881.

1376. Letter lost; Whitman also wrote on this date to Sylvester Baxter, to thank him for the "fervid and stirring criticism" of *Leaves of Grass* in the Boston *Herald,* 30 October 1881 — *The Correspondence of Walt Whitman,* III, 251–252.

1377. Copyright blank lost?

1378. Robert Collyer was mentioned by Whitman in May 1888, when he told Horace Traubel that Collyer asked, "Why write poetry any more? All the songs were long ago sung," to which Whitman had no answer; but he did say that "Collyer's not deep but he's damned cute — for the preacher class very damned cute . . . Collyer is a kind of reduced Beecher — a Beecher with much of the grace lopped off." — *With Walt Whitman in Camden,* I, 120.

1379. Both letters, Whitman's to Hannah Heyde, and Louisa Orr Whitman's to Whitman, are lost.

1380. In the Trent Collection, Duke University Library — printed in *Faint Clews & Indirections* (Durham, North Carolina, 1949), p. 55 — is this paragraph:

N Y Mott Haven
Nov 3 '81

I am writ'g this at Mott Haven station, wait'g for the downward cars — going back to Camden, after an absence of three months. The last twelve days, stopping at the hospitable house of Mr. and Mrs. J[ohn] H J[ohnston] here having an easy & restful time. [Rest of paragraph canceled.] Sent "My Long Island Antecedents" to North American Review [rejected]. Just read a most live, affectionate, and        criticism on the new L[eaves] of G[rass] in last Sunday's Boston Herald, by Sylvan [Sylvester Baxter, "Leaves of Grass," *Sunday Herald,* 30 October 1881]

1380. W. B. Merrill's piece in the Philadelphia *Press* not located.

1381. See Whitman's "On Ossianic Night — Dearest Friends" in *Specimen Days,* which begins, "*Nov.* '81. — Again back in Camden." — *Prose Works 1892,* I, 282–283.

1382. For the article on Whitman's antecedents the *North American Review* did not print?

1383. Harry Stafford's address at this time was in care of Sheriff T. B. Gibbs, Berlin, New Jersey.

sent the two sheets (new poems) to Dr Bucke

[in blue pencil:]

to Osgood[1384] to send book to Chas E Shepard      sent  recd
to Arthur Leibkeucher,[1385] care Krementz & Co
        Newark N J
to Chas E Shephard [1386] – visit from Dick Labar[1387]
to J H Johnston[1388]

---

7     sent circulars (enc: slips of the new pieces) with postals to
Rossetti – Conway – Symonds[1389]

Nov. Scribner[1390] to Hannah – L of G to Mary[1391]

---

8   letter to Critic promising Notes by Nov 20 [1392]

ordered new black overcoat $12

went last night to see Fra Diavolo – Phil:

[212]

from W S Kennedy[1393] [not WW's hand]      [Card of Robt. J. Grigg, with
735 Cambridge street                        Garitee, Masten & Allen, Tower
~~7 Waterhouse St~~                          Hall Clothing Bazaar, 518 & 520
        Cambridge                            Market Street, Phila.]
        [not WW's hand]
     Mass.

---

1384.  Letter lost.
1385.  Arthur E. Lebknecker (not Leibkeucher) was sent a copy of the 1881 *Leaves of Grass* on 27 December 1881 (see entry that date, below); see *The Correspondence of Walt Whitman*, III, 252.
1386.  Letter lost.
1387.  Richard E. Labar was Whitman's friend in the Philadelphia *Public Ledger* office.
1388.  Letter: *The Correspondence of Walt Whitman*, III, 252.
1389.  These post cards to Whitman's English friends, William Michael Rossetti, Moncure D. Conway, and John Addington Symonds are all lost.
1390.  *Scribner's Monthly* for November 1880 (not 1881) contained Edmund Clarence Stedman's "Walt Whitman": could Whitman have sent his sister Hannah Heyde this issue?
1391.  Mary was undoubtedly Whitman's sister Mrs Mary Van Nostrand.
1392.  This refers to Part V of "How I Get Around at 60, and Take Notes," which appeared in *The Critic* on 3 December 1881 (see footnotes 1073 and 1077).
1393.  In the Trent Collection, Duke University Library, is a MS (printed in *Faint Clews & Indirections* [(Durham, North Carolina, 1949], p. 64), with his notation by William Sloane Kennedy: "Found among the papers of Walt Whitman by Horace Traubel, one of his executors. It is in Whitman's handwriting, & was written in 1881. Given to me by Traubel at the dinner in Boston of the Walt Whitman Fellowship Association on Walt's birthday, May 31, 1896, at Hotel Belleview." Whitman's brief note reads:
    Among my special        young men *littérateur* friends are W S Kennedy 7 Waterhouse street Cambridge, Mass: A young college chap —— Greek, Latin, &c —— accepts L of G. — yet bolts at the sexual part —— *but I consider Kennedy as a real & ardent friend both of* self & book

Harry and Clarence Whittaker[1394] are at
Wanamaker's, 13th & Market, Nov. '81

| | |
|---|---|
| [Card of R. M. Ware, counsellor at law, Mullica Hill, N. J.] [1395] | [On slip of paper, not in WW's hand:] From W. A. Eddy / 133 East 16th St. / New York City / |

| | |
|---|---|
| Mr & Mrs Wolf   Emily<br>  2217 Locust Street | Critic Dec 3 [1396]<br>W M Rossetti |
| R W Cooper<br>  N Y Life Ins: office<br>    346 Broadway<br>       N Y | M D Conway<br>Mrs F B Sanborn<br>Dr Edward Emerson<br>H J Bathgate, Oakenholt Hall |
| Elmer Santee    youth 19 – 20<br>  in Test's Drug Store[1397] | near Flint, Eng: |

Jan '82

                                              [in red pencil:]                    [213]
'81 – Nov:                            in  Camden

                                                          [in blue pencil:]
9 – sent new L of G to Helen Price with letter card    recd [1398]

      sent circs, enc. the new pieces, also letter cards to
          Rudolf Schmidt – Edward Carpenter – T W H Rolleston[1399]

10  Sent a copy in paper, & another in sheets to T W H
                                            [in red ink:]
       Rolleston   29 Lang Strasse, Dresden    rec'd
              [in blue pencil:] recd    paid $1.73 for Sunday Times
      "  a copy L of G. to Hannah         for I. J. & stopt it[1400]

1394. Clarence ("Clarry") Whittaker was among those whom Whitman wrote to on 1 November 1879 from St Louis, Missouri, on his western trip; letter lost.
1395. Whitman's note to R. M. Ware, 23 November 1881, is lost.
1396. This issue of *The Critic* contained Whitman's "How I Get Around at 60, and Take Notes" (Part V): see footnote 1392, above. Of the five people to whom Whitman sent copies, Rossetti, Conway, and Bathgate were long-time British friends; Mrs Franklin Benjamin Sanborn was the wife of the abolitionist (see footnote 1337); and Dr Edward Emerson was the son of Ralph Waldo Emerson whom Whitman saw in Concord, Mass. in September 1881 at Mr and Mrs Sanborn's.
1397. As Whitman had done so many times before, he apparently here wrote down the name of a young man he met in a drug store, this time using one name instead of several.
1398. A one-line fragmentary transcript of this letter — from *The Autograph*, I (December 1911), 33, is in *The Correspondence of Walt Whitman*, III, 252; for Helen Price, see footnote 287 and entry for 23 July 1881, above.
1399. Letter to Edward Carpenter: *The Correspondence of Walt Whitman*, III, 253. The letter to Rudolf Schmidt and T. W. H. Rolleston are lost; however, Rolleston's reply, 28 November 1881, is in Horst Frenz's *Whitman and Rolleston: A Correspondence* (Bloomington, Indiana, 1951), pp. 43–47.
1400. This is a subscription for Ida Johnston, daughter of Colonel John R. Johnston, the

Friday evn'g – visit through the Ledger office   with
Dick Labar – the scene in the Press Room with
all the four big (6 and 4 cylinder) presses going at once

11 – the magnificent notice in the Springfield Republican
of Nov. 8 [1401] — visit afternoon from Percy Ives[1402]

13 – note of thanks &c. to Springfield   Republican[1403]

14 – papers to Mrs Drake – Harry Stafford –
note to Mr Jenkins – American[1404]

15   Sent (at John Burroughs request) the new Vol. to Mrs Sara
A Booth, 150 Crown St. New Haven, Conn:
[in blue pencil:]
postal to John Burroughs[1405]   recd

16   Emerson notes to Critic $16 [1406] postal to Ruth Stafford [1407]

20 – cards of thanks to Boston Globe and N Y Sun[1408]

21 – sent back proof (Emerson visit) to Critic[1409]
letter to Dr Bucke[1410] – / father's & mothers pictures

saw and talked with     \ to Gutekunst, photo-types[1411]
H W Beecher at ferry house[1412]

Camden artist, a subscription Whitman had been paying for during several years.
    1401.   This was of course a review of the just published edition of *Leaves of Grass*, issued by James R. Osgood & Company.
    1402.   The young artist who painted portraits of Whitman (see footnotes 1007 and 1011).
    1403.   Letter: *The Correspondence of Walt Whitman*, III, 253.
    1404.   Letter to Howard M. Jenkins lost.
    1405.   Post card lost.
    1406.   Although this piece in *The Critic* for 3 December 1881 is entitled "How I Get Around at 60, and Take Notes," Part V, Whitman refers to it here as "Emerson notes" and below as "Emerson visit"; when he revised it for *Specimen Days* he called it "A Visit at the Last, to R. W. Emerson" — see *Prose Works 1892*, I, 278–282. (Latter parts of the revised piece are entitled "Other Concord Notations" and "Boston Common — More of Emerson.")
    1407.   Post card lost.
    1408.   E. P. M.'s long review, "Walt Whitman and the Poetry of the Future," was in the New York *Sun*, 19 November 1881.
    1409.   See footnote 1406.
    1410.   Letter lost.
    1411.   F. Gutekunst was the Philadelphia photographer who made many portraits of Whitman.
    1412.   Henry Ward Beecher (1813–1887), the well-known Brooklyn preacher and brother of Harriet Beecher Stowe, one of the most popular orators of his day on political, social, and

23   Note to R M Ware   Mullica Hill [1413]

25   left copy of L. of G. for W H Thorne, <u>Times</u> office

26   sent circ: to C H Greene, box 141, Rochester N Y at
       his request – also printed slips ⌈ recd 50 <u>Suns</u>[1414]

28   sent letter to Mrs Gilchrist[1415]

[in blue pencil:]

Dec. 3 – my Emerson[1416] visit article ($16) printed in <u>Critic</u>    paid [1417]

4       the newspapers extract from it pretty freely[1418]

–  sent papers to Smith Caswell [1419]

3   Harry here[1420]

religious subjects, but whose reputation was injured in 1874 by a suit for adultery, even though the jury disagreed. Dr Bucke and his sister, Matilda Gurd, heard him in Brooklyn in October 1881 when they were in New York visiting, among others, Walt Whitman. In May 1873 Whitman wrote his mother that a paper, *Woodhill and Claffin's Weekly,* contained a piece about the Beecher and Tilton scandal: "it is very coarse — I think Beecher a great humbug, but I don't believe there is any truth in that piece — (but of course don't know) — " (*The Correspondence of Walt Whitman,* II, 219; see also II, 104; I, 42–43n, for sources of Whitman's comments on Beecher.)

1413.   See footnote 1395.

1414.   Undoubtedly the New York *Sun* for 19 November 1881 (see footnote 1408, above).

1415.   Letter: *The Correspondence of Walt Whitman,* III, 253–254. See also Mrs Anne Gilchrist's letters to Whitman, in part, III, 254n, in the Library of Congress, in the Feinberg Collection, and in Thomas B. Harned, *The Letters of Anne Gilchrist and Walt Whitman* (1914), pp. 203–204 (letter of 14 December 1881).

1416.   In the Trent Collection — and published in *Faint Clews & Indirections* (Durham, North Carolina, 1949), pp. 28–29, is this opinion of Emerson by Whitman:

His idea of God (as in the oversoul) is beautiful & tender & orthodox, but is not the modern Scientific idea, now rapidly advancing, far more sublime & resplendent, and reflect'g a dazzl'g light upon Democracy, its twin, but the old old Oriental idea of God, taken up by the Ecclesiasticism of the middle ages, and still continued by the fossil churches of the present day

he has a large substrata of Greek and Latin and also of English — with some German and other — but says little of America, and it not only plays no important figure in his writings as a whole, but hardly appears there

☞   It is certain that the time comes when all merely intellectual writ'g, however fine, has been passed beyond, and ceases to attract or nourish.

Emerson — the poems

— it is all crystal, all a glassy clear stream of thought distilled, —
— we want — not a bit of Homeric, Shakespearean Rabelaisian red blood, heat, brawn, animality as in

1417.   See footnote 1406.

1418.   Whitman sent "fair proofs" of his Emerson articles to papers: see his letter to an unidentified editor in *The Correspondence of Walt Whitman,* III, 254.

1419.   John Burroughs's hired man at Esopus.

1420.   Harry Stafford, then working as a telegrapher in Berlin, New Jersey.

8    paid Ed. Morgan $3.50 for printing (paid $13.50 altogether)

[214]

Jo McHenry, 92 Market st. ("tripper") age 22 – Dec 9 '81 [1421]
      leaves ferry abt 4 ¹⁰ & 6 p m   admires the sunset

---

Standish O'Grady   11 Lr Fitzwilliam St   Dublin Ire
                  [in red ink:]
      his letter to me Oct 5 '81 – sent him pictures[1422]

---

David Bogue, St Martin's Place, Trafalgar Sq[1423]
      (? Charing Cross) – London, Eng:   Dec 10 '81

---

                                    [address in red ink]
            in the car paid no fare   756 Mt Vernon St:
Walter Dean   lad 14 or 15 (in Wanamakers.)   Dec 12
      met him again, March 21 – he is a fine boy [line in red ink]

---

Harry Caulfield, 19, printer, "the Sentinel" – father
      dead, 8 yr's, has mother & two sisters – is from Harrisburgh

---

Albert Thompson, driver, Stevens st.   Dec. '81 –

---

J   FitzGerald Lee, Bismarckplatz 10 – Dresden
                     [in red ink:]
            Saxony.     has left Dresden[1424]

---

Kindling wood place – 415 Spruce Camden

---

1421.   Once again, on this left-hand page, are names of young men, with some addresses and brief descriptions or other details; with — on this occasion — three other names of a different sort; Standish O'Grady, David Bogue, and J. FitzGerald Lee. (Whitman spells it "FitzGerald.")

1422.   Standish James O'Grady was an Irish poet, author of "Walt Whitman: the Poet of Joy" in the December 1875 *Gentleman's Magazine*: see footnote 118, above. O'Grady used the pseudonym of Arthur Clive: see *The Correspondence of Walt Whitman*, III, 21, 27, and Horace Traubel's *With Walt Whitman in Camden*, I, 398–400 (which includes O'Grady's long letter of 5 October 1881; Whitman sent him his photograph on 14 December 1881).

1423.   David Bogue became Whitman's publisher in England when Trübner & Company bowed out: see Whitman's letter to James R. Osgood & Company, 8 December 1881, in *The Correspondence of Walt Whitman*, III, 255; and to David Bogue, 14 December 1881, *ibid.*, III, 257.

1424.   Dr J. Fitzgerald Lee, a student and friend of T. W. H. Rolleston, asked Whitman's permission to translate *Leaves of Grass* into Russian — see his letter, 28 November 1881, in *Whitman and Rolleston: A Correspondence* (Bloomington, Indiana, 1951), pp. 48–50; and Whitman's reply, 20 December 1881, in *The Correspondence of Walt Whitman*, III, 259–260.

Howard Atkinson, tall, sandy, young, country fied
$\quad\quad\quad$ Dec. '81 $\quad\quad\quad$ driver, Stevens – also 5th

Grant Whittle, Feb 10 '82

Burroughs Smith (from Penn'sgrove)

David McCoy, (29) Market st driver – Sept 15 '82 –

Clement – – boy Stevens st cars – night

[215]

'81 – Dec: $\quad$ rec'd $80.50 from Trübner & Co. They have declined
8th $\quad$ – to act as publishers & agents in England for L of G. & J
$\quad\quad$ Childs has made David Bogue, St. Martin's Place, Trafalgar
$\quad\quad$ Square, publisher ☞ see J C's letter Nov. 19 '81 [1425]

wrote to J Childs – wrote to Osgood [1426] – sent rec't to <u>Trubner</u>

9 $\quad$ death of J W Forney [1427]

[First word in blue pencil:]
10 $\quad$ sent $\quad$ Mrs D C Peck, 314 State St Bridgeport Conn
$\quad\quad\quad\quad\quad\quad\quad\quad\quad\quad\quad\quad$ [in blue pencil:]
$\quad\quad$ the two Centennial Vols. $\quad$ Pay to be sent $\quad$ recd $\quad$ paid

L of G to Mr McKean (Ledger) with slips

L of G, (three Vols) to W H Thorn, <u>Times</u>

12 – J. W. Forney's funeral [1428]

14 $\quad$ wrote to David Bogue, with list of names in Eng: [1429]
$\quad\quad$ to send circular to – (sent 6 circulars)

---

1425. Joseph Child's letter, 19 November 1881, is lost, but see footnotes 1375 and 1423, and Benjamin H. Ticknor's letter to Whitman, 10 December 1881, in *The Complete Writings of Walt Whitman* (1902), VIII, 286–287.

1426. Letters to Josiah Child and to James R. Osgood & Company are in *The Correspondence of Walt Whitman*, III, 255.

1427. Colonel John W. Forney was a good friend of Whitman's (see footnote 193); he published the Philadelphia *Progress* and accompanied the poet on his western trip in 1879. Whitman commented briefly on Forney in his letter to Ruth Stafford, 11 December 1881, in *The Correspondence of Walt Whitman*, III, 256.

1428. See previous footnote.

1429. Letter (but not the list of names in England): *The Correspondence of Walt Whitman*, III, 257.

wrote to Mrs Peck    Bridgeport about lost p o order[1430]

[overwritten in blue pencil:]    paid

---

16    Mr C sent $5 for charitable purposes[1431]

---

Note from Osgood & Co: they are willing I should
sell the '76 edition copies left [1432]

---

18    sent L of G. & slips to A C Swinburne[1433] care Chatto
& Windus, 214 Piccadilly London

---

sent letter to Ben Ticknor[1434]
papers to Mrs Berry – rec't to Mrs D C Peck

---

rec'd [in red ink]
sent L    of    G to Rudolf Schmidt – also letter – [1435]

"    papers to Richard Fetters – Smith Caswell –

---

19    sent L    of    G & circs to Steingrimar    : Thorsteinsson[1436]

1430.  Letter lost.
1431.  Letter lost, but most likely from George W. Childs.
1432.  See Whitman's letter asking about selling the 1876 edition in *The Correspondence of Walt Whitman*, III, 256.
1433.  Algernon Charles Swinburne (1837–1909) was, after Tennyson and Carlyle, the most important of the English authors in Whitman's "orbit," though his attitude toward the American changed very markedly over the years, caused perhaps by Theodore Watts-Dunton's curbing Swinburne's early rebellion generally. In 1868 Swinburne wrote in his Blake essay that Whitman's "Lilacs" was "the most sweet and sonorous nocturn ever chanted in the church of the world," and in 1871 he wrote the often-quoted lyric, "To Walt Whitman in America": Whitman's response to all this can be seen in his comments in *The Correspondence of Walt Whitman*, II, 16, 20, 22, 161. As seen here, on 18 December 1881, Whitman sent Swinburne a copy of the Osgood edition of *Leaves of Grass,* yet on the same day he declined Benjamin Ticknor's suggestion that he (Whitman) solicit Swinburne to write a notice about *Leaves of Grass*: see *The Correspondence of Walt Whitman*, III, 258. As late as December 1884, Swinburne sent a personal message to Whitman through Edmund Gosse (see *ibid.,* III, 384n, and the letter in the Feinberg Collection). However, in the August 1887 *Fornightly Review* Swinburne made his "recantation" (Gosse's term), comparing Whitman's Eve to "a drunken apple woman, indecently sprawling in the slush and garbage of the gutter amid the rotten refuse of her over-turned fruit-stall." This understandably outraged Whitman's friends but his own reaction was much calmer: "Ain't he the damnedest simulacrum!" See Gay Wilson Allen, *The Solitary Singer,* pp. 392, 430–431, 445–446, 526–527, for a summary of the whole story; William Sloane Kennedy, *The Fight of a Book for the World,* pp. 22–24; Harold Blodgett, *Walt Whitman in England* (Ithaca, New York, 1934), pp. 103–121; W. B. Cairns, "Swinburne's Opinion of Whitman," *American Literature*, III (May 1931), 125–135; and W. S. Munroe, "Swinburne's Recantation of Walt Whitman," *Revue Anglo-Américaine,* VII (August 1941), 138–141. Swinburne is mentioned more than forty times in Horace Traubel's *With Walt Whitman in Camden.*
1434.  Benjamin H. Ticknor was a member of the publishing firm, James R. Osgood & Company, Boston; Thomas B. Ticknor was another from the same family in the company; George Ticknor (1791–1871), the historian and scholar, and William Davis Ticknor (1810–1864), his cousin and founder of Ticknor & Fields, were both dead by this time. Although Whitman began his letter, "My dear Ben: Ticknor," their relationship was always of a business nature. Letter: *The Correspondence of Walt Whitman*, III, 258.
1435.  Letter: *The Correspondence of Walt Whitman*, III, 257–258.
1436.  Steingrimar Thorsteinsson (1831–1913) was an Icelandic classical scholar; see *The Correspondence of Walt Whitman*, III, 258n.

Reizjavik, Iceland, Rudolf ~~Semdt~~ Schmidt's
friend
rec'd book from him [line in red ink]

"the Icelandic poet"

sent Lit World (review of Scandinavian books) to Rudolf Schmidt

rec'd [in red ink]
20  sent letter ∧ (preface to Russian translation) to
J FitzGerald Lee, Bismarckplatz 10  Dresden,
Saxony — also L of G [1437]

letter to Tommy Nicholson – to Ben Ticknor[1438]

met Wm McMichael on 13th st – his talk

[in red ink:]
sent W S Kennedy 3 vols L of G, also other matter   recd

[216]

| [Card of J. M. Stoddart & Co.] [1439] | Gloves – Christmas 81–'2 [1442] |
|---|---|
| [twelve lines in red ink:] | John Copper |
| Sent "Wilde & Whitman" [1440] to | Charley Van Mater |
| Dr Bucke | John Severn |
| John Burroughs | Charles Wood |
| David Bogue | Al Thompson |
| Osgood | Howard [in pencil] |
| Rolleston | Burroughs Smith [in pencil] |
| Rossetti | |
| W S Kennedy | |
| Hannah | |
| Jessie  St L | |
| Mary Johnston | |
| Standish O'Grady[1441] | |

1437.  See footnote 1424; this Russian translation by Lee was never published, but Dr P. Popoff, in "Walt Whitman," *Zagranichy Viestnik* [The Foreign Messenger, Russia], March 1883, did translate "O Captain! My Captain!," "Manhattan Arming"(?), and "Song of the Broad-Axe," and parts of the following, "Inscriptions," "Starting from Paumanok," "Song of Myself," and "Drum Taps." There were numerous Russian versions of *Leaves of Grass* from 1911 on.

1438.  Both letters lost.

1439.  Joseph M. Stoddart (1845–1921) was the publisher of *Stoddart's Encyclopaedia America* and (in 1880) *Stoddart's Review,* which merged (in 1882) with *The American*; he later edited *Lippincott's Monthly*. On 18 January 1882, he visited Whitman in Camden with Oscar Wilde (see entries below).

1440.  "Wilde and Whitman" was an interview in the Philadelphia *Press,* 19 January 1882 (see entry below for 18 January 1882).

1441.  Of the 11 people listed here, only the last two are not among those to whom Whitman sent articles and material by or about him; for Standish O'Grady see footnote 1422; May Johnston is the daughter of John H. Johnston of New York City.